Paradox 4
Made Easy

Edward Jones

Osborne McGraw-Hill

Berkeley   New York   St. Louis   San Francisco
Auckland   Bogotá   Hamburg   London   Madrid
Mexico City   Milan   Montreal   New Delhi   Panama City
Paris   São Paulo   Singapore   Sydney
Tokyo   Toronto

Osborne **McGraw-Hill**
2600 Tenth Street
Berkeley, California 94710
U.S.A.

For information on translations or book distributors outside of the U.S.A., please write to Osborne **McGraw-Hill** at the above address.

Paradox 4 Made Easy

1234567890 DOC 998765432

ISBN 0-07-881766-8

Publisher

Kenna S. Wood

Acquisitions Editor

Elizabeth Fisher

Associate Editor

Scott Rogers

Project Editor

Nancy Pechonis

Technical Editor

David Nesbitt

Copy Editor

Carol Henry

Indexer and Proofreader

Valerie Haynes Perry

Computer Designer

Helena Charm

Word Processing

Lynda Higham
Carol Burbo

Cover Design

Mason Fong

The database and program files used in this book are available on diskette. The complete cost of the diskette package is $20.00, which covers the costs of duplication, postage, and handling. (Add $3.00 for Canadian or $5.00 for other foreign orders; foreign orders should be payable in U.S. funds.) To order the diskette package, use the form below.

Please send me the diskette that accompanies Paradox 4 Made Easy. My payment of $20.00 ($23.00 Canadian or $25.00 foreign) is enclosed. My disk size is

( ) 5.25 inch   ( ) 3.5 inch

Name _____

Address _____

City _____ State _____ ZIP _____

Foreign orders must be payable in U.S. funds. Sorry, no credit card orders or purchase orders.

Send payment to:

Nikki Jones
P.O. Box 74
Nashville, NC 27856

This offer is solely the responsibility of Nikki Jones & Co. Osborne **McGraw-Hill** takes no responsibility for the fulfillment of this offer.

Contents

Acknowledgments

Any technical book represents the combined efforts of a number of people, and this one is no different. Thanks to Liz Fisher, Acquisitions Editor at Osborne/McGraw-Hill, who conceived the project and artfully guided it around a maze of other projects, schedule conflicts, and the assorted road-blocks that have a way of appearing during book production. Thanks to Scott Rogers, Associate Editor at Osborne/McGraw-Hill, for his coordination efforts. Thanks also to Nancy Pechonis and Carol Henry for their work on the book. Thanks to David Nesbitt for his thorough technical review. Finally, no small amount of thanks to the people at Borland, for proving that it is still possible to produce software that one can get excited about.

Introduction

In a short period of time Paradox has established itself as the number two player among database managers for IBM-Compatible PCs. Considering the intense competition in the software industry, this says a lot about the nature of Paradox. It is that nature—the ability to provide true database power along with ease of use—that this book is designed to imitate from the ground up.

Since the beginning of the PC software industry, database management programs have earned a reputation for being difficult to use. Paradox, with its highly visual interface and its query-by-example technology, is very different. It has gained a strong following among corporate users because you need not be a "programming guru" to decipher its use. And even though it is easy to use, Paradox offers a great deal of relational database management power. This book is designed to help you utilize that power.

What is in this book? Chapter 1 offers an introduction to Paradox by showing ways in which the product can be used and by describing the features and capabilities of the product. In Chapter 2, important tips are offered on the subject of database design, and you are introduced to some basic database concepts.

You will quickly begin putting Paradox to use in Chapter 3, which details how to get started with the program, how to create a database, and how to add records, perform simple queries, and print simple reports. Chapter 4 further explores the concept of managing your data, showing you how to edit records, find and delete records, change the layout of a table, sort a table, and view multiple tables simultaneously.

Chapter 5 covers the use of custom forms, a flexible feature which allows you to display your data in a variety of formats. In Chapter 6, you are introduced to the significant power offered by Ask, the Paradox option that uses query-by-example technology to find the data you are looking for. Chapter 7 presents the basics of creating reports, and Chapter 8 covers the use of graphics. Chapter 9 describes how you can work with relational information while using Paradox.

In Chapter 10, you will learn how to use macros, called *scripts*, to automate frequently used procedures. Chapter 11 covers file management, showing how your tables can be easily modified, and describing how you can perform helpful DOS functions without exiting Paradox. Chapter 12 takes a further look at the complex subject of reporting, continuing where Chapter 7 left off by showing you techniques for free-form reports, mailing labels, invoices, and other specific report formats.

Chapter 13 introduces the Paradox Application Workshop, a feature of Paradox that writes complete applications for you. Chapter 14 provides an introduction to PAL, the Paradox Application Language, which is used for writing complex programs within Paradox. Chapter 15 provides important tips and techniques that will help you make optimal use of Paradox on a local area network. Chapter 16 provides instructions for building two sample Paradox applications.

Appendix A contains a complete, alphabetized listing of Paradox commands. Finally, Appendix B provides instructions for running Paradox under Microsoft Windows.

The style of this book encourages learning-by-doing. You will get the best results if you have your PC and your copy of Paradox at hand as you follow along with the practice sessions that are included in most chapters. However, ample illustrations have been provided, so even if you do not have a PC or Paradox, you can still become familiar with the program by reading this book.

1

What Is Paradox?

Welcome to Paradox, a true high-performance database manager for the IBM PC and compatible machines. If you have never used a relational database manager for a microcomputer before, you can feel confident that your choice of Paradox as a database management tool is an excellent one. If you have used other relational database managers prior to Paradox, you are in for a major change in expectations.

For the first decade of personal computer use, relational database managers all shared a very common trait, often expressed as "no pain, no gain." These powerful programs were universally difficult to use. While advances gradually made these programs easier to use, it was still the case that if you wanted real power in a database manager, you had to sacrifice ease of use.

Paradox has changed all that. The word "paradox" is defined as "something that cannot be, but is," and Paradox lives up to its name. High-powered database managers are not supposed to be easy to use, but Paradox is.

Paradox includes a series of well-designed menus, and offers a query-by-example feature that makes asking for specific data a simple task. Paradox normally displays information in one or more *tables*, each contained within a window, as shown in the example in Figure 1-1. The data in each table is

Figure 1-1.   *Paradox in use*

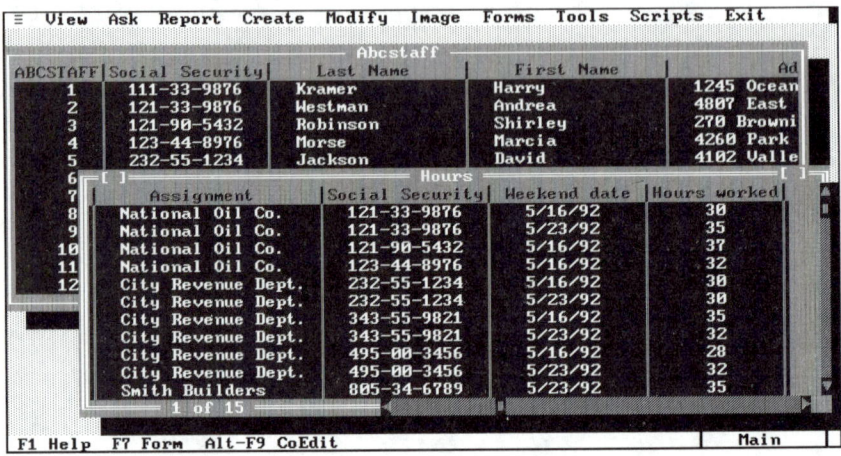

organized in *fields,* or categories. If these terms are unfamiliar to you, don't worry. They will be covered in more detail later in this chapter. You can use Paradox to create databases of tables containing the necessary fields. And by using the custom forms capability built into Paradox, you can display information in a format that best meets your needs.

How You Will Use Paradox

From the very start, Paradox will prove easy to use. Thanks to an automatic installation procedure, the program installs itself on your hard disk, creating the needed subdirectory for you. When you load the program, Paradox displays a *main menu* at the top of the screen (Figure 1-2). This menu provides access to all of Paradox's powerful features.

If you have used other Borland programs, or most any program under Microsoft Windows, you will find the Paradox menu design familiar. With these programs, you can select a menu choice by typing the first letter of the

Figure 1-2.   *The Paradox main menu*

command or by highlighting the choice with the cursor keys and pressing (ENTER). Mouse users can also click on a desired menu option. Most menu options, when selected, will display an explanation of the choice on the Status Bar, which appears at the bottom of the screen.

Creating a table in which to store your data is a simple task. After choosing the Create option from the main menu, you enter a name for the table. You then define the names and types of fields (categories) you will use. Unlike the limits imposed on you by competing programs, Paradox field names can be up to 25 characters in length and can include spaces. Six different data types can be used in Paradox: alphanumeric (combinations of alphabetic and numeric characters), memo (used to store large amounts of alphanumeric text), number, currency, date, and short number (a special type of number field that stores values between –32,767 and 32,767). Figure 1-3 shows the process of creating a table in Paradox.

Once your table exists, you can select the Modify option from the main menu and choose Data Entry from the next menu that appears. You are then ready to begin entering data into the table. Paradox lets you enter data into

Figure 1-3.   *Creating a Paradox table*

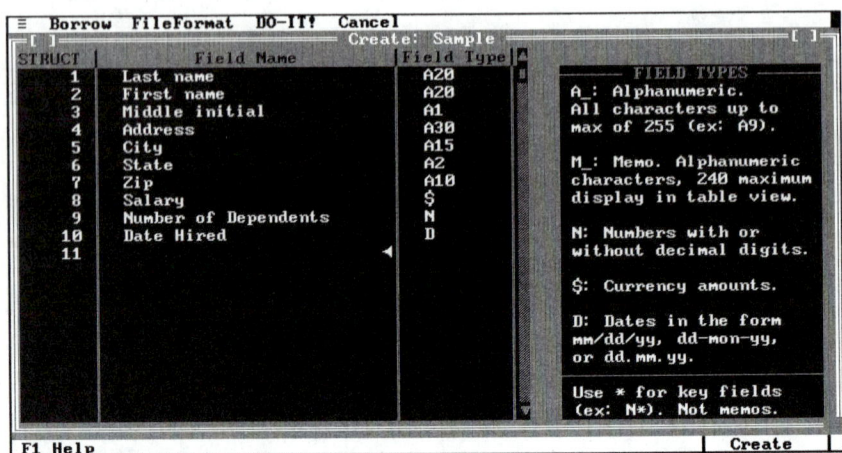

a table-like view or into a form. You can quickly create a standard form for any table by pressing a single function key, (F7). You can also design custom forms, which contain fields at the locations you desire, as well as borders or descriptive text.

To perform *queries* within Paradox that will extract data from your table, you can use the Ask command on the main menu. After using the Ask command to display a Query Form, you check off the fields you want to see in the query *answer,* and you enter matching data in any fields of the Query Form to isolate the subset of records. Figure 1-4 shows a Query Form and the resulting answer to the query.

To get more detailed information from your Paradox tables, you will want to build detailed reports. Paradox provides a report *hot key* that lets you create a quick tabular-style report simply by pressing (ALT)-(F7). If you need additional flexibility, you can use the powerful built-in Report Designer to design custom reports in either a tabular or a free-form format.

Paradox also offers powerful presentation graphics. Numeric data contained in a Paradox table can be visually represented in the form of a graph.

Figure 1-4. *Example of a query*

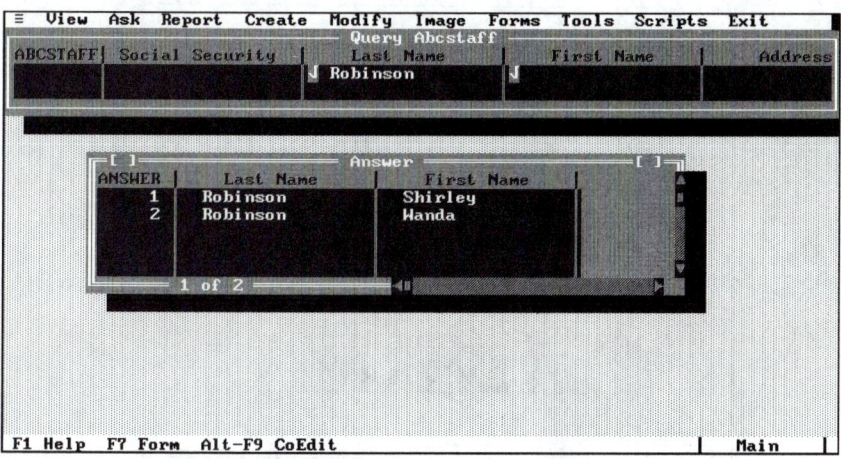

Paradox offers a wide variety of graphs, including bar, pie, line, and marker graphs. The graphs that you create can be displayed or printed, and you can customize many parts of a graph, such as the colors of various objects, shading, and the fonts used for labels within the graph. Figure 1-5 shows an example of a graph created with Paradox.

Finally, advanced users will find no shortage of available power in Paradox. You can make use of *scripts,* which are automated actions stored in a file that Paradox carries out as if individual commands had been entered at the keyboard. Paradox scripts are stored in *PAL,* the Paradox Application Language. You can use PAL to build complete, menu-driven custom applications that novices can use without special training. On the other hand, if you have no desire to learn to write applications in this or any other language, you can use the Paradox Application Workshop, an automated system that writes a Paradox application for you after you use a series of menus to answer questions about the application.

Figure 1-5.   *A Paradox graph*

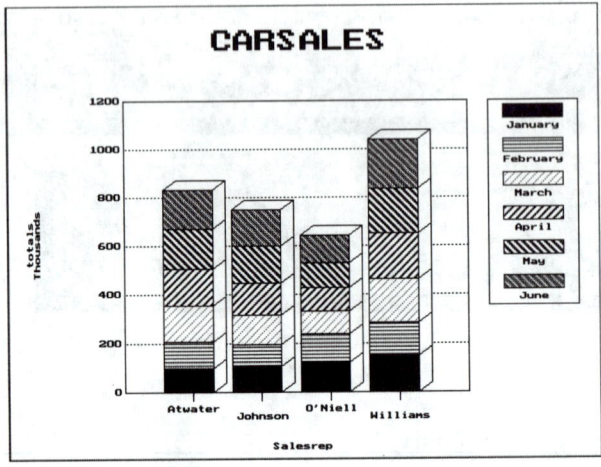

Using Paradox on a Network

You can use Paradox on a local area network, and the program can be used by multiple users as easily as it can by single users. Unlike some database managers, Paradox automatically handles most network tasks in the background, leaving users free to manage data. Paradox automatically places and removes the types of network locks that will prove most beneficial. You always have the option of manually placing more restrictive types of network locks on a table, but it is not necessary to think about this as you would have to with competitive packages. Paradox also updates data viewed by one network user as another user makes changes to that data.

What Is a Database?

Although "database management" is a computer term, it can also apply to the ways in which information is cataloged, stored, and used. At the center of any information management system is a *database.* Any collection of related information grouped together as a single item, as in Figure 1-6, is a database. A metal filing cabinet containing customer records, a card file of names and phone numbers, and a notebook with a penciled listing of a store's inventory are all databases. However, a filing cabinet or a notebook does not itself constitute a database; the way information is organized makes it a database. Objects like cabinets and notebooks only aid in organizing information, and Paradox is one such aid.

Information in a database is usually organized and stored in the form of *tables,* which are made up of rows and columns. For example, in the mailing list shown in Figure 1-6, each row contains a name, an address, a phone number, and a customer number. Each row is related to the others because they all contain the same types of information. And because the mailing list is a collection of information arranged in a specific order—a column of names, four distinct columns of address information, a column of phone numbers, a column of customer numbers—it is a table. One or more tables containing information arranged in an organized manner is a database.

Within a database, the rows in a table are called *records,* and the columns are called *fields.* The one-table database in Figure 1-6 is organized much like an address filing system kept in a box of 3 X 5 file cards. This similarity is illustrated in Figure 1-7. Each file card is a single record, and each category of information on a card is a field.

Figure 1-6.   *A simple database*

Name	Address	City	State	ZIP	Phone No.	Cust. No.
J. Billings	2323 State St.	Bertram	CA	91113	234-8980	0005
R. Foster	Rt. 1 Box 52	Frink	CA	93336	245-4312	0001
L. Miller	P.O. Box 345	Dagget	CA	94567	484-9966	0002
B. O'Neill	21 Way St. #C	Hotlum	CA	92346	555-1032	0004
C. Roberts	1914 19th St.	Bodie	CA	97665	525-4494	0006
A. Wilson	27 Haven Way	Weed	CA	90004	566-7823	0003

Figure 1-7.   *Each card represents a record; information is separated into fields.*

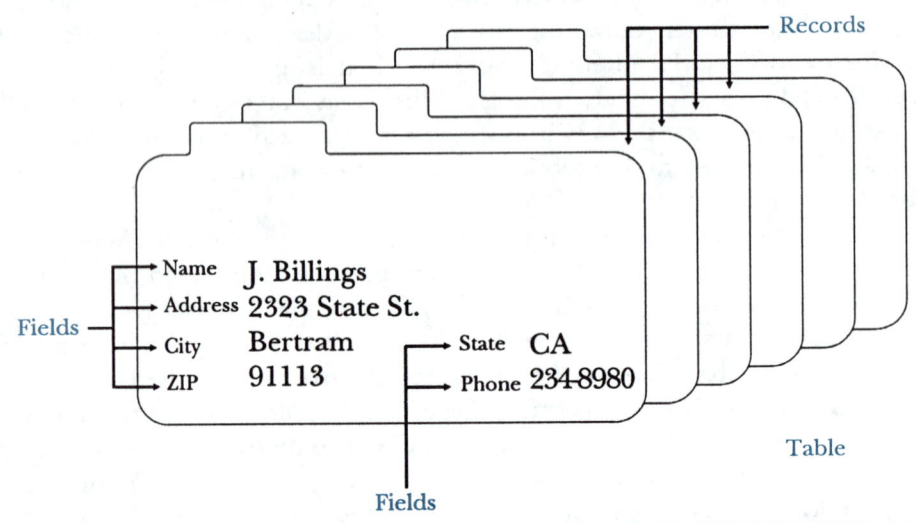

A field may contain any type of information that can be categorized. In the card box, each record contains six fields: name, address, city, state, ZIP code, and phone number. Since every card in the box has the same type of information, the card box is a database. Figure 1-8 identifies a record and a field in the mailing list database.

Using a Database

In theory, any database is arranged in such a way that information is easy to find. In Figure 1-8, for example, names are arranged alphabetically. If you wanted to find the phone number of a customer, you would simply locate the name and read across to the corresponding phone number.

You are already interested in how a computerized filing system or a database system can make information storage and retrieval more efficient than a traditional filing system. You will find that Paradox offers many advantages. A telephone book, for example, is fine for finding telephone

1

Figure 1-8. *A record and a field of a database*

Name	Address	City	State	ZIP	Phone No.	Cust. No.
J. Billings	2323 State St.	Bertram	CA	91113	234-8980	0005
R. Foster	Rt. 1 Box 52	Frink	CA	93336	245-4312	0001
L. Miller	P.O. Box 345	Dagget	CA	94567	484-9966	0002
B. O'Neill	21 Way St. #C	Hotlum	CA	92346	555-1032	0004
C. Roberts	1914 19th St.	Bodie	CA	97665	525-4494	0006
A. Wilson	27 Haven Way	Weed	CA	90004	566-7823	0003

Field (points to City column)

Record (points to B. O'Neill row)

numbers, but if all you have is an address, and not the name of the person
who lives there, the telephone directory becomes useless for finding that
person's number. A similar problem plagues conventional office filing systems. If the information is organized by name, for example, and you want to
find all of the clients located in a particular area, you are in for a tedious
search. In addition, organizing massive amounts of information into written
directories and filing cabinets can consume a great deal of space.

A manual database can also be difficult to modify. For example, adding
a new phone number to the listing may mean rearranging the list. If the phone
company were to assign a new area code, someone would have to search for
all of the phone numbers having the old area code and replace each with a
new one.

When a database is teamed with a computer, many of these problems are
eliminated. A computerized database provides speed: finding a phone number from among a thousand entries or putting a file in alphabetical order
takes just seconds with Paradox. Also, a computerized database is compact: a
database with thousands of records can be stored on a single floppy disk.
Finally, a computerized database is flexible: it enables you to examine infor-

mation from a number of angles, so you can, for example, search for a phone number by name or by address.

Tasks that are time-consuming when done manually are more practical with the aid of a computer. In principle, a database in a computer is no different from a database recorded on paper and filed in a cabinet. But the computer does the tedious work of maintaining and accessing a database, and it does it quickly. A program that enables you to do all of this is known as a *database management system,* or *DBMS* for short.

Relational Databases

There are a number of systems that store in a computer, but not all of these are *relational* database management systems. A word-processing program can be used to organize information in the form of a list; however, it will offer only limited flexibility. You must still sort, rearrange, and access the information. Moving a level above word processors, you get to the simple file managers and the spreadsheets with simple database management capabilities. Most file managers (and spreadsheets) can perform sorting and other data management tasks.

Relational database managers can also store information in computer files. However, in addition to being more sophisticated than file managers, they can access two or more tables simultaneously by linking records on a common field, such as a customer number or an account code. By comparison, file managers can access only one table at a time. This type of constraint can be severely limiting. If a file manager is accessing information from one table, but needs three pieces of information from a second table, it cannot continue unless the second table is available. Only when the file manager has finished with the first table can it proceed to the second table. But what good is this when the file manager needs information from both tables simultaneously? The only solution is to duplicate the three fields from the second table in the first table. Fortunately, this is not necessary with a relational database manager like Paradox.

Let's look at an example. Suppose a computerized mailing list stores customer information for a warehouse that distributes kitchen appliances.

The warehouse database also contains a separate file with a table for customer orders; this table includes fields for customer number, merchandise number, price per unit, quantity ordered, and total cost. The mailing list and the customer order table comprise a relational database because they have the customer number field in common, as shown in Figure 1-9. By searching for the customer number in the mailing list and matching it to the customer number in the order table, the database manager can determine the name and location of a purchaser from one database file, and find out what the purchaser ordered and the total cost of the purchase from another database

Figure 1-9.   *Relationship between tables*

Mailing List

Name	Address	City	State	ZIP	Phone No.	Cust. No.
J. Billings	2323 State St.	Bertram	CA	91113	234-8980	0005
R. Foster	Rt. 1 Box 52	Frink	CA	93336	245-4312	0001
L. Miller	P.O. Box 345	Dagget	CA	94567	484-9966	0002
B. O'Neill	21 Way St. #C	Hotlum	CA	92346	555-1032	0004
C. Roberts	1914 19th St.	Bodie	CA	97665	525-4494	0006
A. Wilson	27 Haven Way	Weed	CA	90004	566-7823	0003

Customer Orders

Cust. No.	Merchandise No.	Price per Unit	Quantity	Total Price
0001	15A	1500.00	5	7500.00
0001	15B	1750.00	10	17500.00
0002	311	500.00	3	1500.00
0003	555	1000.00	4	4000.00
0004	69	650.00	7	4550.00
0005	1111	300.00	2	600.00
0006	15A	1500.00	1	1500.00

file. A database manager that can draw information like this, from different tables linked by a common field, is known as a *relational database manager.*

To handle the same task with a file manager would be very difficult—when the time came for the merchandise to be shipped, a file manager could not automatically match each purchase with the appropriate address from the mailing list. The only alternative would be to combine the two tables, but this would result in a clumsy and inefficient database. For example, to represent both of R. Foster's purchases, you would have to duplicate his name, address, and phone number, as shown in Figure 1-10. (If R. Foster had purchased 100 merchandise items instead of two, the extra typing would take much longer, and the many duplicate entries would use up valuable disk space.)

How Paradox Compares to the Competition

Paradox is one of a number of competing products in a market built on the popularity of the IBM PC and its descendants, and on the usefulness of relational database managers for microcomputers. There are many excellent products on the market that are comparable in power to Paradox, including dBASE IV, R:base, Revelation, FoxPro, and others. All of these products offer relational database management, integral programming languages for applications development, and similar top-of-the-line features. However, Paradox excels at providing the features and the power while maintaining a simple, friendly user interface.

A major difference between Paradox and its competitors is the highly visual nature of the program. Some database managers force you to build strings of commands to carry out operations; these commands must follow a precise syntax. (Some products offer menu systems that help you build parts of the commands, but you must nevertheless supply the commands correctly to carry out your tasks.) In comparison, Paradox lets you perform much of your work by manipulating objects on the screen. And if you are interested in custom applications, the Paradox Application Workshop (described in Chapter 13) makes it easy for non-programmers to create complex custom applications that are free of "bugs."

Figure 1-10. *Combined customer order/mailing list database. (Unnecessary customer number field was eliminated.)*

Name	Address	Phone No.	Merchan- dise No.	Price per Unit	Quantity	Total Price
J. Billings	2323 State St. Bertram CA 91113	234-8980	1111	300.00	2	600.00
R. Foster	Rt. 1 Box 52 Frink CA 93336	245-4312	15A	1500.00	5	7500.00
R. Foster	Rt. 1 Box 52 Frink CA 93336	245-4312	15B	1750.00	10	17500.00
L. Miller	P.O. Box 345 Dagget CA 94567	484-9966	311	500.00	3	500.00
B. O'Neill	21 Way St. #C Hotlum CA 92346	555-1032	69	650.00	7	4550.00
C. Roberts	1914 19th St. Bodie CA 97665	525-4494	15A	1500.00	1	1500.00
A. Wilson	27 Haven Way Weed CA 90004	566-7823	555	1000.00	4	4000.00

System Requirements

To use Paradox, you will need an IBM-compatible personal computer that uses an 80286 (or better) processor. Paradox cannot be used on XT-class machines with 8088 or 8086 processors, because the program requires the use of protected mode, a mode of operation that is possible only on computers with 80286 or better processors. Paradox also requires a minimum of one megabyte of memory (640K installed as base RAM, and an additional 384K as extended memory). Your computer must be equipped with one floppy disk drive and one hard disk drive. Any personal computer that is compatible with the IBM PC and meets the above requirements should be able to run Paradox. You must be using DOS 3.1 or higher. Paradox can be used with either a monochrome or a color monitor, and is compatible with most popular printers. Paradox is designed to take advantage of extra memory; it can be used with the AST RAMPage, Intel Above Board, or any other memory board that meets the EMS (LIM) or EEMS specifications. Extended memory of up to 16MB is supported by Paradox.

To use Paradox or the Paradox LAN Pack on a local area network, you will need workstations with a minimum of 640K of memory; any combination of disk drives (or no drives); and DOS 3.1 or above. The operating system can be any of the following:

- Novell Advanced Netware, version 2.0A or higher
- IBM PC Network or Token Ring Network with IBM PC Local Area Network Program, version 1.12 or higher
- 3Com 3Plus Share Network, version 1.5 or higher
- AT&T StarGROUP for DOS, version 3.1 or higher
- Microsoft LAN Manager, version 2.0 or higher
- Banyan VINES network, version 2.10 or higher
- DEC Pathworks network, version 1.0 or higher

(Other networks that are NETBIOS compatible with those listed here may work with Paradox, but they may not have been tested, and support may be limited.)

Specifications

Specifications for Paradox include the following:

Maximum number of records: 2 billion
Maximum number of fields: 255

1

Maximum number of characters per field:	255
Maximum number of characters per unindexed record:	4000
Maximum number of forms per table:	15
Maximum number of reports per table:	15

2

Database Design

At this point, you may be anxious to load Paradox into your computer and begin using the program. However, you should resist the temptation to use Paradox for a task you have never done on a computer before. There is an excellent reason for approaching the job of designing a database with patience: planning is vital to effective database management. Many a buyer of database management software has gotten started with the software, created a database, and stored data within that database only to discover that the database did not provide all of the needed information. While powerful databases like Paradox let you make up for mistakes committed during the design process, correcting such errors can nevertheless be a tedious job. To help you avoid such time-consuming mistakes, this chapter focuses on the design of a database.

Creating a database without proper planning often results in a database with too many or too few fields.

Note

Database design requires that you think about how the data should be stored and how you and others will ask for data from the database file. During this process, your problem (which Paradox was purchased to help solve) will be outlined on paper. Just as one would not haphazardly toss a bunch of files into a filing cabinet without designing some type of filing system, one cannot place information into a database file without first designing the database. As you design it, you must define the kinds of information that should be stored in the database.

Output requirements can be a significant help in designing your database. Decide what you want to get from a database, in the form of printed reports, screen forms, or graphs. Thinking about your output needs will help you better plan what goes into your database.

Tip

Data and Fields

"Data" and "fields" are two important terms in database design. Fields are the types of data that make up the database. A field is another name for a category, so an entire category of data, such as a group of names, is considered to be a field. Names, phone numbers, customer numbers, descriptions, locations, and stock numbers are common fields that your database might contain. *Data* is the information that is stored in the fields you have defined. An individual's last name (Smith, for example) is data.

In addition to thinking about what kinds of information will go into the database, you must give careful consideration to the ways in which information will come out of the database, or *output*. Output most often comes from a database in the form of *reports*. A report is a summary of information. When you ask the computer for a list of all homes in the area priced between $100,000 and $150,000 or for a list of employees earning less than $15.00 per hour, you are asking for a report. When you ask for John Smith's address, you are also asking for a report. Whether the computer displays a few lines on the screen, a graph, or hundreds of lines on a stack of paper, it is providing a report based on the data contained within the database file.

The practice sessions in this book demonstrate how you can design and use a database. The problems and needs of a hypothetical company called

ABC Temporaries will be used throughout the book to illustrate the effectiveness of Paradox for database management. ABC Temporaries is a temporary services firm that must not only keep track of the number of employees working for each of its client companies, but must also track which client companies its temporary employees are assigned to.

For some time, ABC Temporaries has handled this task by using ordinary 3 X 5 file cards, but the paperwork load has finally grown too large to be efficiently handled in this manner. A major task at ABC Temporaries is to track just how much time each temporary employee spends at a particular client company so that accurate bills can be generated. The relational capabilities of Paradox will make such tracking a simple matter.

Successive chapters of this text will show how the staff at ABC Temporaries uses Paradox to manage information. By following along with these examples, you will learn how to put Paradox to work within your particular application.

Three Phases of Database Design

Designing a database file, whether for ABC Temporaries or for yourself, involves three major steps:

1. Data definition (an analysis of existing or required data)
2. Data refinement (updating your original analysis)
3. Establishing relationships between fields

Data Definition

During the first phase of database design, you must make a list, on a piece of paper, of all the important fields involved in your application. To do this you must examine your application in detail and determine exactly what kinds of information must be stored in the database.

In discussing the design for the database, the staff at ABC Temporaries determined that certain items must be known about each temporary worker: the name of the employee, the employee's address, date of birth, date hired, and salary, and the name of the client firm the employee is assigned to. The staff also needs a Comments field, where textual descriptions of an employee's performance can be recorded. The resulting list of fields is shown in Figure 2-1.

During this phase of database design, you should list all the possible fields your database might contain. Listing more fields than your particular application actually needs is not a problem—unnecessary fields will be eliminated during the data refinement phase.

Data Refinement

In the data refinement phase you refine your initial list of fields so that the fields form an accurate description of the types of data needed in the database. It is vital to include at this stage suggestions from as many other users of the database as possible. The people who use the database are likely to know what kinds of information they need to get from the database. When the staff of ABC Temporaries took a close look at their initial list of fields, for example, they realized that most of the refinements were obvious. The Address field, for example, needed to be divided into street address, city, state, and ZIP code.

Such division of an initial field into more than one field is particularly important when record sorting or selection based on those fields will occur. Any item used to sort or select records should be in a field by itself.

Figure 2-1.   *Initial list of fields*

```
Fields

1. Employee name
2. Employee address
3. Employee salary
4. Assigned to firm
5. Date of birth
6. Date Hired
7. Comments
```

2

In your own case, some refinements may quickly become evident and others may not. Going over your written list of fields will help make any necessary refinements more obvious. For example, when the staff of ABC Temporaries further examined the initial field list, they realized that the index-card system contained multiple occurrences of employees with the same last name. To avoid confusion, the Name field was further divided into separate fields for last name and first name. Suggestions were also made to add the phone number, salary, number of dependents, and hourly billing rate charged to the client. Figure 2-2 shows the refined list of fields.

Before designing a database, get suggestions from those who will use it.

Tip

Establishing Relationships Between Fields

During the third phase of database design, drawing relationships between the fields can help determine which fields are important and which are not

Figure 2-2.   *Refined list of fields*

```
Fields

 1. Employee last name
 2. Employee first name
 3. Street address
 4. City
 5. State
 6. ZIP code
 7. Phone
 8. Salary
 9. No. of dependents
10. Assigned to firm
11. Rate charged to firm
12. Date of birth
13. Date hired
14. Comments
```

as important. One way to determine such relationships is to ask yourself the same questions that you will ask your database. If a manager wishes to know how many different employees worked on temporary assignments for Mammoth Telephone & Telegraph, the database must draw a relationship between an employee identifier (such as the social security number) and the names of the clients for whom that employee worked.

Relationships can be more complex. The company president might want to know how many employees worked as data entry operators for Mammoth Telephone between July and October. The database management system must compare the "client worked for" fields with fields for the type of job and the time the job was performed. These types of questions can help reveal which fields are unimportant so that they can be eliminated from the database.

During this phase you must determine which relationships between data (if any) will call for the use of multiple tables. Keep in mind that Paradox is a relational database, which means that the data within one table can be related to the data in another. When designing a database, you should not lose sight of the opportunities that relational capabilities offer you. Too many users use relational database management software to create bulky, non-relational databases—an approach that drastically increases the amount of work involved.

The proposed staff table to be used by ABC Temporaries has fields that will be used to describe each employee. A major goal of computerizing the personnel records at the firm is to provide automated billing. By creating another table that shows which employees have worked at a given assignment during a certain week, the company can easily generate bills for the services that ABC Temporaries provides to its clients. If the ABC staff took the nonrelational approach of adding a "week ending" date field and a "number of hours worked" field, they could store all of the information needed in each record. However, they would also have to fill in the name and address, as well as other information, for each employee, week after week. A better solution would be to create two tables, one containing the fields described, detailing each employee, and the other containing the number of hours worked, a "week ending" date, the client the work was done for, and a way of identifying the employee. You should consider breaking a database into separate tables whenever one or more tables contain redundant data—data that is the same for a large number of records.

As you establish the relationships, you may determine that additional fields are necessary. In the case of ABC Temporaries, employees are identified by social security number, so an appropriate field was added to the proposed list of fields. The result is shown in Figure 2-3. This finalized list of fields is the basis for a table that will be created in Chapter 3.

During the design phases, potential users should be consulted to determine what kinds of information they will expect the database to supply. Just what kinds of reports are wanted from the database? What kinds of queries will employees make of the database? By continually asking these types of questions, you will think in terms of the tasks your database must perform, and this should help you determine what is important and what is unimportant.

You may have noticed that throughout the entire process, the specific data, such as employees' names, addresses, and so forth, has not been discussed. It is not necessary to identify any specific data at this point; only the fields need to be defined. Once you have finalized a given design, you should test that design using samples of existing data. Testing with real data

Figure 2-3.   *Final list of fields*

```
Fields

 1. Employee social security number
 2. Employee last name
 3. Employee first name
 4. Street address
 5. City
 6. State
 7. ZIP code
 8. Phone
 9. Salary
10. No. of dependents
11. Assigned to firm
12. Rate charged to firm
13. Date of birth
14. Date hired
15. Comments
```

can reveal problems with the original database design, such as foreign postal codes (in a field designed for U.S. ZIP codes) or name titles (M.D. and so on) that were not planned for.

Look at examples of your data before finalizing your list of fields.

Keep in mind that even after completion of the database design phases, the design of the database file is not set in stone. Changes to the design of a database file can be made later, if necessary. However, if you follow a systematic approach toward database design for your application, you will avoid creating a database that fails to provide much of the information you need and that must, therefore, be extensively redesigned. Although Paradox lets you change the design of a table at any time, such changes are often inconvenient to make once the database has been designed.

Here is an example. If you were using Paradox to create a database file for a customer mailing list, you might include fields for names, addresses, cities, states, and ZIP codes. At first glance, this might seem sufficient. You could then begin entering customer information into the database, and gradually build a sizeable mailing list. However, suppose your company later decided to begin telemarketing, based on the same mailing list. You might suddenly realize that you had not included a field for telephone numbers. Using Paradox, you could easily change the design to include the new field, but you would still face the mammoth task of going back and adding a telephone number for every name in the mailing list. If this information had been added as you developed the mailing list, you would not face the inconvenience of having to enter the phone numbers as a separate operation. Thus, planning carefully and taking sufficient time during your database design process can help you avoid later pitfalls.

3

Getting Started

The Paradox software package includes assorted manuals and quick reference guides, and several disks. The exact number of disks varies, depending on your disk format (5.25-inch or 3.5-inch) and on your version of Paradox. The disks are divided into two groups: those that contain the Paradox Application Workshop, and those that do not. (The Paradox Application Workshop is an automated system for building applications; it is covered in more detail in Chapter 13.) If you have not yet installed Paradox on your system, you can place all the disks labeled Paradox Application Workshop aside until later.

Installing Paradox

Installing Paradox on a hard disk is a simple matter, thanks to the installation program contained on the Installation disk, and the detailed instructions in the *Getting Started* booklet packaged with your Paradox software. If you do not have the *Getting Started* booklet handy, you should locate it now. Because versions of Paradox change and the instructions may change along with the software updates, you should refer to your latest Paradox documentation for detailed specifics on installing the program. This book provides only basic instructions and some general tips regarding installation.

The Paradox installation program will create the necessary subdirectory on your hard disk and copy the needed files into that subdirectory. Before beginning the installation, make sure that you have at least 3MB of free disk space to install Paradox in its "minimum configuration" (that is, without the optional software described during the installation process). You will need at least 6MB of free disk space to install Paradox with all its optional software. Beyond what is required for Paradox, you will certainly need adequate space for storage of your databases, and for sorting tables. If you are using Paradox for the first time, you should also be aware of the memory requirements of the program: Paradox requires 640K of installed memory.

Note

You can find out the amount of free disk space by using the DIR command; the description, "XXXXX bytes free" that appears at the bottom of the directory listing indicates the amount of free space remaining.

To install the program, turn on your computer and get to the DOS prompt in the usual manner. The default drive should be your hard disk drive; if it is not, change it to the hard disk before attempting to install Paradox. For example, if your hard disk is drive C, type **C:** and press (ENTER) to change the default to drive C. Then, perform the following steps:

1. Insert the Installation Disk into drive A.

2. Enter the following command to start the installation process:

    A:INSTALL

3. Follow the instructions that appear on the screen, or those contained in the Getting Started booklet, to complete the installation process.

During the installation process, the installation program creates a directory (called \PDOX40 unless you specify a different name), and it copies Paradox into that directory. The installation program also checks for the presence of a file called CONFIG.SYS in the root directory of your hard disk;

if one is not present, the installation program adds one. If CONFIG.SYS is already present, the installation program checks it for the presence of two commands, FILES = 40 and BUFFERS = 40, and adds these commands, if necessary, to the file. This configuration is needed by Paradox.

Starting Paradox

If you are starting Paradox for the first time after installation, reboot (restart your system) to insure that any values in the CONFIG.SYS file that were modified by the installation program will be used. You can press CTRL ALT DEL simultaneously to reboot your system.

When the DOS prompt appears, you must first switch to the subdirectory containing the program (usually C:\PDOX40); then enter **PARADOX** from the DOS prompt. As an example, if your hard disk is drive C, and the program is stored in a subdirectory named PDOX40, you would start the program by entering the following commands from the DOS prompt:

```
CD\PDOX40
PARADOX
```

After the program starts, you will briefly see an introductory screen and a copyright message. In a moment, the working screen for Paradox, called the *desktop,* will appear as shown in Figure 3-1.

About the Desktop

The screen can be divided into three general areas: the menu, which appears at the top of the screen and contains the Paradox menu choices; the desktop, which is the large area in the center of the screen (and is currently empty), and the *status bar* occupying the bottom line of the screen. Paradox will display various messages within the status bar to help you as you use the program.

Figure 3-1.   *The Paradox desktop*

The top line of the desktop shows a series of menu choices. Paradox uses a detailed system of menu commands that let you easily select various options for creating databases, adding and changing information, printing reports, and performing most Paradox functions.

The cursor will always highlight the currently available command or option, or the field or characters you may be selecting or editing. The ⊖ and ⊖ keys may be used to move the cursor around the screen. Mouse users can click on any menu command to select it. (Mouse operations are discussed in greater detail in the later section, "About the Mouse.")

The Menu Key (F10)

When Paradox is first started, the cursor highlights the View command on the menu, but you will find that during other operations, the cursor may be elsewhere (such as within a table). Though mouse users can always activate a command by simply clicking on it, keyboard users will want to make use of the Menu key (F10) for this task. Whenever the menu is not active (meaning that the cursor is not present somewhere in the menu), you can press (F10) to activate the menu. You can then use the (←) and (→), followed by (ENTER), to choose a menu command.

Try pressing (→) once now, and you will see the highlighted menu option change from View to Ask. At the same time, the explanation of the command appears in the status bar at the bottom of the screen. Continue pressing (→) or (←), and notice the various commands.

Pressing (ENTER) with any command highlighted will select that command. For example, if you use the arrow keys to highlight the Report option and then press (ENTER), the available choices for reports will appear as a menu. (You can press the (ESC) (Escape) key to exit the Report menu.) Note that you can also select a command by typing the key for the first character of its name. For instance, you can enter **T** to display the options for the Tools command. Mouse users can select menu options by clicking on them. If an additional menu opens, mouse users can drag (click and hold down the left mouse button while moving the mouse) to select from the additional menu options.

You can press (ESC) *at any open menu to close that menu.*

Remember

About the Paradox Menu Structure

Much of your interaction with Paradox will be through the program's system of menus. The main menu, shown here, is always the first menu you see when you load Paradox.

```
≡  View  Ask  Report  Create  Modify  Image  Forms  Tools  Scripts  Exit
```

The commands available from the main menu provide access to the major operations within Paradox. Paradox uses *pull-down menus* to list these operations, meaning that you can "pull down" options menus from the menu bar at the top of the screen. Sometimes, choosing an option on one pull-down menu will cause an additional menu to appear.

When the main menu is visible, you are in what is referred to as Main mode. When you select Report, Create, Modify, or Forms from the main menu and then begin to work with the chosen object (such as a report, a table, or a form), you are then in one of the lower-level modes of Paradox. Each lower-level mode has its own menu, and when you are in a lower-level mode, that menu will replace the main menu. You can always tell what mode of Paradox you are in by looking at the status bar. To finish your work in a lower-level mode and return to the main menu, you must choose DO-IT! ((F2)), or select Cancel from the lower-level menu. You can also click the Close box of a window, or press the Close Window key ((CTRL)-(F8)), or choose Close from the System menu (described shortly). These actions are all equivalent to choosing Cancel from the lower-level menu.

In addition to the obvious main menu commands (View, Ask, Report, Create, and so on), there is a System menu available; it is represented by the three horizontal lines shown at the far left side of the main menu. The available choices of the System menu will make more sense later in the book, after you are accustomed to working with multiple tables open in separate windows. For now, though, it is helpful to know how to open the System menu so you can make choices it later. Mouse users can open the System menu by clicking on its symbol on the main menu; from the keyboard, you can press (ALT)-(SPACEBAR). Another (rather unwieldy) method for keyboard users is to press (F10) to activate the main menu, use the (←) to move the cursor to the System menu, and then press (ENTER).

Dialog Boxes and File Boxes

The Paradox commands often display *dialog boxes* when you make an option selection; here is an example:

Appropriate selections can be made from the dialog box by using the keyboard or the mouse, or a combination of both. Keyboard users can press (TAB) to move around between the fields of a dialog box and/or *buttons* of a dialog box. Responses to prompts in Paradox can be typed into the appropriate fields in the dialog box; buttons (such as the OK or Cancel buttons) can be selected by tabbing to the button and pressing (ENTER). Mouse users can click in a field and begin typing, or click on a desired button to select that button.

One particular type of dialog box that appears often in Paradox is the *file box*, an example of which is shown here.

```
Next
Maximize/Restore
Size/Move
Close
Window

Interface
Desktop              ▶
Video                ▶

Editor               ▶
Utilities            ▶

About
```

Paradox displays this box or a similar variation of it whenever you need to enter or choose a filename from a list of available files.

If Paradox is asking for a name in order to select an existing file, you have two options. You can type a filename in, if you know its exact spelling. Or you can press (ENTER) without entering a name (or click on the OK button with the mouse), and a list of available filenames will appear in the file box. You can then highlight the desired name and press (ENTER) to choose OK, or click on the desired name and then click on the OK button.

Note

Mouse users should remember that double-clicking within Paradox, as in many other software programs, often selects an action and confirms that action. For example, if a list of files is visible in a File box, you can double-click on a specific filename. This action is equivalent to clicking on the filename, then clicking on the OK button to confirm the selection.

About Compatibility Mode

Version 4 of Paradox can operate in one of two modes: its *standard* mode, and what is known as *compatibility* mode. In standard mode, Paradox looks and behaves as outlined throughout this book. When in compatibility mode, Paradox takes on the menu interface used by earlier versions (specifically versions 3.0 and 3.5) of Paradox. Users of earlier versions may prefer the feel of the menus in this mode, but keep in mind that you give up many excellent features of version 4 when in compatibility mode (such as movable, scrollable windows).

You can switch to compatibility mode at any time by opening the System menu with the mouse or with (ALT)-(SPACEBAR), and then choosing Interface from the menu. From the next menu to appear, choose Yes to switch to compatibility mode. If you are already in compatibility mode and you want to switch back to standard mode, press (ALT)-(SPACEBAR). From the next menu to appear, choose Interface, then Yes, and you'll return to standard mode.

It is not a good idea to switch modes while you are making edits to a Paradox object (such as a table of data), because any changes to unsaved objects are lost when you switch between standard mode and compatibility mode.

Caution

About the Keyboard

If you're already familiar with the PC keyboard, you can skip this section.

Note

Paradox uses a number of special-purpose keys for various functions. In addition to the ordinary letter and number keys, you'll use the *function keys* often, and we'll look at them more closely later in this chapter. On most IBM PCs and compatible computers, the function keys are the double row of grey keys at the left side of the keyboard, as shown on the example in Figure 3-2. On many newer keyboards, the function keys are placed in a horizontal row at the top of the keyboard, as shown on the example in Figure 3-3. The function keys on the older PCs are labeled (F1) through (F10), for Function 1 through Function 10. The newer machines have twelve function keys, labeled (F1) through (F12).

Figure 3-2.   *The IBM PC keyboard*

Usually positioned on the left side of the keyboard are five often-used keys: the (ESC) (Escape) key; the (TAB) key (it may have two arrows on it rather than (TAB)); the (SHIFT) key (it may show a hollow upward-pointing arrow rather than (SHIFT)); the (CTRL) (Control) key; and the (ALT) (Alternate) key. Some keyboards have the (ESC) key in a different location, and there may be another

Figure 3-3.   *The enhanced IBM PC keyboard*

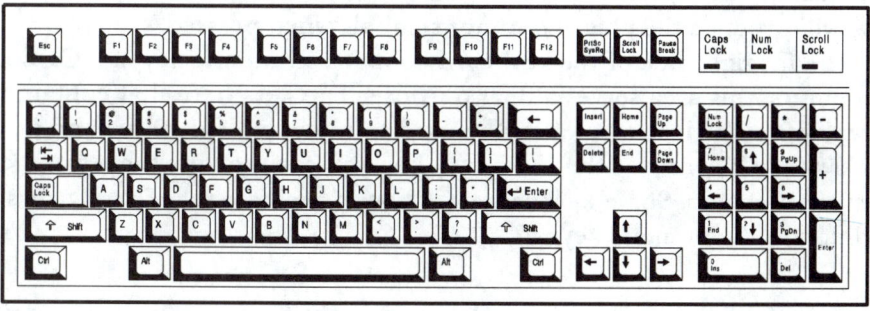

(SHIFT) key and another (CTRL) key on the right side of the keyboard. Locate these keys before going further, as they will prove helpful for various operations.

The (ESC) *key is your most useful key whenever you are somewhere you don't want to be in the menu structure or on the screen. In many cases, repeatedly pressing* (ESC) *will get you all the way out of an operation.* (ESC) *won't, however, undo or cancel an edit session.*

Tip

You will also want to locate the template supplied with your Paradox package, and place it where you can refer to it for the uses of the function keys. Function key operations will be discussed in later chapters as you work through this book.

Toward the right side of the keyboard, there is another (SHIFT) key. Usually located below the right (SHIFT) key is a key labeled (CAPS LOCK). It is used to change all typed letters to uppercase, but it does not change the format of the numbers in the top row of the keyboard. Keyboards on newer IBM PCs and many compatibles may have the (CAPS LOCK) key located somewhere near the left (SHIFT) key. Just above the right (SHIFT) key is the (ENTER) (or (RETURN)) key; it performs a function that is similar to the Return key of a typewriter. Above the (ENTER) key is the (BACKSPACE) key.

On the right side of the keyboard, in the numeric keypad area, is a key labeled (DEL). The Delete key can be used to delete characters or other objects when in Paradox. Finally, the far right side of the keyboard has two grey keys one with a plus (+) and one with a minus (–). In most circumstances, these keys will produce the plus and minus symbols when pressed.

The far right side of the keyboard contains a numeric keypad. On some computers, this area serves a dual purpose. The keys here that contain up, down, left, and right arrows can be used to move the cursor around in the workspace. Or, pressing the (NUM LOCK) key, you can then use these same keys to enter numbers. Some keyboards will have a separate set of arrow keys, in addition to the numeric keypad.

When (NUM LOCK) *is active, the arrow keys on many keyboards create numbers instead of moving the cursor. If you press an arrow key and get an unwanted number, check*

Remember *the status of the* (NUM LOCK) *key.*

About the Mouse

Although Paradox is designed to operate without a mouse, you can make good use of a mouse, if one is installed on your system. There are three basic operations you will perform with the mouse: pointing, clicking, and selecting (also called dragging). The mouse controls the location of a special cursor called the *mouse pointer*. In Paradox, the mouse pointer is shaped as a small, rectangular block.

To point at an object with the mouse, simply roll the mouse in the direction of the object. As you do so, the mouse pointer moves in the same direction on the screen. The term *clicking* refers to pressing the left mouse button. By pointing to objects and clicking on them, you can select many of the objects in Paradox. The term *dragging* refers to pressing and holding down the left mouse button while moving the mouse. This is commonly done to choose menu options within Paradox.

If you have just purchased a mouse to use with Paradox, a few hints are in order. Most mice require software drivers that must be installed before the mice will work properly; for details on installing your mouse driver software, refer to the instructions packaged with your mouse. Obviously, you'll need a clear surface on your desk to manipulate the mouse. What is not so obvious is the fact that some desk surfaces work better than others. A surface with a small amount of friction seems to work better than a very smooth one; commercial mouse pads are available if your desktop is too smooth to obtain good results.

The mouse will probably require cleaning from time to time. (Some mice do not require regular cleaning, so check your manual to be sure.) If you turn the mouse upside down, you will probably see instructions on removing the large ball inside for cleaning. A cotton swab dipped in alcohol works well for cleaning the ball. If your mouse uses an optical sensor design instead of a large ball underneath, you should refer to the manual that accompanied the mouse for any cleaning instructions.

Using the Function Keys

Function keys are used for a variety of tasks within Paradox. Table 3-1 shows the purpose of each function key and function key combination. Many

Table 3-1.   *Function Key Assignments*

Key	Name	Function
(F1)	Help	Displays help information
(F2)	DO-IT!	Performs current operation
(F3)	Up Image	Moves up by one image
(F4)	Down Image	Moves down by one image
(F5)	Example	Enters a query example
(F6)	Check	Includes current column in query result
(F7)	Form	Toggles between Form view and Table view
(F8)	Clear	Clears current image
(F9)	Edit	Starts Edit mode
(F10)	Menu	Activates menu (when menu is inactive)
(ALT)-(F3)	Instant Script Record	Begins/ends recording
(ALT)-(F4)	Instant Script Play	Begins playback
(ALT)-(F5)	Field View	Permits cursor movement within field
(ALT)-(F6)	Check Plus	Includes all records, along with duplicates
(ALT)-(F7)	Instant Report	Prints report based on current table
(ALT)-(F8)	Clear All	Clears all images
(ALT)-(F9)	CoEdit	Starts CoEdit mode
(CTRL)-(F6)	Check Descending	Same as Check, but also sorts in descending order
(CTRL)-(F7)	Graph	Draws graph based on current column
(SHFT)-(F6)	Group By	Groups field, but does not display values in the query answer

of the terms in the table may not make sense at this point, bu[t]
explained in further detail throughout this text.

Getting Help

Should you need help, Paradox provides detailed information on subjects
ranging from basic Paradox concepts to programming in PAL (the Paradox
Application Language), all of which is stored in a Help file that is accessed
through Paradox. A series of menus will assist you in finding the information
you are searching for. For example, if you are working with Paradox and need
information on a certain key combination you cannot recall, you can press
the Help ((F1)) key and choose the Keys choice from the main menu within
the Help System for a more detailed explanation. Mouse users can also click
on "F1 Help" in the lower-left corner of the screen to access Help. If you press
(F1) now, you will see the help screen shown in Figure 3-4.

At any point in Paradox, pressing (F1) *reveals a help screen.*

Note

The Help System uses the same type of menu bar as the rest of Paradox,
and you can select from among these options in the same manner. The Help
System is divided into six basic areas, shown in Table 3-2. You can choose
from any of the six areas by selecting the choice from the menu (again, either
with the mouse, or by typing the first letter in the name of the choice or by
highlighting the choice with the cursor keys and pressing (ENTER)). Mouse users
can click on the options shown in red at the bottom of the screen.

Once you select any one of the six areas, another help screen will appear.
It will usually display additional choices of help topics, which can be selected
in the same manner. From any of the help screens, you can select the Paradox
option from the menu to exit the Help System and return to the program, or
you can press the (ESC) key to move to the previous menu.

One particular area of the Help System that you may find useful is the
Help Index, which is arranged by topic in alphabetical order. To view this
index, go to the main Help System menu and choose Index from the menu.

Figure 3-4.   *Help screen*

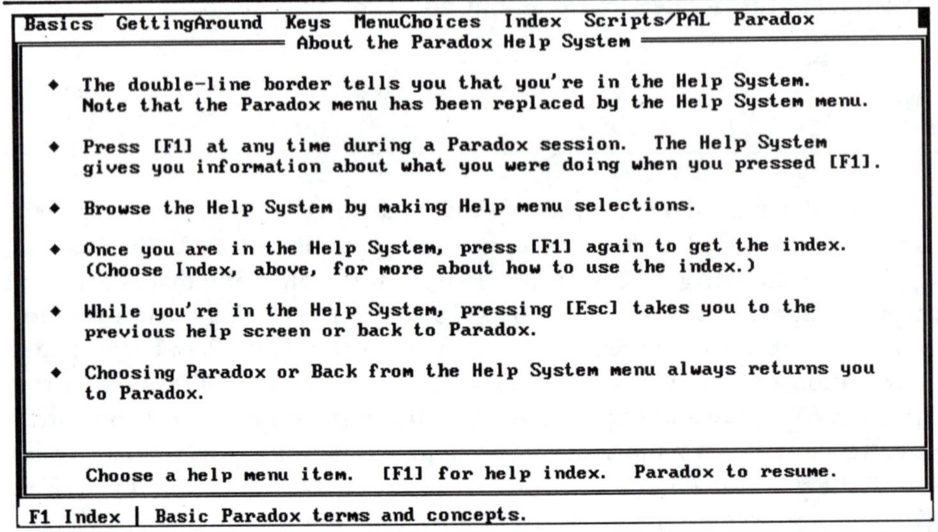

```
┌─────────────────────────────────────────────────────────────────────┐
│Basics  GettingAround  Keys  MenuChoices  Index  Scripts/PAL  Paradox  ▐
│╔══════════════════ About the Paradox Help System ═══════════════════╗│
│║                                                                    ║│
│║  ◆  The double-line border tells you that you're in the Help System.║│
│║     Note that the Paradox menu has been replaced by the Help System menu.║│
│║                                                                    ║│
│║  ◆  Press [F1] at any time during a Paradox session.  The Help System║│
│║     gives you information about what you were doing when you pressed [F1].║│
│║                                                                    ║│
│║  ◆  Browse the Help System by making Help menu selections.         ║│
│║                                                                    ║│
│║  ◆  Once you are in the Help System, press [F1] again to get the index.║│
│║     (Choose Index, above, for more about how to use the index.)    ║│
│║                                                                    ║│
│║  ◆  While you're in the Help System, pressing [Esc] takes you to the║│
│║     previous help screen or back to Paradox.                       ║│
│║                                                                    ║│
│║  ◆  Choosing Paradox or Back from the Help System menu always returns you║│
│║     to Paradox.                                                    ║│
│║                                                                    ║│
│╚════════════════════════════════════════════════════════════════════╝│
│                                                                       │
│      Choose a help menu item.   [F1] for help index.   Paradox to resume.│
├───────────────────────────────────────────────────────────────────────┤
│ F1 Index │ Basic Paradox terms and concepts.                          │
└───────────────────────────────────────────────────────────────────────┘
```

Another screen that details how the index can be used will appear, and from this screen you can press (F1) to display the Help Index, shown in Figure 3-5.

You can use the (PGUP) and (PGDN) keys or the (↑) and (↓) keys to browse through the Help Index. Any specific topic preceded by a period has an accompanying help screen, which can be displayed by pressing (ENTER). After

Table 3-2.   *The Six Areas of the Help System*

Help Area	Features or Concepts Explained
Getting Around	Movement between menus, between tables, and within the Help System
Keys	The Paradox keyboard
Menu Choices	All menu choices
Index	All help topics (displayed in order Form)
Scripts/PAL	Script editing; programming with PAL
Paradox	Basic terms and concepts

Figure 3-5. **Help Index**

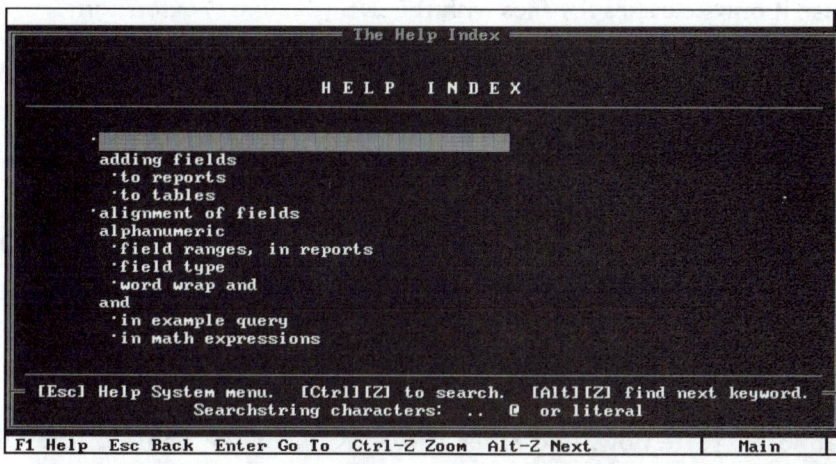

reading the information, you can select Paradox from the menu to resume using the program, or you can press (F1) to get back to the Help Index.

To gain a familiarity with the Help System, you may wish to take a few minutes to browse through the help screens. When you are done viewing the screens, choose Paradox from the menu to get back to the program.

Creating a Table

As mentioned in Chapter 1, Paradox stores data in the form of tables. To create a table, choose Create from the main menu. Remember, you can click the Create option, use the cursor keys to highlight the Create option and then press (ENTER), or type the first letter of the desired menu name (in this case, C for Create).

Once you choose Create from the menu, Paradox displays a dialog box, asking you for the name of the table. Each table must have a name, and the name must conform to the rules for all DOS filenames. A *filename* can include letters, numbers, or the underscore character. It cannot contain more than eight characters. Paradox automatically assigns table names the .DB extension because it only searches for files with the .DB (database) extension.

Note that Paradox uses temporary tables named ANSWER, STRUCT, and KEYVIOL at various times. Other reserved names include CHARTEMP, KVTEMP, RESTTEMP, DELTEMP, PASTTEMP, SORTQUES, INSTEMP, and PRBTEMP. You should not try to assign these names to any tables that you create.

Table names should be unique. If you specify a name that is already in use, Paradox warns you and asks for confirmation.

Tip

Working with the Table Structure Image

Choose Create now, and enter **ABCSTAFF** for the name of the table. Within a moment, Paradox displays a screen known as the table structure image (which is shown in Figure 3-6). This screen contains areas in which you define both the names of the fields and the field types.

When naming a field, use a name that best describes the contents of that field. Like names for tables, field names can be composed of letters and numbers. However, you have considerably more flexibility in naming fields than tables. Field names can be up to 25 characters in length, and they can contain spaces (however, they cannot start with a space). You can include any printable character except for double quotation marks, square brackets, left and right parentheses, curly braces, or the -> character combination. Although Paradox lets you create long field names, it is a good idea to keep them relatively short. Doing so will keep the headings in your simpler reports from occupying too much space.

While the table structure image is visible on your screen, note that the menu structure has changed. Because you are in Create mode, you see the Create menu at the top of the screen, containing four menu options: Borrow, File Format, DO-IT!, and Cancel.

- The Borrow option lets you borrow the structure of an existing table; you can use this option to base a new table's design on the structure of an existing table.

Figure 3-6.   *Table structure image*

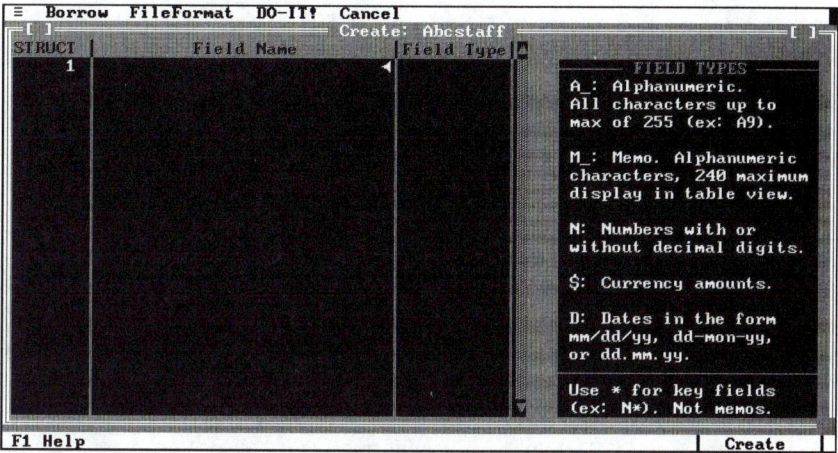

- The FileFormat option lets you change the format in which Paradox will save the table: Standard or Compatible. The default option for this choice is the Paradox 4 (Standard) file format; if you ignore the FileFormat menu choice, your new tables are automatically saved under Paradox 4 file format. If you choose Compatible, the table is saved under the earlier (Paradox 3.5 and older) file format. (Earlier versions of Paradox did not support memo fields, so if your table uses memo fields, you should not try to save it in compatible file format.)

- The DO-IT! and Cancel options perform the same tasks as elsewhere in Paradox; choosing DO-IT! saves the table structure, and Cancel cancels the operation.

Now that you have learned some of the Paradox basics, let's return to the example created in Chapter 2 for ABC Temporaries and begin to create a table. The first attribute on the list is the employee's social security number, so enter **Social Security** for the first name in the Field Name column. Once you press (ENTER), the cursor automatically moves over to the Field Type column. Here Paradox allows the entry of six types of fields. They are as follows.

- *Alphanumeric fields* are used to store any characters, including letters, numbers, special symbols, and blank spaces, up to 255 characters. You define a field as an alphanumeric field by entering the letter A in the Field Type column of the table structure image, next to the field name. You must also specify the width of the field, by entering a number from 1 to 255 beside the letter A. Hence, to define an alphanumeric field 12 characters wide, you would enter **A12** in the Field Type column. If you enter field type A without including the width indicator, Paradox will ask you to specify a width for the field.

- *Memo fields* are used to store memos, or large amounts of alphanumeric information. There is a theoretical limit to the size of a memo field, but that limit is so large (64 megabytes maximum per record) that you can store virtually any needed text in a memo field. Memo fields are typically used to store comments that vary greatly in length, such as descriptions of a product or written evaluations of employees.

- *Number fields* use numbers, with or without decimal places. You can enter numbers of up to 15 significant digits, so unless you are performing scientific calculations, you should not have a problem with numerical accuracy. (If you enter numbers with more than 15 digits, they are automatically rounded and stored under scientific notation by Paradox.) By default, Paradox displays numbers without commas and with up to two decimal places. Negative numbers are displayed with a minus sign preceding the number (and in red if you have a color monitor).

- *Currency fields* are special number fields designed to display currency values. Paradox automatically formats any value stored in a currency field with two decimal places, and with commas as thousands separators. (You can change the type of separator by choosing International Sort Order through the Custom Configuration Program. See your Paradox documentation for details about using the Custom Configuration Program.) The currency format also automatically puts parentheses around any negative number stored in the field.

Note

One point to remember with currency fields is that the formatting affects how the data is displayed, but it does not change the internal value of the data itself. For example, if you entered a value of 553.4572 into a currency field, it would be displayed as 553.46. However, Paradox would internally store the value as originally entered, and would use this internal value in any calculations based on that field.

- *Date fields* are used to store dates. Paradox lets you enter the dates in any of four formats: mm/dd/yy, dd-mon-yy, dd.mm.yy, or yy.mm.dd. Paradox defaults to dates in the twentieth century; for other dates, you can enter all four numbers of the year as part of the date. Paradox automatically checks the validity of a date as you enter it. If you attempt to enter a date that cannot exist (such as 63/85/1993) into a date field, Paradox will beep and display an error message.

  You can perform arithmetic on a date field (such as adding or subtracting a number of days to or from a date to get another date), and you can perform queries (select subsets of tables) based on a date or a range of dates. While Paradox accepts dates between 1/1/100 and 12/31/9999, amateur genealogists and others concerned with dates far in the past should note that date tracking in Paradox is based on the Gregorian calendar in present use, so dates earlier than the sixteenth century may vary when compared to the calendar you decide to use.

Paradox also offers another type of field, which does not appear in the Field Types descriptions on the right side of the screen. These are *short number fields,* a special type of field used for storing short numbers, or numbers within the range from –32,767 to +32,767. You should not use a short number field unless you are an advanced Paradox user or developer; although this type of field takes less space in a database, there are serious limitations affecting the display of short number fields in Paradox forms.

Note

Use numeric fields for numbers that must be calculated. If a field that contains numbers will not be used in calculations, define that field as an alphanumeric field. Such fields commonly contain such items as Social Security numbers, part numbers, phone numbers, and so forth.

Most fields in a table will be either of the alphanumeric or the number type, although there will undoubtedly be times when you will need most or all of the different field types that Paradox offers.

Returning to our example, since the Social Security field will contain alphanumeric characters, enter **A** (for alphanumeric) and press (ENTER). Note that when you press (ENTER), Paradox asks for the field width. Remember, alphanumeric fields can be up to 255 characters in length. In Chapter 2, ABC Temporaries calculated that the Social Security field would require 11 characters, so type **11** but do not press (ENTER).) Add an asterisk (*) to designate the field as a key field (as explained in the next section), and *then* press (ENTER).

The Key Field Concept

Paradox lets you define one or more initial fields as *key fields,* which Paradox will treat differently from non-key fields. Probably the most important thing to remember is that key fields will contain unique information; Paradox will not let you put the same entry into the key of two records. Also, when designing the structure of the table, note that you *must* place all key fields together, beginning at field number 1. (You cannot place key fields in a random order all over the structure of a table.) When you save the file, records are arranged by key field. The requirement that key-field data be unique means you should be careful when deciding what should be a key field. If the first two fields of a table were Last name and First name, making both fields key fields would mean you could never enter two records with an identical last and first name. In such a case, you might want to use a combination of Last Name, First Name, and Middle Name as key fields. Also, remember that you don't have to make any field a key field; doing so can boost performance but is not generally required.

In addition to preventing duplications, designating a field as a key field causes Paradox to keep an internal index that helps to speed sorts and queries that are based on the contents of that field. Since social security numbers are unique, the asterisk is placed after the field type to designate the field as a key field, as shown in Figure 3-7.

Let's continue with our example. Enter **Last Name** for the second field name. When the cursor moves to the Field Type area, enter **A15** to designate the field type and width at the same time. (This saves you the trouble of

Figure 3-7. *Key field designation*

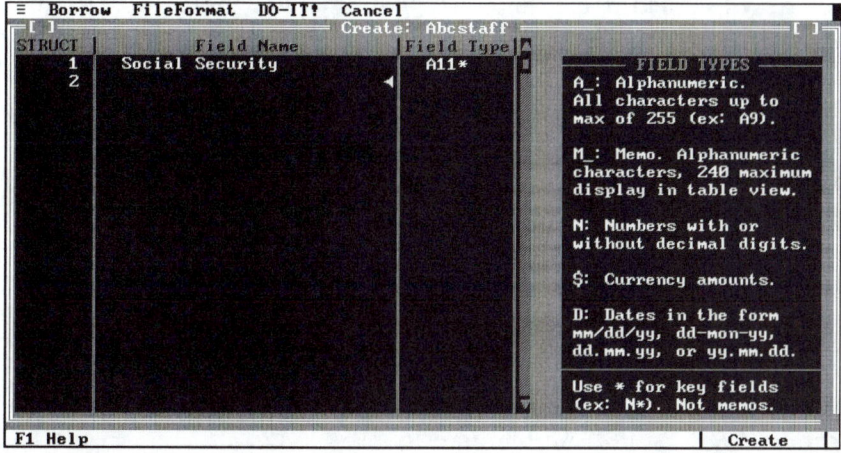

pressing (ENTER) and waiting for Paradox to ask for the field width.) For the third item in the attribute list, the employee's first name, enter **First Name**. Again, when the cursor moves to the Field Type area, enter **A15**. Moving down the list, enter **Address** for the fourth field definition and **A25** for the field type and width. For the fifth field enter **City** and **A15**. For the next field enter **State** and **A2**.

The next field will be ZIP Code. ZIP codes consist of numbers, so at first you might think you should use the numeric field type. However, this is not really practical. If you make use of the nine-digit business ZIP codes, Paradox will not allow the entry of the hyphen. It will also delete beginning zeros in ZIP codes such as 00123. You will never use a ZIP code in a numerical calculation, so it makes sense to store the ZIP code as an alphanumeric field rather than as a numeric field. A number stored in an alphanumeric field cannot be used directly in a numerical calculation, although you can convert the value to a number with a Paradox function. Now enter **ZIP Code** as the field name. Enter **A10** to designate an alphanumeric field ten characters wide.

You may recall from Chapter 2 that two fields in the personnel database take the form of dates. Paradox lets you use date fields to enter these dates. Enter **Date of Birth** for the name of the field, and type **D** in the Field Type column to indicate a date field. Enter Date Hired for the name of the field, and type D in the Field Type column to indicate a date field.

For the next field name, enter Dependents. For the field type, enter N for numeric. You may notice that unlike some database managers, Paradox does not require you to specify the width of a numeric field or the number of decimal places needed to store the number. Paradox will make allowances for storing the number automatically.

Enter Salary for the name of the next field, and enter a dollar sign ($) to designate this field as a currency field. This field will be used to track the salaries of the employees in dollar amounts. Finally, enter the remaining information for the next three fields, as shown here:

Field Name	Type	Width	Key field?
Assignment	Alphanumeric	20	No
Hourly Rate	Currency		No
Phone	Alphanumeric	12	No

For the final field name, enter Comments. For the field type, enter M for memo. Then press (ENTER), and you'll note that Paradox asks you for the length (up to 240 characters) of the memo field. As explained earlier, Paradox lets you store a virtually unlimited amount of text in a memo field—so why must you enter a length?

Paradox needs a specific length for the memo field due to the way Paradox stores data that you place in those fields. The number that you enter in response to this prompt does not limit the actual size of the memo field in any way, but it does affect how much of the memo will be visible when in Table view (the normal way Paradox data is displayed). In Table view, a maximum of 240 characters of a memo field's contents can be viewed; the rest of the field can be seen by changing to Field view, a topic that will be discussed later. Thus, if you enter 50 in response to the prompt, the first 50 characters of the memo field will be visible from Table view. For this example, enter 25.

Correcting Your Entries

If you make any mistakes while defining the structure of the table, you can correct them before you complete the table definition process. Consider a few examples:

- *Changing an Entry* If you make a typing error while defining the table, use the cursor keys to move to the field name or field type entry containing the mistake (or click in the offending entry), and use the (BACKSPACE) key along with the appropriate character keys in order to make the desired corrections. If the error is near the beginning of the entry or the entire entry is incorrect, you can press (CTRL)(BACKSPACE) to clear the entire entry. You can also use (DEL) to delete a character.

- *Adding a Row* If you have forgotten to add a field definition, you can insert a blank row anywhere in the table structure by using the (INS) key. Move the cursor to the location where you want to insert the blank row, and press (INS). A blank row appears, and existing rows below it in the table structure are moved down automatically.

- *Deleting a Row* If you have defined a field and decide it is not needed, move the cursor to any location on that row and press (DEL). The row containing the field is deleted, and any fields underneath move up to fill the space in the table structure.

- *Restructuring an Existing Table* If you have already saved the definition for a table, but you want to change the table's design, you must restructure the table. This process is described in Chapter 6.

Completing the Table Definition

To tell Paradox that you have finished defining the table structure, choose DO-IT!. You will briefly see the message "Creating ABCSTAFF," and then the main menu will reappear.

Displaying a Table Structure

You could begin entering the records for the employees of ABC Temporaries at this time, but instead, display the table structure first. If you cannot recall the precise fields you used when creating a table, or if you cannot remember what a particular table is used for, you can get an idea by displaying the table's structure. From the menu, you can use Tools/Info/Structure to examine the structure of a table.

From the main menu, type **T** to open the Tools menu, and then choose Info. From the next menu that appears, choose Structure. Paradox will ask for a table name. Pressing (ENTER) at this point will display a list of all tables contained in the Paradox subdirectory of your disk. Select ABCSTAFF from the list of available tables by pressing (ENTER), or clicking on the name ABCSTAFF and then on OK. Paradox will show the table's structure within a temporary table named STRUCT, as shown in Figure 3-8.

Since you will not need to retain this data permanently, press Clear Image ((F8)) to clear the display. You now have the new table, but it remains empty. To add records to the table, you will use the Edit command, found within the Modify menu.

The Edit Command

The Edit command can be used both for editing existing records and for adding new records to a table in Paradox. (There are other ways to add records to tables and these will be considered later.) To try this command,

Figure 3-8.   *Table structure for ABCSTAFF*

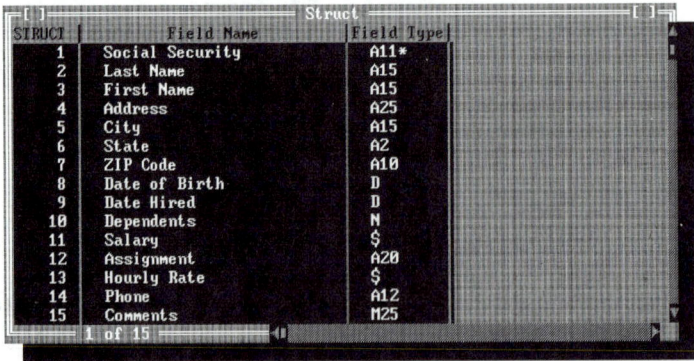

choose Modify from the main menu. On the Modify menu one of the available choices is Edit.

Select the Edit command. (Note that (F9) can be used as a shortcut for the Edit command.) Paradox will ask you for the name of the table you wish to edit; you can enter the table name, or you can press (ENTER) to display all available tables. Mouse users can click on the OK button. Press (ENTER) and choose ABCSTAFF from the list, or enter **ABCSTAFF** and press (ENTER). In a moment, the ABCSTAFF table will appear. In the lower-right corner of the screen you'll see the word "Edit," informing you that Paradox is now in Edit mode. The cursor is flashing in the Social Security field.

For each field in the record, enter the following information, pressing (ENTER) after each entry is completed. In the two currency fields, you don't need to type decimal places if there are no cents in the amount.

Social Security:	**123-44-8976**
Last Name:	**Morse**
First Name:	**Marcia**
Address:	**4260 Park Avenue**
City:	**Chevy Chase**
State:	**MD**
ZIP Code:	**20815-0988**
Date of Birth:	**3/01/54**
Date Hired:	**7/25/85**
Dependents:	**2**
Salary:	**8.50**
Assignment:	**National Oil Co.**
Hourly Rate:	**15.00**
Phone:	**301-555-9802**
Comments:	**Experienced in accounting.**

Once the record has been completely filled in, you will notice that the cursor automatically moves down to the row that will contain the next record. If you make a mistake during the data entry process, you can reach the offending field with the cursor keys and use the (BACKSPACE) key to correct and retype the entry.

Entering Data in a Memo Field

If you press (ENTER) after entering the phone number and then try to type something in the Comments memo field, you will notice that Paradox beeps, and displays the following message near the bottom of the desktop:

```
Press [Alt][F5] or [Ctrl][F] if you want to edit a Memo field
```

Because you are working in a memo field, you must enter data a little differently.

Whenever the cursor is in a memo field (as it is now), you are at the entry point for a *memo window* that can hold large amounts of text (up to 64 MB per record). To enter the memo window you can press Field view ((ALT)-(F5) or (CTRL)-(F)). Mouse users can double-click on a memo field to enter the field. Press (ALT)-(F5) now, and you will see a window like that in Figure 3-9, where you can type the contents of the Comments field.

Like all windows in Paradox, the memo window can be resized or moved around with the mouse. The Paradox Editor lets you type here as you would with any word processor. You needn't press (ENTER) at the end of each line; the Editor automatically moves the cursor to the next line. The (BACKSPACE) key erases any mistakes, and you can use the arrow keys to move the cursor around the screen for editing. For the Comments field of your example record, type the following now:

```
Experienced in accounting, tax preparation, has MBA in business management.
```

When you have finished typing this text, you will need to switch back to Table view. You can do so by choosing DO-IT! with the keyboard or the

Figure 3-9.   *Memo window for Comments field*

mouse. Use either of these methods now to close the memo window and return to Table view.

Press (ENTER) now to move the cursor to the first field for the next record, and proceed to fill in the next few records for the ABC Temporaries staff table, as shown in Figure 3-10.

Remember

Use (ALT)-(F5) *or* (CTRL)-(F) *to add data to the memo fields, then choose DO-IT! when you are done.*

Moving Around in the Table

During your data entry, you can use various combinations of the cursor keys to move around in the table. Table 3-3 explains the function of the cursor movement keys.

Of course, mouse users can move around the table by simply clicking in the desired field of the table. Use the scroll bars, if necessary, to move between the records of a large table. (Scrolling techniques with the mouse are covered later, in "Scrolling the Contents of a Window.")

If, during your editing, you move the cursor to the last field of a record and attempt to move beyond that field, Paradox will "wrap" the cursor around

Table 3-3.   *Cursor Movement Keys Used During Editing*

Key	Cursor Movement
(←)	Left one field
(→)	Right one field
(↑)	Up one record
(↓)	Down one record
(HOME)	To first record of current field
(END)	To last record of current field
(TAB)	Right one field
(SHIFT)-(TAB)	Left one field
(ENTER)	Right one field
(CTRL)-(HOME)	To first field of current record
(CTRL)-(END)	To last field of current record

Figure 3-10.   *Additional records for ABCSTAFF*

Social Security: 121-33-9876
Last Name: Westman
First Name: Andrea
Address: 4807 East Avenue
City: Silver Spring
State: MD
ZIP Code: 20910-0124
Date of Birth: 5/29/61
Date Hired: 7/04/90
Dependents: 2
Salary: 15.00
Assignment: National Oil Co.
Hourly Rate: 24.00
Phone: 301-555-5682
Comments: Did well on last two assignments.

Social Security: 232-55-1234
Last Name: Jackson
First Name: David
Address: 4102 Valley Lane
City: Falls Church
State: VA
ZIP Code: 22044
Date of Birth: 12/22/55
Date Hired: 9/05/91
Dependents: 1
Salary: 7.50
Assignment: City Revenue Dept.
Hourly Rate: 12.00
Phone: 703-555-2345
Comments: Absentee rate high.

Social Security: 901-77-3456
Last Name: Mitchell
First Name: Mary Jo
Address: 617 North Oakland Street
City: Arlington
State: VA
ZIP Code: 22203
Date of Birth: 8/17/58
Date Hired: 12/01/91
Dependents: 1
Salary: 7.50
Assignment: Smith Builders
Hourly Rate: 12.00
Phone: 703-555-7654
Comments: Too new to evaluate, but has excellent references from temporary
agency in Chicago, IL, where she lived previously.

to the first field of the following record. If you attempt to move the cursor below the last record in a table, Paradox assumes that you want to add a new record, and will add a new blank line below the last record.

Saving the Information

As long as you are in Edit mode in Paradox, the information that you have entered has not been saved on your disk. Choose DO-IT! now, and the edits will be saved.

Editing on a Network

If you are editing tables on the shared drive of a local area network, you will want to avoid using the Edit command. Whenever you choose Modify/Edit on a network, Paradox automatically locks the entire table, meaning other users cannot access that table for any reason until you finish your editing. On a network, use the Modify/CoEdit command rather than Modify/Edit. See Chapter 15 for more details about network use of Paradox.

About the Windows on the Desktop

Now that you have an existing table in Paradox, it will be helpful to consider the subject of *windows* on the desktop. Paradox displays your data in the form of tables, and each table occupies an individual window. Later, as you create additional tables, you will learn how you can manipulate multiple windows on the screen. But for now, let's explore techniques for moving and sizing a table window. You can do so with the mouse, or with the Maximize/Restore and Size/Move commands of the System menu.

Mouse users will find the windows in Paradox to be particularly helpful, because you can use your mouse to easily move and resize the windows.

Tip

You learned earlier in the chapter that the System menu is located at the far left side of the main menu, and is represented by three small horizontal lines. You can open the System menu by clicking on this indicator with the mouse, or you can press (ALT)-(SPACEBAR). When you open the System menu, you see these choices:

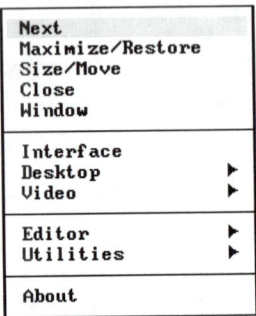

Some of these commands will be discussed later, when you are working with more than one window on the desktop. For now, note the the Maximize/Restore, Size/Move, and Close commands.

Maximizing and Restoring a Window

The Maximize/Restore option *maximizes* the active window (enlarges it to fill the entire screen); or, if the window is already maximized, this command restores the window to the size it was before it was maximized. There are also two alternate ways to maximize or restore a window's size: you may use the Maximize/Restore icon, or the Maximize/Restore key ((SHIFT)-(F5)). Mouse users can click on the Maximize/Restore icon (the small arrow located at the right end of the window's title bar) to maximize or restore a window. Pressing (SHIFT)-(F5) repeatedly will also maximize and restore a window. Try any of these methods now, and note their effect.

Sizing and Moving a Window

The Size/Move command is used to resize or move a window. When you select this command from the System menu, Paradox asks you to use the

(SHIFT) key along with the cursor keys to resize the window, and to use the cursor keys alone to move the window. When you are finished resizing or moving the window, press (ENTER). You can also press the Size/Move key ((CTRL)-(F5)) to resize or move a window.

Mouse users have a decided advantage here; it is much easier to resize or move a window with the mouse than with the keyboard. With the mouse, there is no need to select a command from the System menu. To resize a window, just click and drag the window's resizing corner (the lower-right corner of the window) to stretch or shrink the window as desired. To move a window with the mouse, click and drag anywhere in the window's title bar (the top border); the entire window will move along with the title bar as you drag it.

Scrolling the Contents of a Window

Another advantage of the mouse is that it enables the use of the *scroll bars* to scroll the contents of a table. The vertical scroll bar is located at the right edge of a table's window, and the horizontal scroll bar is located at the bottom edge. Clicking on the up-arrow and down-arrow buttons at the top and bottom of the vertical scroll bar scrolls the table upward and downward, respectively. Clicking on the left-arrow and right-arrow buttons at the left and right ends of the horizontal scroll bar scrolls the table to the left and right, respectively. And you can cause a relative movement within a table by dragging the *scroll box* (the rectangular boxes located within both scroll bars) to a desired location. For example, if you drag the vertical scroll box halfway down the vertical scroll bar and release the mouse button, you will scroll halfway down the records in the table.

Closing a Window

One way to close a window is by choosing Close from the System menu. There are easier ways to do this; you can also click on the Close box (at the left end of the window's title bar), or you can press the Close key ((CTRL)-(F8)).

Table View Versus Form View

Viewing and entering records as you have been doing gets the job done, but as you can see, it is impossible to view all of the fields in the table at the same time—they will not all fit on the screen. Paradox normally displays information in table view, because most users find it easier to grasp the concept of a database when it is shown in this fashion. It is easy to see a number of records, and the records and fields are clearly distinguished. However, not being able to see all of the fields also presents a clear drawback. For example, when you are viewing the name of an employee, you will find that the City, State, and remaining fields are hidden. To view these fields, you could use the ⊙ key, but then the Name fields disappear off to the left side. This makes it hard to recall which line containing Date Hired, Date of Birth, Salary, and so on matches a particular employee name.

To avoid this problem, some database managers display information in an on-screen form rather than in a table. Paradox provides the flexibility of using either method. You can quickly move between the two with the Form Toggle ((F7)) key. Press (F7) now, and Paradox will display the record in a form view, as shown in Figure 3-11.

Moving around in the table is different in Form view than it is in Table view. Try (PGUP) and (PGDN), and then try using the ⊙ and ⊙ keys. Whereas

Figure 3-11.   *Form view of a record*

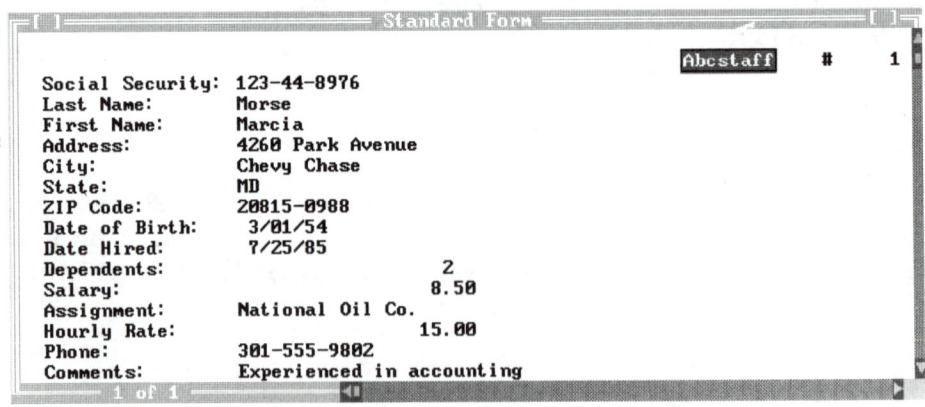

in Table view, (PGUP) and (PGDN) move you up and down by a screenful of records, they now move you up and down one record at a time. And the arrow keys now move the cursor between fields instead of between records. While viewing the records in either view, you can use the (F7) key to switch back and forth between the windows containing Table and Form views.

Use the view of your choice to proceed, and add the remaining records to the table as shown in Figure 3-12. If you're using the form, use the (PGDN) key to get to a new, blank record. If you prefer table view, use the cursor keys to get to the blank line below the last record. Remember, you can use (ALT)(F5) or (CTRL)(F) to edit the memo fields. After the last record has been entered, press the (F2) key to save the records.

An Introduction to Queries

Your data is now stored in Paradox, ready for use. Later chapters will explain how you can make use of data once it has been entered into a table, but a quick introduction, to describe how you will ask Paradox for information and produce simple reports, is appropriate.

Database users frequently need to obtain sets of facts. Suppose you need a list of all employees living in Maryland. Paradox makes such a query simple with its Ask command. To quickly try an example, choose Ask from the main menu. (If the main menu isn't visible, you are probably still in Edit mode; press (F2).) Paradox will ask for the name of the table you are asking about; enter **ABCSTAFF** and a Query Form will appear at the top of the desktop, as shown in Figure 3-13. The use of the Query Form is covered in more detail in Chapter 6.

By moving the cursor to each desired field and pressing (F6), you place check marks in the fields that you want to have included in the answer Paradox will provide. You also type a matching criteria to select the desired records in the field of your choice. To see how this works, use the mouse or the (←) or (→) to place the cursor in the first row of the Last name field, and then press (F6). When you do this, a check mark will appear in the field. Move to the first row of the First name field and press (F6) again; then do the same for the City and State fields. This action tells Paradox that you will want to see

Figure 3-12.   *Remaining records for ABCSTAFF*

Social Security: 121-90-5432
Last Name: Robinson
First Name: Shirley
Address: 270 Browning Ave #3C
City: Takoma Park
State: MD
ZIP Code: 20912
Date of Birth: 11/02/64
Date Hired: 11/17/91
Dependents: 1
Salary: 7.50
Assignment: National Oil Co.
Hourly Rate: 12.00
Phone: 301-555-4582
Comments: Too new to evaluate.

Social Security: 343-55-9821
Last Name: Robinson
First Name: Wanda
Address: 1607 21st Street, NW
City: Washington
State: DC
ZIP Code: 20009
Date of Birth: 6/22/66
Date Hired: 9/17/87
Dependents: 0
Salary: 7.50
Assignment: City Revenue Dept.
Hourly Rate: 12.00
Phone: 202-555-9876
Comments: Client satisfaction with employee's work is consistently high.

Social Security: 876-54-3210
Last Name: Hart
First Name: Edward
Address: 6200 Germantown Road
City: Fairfax
State: VA
ZIP Code: 22025
Date of Birth: 12/20/55
Date Hired: 10/19/86
Dependents: 3
Salary: 8.50
Assignment: Smith Builders
Hourly Rate: 14.00
Phone: 703-555-7834
Comments: Absence rate has been very excessive.

Figure 3-12. *Remaining records for ABCSTAFF* (continued)

Social Security: 909-88-7654
Last Name: Jones
First Name: Judi
Address: 5203 North Shore Drive
City: Reston
State: VA
ZIP Code: 22090
Date of Birth: 9/18/61
Date Hired: 8/12/90
Dependents: 1
Salary: 12.00
Assignment: National Oil Co.
Hourly Rate: 17.50
Phone: 703-555-2638
Comments: Performed well on last four assignments.

the Last Name, First Name, City, and State fields included in the list Paradox provides in response to your query.

With the cursor still in the State field, type **MD** to tell Paradox that you want the query to select only those records that contain the letters MD in the State field. What you have just done is all that you need do to provide Paradox with a query. There are no arcane commands or strange syntax to try to decipher; just check the fields you need to see, fill in an example of what data you want in any desired field, and choose DO-IT! to perform the query.

If you have not yet done so, choose DO-IT!. Paradox will perform the query and then will display the results in a temporary table named ANSWER. This table appears on the desktop atop the existing windows, as shown in

Figure 3-13. *Query Form*

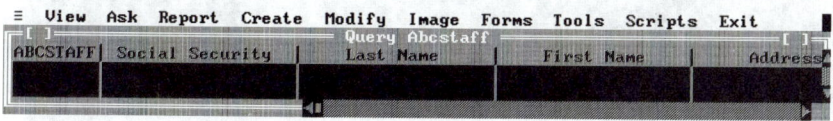

Figure 3-14. (If your results do not match the ones shown, check the entry in the State field of the query to be sure that the entry matches the way you originally entered MD in the table. Click in the Query window with the mouse or use Up Image, (F3) to move back to the Query Form, then correct any typos and, finally, press (F2) to retry the query.)

Chapter 6 provides more details on how you can design queries to retrieve specific information.

Note

Getting an Instant Report

If you need a quick printed report of the results of a query, or of any table, you can easily get one by pressing the (ALT)-(F7) key combination, the Instant Report key. If you have a printer, make sure it is turned on and that paper is loaded. Then press (ALT)-(F7). You should get a printed report based on the

Figure 3-14.   *Results of the query*

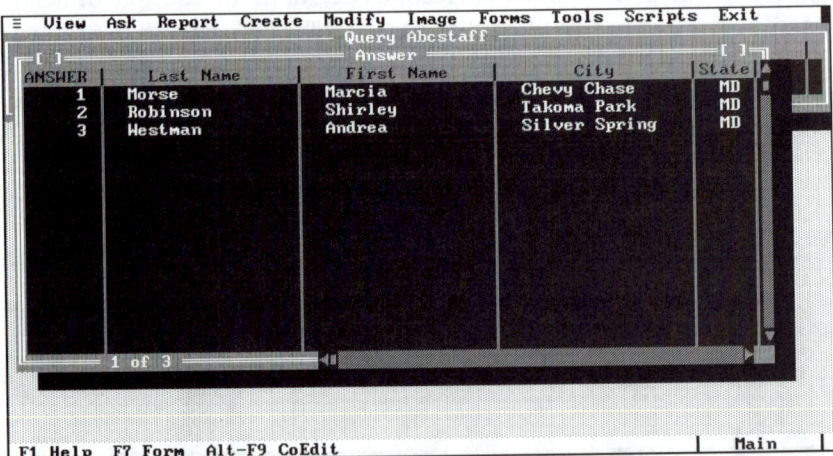

temporary table created by the query. The report will resemble the example shown here:

```
5/12/92               Standard Report          Page   1


Last Name          First Name    City               State
- - - - - - - - -  - - - - - - - - -  - - - - - - - - - - -    - - - - - -
Morse              Marcia        Chevy Chase        MD
Robinson           Shirley       Takoma Park        MD
Westman            Andrea        Silver Spring      MD
```

Click on the Close box for the ANSWER and QUERY tables to put them away, leaving ABCSTAFF open. Or, if you are not using a mouse, press Clear All ((ALT)-(F8)) to clear the results of the query and to clear the Query Form. Then choose View, and enter ABCSTAFF for the name of the table. The screen will again display the table you created during this chapter.

You can also use Instant Report to produce a report of your entire database. Turn on your printer, load paper if necessary, and press (ALT)-(F7). This time, you should get a printed report based on the ABCSTAFF table created by the query. The report will resemble the example that is shown in Figure 3-15.

You can produce very detailed reports in Paradox. Such reports can include customized headers and footers, customized placement of fields, word wrapping of large amounts of text, and numeric results based on calculations of fields. Such reports are covered in detail in Chapter 7.

Getting an Instant Graph

Paradox can also be used to produce presentation graphs. You will learn more about this subject in Chapter 8, but for now, keep in mind that an instant graph can provide a quick look at the presentation capabilities of Paradox. To display an instant graph, first use the View command to view the table you wish to graph. Then, simply place the cursor in the numeric field to be graphed and press (CTRL)-(F7). As an example, perhaps you would like to see a bar graph showing the staff salaries. First use the mouse or the (→) key to move the cursor to any record in the Salary field, and then press (CTRL)-(F7).

Figure 3-15.   *Results of Instant Report using ABCSTAFF table*

```
6/12/92                           Standard Report                    Page   1
```

Social Security	Last Name	First Name	Address
121-33-9876	Westman	Andrea	4807 East Avenue
121-90-5432	Robinson	Shirley	270 Browning Ave #3C
123-44-8976	Morse	Marcia	4260 Park Avenue
232-55-1234	Jackson	David	4102 Valley Lane
343-55-9821	Robinson	Wanda	1607 21st Street, NW
876-54-3210	Hart	Edward	6200 Germantown Road
901-77-3456	Mitchell	Mary Jo	617 North Oakland Street
909-88-7654	Jones	Judi	5203 North Shore Drive

City	State	ZIP Code	Date of Birth	Date Hired	Dependents
Silver Spring	MD	20910-0124	5/29/61	7/04/90	2
Takoma Park	MD	20912	11/02/64	11/17/91	1
Chevy Chase	MD	20815-0988	3/01/54	7/25/85	2
Falls Church	VA	22044	12/22/55	9/05/91	1
Washington	DC	20009	6/22/66	9/17/87	0
Fairfax	VA	22025	12/20/55	10/19/86	3
Arlington	VA	22203	8/17/58	12/01/91	1
Reston	VA	22090	9/18/61	8/12/90	1

Salary	Assignment	Hourly Rate	Phone	Comments
15.00	National Oil Co.	24.00	301-555-5682	Did well on las
7.50	National Oil Co.	12.00	301-555-4582	Too new to eval
8.50	National Oil Co.	15.00	301-555-9802	Experienced in
7.50	City Revenue Dept.	12.00	703-555-2345	Absentee rate h
7.50	City Revenue Dept.	12.00	202-555-9876	Consistently hi
8.50	Smith Builders	14.00	703-555-7834	Absence rate ha
7.50	Smith Builders	12.00	703-555-7654	Too new to eval
12.00	National Oil Co.	17.50	703-555-2638	Performed well

Figure 3-16 shows the resulting graph. (Note that the social security numbers run together; Chapter 8 will detail ways in which you can correct this.) For now, press any key to exit the graph.

If this is a good time for a break, from select Exit the main menu, choose Exit, and choose Yes. Note that whenever you exit Paradox, any temporary tables (such as ANSWER) are normally lost.

Figure 3-16. *An instant graph*

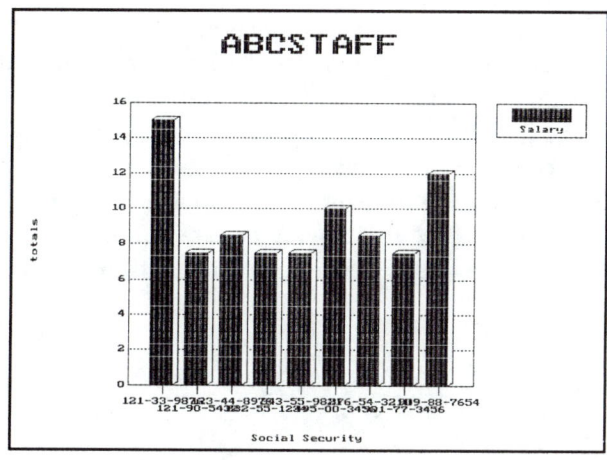

Now that you have a table containing data, you will want to know how you can manipulate that data to better obtain the results you want. The next chapter covers this area in more detail.

Always exit from Paradox by choosing Exit from the menu. Never exit by turning off your computer while still in Paradox!

Caution

About Tables, Objects, and Families

As you have learned, Paradox stores your data in the form of tables, made up of rows (records) and columns (fields). Each table is stored as a DOS file, under the name you assign the table, plus a filename extension of .DB. However, tables are not the only objects you will work with in Paradox. In Paradox, each table can have a number of *objects* associated with it. These objects may include custom forms used for viewing data in the table, custom reports for printing data, and indexes that help maintain the order in which the records are displayed.

A table, along with the collection of objects associated with that particular table, are referred to collectively as a *family*. Besides containing the table, forms, and reports, a table's family may also contain image settings (settings that control how the data is displayed), validity checks (rules that control how data can be entered), a primary index (used to maintain the order of records by a key field) and secondary indexes. The associated objects are stored in files with the same name as that given to the table; only the filename extensions differ. Table 3-4 shows the extensions used for files of various objects under Paradox.

Temporary Tables

During normal operations, Paradox often creates *temporary tables*. For instance, whenever you perform a query, Paradox stores the results of the query in a temporary table called ANSWER. And, during the process of designing a table's structure, Paradox stores the design in a temporary table called STRUCT. The temporary tables that Paradox may create during various operations are

ANSWER	INSERTED
CHANGED	KEYVIOL
CROSSTAB	LIST
DELETED	PROBLEMS
ENTRY	STRUCT
FAMILY	

Caution

At this time, it is not important to know what these tables are used for. Remember these names, however, as you should never use them to name any of your own tables. If you do, Paradox can overwrite the data in your table when it creates its own temporary table using the same name.

Table 3-4. *Extensions Used by Paradox Object Files*

Object	Extension
Paradox table	.DB
Memo field file for table	.MB
Form	.F; or .F1 through .F14
Report	.R; or .R1 through .R14
Image settings	.SET
Validity checks	.VAL
Primary index	.PX
Secondary indexes	.Y01, .Y02,...; or .X01, .X02,...

Quick Summary

To start Paradox   Switch to the directory containing your data files, and set a path to the directory containing Paradox. Then enter **PARADOX** at the DOS prompt.

To get help   From anywhere in Paradox, press (F1).

To create a table   From the main menu, choose Create. Enter the name for the table. When the table structure image appears, enter the desired field names and field types. (Remember, with alphanumeric fields, you must include a number that indicates the width of the field; for example, A12 indicates an alphanumeric field that is 12 characters wide.) Add an asterisk after the field type if you wish to indicate that a field is a key field. When you are done defining the table, choose DO-IT! ((F2)) to save the table definition.

To add data to a table   From the main menu, choose Modify, then choose DataEntry. Enter the name of the table (or press (ENTER), and choose from the list of tables which appears). You can proceed to enter the data directly while in Table view. To change to a form for the data entry, press Form Toggle ((F7)).

To get an instant report   While viewing the table, make sure your printer is ready, and press Instant Report ($\boxed{\text{ALT}}$-$\boxed{\text{F7}}$).

To get an instant graph   While viewing the desired table, place the cursor in the field to be graphed, and press Instant Graph ($\boxed{\text{CTRL}}$-$\boxed{\text{F7}}$).

4

Managing Your Database

As you work with your data within Paradox, you will find that much of your time is spent adding new records, finding specific information, making changes, rearranging records, producing simple lists, and performing similar tasks that keep your database current. This chapter will show you how you can perform those tasks effectively.

Listing Existing Tables

The Info choice on the Tools menu provides you with information about Paradox tables and any forms and reports you build that are associated with tables, as well as other information of interest to network users. To keep track of your tables and other assorted files, you can use the Tools/Info/Inventory option. Choose Tools/Info/Inventory/Tables from the main menu, and Paradox will ask you for the name of the desired directory. Click on OK or press (ENTER) to accept the default directory (the one currently in use), and Paradox will display a LIST table, which shows the names of all tables and their creation dates. Figure 4-1 gives an example of a LIST table. Here,

Figure 4-1.   *LIST table*

Paradox displays information in the form of a temporary table. As with all tables, you can clear the information from the screen by pressing Clear Image ((F8)), or you can click on the Close box of the table's window.

Other menu choices from Tools/Info/Inventory are helpful for locating other files contained on your disk. The Info choice lets you view files without having to leave the program and return to DOS. Choose Tools/Info/Inventory/Files from the main menu, and Paradox will respond with a dialog box asking you to enter a pattern, as shown here:

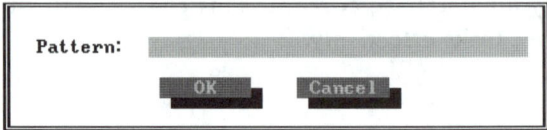

At this point, click on OK or press (ENTER) to see a table containing all files in the current (PDOX40) subdirectory. Or you can enter any accepted DOS wildcards and extensions to limit the types of files viewed. For example, entering **.f** would display all files with the extension of .F, which are standard screen form files used by Paradox. If there are too many filenames to be viewed on a single screen, use the (PGUP) and (PGDN) keys to view more.

You can also enter other directory names at this prompt to see the contents of other subdirectories on your hard disk. This can be particularly useful if you keep different Paradox databases in multiple subdirectories on your hard disk. Figure 4-2 shows a sample of the list of files obtained by

Figure 4-2. *LIST table containing all files*

pressing (ENTER) to view all files. Pressing Clear Image ((F8)) or clicking on the Close box clears this list from view.

More About Editing

Chapter 3 provided an introduction to editing records within Paradox. Because updating information is a major task with any database, it is worth the time you spend to learn the ways you can edit with Paradox.

Paradox lets you edit records in two ways: by pressing the Edit ((F9)) key after you select View from the main menu, or by choosing Modify from the main menu and selecting Edit. If you choose View from the main menu, Paradox prompts you for a table name. You can enter the table name directly, or press (ENTER) or click on OK to view a list of tables. Then, choose the desired table from the list. Once the table appears, press Edit ((F9)) and you are in Paradox's Edit mode, as Figure 4-3 demonstrates. As an alternative method, use the keyboard or the mouse to choose Modify from the main menu, and then choose Edit from the next menu that appears. (Another menu choice

Figure 4-3.   *ABCSTAFF table in Edit mode*

```
 ≡  Image  Undo  ValCheck  DO-IT!  Cancel
[ ]                          Abcstaff                            [ ]
ABCSTAFF│Social Security│    Last Name    │    First Name    │     4807 E
    1      121-33-9876◄    Westman          Andrea            4807 E
    2      121-90-5432     Robinson         Shirley           270 Br
    3      123-44-8976     Morse            Marcia            4260 P
    4      232-55-1234     Jackson          David             4102 V
    5      343-55-9821     Robinson         Wanda             1607 Z
    6      495-00-3456     Abernathy        Sandra            1512 R
    7      876-54-3210     Hart             Edward            6200 G
    8      901-77-3456     Mitchell         Mary Jo           617 No
    9      909-88-7654     Jones            Judi              5203 N



         1 of 9



 F1 Help  F7 Form                                              Edit
```

available at this point, called CoEdit, is used for editing on a network; this is
described in greater detail in Chapter 15.)

Whenever you are in Edit mode, Paradox informs you of this fact by
displaying "Edit" in the lower-right corner of the status bar. As you learned
earlier, you can press Form Toggle ((F7)) to move back and forth between
Table view (which shows you the records in a tabular fashion) and Form view
(which shows the records one at a time in an on-screen form).

While you are in Edit mode, the cursor is always at the *end* of the current
field. You cannot move the cursor to individual characters while you are in
this mode, but you can use the (BACKSPACE) key as necessary to delete
characters, and retype them in order to correct mistakes. (A way to do a full
cursor edit is described shortly.) As a helpful shortcut, you can also use the
(CTRL)-(BACKSPACE) key combination to delete an entire value in any field.

When editing, use (F7) to move between Form view and Table view.

Remember

Editing in Field View Mode

While editing, you may come across an error at or near the beginning of a field, and you may prefer to correct that character without backspacing over the entire field. Paradox has a special key, Field View ((ALT)-(F5) or (CTRL)-(F)), for this purpose. You may recall using the Field View key for entering data in memo fields; you can also use this same key to edit any field. Just place the cursor at the desired field and press Field View ((ALT)-(F5) or (CTRL)-(F)). (Mouse users can double-click on the desired field.) The cursor assumes the shape of a small rectangle, and the keys listed in Table 4-1 can then be used for editing. When you are done editing in Field View mode, just press (ENTER) and you will be back in normal Edit mode.

Inserting and Deleting Records

The (DEL) and (INS) keys perform more powerful functions in Paradox 4's Edit mode than you might be accustomed to in other PC programs, so be careful with these keys. In Edit mode, the (DEL) key deletes records, and the (INS) key inserts blank records. To delete an existing record, place the cursor in any field of the record and press the (DEL) key. The record is removed from the table, and the next record below it (if there is one) assumes the deleted record's place in the table. You can use the Undo command to reverse a

Table 4-1. *Editing Keys Available in Field View Mode*

Name of Key	Results While in Field View Mode
(←) (→)	Moves from character to character
(HOME)	Moves to beginning of field
(END)	Moves to end of field
(DEL)	Deletes character at cursor location
(INS)	Switches between insert and overwrite modes
(ENTER)	Leaves Field view

deletion, if desired. Once you save the edits by pressing (F2) or choosing DO-IT! from the menu, the deletions become permanent.

The (INS) key in Edit mode inserts a new blank record just above the current record in the table. For example, if you place the cursor at the third record of a table and then press (INS), a blank space will open between records 2 and 3, as illustrated below, and you can proceed to enter a new record in the blank space. (INS) is useful when you want to duplicate information into a new record from the previous record.

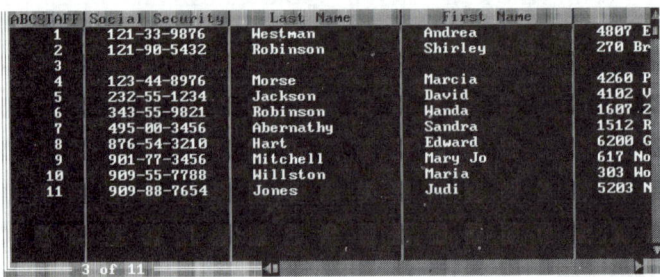

Although using the (INS) key is one way of keeping your table records in order, don't be concerned about how to insert new records in a particular order in a table. It is much easier to add as many records as you want at the end of the table, or by using the DataEntry menu option (described shortly), and then let the powerful sorting features of Paradox do the work of keeping your records in order.

Tip

Another quick way to add a record while in Edit mode is to move to the last record of a table and press (↓). The cursor will move to the next blank record, and you can proceed to add the information.

Using the Undo Command in Edit Mode

During editing, the main menu provides an Undo command. This command lets you undo the last change made to the table. You can choose Undo from the menu, or you can use the Undo key ((CTRL)-(U)). The Undo command always reverses the effects of your last action. If your last change was to edit a field of a particular record, choosing Undo will restore the original value in the field. If your last change was to delete a record, Undo will reinsert the deleted record.

Since Undo can only be used to reverse the last action, there may be situations where Undo is not helpful. If, for example, you accidentally delete a record and then do some other editing before you notice your error, the Undo command will not help. You can still regain the deleted record by choosing Cancel from the menu to cancel the effects of the edits; however, this action would cancel any other edits you have made, restoring the table to its status before you entered Edit mode.

Ending Editing with DO-IT!

Once you have completed your edits, you can exit Edit mode and save your changes simultaneously by pressing the DO-IT! ((F2)) key or by choosing DO-IT! from the menu. When you choose DO-IT!, Paradox writes the changes to disk and returns the cursor to the main menu. To cancel your edits without saving the changes, choose Cancel from the main menu.

A Reminder to Network Users

Note

If you are using Paradox on a network, remember that the use of Edit mode causes the table to be locked to all other users until you complete your editing. If you are on a network, it is wise to use the CoEdit command rather than the Edit command. See Chapter 15 for more details on networks and the use of CoEdit.

Hands-On Practice: Adding and Editing Records

To try adding a new record to the ABC Temporaries table, first choose Modify, then choose Edit. Enter **ABCSTAFF** in response to the name for the table, and Paradox will place you in Edit mode. Move the cursor past the last entry with the (↓) key, and a new record number will appear on the blank line. Enter the following information to fill in the new record:

Social Security: 495-00-3456
Last Name: Abernathy
First Name: Sandra
Address: 1512 Redskins Park Drive
City: Herndon
State: VA
ZIP Code: 22071
Date of Birth: 10/02/59
Date Hired: 02/17/92
Dependents: 1
Salary: 10.00
Assignment: City Revenue Dept.
Hourly Rate: 18.00
Phone: 703-555-7337
Comments: Too new to evaluate.

Secondly, suppose that while you are in Edit mode, you learn that Ms. Shirley Robinson has moved to a different apartment on the same street, and you wish to correct the address without retyping the entire line. Move the cursor to the address for Shirley Robinson and press Field View ((ALT)-(F5)). Change the address to **267 Browning Ave, #2A**, and then press (ENTER) to leave Field View mode. You have made the needed additions and changes, but they have not been saved to disk; if you were to shut off the PC (never a good thing to do while inside a program), the changes would be lost. To save your changes, choose DO-IT!, and the edits will be written to disk.

Using the DataEntry Option to Add Records

Although you can add records to a table when you are in Edit mode, that is not the best way to do it. As you have seen, Edit mode lets you change or delete records, something you normally do not do while adding new records. In Edit mode, there is always the possibility that you might hit the wrong key and make a change to an existing table. For adding a large number of records, Paradox provides the DataEntry option, available from the Modify menu. The difference between using DataEntry and Edit is that existing records are not displayed when you use DataEntry, so you cannot delete or alter those records.

To add records with the DataEntry option, select Modify from the main menu and then choose DataEntry from the next menu. Paradox will prompt you for the name of the table into which you wish to enter data; enter the desired name, or press (ENTER) to see a list of tables. Once you have chosen the desired table, a blank table in DataEntry mode will appear, as shown in Figure 4-4. You will use this table for adding new records.

When you use DataEntry mode, Paradox creates a temporary table named ENTRY with a structure that matches the table you selected. All of the new records that you enter will be stored in this temporary table. After adding the last record, you may want to use (ALT)-(F7) to get an instant report of the temporary table; you can then check your work for any errors. Once you complete the record entry, choose DO-IT!, and the new records are inserted automatically into the permanent table.

Note to Network Users   If you are using Paradox on a network, you should be aware of the "lockout-after-DataEntry" syndrome. On a network, it is possible to begin data entry with the DataEntry command, and later find yourself unable to complete the data-entry process because someone else has locked the original table. In such cases, you can use the KeepEntry command to save the temporary table until you can add the records to the original table.

Figure 4-4. *Table used for data entry*

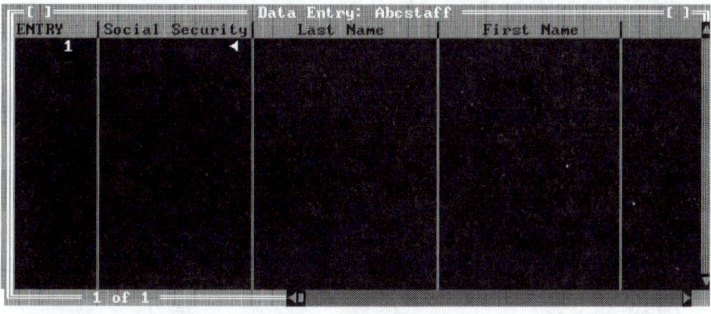

See "Dealing with the Lockout-After-DataEntry Syndrome" in Chapter 15 for more details on this potential problem.

Keyed Tables and Key Violations

When you are adding data using DataEntry, a problem may arise when you are working with a table containing key fields and you attempt to add a record that has the same key field value as that of an existing record in the original table. (There can be only one occurrence of a given key field value in the records of any table.) Paradox resolves this problem by placing any records with conflicting key values in a special table called KEYVIOL.

It's easier to demonstrate this problem by means of an example, so try working through the following steps. First, assume that you want to add two new records to the ABCSTAFF table, using the DataEntry command. Choose Modify/DataEntry from the main menu. When prompted for a table name, enter ABCSTAFF. In a moment, the new empty ENTRY table appears, as shown earlier in Figure 4-4. Using the same keys that you use for editing elsewhere in Paradox, add the following two records. Note that one of the records has an intentional mistake: the social security number for Mr. Harry Kramer is identical to the existing record for Ms. Westman in the original ABCSTAFF table.

> Social Security: 121-33-9876
> Last Name: Kramer
> First Name: Harry
> Address: 1245 Ocean Pine Way
> City: McLean
> State: VA
> Zip: 22304-1234
> Date of Birth: 5/12/72
> Date Hired: 5/3/92
> Dependents: 0
> Salary: 7.50
> Assignment: Smith Builders
> Hourly Rate: 12.00
> Phone: 703-555-4323
> Comments: Too new to evaluate.

Social Security: 909-55-7788
Last Name: Willston
First Name: Maria
Address: 303 Woodstock Ct. #1A
City: Potomac
State: MD
Zip: 22117
Date of Birth: 2/13/70
Date Hired: 5/15/92
Dependents: 1
Salary: 10.00
Assignment: National Oil Co.
Hourly Rate: 14.00
Phone: 301-555-2378
Comments: Too new to evaluate.

After entering the data and checking your work, choose DO-IT!. Paradox flashes a message near the bottom of the screen, "Adding records from ENTRY into ABCSTAFF." However, Paradox will not add the record for Mr. Kramer into the ABCSTAFF table, because Ms. Westman's record already exists with that key value (social security number). Instead, Paradox creates a new temporary table called KEYVIOL, and enters the record for Mr. Kramer into that table, as shown in Figure 4-5. This occurs because there is already a record with the same social security number in the ABCSTAFF table.

Whenever you enter records into a keyed table using DataEntry, Paradox checks to make sure none of the table records have the same key value; if any do, they are deposited into the KEYVIOL table. You can then edit the entries in the KEYVIOL table to correct them (or simply delete them if the record is an accidental duplication of existing data). Once you have made the necessary corrections to the KEYVIOL records, you can use the Tools/More/Add command to add the edited records to the primary table.

In our example, with the cursor in the KEYVIOL table, press (F9) to begin editing. Change Mr. Kramer's social security number to 111-33-9876, and press (F2) to complete the edits. Choose Tools/More/Add from the menu. A dialog box appears, asking for the name of the source table; enter KEYVIOL as the name. The next prompt that appears asks for the name of the target table; enter ABCSTAFF. Another menu appears with two choices: New

Figure 4-5.   *KEYVIOL table*

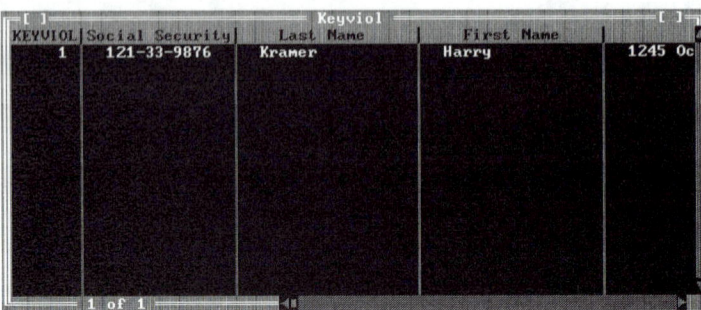

Entries and Update. Choose New Entries by pressing (ENTER), and the record for Mr. Kramer will be moved from the KEYVIOL table to ABCSTAFF, as shown in Figure 4-6.

   Notice that the record you've copied into the ABCSTAFF table also remains in the KEYVIOL table; however, since KEYVIOL is a temporary table, it will automatically be discarded when you exit from Paradox. And you can close the window containing the KEYVIOL table window at any time, through the usual methods.

Tip

As the prior example demonstrates, Modify/DataEntry provides a safer way to add records into keyed tables than does the Edit command. With Edit, you risk overwriting a record if you attempt to enter another record with the same key value; the new record will replace the old one. With DataEntry, however, the new record with the conflicting key value will always be placed in the KEYVIOL table.

Helpful Shortcuts

   While adding new records, you may find certain "shortcut" key combinations offered by Paradox to be quite useful. One such shortcut is the Ditto

Figure 4-6. *ABCSTAFF table with record added from KEYVIOL*

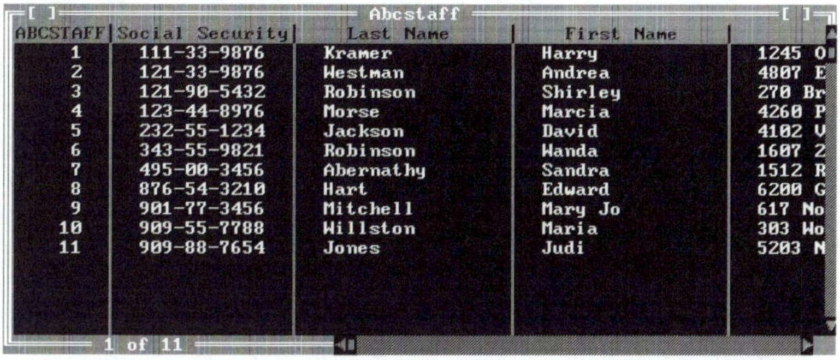

Abcstaff

ABCSTAFF	Social Security	Last Name	First Name	
1	111-33-9876	Kramer	Harry	1245 O
2	121-33-9876	Westman	Andrea	4807 E
3	121-90-5432	Robinson	Shirley	270 Br
4	123-44-8976	Morse	Marcia	4260 P
5	232-55-1234	Jackson	David	4102 V
6	343-55-9821	Robinson	Wanda	1607 2
7	495-00-3456	Abernathy	Sandra	1512 R
8	876-54-3210	Hart	Edward	6200 G
9	901-77-3456	Mitchell	Mary Jo	617 No
10	909-55-7788	Willston	Maria	303 Wo
11	909-88-7654	Jones	Judi	5203 N

1 of 11

key combination ((CTRL)-(D)), used to repeat a prior entry without retyping. Pressing (CTRL)-(D) when in a blank field of a new record will tell Paradox to repeat the entry stored in the field immediately above. Another useful shortcut key, which only applies to date fields, is the (SPACEBAR). If you press the (SPACEBAR) while in a date field, Paradox will automatically enter the month, then the day, and then the year (as measured by the PC's clock) into the date field.

Hands-On Practice: Using the Shortcut Keys

An example of the usefulness of the shortcut keys is illustrated by ABC Temporaries' hiring of the spouse of an existing employee, Marcia Morse. Instead of manually typing all of the characters for William Morse, you can insert a new record under the one for Marcia Morse and then use the shortcut keys to duplicate much of the information and to enter today's date as the date of hire. If you are not in Edit mode now, go to it by pressing (F9), and move the cursor to the record immediately following the one for Marcia Morse. Press the (INS) key once, and a new record will appear, as shown in Figure 4-7.

Figure 4-7.   *New record inserted into existing table*

Place the cursor in the Social Security field and enter 805-34-6789. Move the cursor to the First Name field and enter William. For most of the remaining fields, you can duplicate the fields in the previous record. In succession, move the cursor to the Last Name, Address, City, State, and ZIP Code fields, and press (CTRL)-(D) each time to duplicate the entry from the prior record. For the Date of Birth field, enter 8/17/52.

For the Date Hired field, press the (SPACEBAR) three times. Each time you do, Paradox will insert part of the current date: the month, followed by the day, and finally, the year. To complete the entry of the new record, enter **1** for Dependents, 7.50 for Salary, Smith Builders for Assignment, and **12.00** for Hourly Rate; then move to the Phone field and again use (CTRL)-(D) to duplicate the prior entry. In the Comments field enter Too new to evaluate.

Finding a Record Quickly

With a table as small as the one we have created in our example so far, you can easily find a record by looking for a specific name within the table. However, when there are hundreds or thousands of names and items in your tables, finding a record will not be that simple. Paradox offers sophisticated query features for selecting one or more records; these features are detailed in Chapter 6. You can also use a quick method, The Zoom key ((CTRL)-(Z)), to search for the first record that contains desired information.

To use the Zoom key, simply place the cursor in the field you wish to search, press (CTRL)-(Z), and enter the value that you wish to search for. Capitalization must be exactly the same here as it is in the record. For example, if you place the cursor in the Social Security field and press (CTRL)-(Z), Paradox will display a dialog box asking for a value, as shown here:

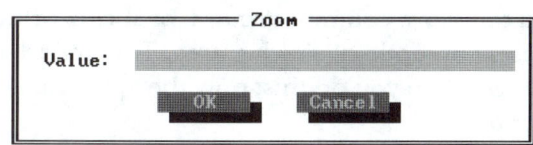

If you enter **876-54-3210**, the cursor will move to the matching social security number, which is for Mr. Hart. In a similar fashion, you can place the cursor in the Last Name field, press (CTRL)-(Z), and enter **Westman** in response to the prompt, and the cursor will move to the record for Ms. Westman. This works well for simple searches or for searches in which you are searching a unique key field (such as Social Security).

Place the cursor in the field you want to search before using the Zoom ((CTRL)-(Z)) key.

Remember

The Zoom key finds the first occurrence of the item, so if you search for Robinson in the Last Name column, you will find the first "Robinson" in the table, which may or may not be the one you are looking for. You could use the (ALT)-(Z) key combination (Zoom Next) to find the next occurrence of the same search value. When you want to do a search based on more than one field (as in a combination of last and first name), you must resort to the more powerful query features offered by Paradox.

Changing the Table's Screen Layout

While working with your data, you may find that you frequently need to see particular kinds of information at a glance. For example, the ABC Temporaries table contains a number of fields, not all of which can be viewed in tabular form at the same time. However, for most day-to-day needs, the staff can get the needed data from four fields: Last Name, Social Security, Phone, and Assignment. If these fields could be viewed at once, most requests for information could be satisfied with one quick glance at the screen.

To meet such needs, Paradox lets you change the appearance of the table on the screen. You can move columns around, or shrink or expand the width of columns, to present an optimal viewing area. The underlying data in your table does not change when you do this; only the appearance of the table on the screen is affected.

Moving Columns

To move a column you use the Move command, available from the Image menu (Figure 4-8). From the main menu select Image and then Move, and Paradox will display a list of the fields in the table. You can select the field you wish to move, and then place the cursor in any field. Press (ENTER), and the field will be moved to where the cursor is, and all other fields will shift to the right. Note that (CTRL)-(R) also can be used to move one column at a time. (CTRL)-(R) is the Rotate key; when you press it, the current column (the one containing the cursor) is rotated, or moved, to the far right side of the table.

Changing Column Widths

You can also change the width of a column to provide additional room for the display of other columns. To change column widths, you use the ColumnSize command, also available from the Image menu. (By now it is probably clear that most of the commands available from the Image menu are used to affect the image on your screen.) From the main menu select Image and then ColumnSize; then you can move the cursor to the column you wish to resize. With the cursor positioned in the desired column, press

Figure 4-8. *Image menu*

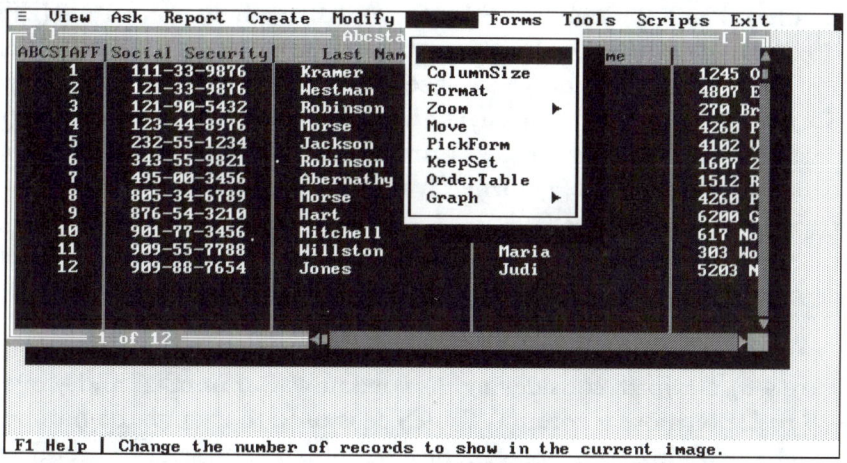

(ENTER). Paradox will tell you to use the (←) and (→) keys to resize the column. As you press the arrow key, the column will expand or contract in width on the screen. (alphanumeric fields can only be contracted; numeric fields can be contracted or expanded.) When the column is the size you want, press (ENTER), and the change will be complete.

Mouse users can easily change column widths. Just click on the vertical line to the right of the desired column, and drag to the left or right to widen or narrow the column.

Note

Changing Column Formats

The Format option lets you change the display format for numeric, currency, and date fields. For numbers and currency fields, Paradox lets you format a column in general format (all numbers justified), fixed number of decimal places, numbers with commas inserted, or scientific (exponential) format. Dates can be formatted as mm/dd/yy, dd-mon-yy (with the month spelled as a three-character abbreviation), dd.mm.yy, or yy.mm.dd.

4

To try reformatting a column, choose Image from the menu and then choose Format. Paradox will ask you to move the cursor to the field to be reformatted. Place the cursor in the Date of Birth field, and press (ENTER). Paradox will next display the four available date formats on the screen. Select dd-mon-yy from the list, and you will see the dates change to the European date format. If you prefer, you can change them back by again pressing (F10) for the menu and choosing Image/Format, reselecting the Date of Birth field, and choosing the mm/dd/yy format from the list of available formats.

Other Image Menu Commands

There are other useful commands available from the Image menu (shown in Figure 4-8), all worth considering. As you know, ColumnSize and Move are used to resize or move a column. TableSize is used to change the number of records that Paradox will display in the current table; this can be useful when you are working with more than one table on the screen. (A later section will show you how this is done.)

The Zoom command (called GoTo in earlier versions of Paradox) is available from the Image menu that you can summon from the main menu, or from the Image menu that is available in Edit mode or DataEntry mode. The Zoom command provides another way to move the cursor to an item. Using Zoom, you can quickly move the cursor to a named field, a specific record, or a field containing a certain value. Zoom can be useful when you are viewing a table with a large number of fields and want to move to a certain field quickly. To use this option, begin your data entry or editing; then press (F10), choose Image, and choose Zoom. The next menu to appear provides three options: Field, Record Number, and Value. Choose Value and enter the desired data to find that value. (Field takes you to a field you give by name, while Record Number takes you to the record number you specify.)

The PickForm command lets you use a specific form to view the table. (Forms will be discussed in greater detail in the next chapter.)

The OrderTable command lets you change the order in which the records appear. (How you can do this is detailed later in this chapter.)

The Graph command lets you change, load, or save graph settings. Graphs will be covered in Chapter 8.

You have read that changes you make in a table with the Image command are not permanent unless you save those changes. Normally, Paradox disposes of any table image settings in effect when you choose Exit from the main menu to leave the program. When you next load Paradox and view the same table, Paradox will use the default table to display the data. With the KeepSet command, accessible from the Image menu, you can save your changes.

To save the image, choose Image from the main menu, and then choose KeepSet. Paradox will briefly display the message "Settings recorded." The current image settings will be saved in a file named after your database, but with an extension of .SET. Thereafter, Paradox will use the image settings recorded in the .SET file.

When you use commands from the Image menu, your changes do not affect the actual data contained in the table; only the appearance of that data is altered. You can, however, save the new image settings with Image/KeepSet.

Remember

Hands-On Practice: Changing the Table's Screen Layout

Since the ABC Temporaries staff wants to see the Social Security, Last Name, Phone, and Assignment fields most frequently, you can move the columns containing these fields to the left side of the table. From the main menu choose Image and then Move, and Paradox will ask for the name of the field to be moved, by displaying a list of fields, as shown here:

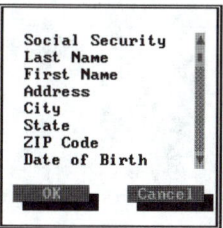

Choose Phone from the list. When you select the field, Paradox will ask you to use (←) and (→) to show the new position for the field. Place the cursor in the First Name field, and then press ENTER to move the field. Paradox will place the Phone field to the left of the cursor, between the Last Name and First Name fields.

Press F10 to activate the main menu, and again choose Image and then Move. For the field, choose Assignment. Place the cursor in the First Name field, and press ENTER. The column containing the employee assignments will be moved to its new location, as shown in Figure 4-9.

One last point noted by the staff of ABC Temporaries is that if the Last Name column were shortened a bit, some of the First Name column would then appear and could be useful. Press F10 to activate the main menu, and choose Image, then ColumnSize. Paradox will ask you to place the cursor in the column to be resized.

Move the cursor to the Last Name column, and press ENTER. Paradox next asks that you use ← and → to change the column's size. Press the ← key five times to shorten the column's width by five characters. Then press ENTER to complete the change. Repeat these steps for the First Name column. To make this change in appearance permanent, press F10 to activate the menu, choose Image, and then choose KeepSet.

Figure 4-9. *New location of columns*

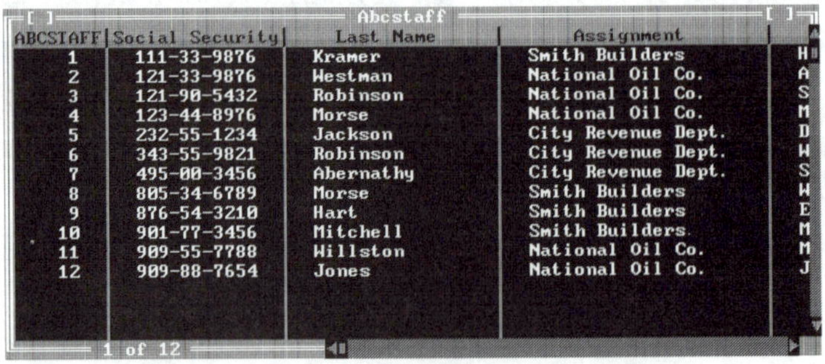

Abcstaff

ABCSTAFF	Social Security	Last Name	Assignment	
1	111-33-9876	Kramer	Smith Builders	H
2	121-33-9876	Westman	National Oil Co.	A
3	121-90-5432	Robinson	National Oil Co.	S
4	123-44-8976	Morse	National Oil Co.	M
5	232-55-1234	Jackson	City Revenue Dept.	D
6	343-55-9821	Robinson	City Revenue Dept.	W
7	495-00-3456	Abernathy	City Revenue Dept.	S
8	805-34-6789	Morse	Smith Builders	W
9	876-54-3210	Hart	Smith Builders	E
10	901-77-3456	Mitchell	Smith Builders	M
11	909-55-7788	Westman	National Oil Co.	M
12	909-88-7654	Jones	National Oil Co.	J

1 of 12

Viewing More than One Table

Because Paradox is a relational database, you can use it to work extensively with multiple tables at the same time. Later chapters will explain how relationships can be drawn between multiple tables. For now, however, the ability to simply view more than one table on the screen will come in handy.

ABC Temporaries needs an additional table that will show how many hours were worked by a given employee for a given firm while on assignment. This table, called HOURS, will be used along with the ABCSTAFF table throughout the remainder of this text, so we will create it in this section.

After some analysis, the management staff at ABC Temporaries decides that the fields shown in Table 4-2 need to be tracked. Note that in this table, a key field designation will *not* be assigned to any field. There will be intentional duplicates in every field in this table; any record may have the same social security number as other records, and the same fact goes for the Assignment, Weekend date, and Hours worked fields.

From the main menu, choose Create to create a new table, and enter **HOURS** for the name of the table. Using Table 4-2 as a guide, create the four fields of the table. When you have finished defining the fields, the structure should look like the example in Figure 4-10. Choose DO-IT!, and the new table will be created. Paradox will return to the display of the existing table you were working with earlier.

Now that you have two tables, you can view both simultaneously. From the main menu, choose View. For the name of the table, enter **HOURS**. The empty table will appear in its own window, as shown in Figure 4-11.

Table 4-2.   *Fields for the HOURS Table*

Field Name	Field Type	Length
Assignment	Alphanumeric	20
Social Security	Alphanumeric	11
Weekend date	Date	
Hours worked	Numeric	

Figure 4-10.   *Structure for the HOURS table*

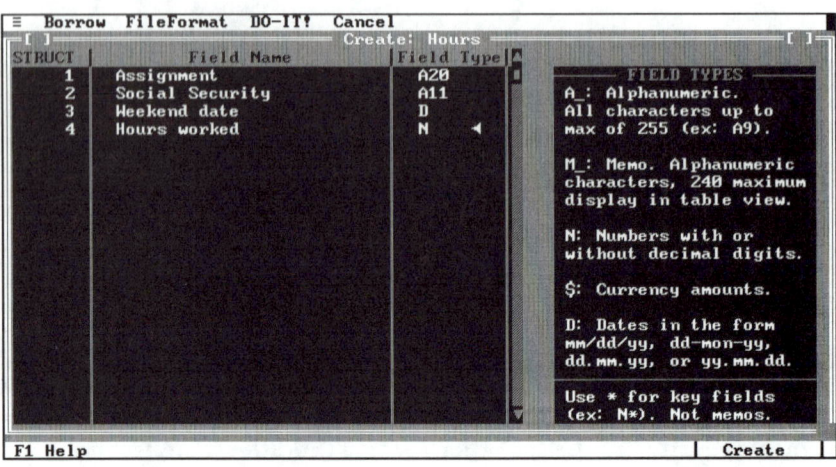

Figure 4-11.   *Two tables in two windows*

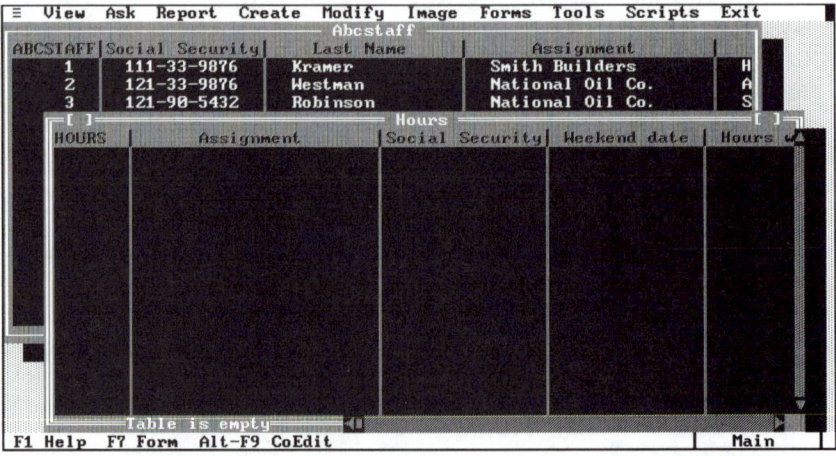

You can tell which table is the current one (in use) in a number of ways. One way is by the presence of a highlighted, double-line border around the table's window. As Figure 4-11 shows, the HOURS table is the active one; the other table window (ABCSTAFF) has only a single-line border. Another way to tell is by the presence of the Close box, the Maximize/Restore icon, and the scroll bar; only active windows will contain these items. A third way to tell is by the presence of the cursor; if you are performing data entry or any editing operation, the cursor will be within the active table.

With the HOURS table currently active, press Edit ((F9)), and the cursor will appear in the first record of the new table. Since you will not be disturbing any existing records, it is safe to add new records from Edit mode. If you prefer to use a form for entry, press (F7) to switch to a form. Add the records shown in Table 4-3 to the new table; remember the helpful shortcut (CTRL)-(D)

4

Table 4-3.   *New Records for the HOURS Table*

Assignment	Social Security	Weekend date	Hours worked
National Oil Co.	909-88-7654	5/16/92	35
National Oil Co.	121-33-9876	5/16/92	30
National Oil Co.	121-90-5432	5/16/92	27
National Oil Co.	123-44-8976	5/16/92	32
City Revenue Dept.	343-55-9821	5/16/92	35
City Revenue Dept.	495-00-3456	5/16/92	28
City Revenue Dept.	232-55-1234	5/16/92	30
Smith Builders	876-54-3210	5/23/92	30
Smith Builders	901-77-3456	5/23/92	28
Smith Builders	805-34-6789	5/23/92	35
City Revenue Dept.	232-55-1234	5/23/92	30
City Revenue Dept.	495-00-3456	5/23/92	32
City Revenue Dept.	343-55-9821	5/23/92	32
National Oil Co.	121-33-9876	5/23/92	35
National Oil Co.	909-88-7654	5/23/92	33

key combination for duplicating data. When you have finished adding the records, choose DO-IT! to save the new records to disk.

With two tables on the screen, as you now have, things get a little more complex. You cannot possibly see all of the records from both tables at the same time, so you must make some decisions about what you want to work with. Of major importance when dealing with more than one table are the Up Image ((F3)) and Down Image ((F4)) keys, which let keyboard users move between images on the screen. Mouse users will find it easier to click in the desired table to make it the active one. Since you are currently viewing tables, these tables are your screen "images." (If you are viewing the records through a form, press (F7) to get back to a table view.) Try pressing (F3) and (F4) repeatedly, and note that the cursor moves back and forth between the two tables. All of your Paradox menu commands will apply to the active table, or the table that the cursor is currently located within.

Hands-On Practice: Resizing a Table

You can resize the tables in order to give more of the screen to one table than to another. For example, you may decide that you only need to see a few employee names at a time, but you would like to view simultaneously as many records of the hours worked as will comfortably fit on the screen.

If you don't have a mouse, to reduce the size of the ABCSTAFF table, first press Up Image ((F3)) so that the cursor is in the ABCSTAFF table. Press (F10) to activate the main menu. Choose Image and then TableSize. Paradox will ask you to use the (↑) or (↓) key to increase or decrease the size of the table in rows. Press (↑) five times, and then press (ENTER). If you have a mouse, click and drag the Resize corner of the ABCSTAFF window to decrease its size by approximately five rows; then release the mouse. You also may want to move the windows around to locations on the screen that suit you; to move a window, click and drag anywhere on the window's title bar. Once you have made your changes, the ABCSTAFF table will assume its new size. An example of how the table might appear is illustrated in Figure 4-12.

Figure 4-12. *Tables after resizing*

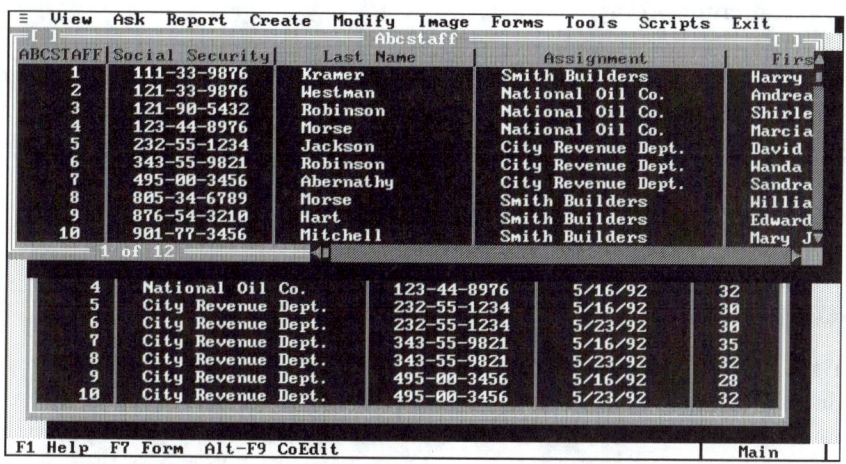

Checking a Field's Validity

A powerful feature of Paradox, called ValCheck, lets you define validity checks—conditions that entries into fields must meet before they will be accepted. Using this feature, you could, for example, specify a minimum and a maximum salary for a salary field, or you could specify that a date field not allow any entries earlier than a certain date. Validity checks apply to records that are changed as well as those that are added. You can even define *lookup tables,* which are other Paradox tables that can be used as cross-references for data entry or editing. (These tables must be created before you use the ValCheck option.) With a lookup table of valid state abbreviations, for example, you could specify that all entries into a state field be accepted only if a match for the entry were found in another database containing the valid state names.

To set validity checks, you use Modify/DataEntry to begin data entry. You then press (F10) for the menu, and choose ValCheck (or click on the ValCheck menu option). For editing, you choose Modify/Edit to begin the editing process, press (F10) for the menu, and choose ValCheck (or click on the ValCheck menu option).

Note

Validity checks can reduce data-entry errors.

Setting Minimum and Maximum Values

As an example, consider setting a minimum and maximum salary for employees of ABC Temporaries. Choose Modify/DataEntry from the main menu. For the name of the table, enter **ABCSTAFF**. (You may or may not want to add data at this time, but you must be in DataEntry or Edit mode to set validity checks. The ValCheck option is reached from the DataEntry or Edit menu.)

Now that you are in DataEntry mode, the menu changes to that of DataEntry mode. You will see that ValCheck is one of the available options. Choose ValCheck now. Paradox presents another menu with two option, Define and Clear. The Clear option clears an existing validity check; the Define option sets new validity checks. Choose Define now. Paradox asks you to move the cursor to the field to which the validity check is to apply. Since you want to limit the possible salaries, use the cursor keys to place the cursor in the Salary field, then press (ENTER). You will see another menu, as shown here:

```
LowValue
HighValue
Default
TableLookup
Picture
Required
Auto          ▶
```

Before you proceed, an explanation about the ValCheck/Define options is in order. (These options will be demonstrated in the sections that follow.) The LowValue and HighValue options are used to specify a minimum and maximum value, as you will do for the Salary field. Such values can be numbers, dates, or even letters. (For example, A for a low value and M for a high value could limit names to those starting with the letters A through M.) The Default option lets you set a default value that Paradox will place automatically in a particular field. (For example, you might want to place the minimum wage as a default value in a salary field if most employees are paid that amount.)

The TableLookup option lets you specify the name of another Paradox table, which will provide acceptable values for the validity check. For example, you might want to limit entries in a ZIP code field to a certain group of ZIP codes. You would create another Paradox table containing only one field with the same field structure, store the acceptable ZIP codes in the records of that table, and use that table's name with the TableLookup option. (Remember— you must first create the table that will serve as a lookup table before you can use the TableLookup option.)

The Picture option lets you specify, using symbols, a valid format that entries must match before they will be accepted. For example, you could limit telephone numbers to a ten-number format, with the area code surrounded by parentheses and the prefix and suffix separated by hyphens, by using a *picture format* like the following:

```
(###)###-####
```

Paradox would then supply the literal characters (the hyphen and parentheses) automatically; the user would not need to type these in each record. You'll read more about using the Picture option in a later section.

You can use any of the symbols shown in Table 4-4 within a picture format.

- The repetition count character (*) is the equivalent of repeating another picture symbol a specified number of times. For example, the following pictures represent the same format—up to ten numeric digits in a field:

```
##########
*10#
```

- The [] brackets for optional elements tell Paradox that the entry in this area is optional. For example, you could specify a picture for a

Table 4-4.   *Acceptable Symbols in a Picture Format*

Symbol	Function
#	Represents any numeric digit
?	Represents any letter
&	Converts letters to uppercase
!	Accepts any characters; converts letters to uppercase
; (semicolon)	Takes the next character literally
*	Repetition count (use to repeat a character)
[]	Specifies items that are optional
{}	Grouping operator
, (comma)	Separates alternate values

telephone number, with the area code as optional, with a format like this one:

```
[###]  ###-####
```

- The comma can be used to separate alternate values, which is useful for multiple-choice types of applications. For example, if four different prices of 1.99, 2.99, 5.99, and 7.99 are the only acceptable entries in a dollar field, you could use a picture like the following:

```
{1.99,2.99,5.99,7.99}
```

- The curly braces are grouping operators. The braces surround any group of acceptable items in a picture.

The Required option on the ValCheck/Define menu is used to specify whether a field may be left blank. Keep in mind that you must move the cursor into the field for the validity check to be tested. Thus, if the user never moves the cursor into a required field, the record could be saved without filling in the required field. A later section will detail more about using Required.

The Auto option can be used to instruct Paradox to automatically move the cursor to the next field as soon as the current field is completely filled with data.

Keep in mind that you can use the various validity check options in combination with others. For example, a field could have a low value, a high value, and be a required field.

Getting back to the ABCSTAFF example, suppose the Salary field needs a minimum (low) and a maximum (high) value. Choose LowValue from the ValCheck menu. In the dialog box that appears, Paradox asks for a value. Enter **4.50** for the minimum value. You will see the message "Low value recorded" appear at the lower-right corner of the screen. Choose ValCheck again from the menu; then choose Define. Since the cursor is still in the Salary field, you can press (ENTER) to select this field again. Choose HighValue and enter **18.00** as the maximum acceptable salary. This time, the message "High value recorded" will appear in the lower-right corner of the screen.

When you are done setting validity checks, you can press (F2) or choose DO-IT! (don't do this yet, because you will be setting more validity checks in the following paragraphs). Choosing DO-IT! records your validity checks in a file with the same name as the table, but with a .VAL extension. The file is read whenever you open a table, and the validity checks are automatically put into effect for further data entry and editing.

Setting a Default Value

At times, you may want to set a default value for a field. Once you set a default value, Paradox automatically enters that value in the field when you add a new record to the table and move the cursor into that field during the data-entry process. In cases where a particular value is the most common entry in a field, this can save significant time during data entry. For instance, if you are creating a table of customer names and addresses, and most of your company's customers live in a particular state, you can enter the name of that state as a default value for the State field. During data entry, the state name would be filled in automatically, and you would only need to make an entry in that field if the state happened to be different from the default.

Paradox automatically enters a default value in a blank field only if you move the cursor into that field during data entry. If you add a new record but never move the cursor into the field that uses the default value, the value will not be entered by Paradox.

For the case of ABC Temporaries, you can try the following exercise to set a default value. In this example, what's desired is a default salary value; since most employees of the agency start at $7.50 per hour, you want this amount to be the default. Click on ValCheck, or press F10 and choose ValCheck from the menu. From the next menu, choose Define. With the cursor still in the Salary field, press (ENTER). When the ValCheck menu appears, select Default. Paradox asks you for a default value for the field; enter 7.50. The message "Default value recorded" near the bottom of the screen tells you that Paradox has set the amount of 7.50 as a default value for the Salary field.

You can set default values in all types of fields. Also, note that for date fields there is a special type of default value available, called TODAY. This value automatically causes the current date (as measured by the PC's clock) to be entered into a date field of a new record. To use TODAY, when you choose Default from the ValCheck menu and Paradox asks you for the default value, just type the word TODAY and press (ENTER). (Of course, for this technique to work properly, your computer's internal clock must be set correctly.)

Using the ValCheck/Picture Option

As mentioned earlier, you can use the Picture option of the ValCheck menu to specify a picture, or a format that the field data must match. A good example of the Picture option at work would be the Social Security field of the ABCSTAFF table. Entries in this field will always have a specific pattern of numbers, separated by hyphens in specific places. Without a pattern controlled by the use of the Picture command, someone could enter a social security number using a different format. For example, the same social security number could be entered in three different ways:

121-33-5678
121 33 5678
121335678

and Paradox would treat records with these entries in the key (Social Security) field as three different records, because the values appear different to Paradox. This could lead to accidental duplicates of the same employee record. You can prevent this kind of duplication by using a picture format that not only restricts the field to precisely eleven characters, but also forces the hyphens to appear at the proper locations automatically. Let's see how it would work.

While still in DataEntry mode, click on ValCheck, or press F10 and choose ValCheck from the menu; from the next menu, choose Define. Move the cursor to the Social Security field, and press (ENTER). The ValCheck menu again appears; choose Picture from the menu. When Paradox asks you to enter the picture, type ###-##-### and press (ENTER). This picture format tells Paradox to accept as a valid entry any three numbers, followed by a hyphen, followed by any two numbers, followed by a hyphen, followed by any three numbers. When data is entered in the field, Paradox will add the hyphens automatically because they are *literal characters* (that is, characters not used as picture symbols as listed in Table 4-4).

There are a number of symbols that you can use when defining formats for pictures. These are described in Table 4-4.

Remember

Using the ValCheck/Required Option

You can use the Required command of the ValCheck menu to indicate that an entry must be made in a particular field of a new record. Once you establish the Required validity check for a particular field, whenever the cursor is moved into that field during data entry or editing, Paradox will not permit the cursor to be moved from that field if it is left blank.

As an example, while still in DataEntry mode, click on ValCheck, or press (F10) and choose ValCheck from the menu; from the next menu, choose Define. Move the cursor to the Last Name field and press (ENTER). The ValCheck menu again appears; choose the Required option. The next menu to appear provides a No option (meaning the field can be left blank), and a Yes option (an entry in the field is required). For this field, enter **Yes**.

As with other types of validity checks, the cursor must enter the field (during data entry and editing) for the validity check to be effective. In other words, if you were to add a new record to the table but you never moved the cursor into the Last Name field, Paradox could not require an entry there. Once the cursor is moved into the Last Name field, however, Paradox will not permit you to leave the field without making an entry.

Using Table Lookup

Now let's try an example of the Table Lookup feature of Paradox, which can be one of the more powerful (and useful) types of validity checks, although it also takes a little planning. With Table Lookup, you are specifying that an entry made in a particular field must match a record in the lookup table. Using Table Lookup can greatly reduce the possibility of data-entry errors, and it can speed up the data-entry process by making it easier for entry operators to find an acceptable value, as the following example demonstrates.

Consider the Assignment field in the ABCSTAFF table. There are only a certain number of clients using the services of ABC Temporaries, so these client names would be the only acceptable entries for the Assignment field. By entering valid client names in a lookup table and setting a validity check to use that table, you can ensure that an incorrect client name is never entered in the Assignment field.

First, exit from the current process of setting validity checks, because you need to create a new table to serve as the lookup table. Choose DO-IT! or press F2 to save the validity checks you established in the prior examples. Next, create a table called NAMES, containing the names of the clients for ABC Temporaries. From the menu, choose Create, and enter **NAMES** for the table name. When the Structure Definition table appears, enter **CLIENT** for the first (and only) field name, and then enter **A20** in the Field Type column. (When you are creating lookup tables for your own use, remember that the field used for the validity check must be the first field of the lookup table.) Press (F2) to save the new table's definition.

From the main menu, choose Modify/DataEntry. When prompted for the name of the table, enter **NAMES**. Add three records to the table, using the following client names in the CLIENT field:

National Oil Co.
Smith Builders
City Revenue Dept.

Press (F2) when done to save the records in the new table. Then, click on the Close box in the window or choose Close from the System menu to put the new table away.

With the new table set up, you can now designate a validity check for the Assignment field of the ABCSTAFF table. From the menu, choose Modify/DataEntry, and enter **ABCSTAFF** as the table name. Choose ValCheck from the menu, and select Define. Move the cursor to the Assignment field, and press (ENTER). From the ValCheck menu that appears, choose Table Lookup.

Paradox now asks for the name of the lookup table; enter **NAMES.** When you do so, Paradox displays a menu with two choices: Just Current Field, and All Corresponding Fields. Selecting the Just Current Field option (which will be used in this example) tells Paradox to check only the value entered in the Assignment field against the values in the lookup table. The remaining option, All Corresponding Fields, tells Paradox to automatically fill any other fields that the current table has in common with the lookup table, using the data from the lookup table. (In our example, the lookup table has no other fields, so this option does not apply. If, however, the ABCSTAFF table had a field called Assignment Address, you could add a field of the same name to the lookup table and store the client addresses in that field; then, whenever Paradox checked the Assignment Address field's validity against the lookup table, it would automatically fill in the address in the ABCSTAFF table.)

For our example, choose Just Current Field from the menu. Now another menu appears, with two choices: Private Lookup, and HelpAndFill. If you select Private Lookup, Paradox will use the lookup table for the validity checks, but will not allow the operator to see the values in the lookup table during data entry. Select HelpAndFill, and Paradox will allow the operator to see the values in the lookup table (by pressing the Help or (F1) key during data entry). If your data in the lookup table is not sensitive or confidential, using the HelpAndFill option can speed up data entry, because the operator

4

can press (F1) and pick the desired entry from the lookup table that appears, to fill in the field. For this example, choose HelpAndFill. The message "Table Lookup Recorded" that appears near the bottom of the screen tells you that the validity check using the table lookup method has been set.

Testing the Sample Validity Checks

You can see the effects of the validity checks you entered in the foregoing examples, by entering a new record. (What data you enter in the record does not matter, as the new record will be discarded shortly.) First, press (F2) to close the Entry table, so that all the validity checks will take effect before you begin data entry. Then, from the menu, choose Modify/DataEntry, and enter ABCSTAFF for the table name. Now try out each validity check.

- When the cursor appears in the first field (Social Security) of the Entry table, type 222334444. As you type the number, the picture format you recorded earlier causes the hyphens to appear in the proper places.

- Move the cursor into the Last Name field, and try to move the cursor out of the field without making an entry. Because you set the Required option for this field, Paradox displays a warning message near the bottom of the screen, saying that an entry is required here. Add any name you like, and then move over to the Assignment field.

- In the Assignment field, enter XYZ Plumbing and press (ENTER). Because of the table lookup validity check you set for this field, Paradox will not accept this value. Your entry flashes once on the screen, and the message, "Not one of the possible values for this field" appears near the bottom of the screen. Delete the entry you made in the Assignment field, and press Help (F1). You will see the lookup table containing the valid client names (Figure 4-13). At the bottom of the screen, a message tells you to "Move to the record you want to select." Move the cursor to the entry for Smith Builders, and press (F2). The lookup table closes automatically, and "Smith Builders" automatically appears in the Assignment field.

Figure 4-13.  *Pressing* (F1) *displays the lookup table for the Assignment field.*

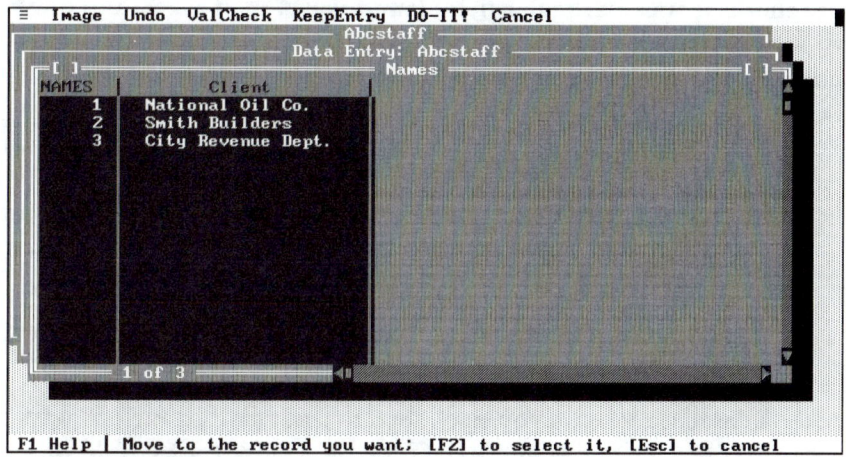

- Move the cursor into and then out of the Salary field. Notice that when you move out of the field, Paradox automatically puts the default value of 7.50 into the field. Move back into the Salary field, and try entering a value of less than 4.50, or a value greater than 18.00. Because of the minimum and maximum values you set for this field (with LowValue and HighValue), Paradox does not allow you to enter values outside the 4.50 to 18.00 range.

The record you've been working with will not be needed in further exercises, so choose Cancel now from the menu, and then choose Yes from the next menu to appear, to cancel the data-entry process without saving the new record.

Clearing Validity Checks

To clear the validity checks you have set for a table, use the ValCheck/Clear command from the menu. (Remember, you must be in the Edit or DataEntry mode to access the ValCheck menu.) Begin editing the desired table, and choose ValCheck/Clear from the menu. Another menu appears with two choices: Field and All. Choose Field if you want to clear the validity checks from a particular field; Paradox will then ask you to move the cursor to the desired field and press (ENTER) to remove the validity checks. If you choose All, Paradox removes all validity checks for the table, and deletes the validity check (.VAL) file from your hard disk.

You can now press DO-IT! ((F2)) to leave DataEntry mode and return to viewing the ABCSTAFF table. The values recorded by the ValCheck options will take effect for any additions or edits you make to the ABCSTAFF table.

Sorting a Table

After a database is built, you may need to arrange it in various ways. For instance, consider the needs of the staff at ABC Temporaries. Judi, who does the accounting, often wants to refer to a list of employees arranged by the amount of salary. Marge, the personnel administrator, prefers to keep a list organized in alphabetical order by name; Bill, who mails assignments and paychecks to the staff, wants to keep a list arranged by ZIP codes. You can arrange a table by *sorting,* which means changing the order of the table.

When Paradox sorts a table, it rearranges all records in the table according to the specified new order. If the table you sort contains a key field, Paradox writes the sorted records to a new table. If the table is not keyed, you are given the option of placing the sorted records in a new table or in the existing table. If you were to sort a table of names arranged in random order, the sorted table would contain all the records that were in the old table, but they would be arranged in alphabetical order, as shown in Figure 4-14.

You must choose one or more fields on which to sort. In some cases, you will need to sort a database on more than one field. As an example, if you sort a database with last names as the sort field, you may get groups of records with the same last names but with the first names in random order. In such a case, you can sort the database with one field (such as last names) as the primary sort field and with another field (such as first names) as the secondary sort field.

Figure 4-14. **Sorting records in a database**

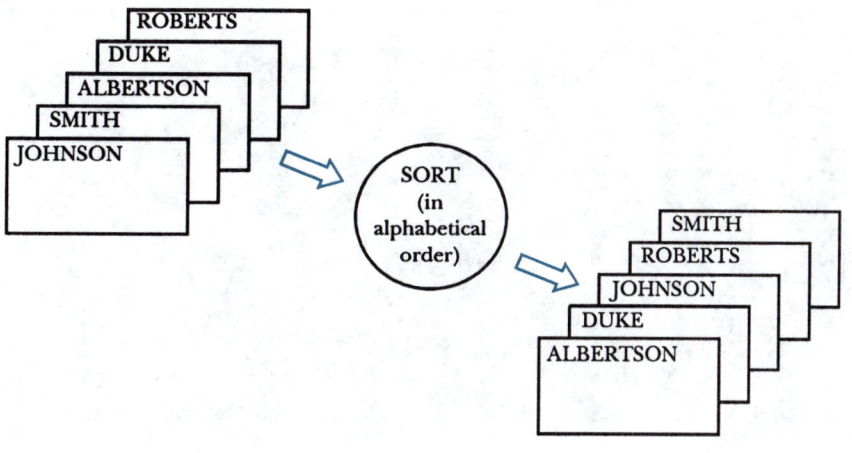

To sort a table, you will use the Sort option of the Modify menu. Activate the main menu with (F10) if necessary, and choose Modify/Sort. Paradox will ask you for the name of the table to be sorted; you can enter the name or press (ENTER) to display a list of tables. If the table you choose to sort has a key field, Paradox will next ask you to give a name to the new table that will result from the sort. If the table is not keyed, you next must choose Same, which places the results of the sort in the same table, or New, which places the results of the sort in a new table. Supply the name for the new table if you are making one, and the Sort Questionnaire will appear (as shown in Figure 4-15).

The Sort Questionnaire allows you to sort a table by any field, or combination of fields, in ascending or descending order. The arrow keys are used to move the cursor among the fields. Numbers indicating the sorting priority (1, 2, 3, and so on) are placed to the left of the fields on which the sort is based. As an example, if you wish to sort a table by ZIP codes, you would place a 1 next to the ZIP Code field. If you wish to sort by ZIP codes and then, where the ZIP codes were the same, by last names, you would place a 1 next to the ZIP Code field and a 2 next to the Last Name field.

Figure 4-15.   *Sort questionnaire*

```
≡  DO-IT!  Cancel
[ ]════════════════════════Sort: Abcstaff ═════════════════════
  Number fields to set up sort order (1, 2, etc.).  If you want a field sorted
    in descending sequence, follow the number with a 'D' (e.g., '2D').
         Ascending is the normal sequence and need not be indicated.


          Social Security
  2       Last Name
  3    ◄ First Name
          Address
  1       City
          State
          ZIP Code
          Date of Birth
          Date Hired
          Dependents
          Salary
          Assignment
          Hourly Rate
          Phone
          Comments


 F1 Help                                                  Sort
```

Indicating the Sort Order

Paradox assumes you wish to sort fields in ascending order. Ascending order means from A through Z if the sorted field is an alphanumeric field, from lowest to highest number for numeric or currency fields, and from earliest to latest date for date fields. In most cases, this is how you will want the table to be sorted. When you prefer descending order, however, you can indicate your preference by adding the letter D beside the number that indicates the sort priority. For example, entering the designation 1D beside the Last name field of a table tells Paradox that you wish to sort on the last names in descending order (the letters Z through A). The designation 1A indicates ascending order. If you omit the letter entirely, Paradox assumes ascending order.

Note

Paradox assumes that uppercase letters are sorted before lowercase ones. Paradox sorts using the ASCII sort order, which is punctuation marks, then uppercase letters, then lowercase letters, then extended characters, in order of the character's ASCII value.

Performing the Sort

Once you have entered the sort designations in the Sort Questionnaire, choose DO-IT!. Paradox will perform the sort, and the results will appear in the new table on your screen.

If you want records in a report to print in a particular order, sort the table first, then produce the report using the sorted table.

Tip

Hands-On Practice: Sorting a Table

4

Things are always clearer with an example, so try one now. Press (ALT)-(F8) to clear any remaining tables from the screen. Then choose the Modify option from the main menu, choose Sort from the Modify menu, and enter **ABCSTAFF** for the name of the table to sort. When Paradox asks for a name for the new (sorted) table, enter **SORTS** as the name. Paradox will then display the Sort Questionnaire.

To satisfy Judi's request for a list of employees arranged by amount of salary, move the cursor down until it is beside the Salary field and enter **1**. The numbers you enter beside the Sort fields indicate the priority of fields, in order of importance, that determine how the table will be sorted. When a table is sorted on a single field, this order has no real meaning, but when you sort a table on more than one field (as you will in later examples), you can use these numbers to choose which fields will take priority over other fields.

Once the criteria for the sort have been entered in the Sort Questionnaire, the sort can be performed. choose DO-IT! and the table will be sorted. The new table will appear, arranged by the amount of salary in ascending order (as shown in Figure 4-16).

If records are added to a table following a sort, the new records are not automatically placed in any sorted order. If you want those records to fall into a proper order, you must again sort the table after the addition of the records.

Note

Figure 4-16.   *Sorted database*

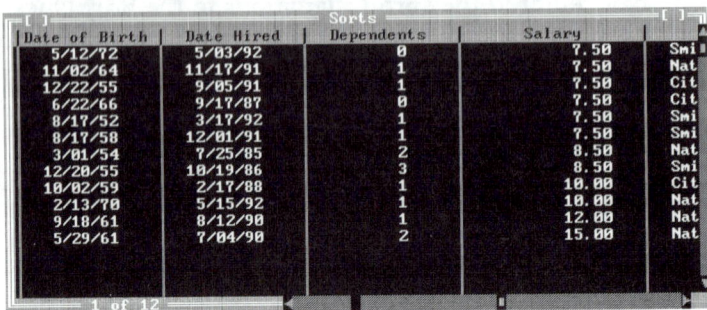

Sorting on Multiple Fields

Let's say you have printed the table and passed it along to Judi, who immediately decides that wherever the salaries were the same, the names should appear in alphabetical order. This requires a sort on more than one field.

Press (F8) to clear the table from the screen. Then again choose the option Modify/Sort from the main menu and enter **ABCSTAFF** for the name of the table to sort. When Paradox asks for a name for the new (sorted) table, enter **SORTS**. Because you are attempting to make use of the same table name as before, Paradox presents a menu displaying two choices, Cancel and Replace. As a precaution, Paradox is asking for confirmation before it will replace the prior table named SORTS with another one. Choose Replace from the menu to tell Paradox to proceed, and the Sort Questionnaire will appear.

Place the cursor beside the Salary field and enter **1**. Then place the cursor beside the Last Name field and enter **2**. Again, since the letter D was not entered in either case, Paradox will assume that ascending order is desired.

The order that you have entered indicates that the table should be sorted in two ways. First, it will be arranged by the salary amount, in ascending numeric order. Second, where salaries are equal, the records will be sorted by last name in ascending alphabetical order. To see the results, press (F2), and the new sorted table will appear, as shown in Figure 4-17. In the figure,

Figure 4-17. *Table sorted by Salary field, then by Last Name field*

the columns have been rearranged to show the Last Name and Salary fields simultaneously.

Changing the Sort Direction

Now assume that Judi is happy with the printed table you have supplied, but Marge would like to see a list arranged by date hired with the earliest dates at the bottom of the list. To sort in descending order, you will need to change the direction of the sort.

Press (F8) to clear the table from the screen, choose Modify/Sort from the main menu, and enter **ABCSTAFF** for the name of the table to sort. When Paradox asks for a name for the new (sorted) table, enter **SORTS** and choose Replace from the next menu that appears. This tells Paradox to proceed, and the Sort Questionnaire will appear.

Since you need to sort on the Date Hired field this time, move the cursor to the Date Hired field and enter **1D**. Then press (F2) to implement the sort. The new table will display the records in order of the date of hire, with the earliest dates at the bottom of the table, as illustrated in Figure 4-18.

Future chapters will demonstrate how you can use Paradox to draw relationships between the two tables you have created, so you can produce

Figure 4-18.   *Table sorted in descending order by Date Hired field*

ZIP Code	Date of Birth	Date Hired	Dependents	Salary
22117	2/13/70	5/15/92	1	10.00
22304-1234	5/12/72	5/03/92	0	7.50
20815-0988	8/17/52	3/17/92	1	7.50
22203	8/17/58	12/01/91	1	7.50
20912	11/02/64	11/17/91	1	7.50
22044	12/22/55	9/05/91	1	7.50
22090	9/18/61	8/12/90	1	12.00
20910-0124	5/29/61	7/04/90	2	15.00
22071	10/02/59	2/17/88	1	10.00
20009	6/22/66	9/17/87	0	7.50
22025	12/20/55	10/19/86	3	8.50
20815-0988	3/01/54	7/25/85	2	8.50

1 of 12

reports showing the fees that should be billed to each of ABC Temporaries' clients.

When you sort a table with a key field, you must sort to a new table. When you sort a table with no key fields, Paradox gives you the option of sorting either to the same table or to a new table.

Remember

Sorting on a Network

When you sort a table on a local area network, Paradox automatically puts what is known as a *write lock* on the table. While a write lock is in effect, other users cannot make changes to the table. Also, if you are sorting the table to a new table, Paradox places a *full lock* on the new table, meaning other users cannot access it in any way until the sort is complete. (For more details on network locks placed by Paradox, see Chapter 15.)

When To Sort

Once you've learned about sorting with Paradox, you should keep a few facts in mind as you decide when and how often to sort a database. Sorting can be time consuming, especially with large files. Sorting also uses a lot of disk space. Each time a sort occurs, Paradox creates a new file that will be as large as the original. For this reason, you must limit the size of the database to be sorted to no more than half the free space on the disk. And adding records to a database merely complicates matters. After you add records, chances are that the database must be resorted to maintain the desired order.

When you need to order a table based on a combination of sort fields, it is easiest to simply sort the table. But if you only need to arrange a table by only a single field, there is another fast, easy way to do so. By choosing Image/OrderTable, you can create an index for that field, as explained in the next section.

4

Creating an Index

In Paradox, an *index* is a separate file containing data based on one field from a table. The file is sorted alphabetically, numerically, or chronologically, and with each entry is the corresponding record number from the table. The record number is used to reference the record in the table. In effect, an index is a virtual sort of the table (see Figure 4-19). Just as a book index is a separate section that indicates where information is located, a Paradox index is a separate file that indicates where individual records are located in the table. When the table is displayed in a window according to the order of the index file, the first record to be displayed is the first record listed in the index; the next record displayed will be the second record listed in the index, and so on.

You can create an index by choosing Image/OrderTable from the main menu. Paradox will ask by what column you wish to order the table. Move the cursor to the desired column, and press (ENTER). (Paradox automatically names the index it will create after the column name you choose.) Next, Paradox displays a dialog box similar to this one:

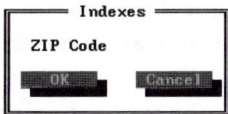

Figure 4-19.   *An index file is a virtual resort of the parent table.*

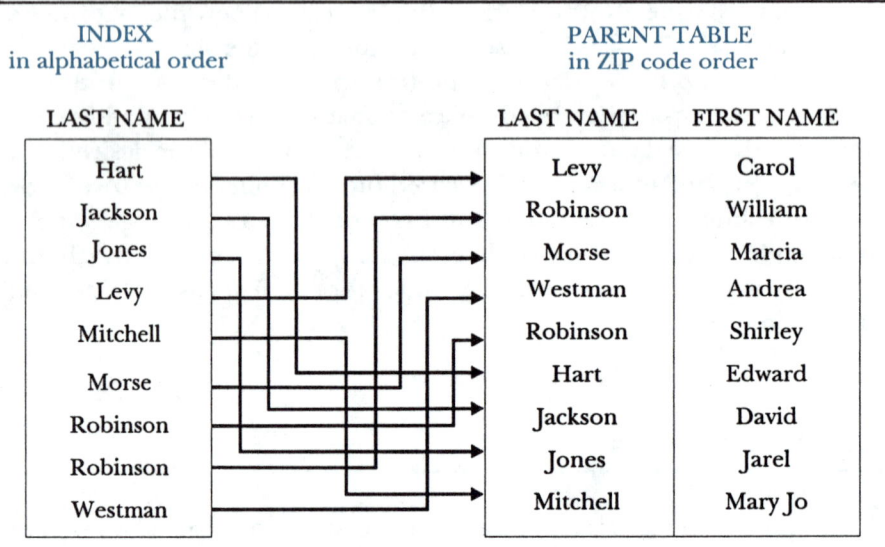

The dialog box gives you two options, OK and Cancel. Choose Cancel to cancel the operation. Choose OK, and Paradox creates an index; the table is redisplayed according to the order of that index.

As an example, open the ABCSTAFF table in a window (if it is not already displayed on your screen). From the main menu, choose Image. Then choose OrderTable. The message shown at the top of the screen reads as follows.

```
Move to the column you want to order by then press RETURN.
```

Place the cursor in the ZIP Code column, and press (ENTER). The dialog box that appears shows that an index will be built on the basis of the ZIP Code column. Choose OK by pressing (ENTER), or by clicking on the OK button. A confirmation dialog box next appears next; choose OK again. When the index is completed, your results should be similar to those shown in Figure 4-20; the records appear in order based on the entries in the ZIP Code column.

If an index already exists for a column and you use Image/OrderTable to order a table based on that column, Paradox will not ask you for confirmation to build the index; instead, it will simply place the existing index back

Figure 4-20.   *Table indexed by ZIP code*

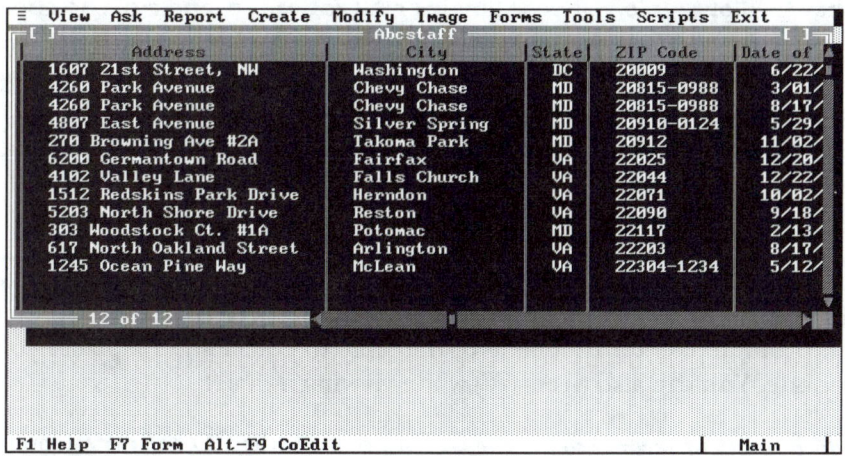

into use. For example, if you choose Image/OrderTable again now, and this time choose the Social Security field as the field to order the table by, you will notice that once you choose OK from the dialog box, Paradox displays the records in social security number order, without building an index. This is because an index for this column already exists. Whenever you specify a field as a key field (as you did during the creation of the ABCSTAFF table), Paradox automatically maintains an index based on that field.

Index Housekeeping

If you use the Image/OrderTable command often, over time you may clutter your hard disk with index files. Having multiple index files will affect your PC's performance to some degree, as Paradox must maintain these indexes as you add, edit, and delete table records. So if you have indexes that are no longer needed, it is a good idea to delete them. This can be done with the Tools/Delete/Index command.

When you choose Tools/Delete from the main menu, an additional menu opens, asking which type of object you want to delete. Choose Index, and you are next asked if you want to delete a single index, or all secondary indexes. (In Paradox, *secondary indexes* are ones you create; a *primary index* is one used by a key field of a table.) Choose Single or All as desired, and a file box opens, asking for the name of the table. Enter the desired table name. If you chose Single, all available indexes for that table will appear and you can select the index to be deleted. If you chose All, all secondary indexes for that table will be deleted.

Quick Summary

To edit records in a table   Choose Modify/Edit from the main menu. When prompted, enter the name of the table to edit. Paradox places you in Edit mode. You can also press (F9) while viewing a table.

To add a group of records to a table   Choose Modify/DataEntry from the main menu. When prompted, enter the name of the table. A new (temporary) table appears, and you can proceed to add records to that table. When done, choose DO-IT!.

To quickly find a record   Place the cursor in the field to search, and press Zoom ((CTRL)-(Z)). Paradox will ask for a search value. Enter the desired value to search for. The cursor will move to the first occurrence of the value. Use Zoom Next ((ALT)-(Z)) to search for repeated occurrences of the same value.

To delete a record   Press Edit ((F9)). Place the cursor in any field of the record to be deleted, and press the (DEL) key.

To sort a table   Choose Modify/Sort from the main menu. Enter the name of the table to be sorted. If asked, choose Same (to sort to the same table) or New (to sort to a new table). If asked, enter a name for the new table. When the Sort Questionnaire appears, enter the numbers indicating the sort order next to the desired fields. Choose DO-IT! to perform the sort.

To index a table   From the main menu, choose Image/OrderTable. Move the cursor to the column that will be used as the basis for the index, and press (ENTER). To build the index, choose OK from the next menu (and, if asked, choose OK from the menu that follows).

5

Using Custom Forms

So far, when adding new records to a table with DataEntry or making changes with Edit, you have used the Form Toggle key (F7) to switch from a table view to a simple on-screen entry form. This form listed the various fields and displayed highlighted areas that contained the actual data. For demonstrating how to add or change data within a database, this approach has been sufficient. However, there can be problems with such a straightforward approach to adding data to a table.

One drawback is the "unfriendly" screen that this approach presents to the computer user. If an ABC Temporaries employee does not know whether the hourly salary or the weekly salary belongs in the Salary field, the help screens and the Paradox manual will not offer any assistance. Another drawback is the lack of editing control you have within Paradox's default entry form. If for any reason you wish to prevent the editing of a particular field, you cannot do so with Edit.

To overcome such limitations, Paradox provides a flexible way to build *custom forms*. A custom form is simply a form of your own design that appears on the screen for data display and entry. Using Paradox, you can build custom forms that resemble printed forms commonly used in an office. Figure 5-1

Figure 5-1.   *Example of a custom form*

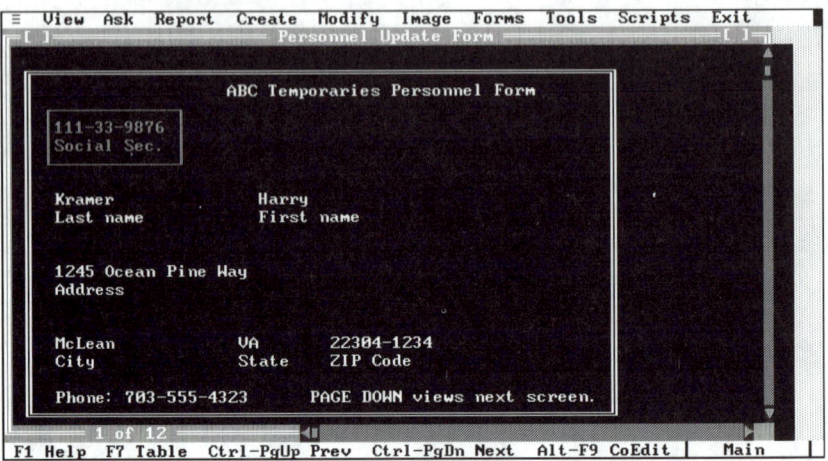

shows an example of such a form. You can also restrict entry by omitting or including certain fields in the form, or by making fields visible but unchangeable. And you can use Image/PickForm to use a specific custom form by default so that the form appears automatically when you use DataEntry and Edit commands.

If you are not already in Paradox, load the program now.

If you desire, you can design forms that resemble the paper forms used in your office.

Note

Creating a Custom Form with the Form Designer

Custom forms are created with the Design command from the Forms menu. There are four basic steps in this process:

1. Choose the table with which the form will be used.
2. Assign a number and a description to the form.
3. Using the screen as a drawing area, place the desired fields and enter any accompanying text and borders.
4. Store the form.

The first step is straightforward. From the main menu, choose Forms and then Design. Paradox will prompt you for a table name; type the desired table name or press (ENTER) and choose the desired table name from the list of available tables.

Paradox will next display a menu containing 14 numbers, along with the letter F, a designation for "standard form." (The standard form is the one that Paradox normally displays when you use the Form Toggle key, (F7), to switch from a table view to a form view. It is generally not a good idea to modify this form. If the standard form does not yet exist, Paradox automatically creates it for any table in use when you press (F7).) The numbers and the letter F are followed by descriptions of form names, as shown here:

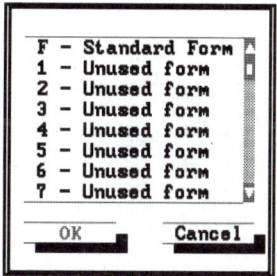

You can assign any of the 14 number choices as names for your custom forms. This provides you with a total of 15 possible forms for each table. If you select a number that has previously been used for a custom form, Paradox will verify that you want to replace the previous form with the new one you are designing.

When you choose a number for the form, Paradox next asks for a description of the form. You can enter up to 40 characters (including spaces) as the description, which will appear as a part of the menu whenever you select a form.

Once you enter the description, a window containing the Form Designer appears, as shown in Figure 5-2. Also, notice that the menu changes, revealing the Form Designer options.

The Form Designer window is a work area where you will draw (design) your custom form. As with all windows in Paradox, you can maximize the window, either by clicking on the Maximize/Restore icon, or by pressing the Maximize/Restore key ((SHIFT)-(F5)).

When designing a form, you may find it helpful to maximize the window; a maximized form gives you more space to work with.

Tip

Press the (INS) key repeatedly, and you will see the cursor switch between a thin line and a solid block shape. The thin line cursor indicates that you are in Insert mode, where typed characters push existing ones to the right. When the cursor is a solid block, you are in Overwrite mode, where typed characters overwrite existing characters.

Figure 5-2.   *Form Designer window and menu options*

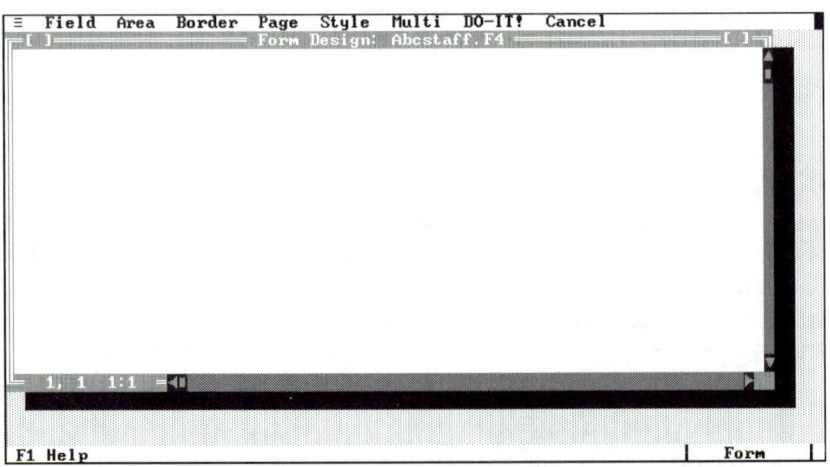

Within the bottom border of the window, at the lower-left, appear two sets of numbers. The leftmost set is the Cursor Position indicator, which indicates the current row and column position (separated by a comma) of the cursor. The second set of numbers are the Page indicator, which shows which page of a multiple-page form currently appears on the screen, and how many pages the form contains. (The current designation, 1:1, indicates that you are on the first page of a one-page form.) Each page of a form is precisely one maximized window in size; later in this chapter, a hands-on practice section helps you work with forms that are larger than one page in size.

When you are in the Form Designer, you cannot use the mouse or the System menu to switch to other windows. You must complete and save the form (or cancel the design

Remember *process by choosing Cancel) before you can work with other windows in Paradox.*

The Form Designer Menus

Let's examine the set of menus that appears when you are in the Form Designer. In addition to the System menu that appears everywhere in Paradox, the remaining menu options are Field, Area, Border, Page, Style, Multi, DO-IT!, and Cancel.

- The DO-IT! and Cancel options perform the same tasks as they do elsewhere in Paradox; in the Form Designer, choosing DO-IT! saves changes you've made to the form, and returns you to the Paradox desktop.

- The Multi option is used in the design of multitable and multirecord forms; these more advanced topics are covered later in this chapter and in Chapter 9.

- The Field menu is used to manipulate fields within the form; various Field options that appear on a submenu let you place fields on the form, erase existing fields, change a field's format, create calculated fields, and wrap the contents of long fields onto multiple lines.

- The Area menu lets you move an entire segment of a form to another area; you can also use this option to erase an area of a form.

- The Border option lets you place borders in the form; you can add single-line, and double-line borders, or borders composed of any ASCII character.

- The Page option lets you insert or delete pages from a multipage form.

- The Style option lets you change the particular display styles used for objects throughout the form. You can change colors, use reverse-video or blinking, and show or hide the names of fields.

Typing and Editing in the Form Designer

To move around the Form Designer window, you'll use editing keys that operate, in most respects, as they do elsewhere in Paradox. Table 5-1 shows the editing keys used by the Form Designer.

Caution

Be aware that in the Form Designer, pressing (SCROLL LOCK) changes the mode of the window so that the cursor keys do not move the cursor, but instead scroll the screen. If you are working on a form and suddenly find that you cannot move the cursor with the cursor keys, you may have accidentally turned on Scroll Lock. Press the (SCROLL LOCK) key to turn it off.

One key combination used in the Form Designer may be new to you at this point: the (ALT)-(C), or Color Palette key. After choosing Style/Color in the Form Designer menus, pressing (ALT)-(C) causes a color palette to be displayed; you can then choose a desired color for the object (field or text) that you are working with on the form. Later in this chapter you'll see how to do this, in "Working with Colors and Intensity."

You can use the editing keys to place descriptive text (such as field names), titles, or instructions anywhere you wish. To add labels or other descriptive text, simply enter the text at the desired location. The (DEL) and (BACKSPACE) keys can be used to remove unwanted characters, and you can move text strings to the right by inserting spaces ahead of the text while in Insert mode. Remember, you can use of the Cursor Position indicator at the bottom-left corner of the window to help position titles or labels within the form. The Style command on the Form Designer menu lets you display text in a special style, for instance, in reverse video, or blinking, or in a different color. The later section, "Adding Some Style," shows you how.

Table 5-1. *Editing Keys Used by the Form Designer*

Key	Action
(HOME)	Moves cursor to first line
(END)	Moves cursor to last line
(CTRL)-(HOME)	Moves cursor to start of line
(CTRL)-(END)	Moves cursor to end of line
(↑)	Moves up one line
(↓)	Moves down one line
(←)	Moves cursor left one character
(→)	Moves cursor right one character
(PGUP)	Moves cursor up one window/screen
(PGDN)	Moves cursor down one window/screen
(INS)	Toggles between Insert and Overwrite modes
(DEL)	Deletes character at cursor
(ALT)-(C)	Toggles color palette on or off (after you choose Style/Color from the menu)

5

Placing Fields

To place fields in the form, use the Field command from the Forms menu. To activate the Forms menu, press Menu ((F10)) while you are in the Form Designer, and choose Field. As mentioned earlier, the Field command is used to place or erase fields from the form, reformat a field's width, edit an expression used in a calculated field, or wrap text within a long field. Figure 5-3 shows the Field menu options.

For each field desired, choose Field from the menu, and then choose Place to place the field. From the next menu that appears, you can choose Regular if you desire a normal field, which can be edited; DisplayOnly for a field in which the contents appear but cannot be edited; Calculated for a field

Figure 5-3.   *Field menu options*

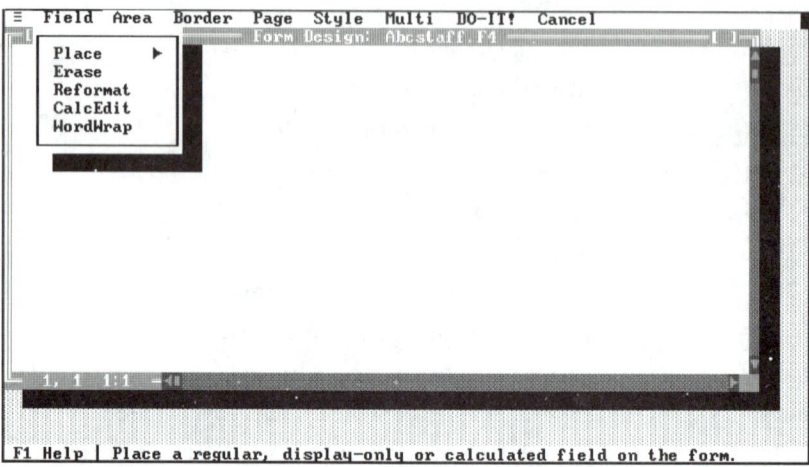

that will contain a value based on a calculation that uses the contents of other fields; or #Record to display the record number.

Field Choices

Regular fields are fields used for normal data entry and editing. They are actual fields from the table, as opposed to temporary values based on a calculation, and each field can be used in a form no more than once. You would not want to edit the same field twice anyway, so there should be no need to place the same regular field on a form more than one time.

Display-only fields contain the same information as regular fields, but they are used only to display the data and cannot be edited. Display-only fields are most common on multiple-page forms, where you want to show pertinent information. An example is showing a customer's name on every page of a four-page form, although the customer's name only needs to be entered or edited on the first page of the form.

Calculated fields are used to display the results of calculations that usually are based on the contents of other fields in the table. When you make a calculated field, Paradox will ask for an expression that provides the basis of the calculation. For example, if your table contained both an hourly salary field named Salary and an hours-worked field named Hours, using the expression [Salary] * [Hours] would display a calculated field containing the result of the Salary field multiplied by the Hours field. The asterisk indicates multiplication and brackets are always used to enclose field names in expressions. Calculated fields will be explained in more detail later in this chapter.

#Record, the final field choice, is used to insert the record number field at the desired location. The record number field will always display the record number of the current record.

Once you choose the type of field, you must in most cases tell Paradox which field will be placed on the screen. If you choose Regular or DisplayOnly, Paradox will show a list of all available fields in the table, and you can select from among the list. If you choose Calculated, Paradox will ask for the expression that provides the basis of the calculation. If you choose #Record, it assumes that you want to show the record number.

Once you choose the field type, Paradox asks you to place the cursor at the starting location for the field. You can use the cursor keys as well as (HOME) and (END) to move the cursor. (You cannot place fields with the mouse; hopefully this minor drawback will be addressed in a later version of Paradox.) (HOME) will move the cursor to the top of the screen, and (END) will move it to the bottom. Moving the cursor past the right edge is a shortcut for moving to the left edge of the screen, and moving the cursor past the left edge gets you to the right edge of the screen. With the cursor at the desired screen location, press (ENTER). A solid underline representing the field will appear. You can use (←) and (→) to adjust the width of the field. The width defaults to the width needed to display the entire field, but you can shorten it and use Field/WordWrap to wrap long text fields. If you shorten a field but do not use WordWrap, you can scroll through data using the (→) key. If you want to shorten a number field, it must be two digits longer than the maximum number currently stored in any record in the database.

5

Drawing Borders

In addition to placing fields and descriptive text on the form, you may wish to add borders. These can be easily added with the Border command from the Forms menu. From the menu, choose Border and then Place to place the border on the screen. Paradox then provides the choices of Single-Line, Double-Line, or a border character of your choice. When you select Other to use border characters of your choosing, ASCII graphics can be used by pressing (ALT) and typing the decimal number from the keypad. (For a listing of ASCII characters, see Appendix D of the PAL manual.) Make the desired selection, and then use the cursor keys to place the cursor at one corner of the border and press (ENTER). Then move the cursor to the other corner, and press (ENTER) again. If the two cursor positions have the same horizontal or vertical coordinate, a line will be drawn using the specified character, or a single or double line. If the coordinates are at different horizontal and vertical locations, a box will be drawn.

Using WordWrap

Depending on your application, you may encounter amounts of text that are too large to fit on a single line of a screen. As an example, consider the following database for tracking billings at a law firm:

Date	Rate	Hours	Description
10/02/92	150	2	Filing, preparation for appeal in case of United States government vs. John Doe
10/16/92	65	6.5	Westlaw, library research on Internal Revenue Service statues and precedents in prior rulings

When entering such data into a form, it would be helpful if the entire Description field could be viewed without your having to scroll with the cursor keys. However, the text is clearly going to extend past a single line in most cases. The solution is to use the WordWrap option, which is available once you select the Field option from the Forms menu.

To wrap a field within a custom form, first reformat the field to the desired width on the form. Then choose Field from the menu, and then WordWrap. Paradox will ask you to move to the desired field. Place the cursor in the field you want to wrap, and press (ENTER) to select that field. Paradox will now display the following prompt:

```
Number of lines: 0
```

Paradox is asking for the maximum number of lines that the wrapped text will be allowed to occupy on the form. Enter the desired number of lines to complete the placement of the wrapped field.

Note that you cannot add fields, text, or borders in the area needed for the maximum amount of wrapped text. For example, if you place a field on line 15 and allow it to wrap to a maximum of 3 lines, down to line 18, you cannot place other fields on line 18 in the area that the wrapped field occupies. If you attempt to do so, Paradox will display a warning message when you attempt to save the form, and you must correct the error before the form can be saved.

Also keep in mind that the maximum field width (the width specified in your table structure) must exceed the displayed width for WordWrap to take effect. To calculate the number of lines needed to wrap text, use the formula

MAX WIDTH/DISPLAY WIDTH = NO. OF LINES.

Wrapped fields can be used for data entry or for editing records. If a value is still too long to fit in the field, you can use Field View ((ALT)-(F5)) to view and edit the entire value. If this happens often, you always have the option of changing the form's design so that still more lines are allowed in the wrapped field.

Saving the Form

When all the desired fields, borders, text, and other elements have been placed, you can press (F2), or choose DO-IT! from the menu, and the form will be stored. To use the form, view a table in the normal manner. From the main menu choose Image and then PickForm, and select the desired form from the list of choices. Use Image/KeepSet to invoke the form automatically.

Hands-On Practice: Designing A Two-Page Personnel Form

Try building a detailed multipage form for use with the ABC Temporaries staff table. Since most updates to the staff table are performed when an employee moves to a new address, the personnel department wishes to use a two-page form for updating records in the table. The first page of the form will display the name and address information for each employee, and the second page will display the remaining information. Since employees do not normally change social security numbers, the personnel manager wants the Social Security field to be display-only. And the manager also wants a "profitability" field, which will contain the result of the salary subtracted from the hourly rate for each employee. When completed, the form will resemble the example shown in Figure 5-4.

To begin designing the form, from the the main menu choose Forms and then Design. Enter **ABCSTAFF** for the name of the table, or press (ENTER) and select ABCSTAFF from the list provided. From the next menu, which shows the 14 available numbers, select 1 to identify the form. Paradox will prompt you for a description of the form. Enter **Personnel Update Form** as the description, and the Form Designer window will appear.

Note that although you can choose a field to place and then move the cursor after you have selected the field, for this example you will first locate the cursor at the desired starting location. Place the cursor at row 5, column 5. This will serve as the starting position for the first field, Social Sec.

Note

The row and column indicators are helpful for determining cursor location when you are designing forms.

Form the Forms menu, choose Field and then Place to insert the first field. This will be the Social Sec. field, which should not be edited, so choose DisplayOnly from the next menu. Paradox will show a list of available fields from the ABCSTAFF table. Choose Social Security from the list, and Paradox will display the following prompt at the top of the screen:

```
Move where you want the field to begin, then press ↵
```

Figure 5-4. *Example of a personnel form*

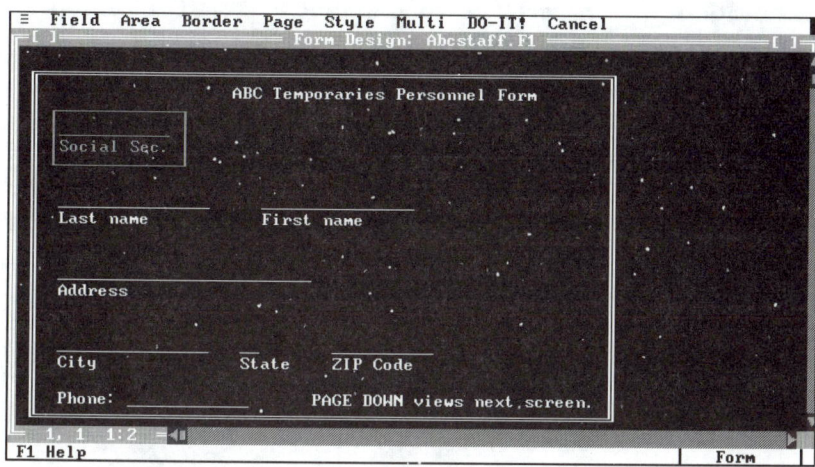

Since you are already at the desired starting position for the field, press (ENTER). A dotted line will appear, indicating the length of the Social Sec. field. It does not need to be lengthened or shortened, so press (ENTER) to accept the current width of the field.

Place the cursor at row 6, column 5, and enter **Social Sec.** as the text. Then move the cursor to row 9, column 5, and from the menu choose Field/Place/Regular to place a regular field at the cursor location. Choose the Last Name field, press (ENTER) to start the field at the current cursor location, and press (ENTER) again to end the field at row 9, column 20.

Now place the cursor at row 9, column 25. From the menu choose Field/Place/Regular. Then select First Name as the desired field. Press (ENTER) twice to place the field at the desired location. At row 10, column 5, enter the heading **Last name**. At row 10, column 25, enter the heading **First name**.

Move the cursor to row 13, column 5. Choose Field/Place/Regular, select Address as the field, and press (ENTER) twice to place the field. Move the cursor to row 14, column 5, and enter the heading **Address**. Use the locations and commands described in Table 5-2 to complete the fields and headings on the first page of the form.

Table 5-2.   *Remaining Field Locations for First Page*

At Location:	Select These Commands:	Then Choose This:
17,5	Field/Place/Regular	City
17,23	Field/Place/Regular	State
17,32	Field/Place/Regular	ZIP Code

At Location:	Enter This Heading:
18,5	City
18,23	State
18,32	ZIP Code
3,22	ABC Temporaries Personnel Form
20,16	PAGE DOWN views next screen.

Two borders are desired. One will be used to visually highlight the employee's social security number, and the other will enclose all of the fields in the first page of the form. Place the cursor at row 4, column 4, and press (F10) to display the menu. Choose Border/Place/Single-Line, and press (ENTER) to start the border at row 4, column 4. Move the cursor approximately to row 7, column 17, so that the Social Sec. field and the entire label are enclosed within the highlighted box, and press (ENTER).

Move the cursor to row 2, column 2. Choose Border/Place/Double-Line and press (ENTER) to begin the border. Move the cursor to approximately row 21, column 58, so that the box encloses all of the fields and the headings, and then press (ENTER) to complete the border. This will complete the first page of the custom form, which should resemble Figure 5-4.

Adding a New Page

Paradox usually adds another page for every 22 lines used in a form to place fields. However, you can add new pages at any time by using the Page command from the Forms menu. From the menu choose Page and Insert. Paradox will display a menu with two options, After and Before. You can insert new pages either before or after the current page in the form. In this case, choose After. The screen will clear, and the Page indicator at the lower-left corner of the screen will indicate that you are now on Page 2 of a two-page form.

To help the employee using the form keep track of which employee's record is being edited, we will need to again display the Last Name and First Name fields. However, there is no need to allow editing, since these fields were editable on the first page of the form. Place the cursor at row 3, column 5, and from the menu choose Field/Place/Display Only. For the field name, choose Last Name, and then press (ENTER) twice to locate the field. Place the cursor at row 3, column 22, press (F10) for the menu, and choose Field/Place/Display Only. For the field name, choose First Name, and then press (ENTER) twice to locate the field.

For the name headings, at row 4, column 5, enter **Last name** and at row 4, column 23, enter **First name**. At row 6, column 5, choose Field/Place/Regular from the menu; then select Date of Birth and press (ENTER) twice to place the field. Move to row 6, column 20, and choose Field/Place/Regular. Select Date Hired, and press (ENTER) twice to place the field. Finally, move to row 6, column 36, choose Field/Place/Regular, select Dependents as the field, and press (ENTER) once.

You will note that the Dependents field displays a full 22 characters. Because this is a numeric field, Paradox allows a maximum of digits for the field, which in this case is overkill. Use the (←) key to narrow the field until a maximum of 8 digits can be displayed, and then press (ENTER) to set the width at 8 digits.

For the headings, at row 7, column 5, enter **Date of birth**. At row 7, column 20, enter **Date hired**. At row 7, column 36, enter **Dependents**. Use the locations and commands described in Table 5-3 to add the remaining fields and headings to the second page of the form.

Adding a Calculated Field

As mentioned earlier in the chapter, Paradox lets you add *calculated fields* to a form. These fields are used to display the results of calculations that are usually based on the contents of other fields in the database. Calculated fields are not actual fields in a database; they do not consume space because they

Table 5-3.   *Additional Field Locations for Second Page*

At Location:	Select These Commands:	Then Choose This:
10,5	Field/Place/Regular	Assignment
13,5	Field/Place/Regular	Salary (adjust width to 8)
13,25	Field/Place/Regular	Hourly Rate (adjust width to 8)

At Location:	Enter This Heading:
11,5	Assignment
14,5	Salary
14,25	Hourly rate

are not stored in any permanent location. Adding a calculated field simply tells Paradox to perform a calculation and to display the results in the calculated field of the form.

When you create a calculated field, Paradox will ask for the expression that provides the basis of the calculation. Such expressions can be up to 175 characters in length. As a part of an expression, you are allowed to use field names that are enclosed in [] brackets and typed exactly as they appear in the table structure; math operators, which include + (addition), – (subtraction), * (multiplication), and / (division); and constants, such as "James," 4.75, or 3/12/92. Here are some examples of valid expressions:

"Mr./Ms. " + [First name] + " " + [Last name]
[Date] + 365
[Hourly salary] * [Hours worked]

As these examples indicate, you can use the + operator to combine text strings (including text stored in alphanumeric fields), and you can add a number of days to a valid date value. You cannot perform calculations between incompatible data types; for example, you cannot add a value in a numeric field to a text string in a character (alphanumeric) field. If you try to base a calculated field on an incompatible operation, or if you misspell a field name used as the basis for the calculation, Paradox will warn you about it by displaying an error message.

Note that in Paradox 4, you can include most PAL functions in calculated fields, as well as in forms and reports. PAL is introduced in Chapter 14.

In our example, the managers at ABC Temporaries desire a "profitability" field, which will display the difference between the hourly rate charged to the customer and the employee's salary. To add a new field to the table for this information would be a waste of time, since the information can be readily obtained by subtracting the salary amount from the hourly rate amount. The result can be displayed as a calculated field.

The calculated field for the hourly profit is still needed. Place the cursor at row 13, column 44. Choose Field/Place/Calculated from the menu. In response to the prompt for an expression, enter the following:

```
[Hourly Rate] - [Salary]
```

Be sure to include the left and right bracket symbols around the field names. Press (ENTER) once to begin the field, use the (←) key to shorten the field width to eight characters, and press (ENTER) again to set the field's width. Finally, place the cursor at row 14, column 44, and enter the heading **Hourly profit**. If you were observant enough to notice that we have forgotten the Phone field, do not add it yet; it will be added to the form later.

Since the Comments field is a memo field, it is a prime candidate for the benefits of the WordWrap feature of the Form Designer. Place the cursor at row 16, column 5, and type **Comments:**. Then, move the cursor to row 17, column 5. From the menu, choose Field/Place/Regular. From the list of fields that next appears, choose Comments. Press (ENTER) once, then press (→) 20 times, to widen the field by an additional 20 characters. Press (ENTER) again to finish placing the field.

Next, choose Field/WordWrap from the menu. Place the cursor anywhere within the Comments field, and press (ENTER). Paradox next displays a dialog box asking you for the maximum allowed number of lines for wrapping the field. Enter **3** as the desired value, and choose OK or press (ENTER). This value allows the Comments field to occupy the current line, and two lines below it.

To draw a border, first place the cursor at row 20, column 58, and choose Border/Place/Double-Line from the menu. Press (ENTER) to start the border.

5

Place the cursor at approximately row 2, column 2, so that the entire form, including the headings, is enclosed by the border, and then press (ENTER) to complete the border.

The completed form only needs to be saved to be ready for use. Select DO-IT! from the menu (or press (F2)) to save the form.

Because calculated fields do not exist in the table, you cannot edit them while viewing the form. Calculated fields are display-only fields.

Remember

Using the Example Form

To use the form you have just created, choose View from the main menu, and enter **ABCSTAFF** as the table to view. Next, choose Image/PickForm from the menu, and select **1**, Personnel Update Form, from the available forms. The Personnel Update Form you just designed will appear in its own window. If you try moving through the form with the arrow keys, you will notice that you cannot move the cursor to the Social Sec. field on the first page of the form or to the Last name and First name fields on the second page—because you set them to display-only. Also, try using the (PGUP) and (PGDN) keys. These will take you between the pages of the form.

Editing an Existing Form

The Change command, available from the Forms menu, allows you to modify existing forms. Any changes that you wish to make to the form can be made in a manner similar to that used to create the form. Use the same options from the Forms menu to place or remove fields, add borders, insert or delete pages, or to change styles.

To change a form, choose Forms/Change from the main menu, enter the name of the table associated with the form, and pick the number assigned to the form from the menu of up to 14 numbers that appears. Once you have chosen the form, the form description you originally entered will appear. You can change the description, or you can press (ENTER) (or choose OK) to accept it without changes. The Forms menu will then appear. You are provided with the same options for placing fields and borders, changing styles, and inserting or deleting pages as you were provided when you originally designed the form. Some specific menu commands that may prove useful when you want to make changes to an existing form are discussed in additional detail here.

Reformatting Fields

If you want to change the width of existing fields, use the Reformat command, available from the Field menu. While editing the form, press (F10) if needed to display the Forms menu, and choose Field/Reformat. Paradox will ask you to select the desired field; move the cursor to the field whose width you wish to change, and press (ENTER) to select the field. You can then use (←) and (→) to adjust the field's width. When you are satisfied with the width, press (ENTER) to set the new field width. When a field will not expand further when you press the (→) key, the field has reached its maximum width.

Moving an Area

If you do not like the location of a portion of your form, you can move it to a new location by using the Move command, available from the Area option of the Forms menu. To do this, begin editing the form as described earlier, and from the menu choose Area/Move. Paradox will ask you to place the cursor on any corner of the desired area; do so, and press (ENTER). Next, move the cursor to the opposite corner. As you move the cursor, the area on the screen will be highlighted.

Once the highlight encloses the desired area, press (ENTER) again. Then use the cursor keys to drag the area to the new location, and press (ENTER) once more to reposition the area. Note that you can use the (PGUP) and (PGDN) keys to move entire areas between pages of a multipage form.

5

Erasing an Area

The Erase command, available from the Area option of the Forms menu, offers a convenient way to erase a portion of a form. Begin editing the form as described earlier. From the menu, choose Area/Erase. Paradox will ask you to place the cursor on any corner of the desired area; do so, and press (ENTER). Next, move the cursor to the opposite corner. As you move the cursor, the area on the screen will be highlighted.

Once the highlight encloses the desired area, press (ENTER) again, press (ENTER) once more to erase the area.

Caution

Though you could undo the effects of the Area/Erase operation by choosing Cancel from the menu, this would also cancel any constructive changes you made while you were editing the form. Be sure that an area of the form is no longer needed before you erase it.

Deleting Fields

If you need to remove an existing field from a form, you can do so with the Change command, available from the Forms menu. While in the Form Designer, choose Field/Erase from the menu, and Paradox will ask you to place the cursor at the field that is to be removed. Place the cursor anywhere in the desired field, and press (ENTER). The field will be removed from the form.

Deleting Pages

In just as final a manner as described above, you can delete pages from a multiple-page form. To do so, edit the form, and use the (PGUP) or (PGDN) key to reach the page that you want to delete. Then choose Page/Delete from the menu. When you select the Delete command and confirm your choice by choosing OK from the next menu to appear, the page will be removed. Although deleting a page is final, you can cancel the effects of the deletion if you cancel the form design process without saving your changes—but you sacrifice any other edits you have performed.

Adding Some Style

You can assign style attributes to selected areas of a form after entering text and placing your desired fields. While designing the form, choose Style from the Forms menu. The options available from the Style menu are Color, Monochrome, FieldNames, and ShowHighlight. (If you are using an older version of Paradox, the choices are Intensity, Blink, Reversal, FieldNames, and Default.)

The Color option lets you select foreground and background colors for a selected area of the form or a border. The Monochrome option lets you set the intensity, reverse, normal, and blink attributes for a selected area of the form or for a border. If you select the FieldNames option, Paradox will superimpose field names on the fields you place on the form. This can be helpful for designing complex screens, because it is easier to identify fields when they are labeled. Once the form has been saved and you begin using the form to add or edit records, the field names are no longer visible. The ShowHighlight option tells Paradox to display the areas of multirecord forms while you are designing or changing a form. You will learn more about multirecord forms later in this chapter.

The Intensity option tells Paradox to show selected text and borders in boldface on monochrome monitors or in color on color monitors. The Blink option causes text and borders to blink, and the Reversal option causes text and borders to be shown in reverse video. The Default option lets you quickly turn off a previously chosen display attribute. This option, when chosen, will turn off blinking and reverse video, disable any display of field names during form design, and restore text and borders to normal intensity. If you want to assign a style attribute to existing text, use the Area option and then select the desired style.

 *Use colors or highlighting to emphasize important fields in your forms.*

Tip

Working with Colors and Intensity

You can change the colors used in a form (unless you have a monochrome system, in which case the color options are ignored by Paradox). With versions of Paradox prior to version 3.0, you do not have the color options, but you can change the intensity and blinking attributes as described earlier by using the Intensity and Blink options of Forms/Style. The rest of this section assumes you are using Paradox version 4 or above.

When you select Style from the Forms menu, you can then select the style and the colors for selected areas of the form or for borders. You might want to use this option to visually highlight a portion of a form; for example, you might want an employee's name to appear in a different color than the rest of the form, or you might want the salary to appear blinking. Recall that selecting the Style option of the Forms menu reveals the following choices.

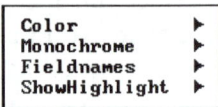

```
Color              ►
Monochrome         ►
Fieldnames         ►
ShowHighlight      ►
```

For changing the visual attributes of part of a form, you are interested in the Color and Monochrome options. If you are using a color system and you want to change the colors for a field, fields, or a border, choose Color. You will then see a menu with two options Area and Border.

If you want the color changes to affect a portion of a form (such as one or more fields), choose Area. Then place the cursor at the start of the area to change the color, and press (ENTER) to begin selecting the area. Move the cursor to the diagonal corner of the area (it will be highlighted as you do so), and press (ENTER) again to mark the end of the area. Once you have marked the area, a color palette showing the available foreground and background colors will appear in the upper-left corner of the screen. Use (↑) and (↓) to change the background color, and use (←) and (→) to change the foreground color. (As you press the arrow keys, the new colors will appear in the selected area on the form; this makes it easier to decide on the most desirable color choice.) When you have selected the desired colors, press (ENTER), and the new colors will take effect. Note that you can color the entire form by selecting Area and blocking out the entire window. You would then enter your text, place fields, and designate other colors, if desired, for specific portions of the form.

Use (ALT)-(C) to toggle the color palette on and off.

Tip

In a similar manner, you can change the colors for the border of a form by choosing Style/Color/Border. Move the cursor to one corner of the border and press (ENTER) to begin selecting it; then move the cursor to the diagonal corner of the border and press (ENTER) to finish defining the border. The color palette will appear in the upper-left corner of the screen. Use the arrow keys to select the desired foreground and background colors, and press (ENTER) when you've found the desired colors.

If you are not using a color monitor, you can still take advantage of the Style/Monochrome option. As with the Color option, selecting the Monochrome option provides you with two choices: Area and Border. Choose Area if you want to change the display attributes for a portion of the screen (such as one or more fields), or choose Border to change the display attributes for a border. Move the cursor to one corner of the area or the border, and press (ENTER); then move the cursor to the diagonal corner of the area or the border, and press (ENTER) to complete the selection. Once you've made the selection, Paradox will tell you to use the (←) or (→) key to switch between the available monochrome attributes, or styles. You can switch between intense display, reverse video, intense and reverse, blinking, nonblinking, and normal (which cancels the effects of intense or reverse if it was chosen earlier). Continue pressing either the (←) or the (→) key until the desired display style appears on the screen. Then press (ENTER) to accept that style of display.

Whatever color and style choices you make are stored when you save the form with the DO-IT! option. You can move forms between systems of the same types and they will be displayed in the same fashion. You can also move forms designed on a monochrome system to a color system and the form will appear in black-and-white, with the same intensity, reverse, or blinking attributes that you designed on the monochrome system.

Taking forms designed on a color system to a monochrome system may present some problems. Paradox saves your color information, and monochrome equivalents for that information, along with the form. However, since you did not design the form on a monochrome system, you have no way of knowing exactly what it will look like on a monochrome system before trying it. Also, some color combinations make data difficult to read on a monochrome system. If you are designing a form on a color system that will be used on monochrome systems, you may want to first use the Video/Colors option of the Custom Configuration Program to see the equivalent monochrome

5

attributes for various colors. For more details on the use of the Custom Configuration Program, see Appendix B.

The same sort of problem can apply to most laptop computers. If you design a form with different colors on a color system and then move that form to a laptop, you may have trouble seeing some of the data clearly on the laptop's screen. If you know laptop users will be using the form, it may be best to stick with white-on-black or black-on-white color combinations.

Hands-On Practice: Editing the Personnel Form

The Change command in the Forms menu lets you make changes to the design of an existing form. From the main menu, choose Forms/Change, and enter **ABCSTAFF** for the name of the table. Paradox will display the list of available forms; choose 1 as the form to edit, and when prompted for a description, press (ENTER) to keep the same description for the form.

For the example form, the phone number needs to be added to the first page of the form. Place the cursor at the start of the descriptive text, "PAGE DOWN views next screen."

With the Area command, you can move portions of the form from one area to another. (Note that the area to which you move an object must be a blank area.) Choose Area/Move from the menu, and press (ENTER) to mark the beginning of the area. Move the cursor to the end of the descriptive text, and press (ENTER) again to define the area. Press (→) 15 times to move the descriptive text to column 57, and press (ENTER) to relocate the area.

Place the cursor at row 20, column 5, and type **Phone** followed by a colon (:) and a space. From the menu, choose Field/Place/Regular, and select Phone from the list of fields. Press (ENTER) twice to place the field. You can also try changing the display characteristics of the Social Sec. field to set off this field visually from the remainder of the form. Place the cursor at the upper-left corner of the border surrounding the Social Sec. field (row 4, column 4). Choose Style from the menu. If you are using a color system, choose Color; otherwise, choose Monochrome.

From the next menu to appear, choose Area. Since the cursor is already at the start of the area you want to change, press (ENTER). Then move the cursor to the lower-right corner of the border surrounding the Social Sec. field and press (ENTER) again.

If you are using a color system, the color palette will appear (unless it has been turned off using the Custom Configuration Program). If the color palette does not appear, press (ALT)-(C) to show it. Use (↑) or (↓) to pick a background color. Press (ENTER) when done, and the new colors will take effect. Then choose DO-IT! from the menu, or press (F2), to save the modified form.

If you are using a monochrome system, use (←) or (→) to display the Intensity-Reversal option, and then press (ENTER) for the option to take effect. Then, choose DO-IT! from the menu, or press (F2), to save the modified form.

If you were viewing the table when you chose the Change command to modify the form, you will again see the records in the table through the form when you complete the change process. Note that the Phone field now appears at the bottom of the first page of the form, as shown in Figure 5-5.

5

Figure 5-5. *Personnel form with Phone field added*

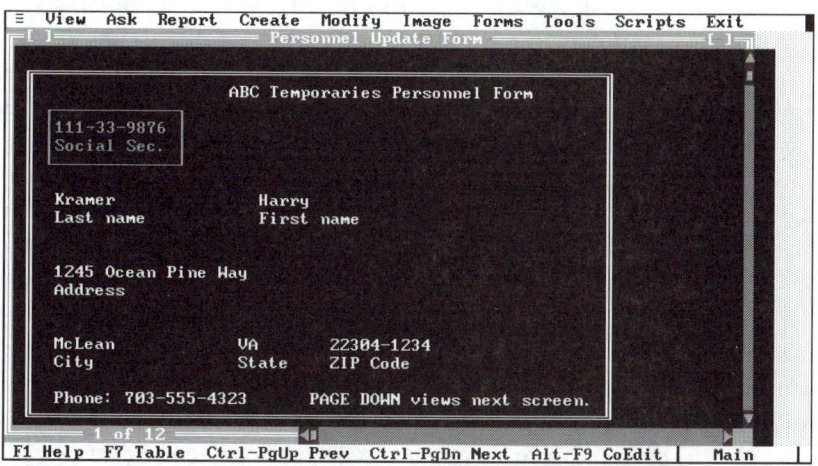

Designing a Form Based on an Existing Form

You can design a new custom form by using another form as the basis for the new form. For example, you might want to use the Paradox standard form as a starting point for a custom form. To do so, choose Tools/Copy/Form from the main menu. From the next menu that appears, choose SameTable. Enter the table name; then, from the menu of available forms that appears, choose the form name to copy (the one on which you want to base the new form's design).

At the next menu, choose a name for the new form. Paradox copies the old form to a new file under the new name. Once this is done, choose Forms/Change from the main menu. Pick the newly copied form by number from the menu that appears. Change the description (if desired), and the copied form will appear in a Form Designer window. You can then proceed to make changes to the design of the form, and save it with DO-IT! ((F2)).

Designing a Multirecord Form

Paradox offers the capability of *multirecord forms*. Such forms show more than one record at a time, much like the tabular display that appears by default when you first begin viewing a table. One important difference between an ordinary table view and a multirecord form is that you can design the form to show the data in the format you prefer. Another important difference is that, as with any form, you can add calculated fields. Note, however, that you cannot have multirecord forms that span more than one page (unlike other types of forms).

Multirecord forms can be very useful when you want to be able to scroll up and down and see many records on the screen at once. They are also useful when a number of records, such as those containing "week ending" dates and hours worked, are related to a single record in another table, such as the name of an employee. Designing this type of multirecord form (a form that is linked to another table) will be covered in Chapter 9.

Any multirecord form has two areas: an *original record*, where fields from the first record to appear are placed on the form, and *copies* of the original record. The copies of the original record appear directly below the original record, as shown in Figure 5-6.

To create a multirecord form, you start designing the form in the usual manner by choosing Forms/Design from the menu, entering a table name, and selecting a number for the new form. After entering the form description, you are placed in a Form Designer window. You next choose Multi/Records and then Define from the menu.

Paradox next asks you to place the cursor at the corner of the region to be used for the original record of the multirecord form. You move the cursor to the start of the area and press (ENTER); then you move the cursor to the diagonal corner of the area, and press (ENTER) again. Paradox then asks you to use (↑) or (↓) to add or delete repeating rows; these are used to display the copies, or additional records, that will appear in the multirecord form. Press

5

Figure 5-6.   *Concept of multirecord form*

Last: Kramer First: Harry
Assignment: Smith Builders Salary: 7.50 Rate: 12.00

Last: Western First: Andrea
Assignment: National Oil Co. Salary: 15.00 Rate: 24.00

Last: Robinson First: Shirley
Assignment: National Oil Co. Salary: 7.50 Rate: 12.00

Last: Xxxxxxx First: Xxxxxxxx
Assignment: Xxxxxxx Xxx., Salary: xx.xx Rate: xx.xx

Multiple records displayed

the arrow keys as many times as necessary, and press (ENTER) when you are finished.

At this point, the original area and the copies area will appear in different colors or styles of highlighting. You can then proceed to use Field/Place as described previously to place the desired fields in the original area. As you place each field, copies of that field will automatically appear in the copies area. Once you have finished placing the fields and adding any desired headings, save the form with the DO-IT! option of the Forms menu. When you select the form with Image/PickForm, you will see multiple records displayed in the form, and you will be able to use the arrow keys to move among the records.

Hands-On Practice: Designing a Multirecord Form

The managers at ABC Temporaries would like to be able to use a tabular form for editing employee records. The fields most often edited are the Salary, Assignment, and Hourly Rate fields, so these fields are to be included in the form. Also, the name fields are needed so the managers will be able to see which employee record is being edited.

Choose Forms/Design from the menu. Enter **ABCSTAFF** as the name of the table. Choose 2 as the form name, and for a description, enter **Tabular form for employees**. In a moment, a new blank Form Designer window opens.

Move the cursor to row 5, column 10. From the Forms menu, choose Multi/Records/Define. Since the cursor is already at the desired starting location, press (ENTER). Move the cursor down 2 lines and to the right 64 spaces. Press (ENTER) again to mark this as the area for the original record.

Paradox now asks you to use (↑) or (↓) to add or delete repeating rows in the region. Press (↓) five times to add room for five additional records. Then press (ENTER). The screen will now contain two highlighted areas: a two-line area for the original record and a ten-line area for the copies. (Depending on your monitor type and your graphics hardware, you may or may not be able to see the distinction clearly. With monochrome monitors, adjusting your contrast may improve the distinction.)

Move the cursor to row 5, column 10, and type the heading, **Last:**. Choose Field/Place/DisplayOnly from the menu. From the list of fields to appear, choose Last Name. Then press (ENTER) twice to place the field at the desired location.

Move the cursor to row 5, column 32, and type the heading, **First:**. From the menu, choose Field/Place/DisplayOnly. From the list of fields to appear, choose First Name. Then press (ENTER) twice to place the field at the desired location.

Move the cursor to row 6, column 10. Type the heading, **Assignment:**. From the menu, choose Field/Place/Regular. From the list of fields to appear, choose Assignment. Then press (ENTER) twice to place the field at the desired location.

Move the cursor to row 6, column 43. Type the heading, **Salary:**. From the menu, choose Field/Place/Regular. From the list of fields to appear, choose Salary. Then press (ENTER) once. Use (←) to shorten the field width to eight characters, and then press (ENTER) again.

Move the cursor to row 6, column 60. Type the heading, **Rate:**. From the menu, choose Field/Place/Regular. From the list of fields to appear, choose Hourly Rate and press (ENTER) once. Use (←) to shorten the field width to eight characters, and then press (ENTER) again. The final line of the original area will remain blank, providing a visual divider between successive records when they appear in the completed form.

Move the cursor to row 4, column 8. From the menu, choose Border/Place/Double-Line. Press (ENTER) to start the border. Move the cursor just to the right and below the other diagonal corner of the highlighted area for the copied records (approximately row 23, column 76) and press (ENTER) again to complete the border.

Save the form with DO-IT! ((F2)). When you are back viewing the table, choose Image/PickForm from the main menu. From the next menu, select 2. You should see the new multirecord form on your screen (Figure 5-7), and you can try using the arrow keys to move among the various records.

You can make changes to a multirecord form at any time in a manner similar to that for other forms. From the Forms menu, choose Multi/Records/Adjust to change the size of the original and copies areas. Use Multi/Records/Remove to remove all copies of an original record from the form. Changing attributes (such as intensity or colors) is done in the same manner as with other forms, as described earlier in this chapter.

5

Figure 5-7.   *Example of multirecord form*

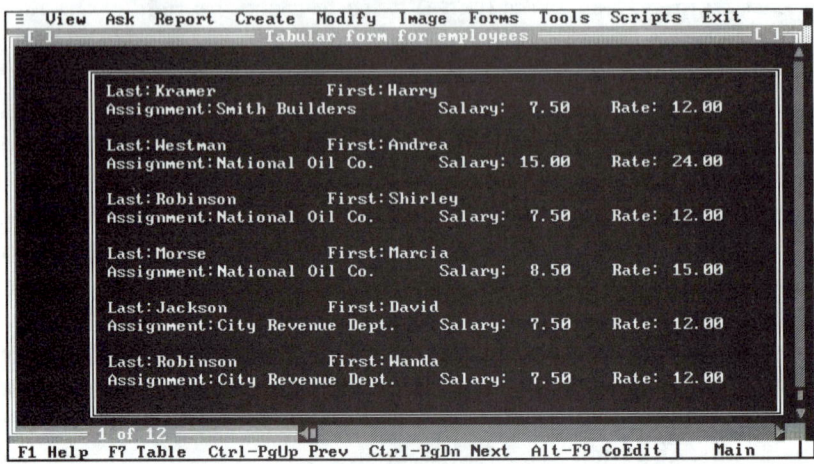

Boxes, Lines, and Your Printer

If you use the (SHIFT)-(PRINT SCREEN) key combination to print screen images to your printer, any form containing lines or boxes created by Paradox may not print out as you might expect. In most cases, the lines on the form will print as alphabetic characters on your printer. Only printers that can print the IBM extended graphic character set will print these lines as they actually appear on a form.

A Note About Files

Paradox stores your screen forms as Paradox objects in disk files. In order to better keep track of the files, it provides the same name as you assigned to the associated table, but with an extension of .F for the standard form, .F1 for the first custom form, .F2 for the second custom form, and so on. You should keep these files in the same directory with other Paradox objects so that the program can find them when you want to use them.

Quick Summary

To design a form   From the menu, choose Forms/Design. Enter the table name on which the form will be based. Choose a number for the form, then enter a description. When the Form Designer appears, place the desired fields and enter any accompanying text or borders. Save the form by choosing DO-IT!.

To modify an existing form   From the menu, choose Forms/Change. Enter the table name on which the form will be based. Choose the number of the existing form; then enter a new description, or press (ENTER) to accept the previous description. When the Form Designer appears, make any desired changes to the form. Save the form by choosing DO-IT!.

To place fields in a form   When in the Form Designer, choose Field/Place from the menu. From the next menu, choose Regular to place fields; Display-Only to place fields which cannot be edited; or Calculated to place fields which are calculations based on other fields, or PAL functions.

To add labels or text to a form   Place the cursor at the desired location, and type the labels or the descriptive text.

To draw borders or lines in a form   When in the Form Designer choose Border/Place from the menu. From the next menu, choose the desired type of border (single line, double line, or a character of your choosing). Place the cursor at one corner of the border (or one end of a line) and press (ENTER); then move the cursor to the other corner or end and press (ENTER) again.

To place a form in use   Choose Image/PickForm from the menu. From the list of available forms that appears. Select the desired form by name.

5

6

The Power of Ask

Now that you have significant sets of data stored within a Paradox database, it is time to examine more complex and better methods to get at the precise data you will need. You have already used the helpful Zoom key CTRL-Z to quickly locate a record, but this is only a simple form of query. You will often need to isolate one or more records that meet a condition. For example, you may need to generate a list of all employees working at a particular assignment, or all employees earning over $8.00 an hour.

In this chapter you will learn to use the main menu's Ask command to compose queries. This powerful Paradox feature uses a query-by-example design and artificial intelligence technology to make complex requests easy for the user. You will not have to think of the arcane logic behind a detailed set of commands, as you must with other database products. With Paradox, you simply check off the fields you want included in the results and provide examples or ranges of the data that you wish to extract. Paradox does the rest for you.

You can also use queries to add or delete records, with the additions or deletions based on the results of the query. You can even update values in one table, based on a query directed to another table.

Displaying a Query Form

Queries are built in a Query Form, which resembles the table you are using to supply the data. To display a Query Form, choose Ask from the main menu, and Paradox will prompt you for the name of the table. Enter the name, or choose a table from the list by pressing (ENTER) and then selecting a name in the list dialog box. The Query Form that appears will be similar to the one that is shown in Figure 6-1.

The Query Form will duplicate the table you choose in its structure. In the example in Figure 6-1, the Query Form was produced from the ABCSTAFF table. Queries of a relational nature are covered in Chapter 9, but for now, note that you can repeat the Ask process for additional tables and make use of examples to link common fields in order to build a query that is dependent on multiple tables.

To fill out a Query Form, you usually need to perform just two basic steps. You select the fields you want displayed in the answer by moving the cursor to those fields and adding a checkmark with the Check Key ((F6)). If you wish to see all of the fields in the answer, you can move to the leftmost field of the Query Form and press (F6) to place a checkmark in all fields. If you place a checkmark in a field and then decide you do not need to see that field in the answer, place the cursor in the field again and press (F6) to remove the checkmark. All existing checkmarks can be removed from a table by moving to the leftmost field and pressing (F6). The (F6) key acts as a *toggle;* if checkmarks exist, they are removed, and if no checkmarks exist, (F6) adds them. Mouse users can add and remove checkmarks by clicking on the F6 indicator that appears at the bottom of the screen.

For the second step, simply enter a matching expression in any desired field, in the same row as the checkmark. (This is only necessary if you want

Figure 6-1.   *Query Form*

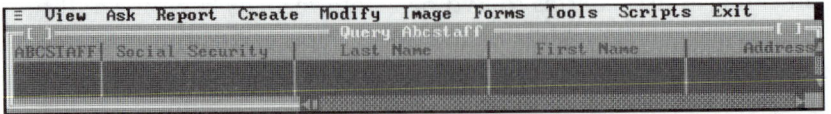

to limit your query to include a specific subset of records; if you want to see all records, you can omit this step.)

As an example, if you wanted to see all employees with a last name of Robinson, you would move the cursor to the Last Name field and type **Robinson** (no quotes are necessary). To select records for employees hired before January 1, 1987, you would enter **<1/1/87** in the Date Hired field. And if you wanted all employees who earned between $7.50 and $9.00 an hour, you could enter **>=7.50, <=9.00** in the Salary field, as shown in Figure 6-2. There are many other variations that can be used, but these are the basic steps for constructing a query.

Performing the Query

Once the Query Form has been filled in, choosing, DO-IT! will perform the query. The results will appear in a new table, which is automatically named ANSWER. Figure 6-3 shows the results of the query described in Figure 6-2.

These steps are all that is necessary, in many cases, to get the kind of information that you need from your database. You can quickly produce reports of critical data by designing a query with the desired fields and filling in any desired conditions to isolate the needed set of matching records. (You may want to limit the fields so they will fit on a single page.) Execute the query with DO-IT!, and the results you need will be displayed in the ANSWER table; then press (ALT)-(F7) for an instant report based on your query. You can move fields in the ANSWER table, if you desire, with Image/Move or by using the Rotate key ((CTRL)-(R)).

Unlike a table, a Query Form always contains four columns (unless you resize the window), regardless of the actual widths of the fields. While the

Figure 6-2.   *Example of filled-in Query Form*

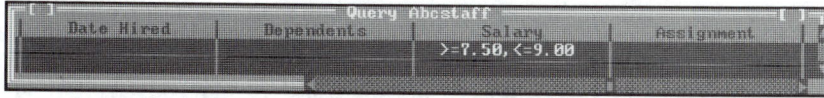

Figure 6-3.   *Results of example query*

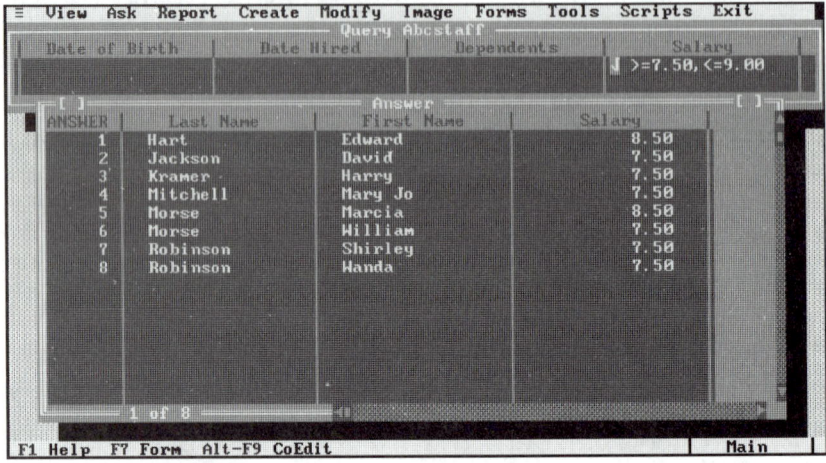

fields in the Query Form may appear narrow, they are no more limited in size than a normal field within a Paradox table. You can enter any valid expression, up to 255 characters in length, into any field of a Query Form. If you wish to see all of the expression as you are entering it, you can use the Field View key ((ALT)-(F5)) to edit the field of the Query Form. (Mouse users can do this by double-clicking on the field.) When using the Field View key, you must press (ENTER) when done, to exit the field view.

Use the Instant Report ((ALT)-(F7)) key if you need to generate a report based on the results of a Query.

Note

Some Query Basics

A later portion of this chapter will demonstrate how you can perform queries like the one just described, using the tables you have created in earlier chapters. Before proceeding to that section, however, you need to learn some basics that apply to all queries.

Working with the Query Form

The Ask command of the main menu is the first step in creating any query; choosing Ask, and specifying a table name, causes the Query Form for that table to appear, as you saw in Figure 6-1. Paradox always places the Query Form at the top of the desktop. A table does not have to be visible on the desktop for you to use the Ask command to display a Query Form. If any tables are visible at the top of the desktop, Paradox places the Query Form atop those tables.

The Query Form appears in a window, and you can use the same window-moving and window-resizing techniques used elsewhere in Paradox. If other windows are visible on the desktop, you can use the Up Image ((F3)) and Down Image ((F4)) keys to move between the Query Form and the other windows; and mouse users can, of course, click in any window to make it the active one.

Cursor movement within a Query Form is the same as it is within a table. You can use the (←) and (→) keys (or (TAB) and (SHIFT)-(TAB)) to move the cursor between fields, and you can use (CTRL)-(←) and (CTRL)-(→) to move one screen to the left or right. The (CTRL)-(END) key combination moves to the right edge of the Query Form, and (CTRL)-(HOME) moves to the left edge. Mouse users can click in any field to place the cursor in that field.

The (↑) and (↓) keys can also be used in a Query Form, to move the cursor up or down by a row. In simple queries, you will want to enter all your checkmarks and selection conditions on the same line. Later, when performing more complex queries using multiple conditions, you'll use (↑) and (↓) to place multiple conditions on more than one line of a query. Note that Paradox won't let you move the cursor down a row in a Query Form until you have made an entry in the existing row.

In simple queries, you'll commonly make two types of entries: checkmarks, and selection conditions or examples. The checkmarks, entered by pressing the Check ((F6)) key, tell Paradox which fields you want to include in the ANSWER table. In the Query Form shown next, checkmarks have been

entered in both the Last Name and First Name columns, and a selection
condition of "Robinson" has been entered in the Last Name column.

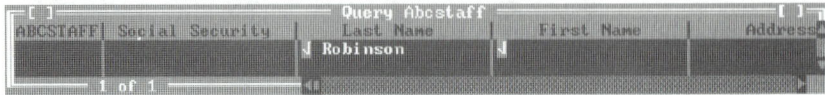

Tip

*You can quickly select all fields in a Query Form by placing the cursor in the far left
column and pressing* (F6).

All queries must have at least one checkmark; Paradox will not let you
process a query that has no fields selected for inclusion in the result. You can,
however, have queries with no selection conditions. If you select fields for the
query but you do not enter any selection conditions, Paradox includes every
record from the original table in the ANSWER table. This technique can be
useful for producing instant reports, in cases where you want to include every
record in the database, but not every field. For example, you might want an
instant report with just the Last Name, First Name, City, and State fields of
the ABCSTAFF table. To do this, you can open a Query Form for ABCSTAFF,
and check these fields for inclusion. If you then choose DO-IT!, without
entering any selection conditions, you will get an ANSWER table containing
all records in the ABCSTAFF table, but with only those fields selected, as
shown in Figure 6-4. You can then press the Instant Report key ((ALT)-(F7)) to
generate a printed report, based on the ANSWER table in use.

Reusing Query Forms

If you perform a query on a table and then decide to query the same table
again immediately, you do not need to open another Query Form. (In fact,
if you try to, Paradox will not open another window; it will instead put the
cursor back in the existing Query Form.) You can reuse existing Query Forms;
just edit or delete the checkmarks and conditions that you want to change,
and enter new checkmarks and conditions as needed.

Figure 6-4. ANSWER table with selected fields from ABCSTAFF table

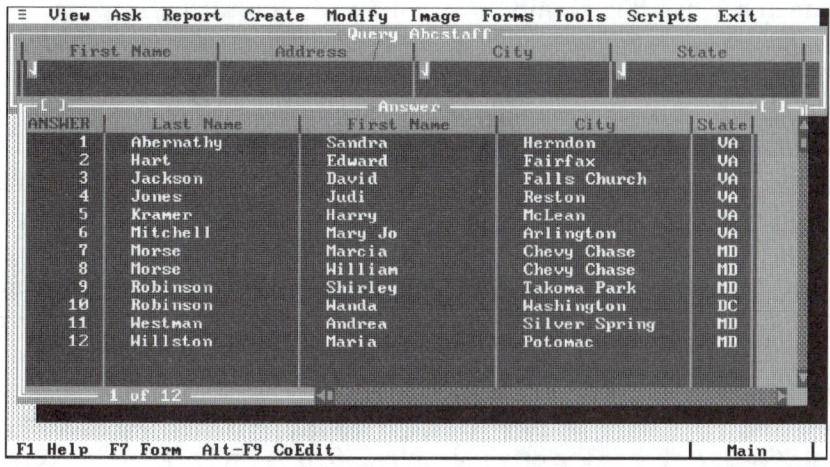

- To remove an existing checkmark move the cursor to the desired column and press F6 again. (The Checkmark key is a toggle, so pressing it repeatedly inserts and removes a checkmark in the current column.)

- To change your selection conditions, move to the appropriate column and use the DEL or BACKSPACE key to edit the existing entries.

If you are done with a Query Form, you can clear it from the workspace by pressing Clear Image (F8).

About the ANSWER Table

With most queries that you perform, the results are placed into an ANSWER table by Paradox. (There are certain types of queries, called *update queries,* that do not produce an ANSWER table; these are explained at the end of this chapter.) An ANSWER table can be manipulated like any other table, but remember that it is a temporary tables and is normally erased whenever you exit from Paradox.

The records in the ANSWER table appear in order based on the first field of the ANSWER table. Where records are identical in the first field, the second field of the ANSWER table determines the order; where records are identical in the second field, the third field of the table determines the order. When Paradox performs a query, it automatically sorts the resulting ANSWER table in ascending order based on every field, with the leftmost field having the most importance. (Of course, you can use the Modify/Sort command to resort the ANSWER table in any order you desire; see Chapter 4 for more on sorting tables.)

You can edit the records in an ANSWER table just as you can edit records in any table in Paradox. However, do not confuse ANSWER table data with the data that is stored in the original table. Changes you make to the contents of an ANSWER table will not affect the records in the original table.

You can perform a query on an ANSWER table, just as you can on any other Paradox table. However, since Paradox only allows one ANSWER table to exist at a time, the results of a query based on an ANSWER table (which are also stored in an ANSWER table) will replace the original ANSWER table. If you want to save an ANSWER table permanently, choose Tools/Rename/Table from the main menu, and when prompted for a table name, enter ANSWER. Then enter a new name for the table.

Valid Query Symbols

The symbols, operators, and reserved words listed in Table 6-1 assist you in building your queries. They let you select records based on a wide variety of numeric conditions, pattern matches, and ranges. Of special interest are the pattern-matching wildcard operators and the blank operator, discussed next. Other symbols and operators, including those used for calculations, are discussed as you work through this chapter.

Table 6-1.   *Valid Query Symbols and Operators*

Symbol or Word	Meaning
+	Addition
–	Subtraction
*	Multiplication
/	Division
()	Operators
=	Equal to
>	Greater than
<	Less than
=>	Greater than or equal to
<=	Less than or equal to
..	Pattern matching for any characters
@	Pattern matching for any single character
like	Similar to (spelling need not be exact)
not	Not a match
blank	Contains no value
today	Date in field matches today's date
average	Average of values
max	Maximum of values
min	Minimum of values
sum	Sum of values
count	Number of values
or	Specifies "or" conditions in a field
as	Specifies name of field in answer
calc	Used with another reserved word, calculates the value specified by that word

Pattern Matching

On occasion, you may need to find a group of records in which the characters match a specific pattern. Paradox lets you use certain *wildcards* as a part of a query expression. Valid wildcard operators are a double-period (..), which represents any number of characters, and the at sign (@), which indicates any single character. The wildcards can be used in alphanumeric, number, or date fields.

As an example, you could use the expression

```
J..n
```

to query a name field for names, which might produce Jackson, Jonson, and James-Albertson. Whenever you base queries on alphanumeric fields, remember that uppercase letters are considered to be different from lowercase ones. However, when you use a wildcard pattern such as the one just shown, case does not matter.

To use the double-period wildcard along with a query of a numeric field, while not confusing Paradox about where the decimal point is, you can enclose the decimal point in quotes. As an example, the expression

```
.."."50
```

could be used to query a currency field for all amounts ending in fifty cents (.50). In this example, the double-period wildcard tells Paradox to accept any characters to the left of the decimal point, as long as the characters "50" appear to the right of the decimal place in the field.

If you need to include any punctuation marks in the pattern, enclose them in double quotation marks.

Remember

For dates, you could enter an expression that is similar to

```
10/../92
```

to qualify records with any day in October of 1992 in the date field.

To see some examples of pattern matching, press Clear All ((ALT)-(F8)) to clear the screen. Choose Ask from the menu, and enter **ABCSTAFF** for the table. Use the (F6) key to place checkmarks in the Social Security, Last Name, First Name, Date Hired, and Salary fields. In the Social Security field, enter this expression:

```
@@@-55-@@@@
```

Press (F2) to implement the query. The resulting records are those that have social security numbers with 55 as the center digits, as shown in Figure 6-5.

Get back to the Query Form with (F3), and press (CTRL)-(BACKSPACE) to delete the entry. (If you accidentally press (DEL) instead of (CTRL)-(BACKSPACE), the entire line will be erased.) Then try this expression in the Last Name field:

    ..n

Press (F2) to process the query, and this time you will see every last name ending in the letter n, as shown in Figure 6-6.

Press (F3) and then (CTRL)-(BACKSPACE) to delete the last entry, and place the following expression in the Salary field:

    ..".."50

Pressing (F2) now displays an answer that shows every employee earning any dollar amount that ends in .50, as shown in Figure 6-7.

Finally, to try some date logic, press (F3). Delete the prior entry with (CTRL)-(BACKSPACE), and enter this expression in the Date Hired field:

    ../../91

6

Figure 6-5.   *Query and answer using the @ wildcard*

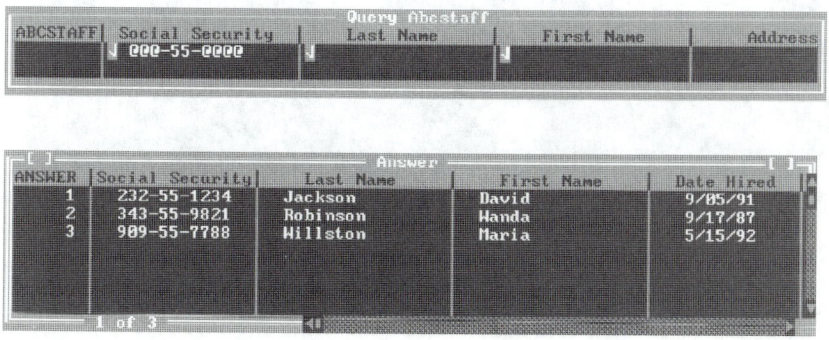

Figure 6-6.   *Query and answer using the double-period wildcard*

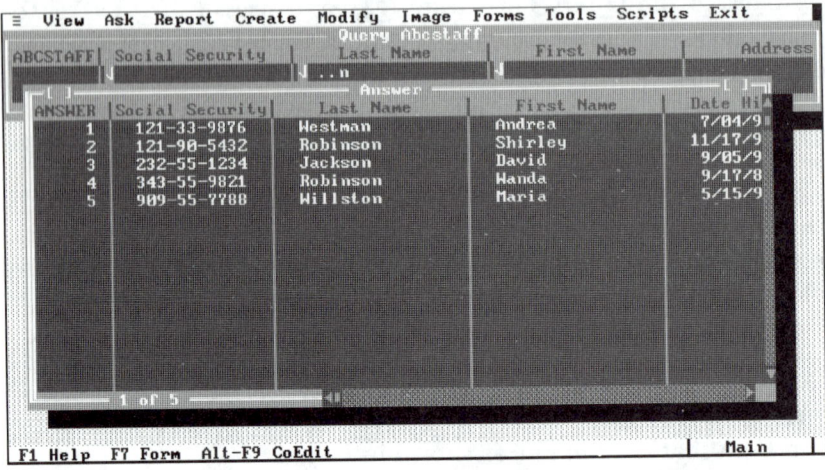

Figure 6-7.   *Query and answer using double-period in a numeric field*

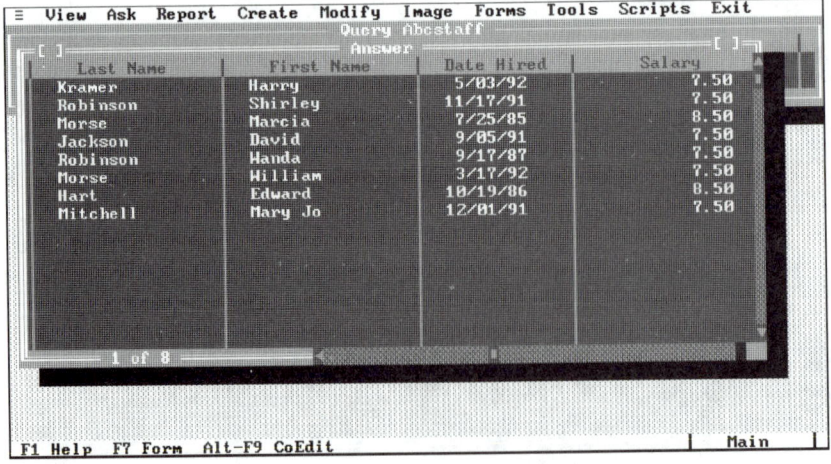

Press (F2) to see all employees hired during the year of 1991, as shown in Figure 6-8.

The Blank Operator

If you need to find records in which there may not be an entry in a particular field, you can use the reserved word "blank" as a part of the expression. This tells Paradox to find records where the field is blank.

Note that this is *not* the same as leaving a field in a Query Form empty. An empty field indicates that it does not matter what is in that field of a particular record. The word "blank" in the query field indicates that the field *must be blank* (contain no entry) before the record will be selected and placed in the ANSWER table.

Figure 6-8. *Query and answer using date logic*

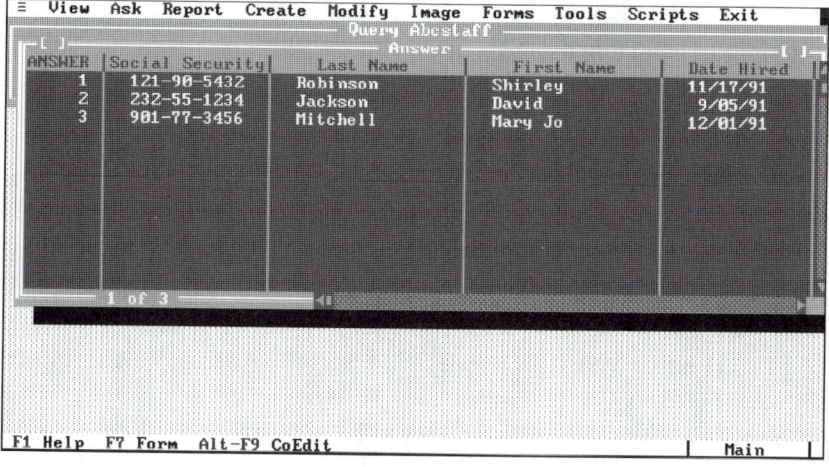

A Warning About Reserved Words and Wildcard Symbols

Because Paradox uses certain reserved words and wildcard symbols (such as blank, like, not, today, *, and @ as shown in Table 6-1), you may someday run into a special problem. You might try to perform a query in which you want a record with a literal word or symbol, but Paradox will think that you are trying to use one that is reserved. For example, you might be searching for a text string that specifically contains the @ sign, but Paradox might take the symbol to mean any single character, possibly providing incorrect results. For such occurrences, you can surround the desired character or word in double quotation marks. As an example, entering **"today"** in a query expression would ensure that Paradox searches for the literal word "today" and not for the date stored in the PC's clock.

Hands-On Practice: Performing Queries

Your first task as the personnel manager for ABC Temporaries is to find a person living in Maryland whose last name is Robinson. Get into Paradox if you are not already there. If a table is currently displayed on the screen, you may want to clear the working area with Clear All ((ALT)-(F8)) so that there is sufficient room on the screen to view both the Query Forms and the temporary ANSWER tables that result.

To begin the query, choose Ask from the main menu and enter **ABCSTAFF** for the table. Once you choose the desired table, the Query Form will appear at the top of the screen. In the query answer you are seeking, you will want to see the Last Name and State fields, so place the cursor in the Last Name field, press (F6) to place th'   **Robinson**. Place the cursor in the First Name field, and press (F6). Then move the cursor to State, press (F6), and enter **MD**. Choose DO-IT! and the answer to the query will appear, as in Figure 6-9.

If your results do not match those of the figure, make sure that your matching criteria in the Query Form matches the actual data in the table. For example, if you are trying to locate a record in which the last name has been

Figure 6-9.   *Results of first practice query*

```
≡  View  Ask  Report  Create  Modify  Image  Forms  Tools  Scripts  Exit
                            Query Abcstaff
     First Name        |       Address        |      City       |      State
                                                              MD
  [ ]                           Answer                                   [ ]
 ANSWER |    Last Name      |    First Name   | State|
     1     Robinson            Shirley          MD




     1 of 1

F1 Help   F7 Form   Alt-F9 CoEdit                              Main
```

entered as Robinson, you cannot find the record if you enter robinson or
ROBINSON in the Query Form.

Since ANSWER is an actual Paradox table, you can treat it like any other
Paradox table; you can add to, edit, or delete its records, and you can generate
reports based on it. The most important difference to remember is that this
table will be erased if you change directories or leave Paradox, and it will be
replaced by the results of successive queries unless you change its name.
Remember, ANSWER is a temporary table. Rename the ANSWER table if
you wish to save its results.

When modifying existing queries, you can use (CTRL)-(BACKSPACE) *to delete an entry
in a Query Form field.*

Remember

Matching on Two or More Fields

To search for records that meet criteria in two or more fields, simply enter
the criteria in the proper format within each field of the Query Form. If, for

example, you need to see the records of all employees who live in Virginia and earn more than $10.00 an hour, you will need to place **VA** in the State field and **>10.00** in the Salary field of the Query Form.

To try this, first press Clear All ((ALT)-(F8)) to clear both the ANSWER table and the existing Query Form. (You could have edited the existing form, but (ALT)-(F8) is the fastest way to clear the entire desktop.) Choose Ask from the main menu, and choose ABCSTAFF for the table. Use (F6) to place checkmarks in the Last Name, First Name, and State fields. While within the State field, enter **VA**. Move to the Salary field and press (F6) to add the checkmark, and then enter **>10.00**. Finally, choose DO-IT! to process the query. The results will appear in the answer, as shown in Figure 6-10.

Including Duplicates

Paradox automatically filters out any records that it considers to be duplicate records. Depending on how you structure your query, this tendency may or may not give you precisely what you want. Try this example to see how Paradox treats duplicates. First press (ALT)-(F8) to clear the table and the Query

Figure 6-10.   *Results of second practice query*

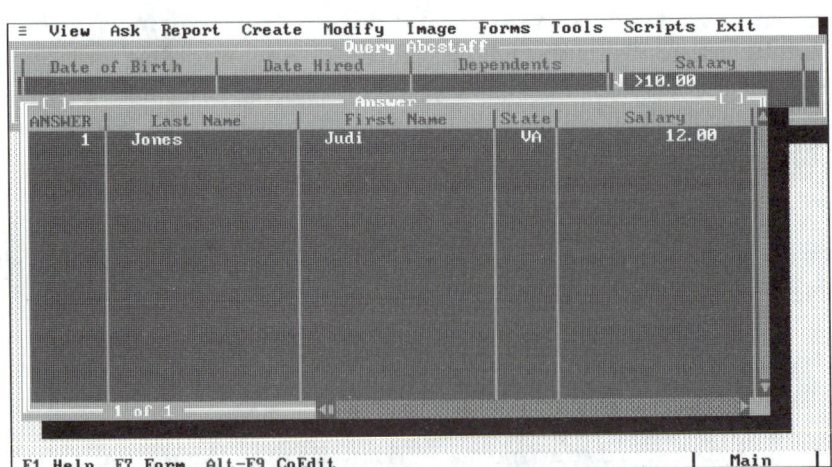

Form. Perhaps you want a quick count of the number of employees living in Maryland. (There are other ways to get a count in Paradox, but for the sake of this example, use this method.) Choose Ask from the main menu, and enter **ABCSTAFF** as the table name. You are only interested in the number of records, so you really do not need to see any fields other than the State field. Move the cursor to the State field, press (F6) to supply the checkmark, and enter **MD**. Press (F2) to process the query, and the results will look like those in Figure 6-11.

If you do not understand how Paradox operates, the answer may seem deceiving. There is obviously more than one employee living in Maryland, yet the answer indicates just one. Because you asked for only the State field in the answer, Paradox considers all other records with MD in the state after the first one found to be duplicates of the first one. Had you asked for more fields than just the State field, Paradox would have displayed additional records, because the other records would not be considered duplicates.

Paradox considers records duplicates when they contain the same values in all the fields included in the ANSWER table.

Note

6

Figure 6-11. *Results of third practice query*

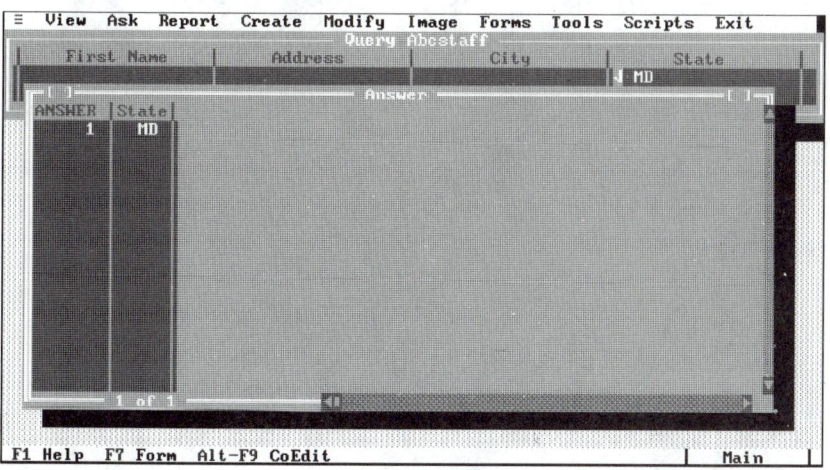

There will be times like this when you have intentional duplicates, as in item numbers from an inventory. You can tell Paradox to display all duplicates by using (ALT)-(F6), instead of (F6), to place a checkmark followed by a plus symbol (+) in the field of the Query Form. In Paradox, this is called the *check-plus.*

To try this, press (F3) to move back to the State field of the Query Form. Press (F6) once to remove the existing checkmark. Then press (ALT)-(F6), and a checkmark followed by the plus symbol will appear. The check-plus tells Paradox to include all records that match the example conditions in the ANSWER table, regardless of what it considers to be duplicates. Press (F2) to process the query. The resulting answer, shown in Figure 6-12, shows how many times an entry of "MD" occurs in the STATE field.

Using Inexact Matches

One very useful feature of the query-by-example nature of Paradox is its ability to use the like operator as a condition for finding inexact matches. For

Figure 6-12.   *Results of practice query with check-plus*

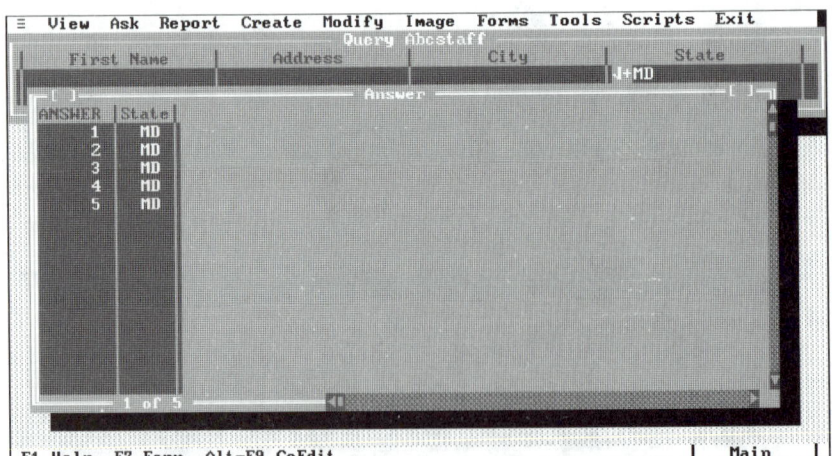

example, the selection condition "like Morrs," when used in the Last Name field of a query of the ABCSTAFF table, should find a record that actually sounds like "Morrs"—in short, Marsha Morse.

Try this now. Press (ALT)-(F8) to clear any existing tables, choose Ask from the main menu, and enter **ABCSTAFF** for the table. Use the (F6) key to place checkmarks in the Last Name and First Name fields. Enter the following in the Last Name field of the Query Form:

```
like Morrs
```

Press (F2) to process the query. The answer should show the records for Ms. Marcia Morse and Mr. William Morse, because the last name "Morse" sounds like "Morrs." This Paradox capability can be quite useful for finding names when you are not quite sure of the spelling. The like operator is also helpful for maintaining mailing lists, where you are trying to weed out accidental duplicates of the same record.

Using Ranges

The range operators, shown with the operators in Table 6-1, are very useful for ensuring that records fall within a selective range. You can use the range operators with all types of Paradox fields; they are by no means limited to numeric values.

Consider a list of employees whose last names fall between the letters M and Z. Press (F3) to move up to the Query Form (you can leave the existing checkmarks intact, or if you have already cleared them, open a new Query Form and place checkmarks in the Last Name and First Name fields). In the Last Name field of the Query Form, enter the following expression:

```
>M,<=Zz
```

This stands for "Greater than M and less than or equal to Zz." Note the inclusion of the second letter z. If it were omitted, Paradox would find names up to Z, but none after the letter Z alone (in effect, omitting all last names of more than one character starting with Z). Press (F2) to process the query, and the results shown in Figure 6-13 will appear.

6

Figure 6-13.   *Results of practice query with operators limiting names*

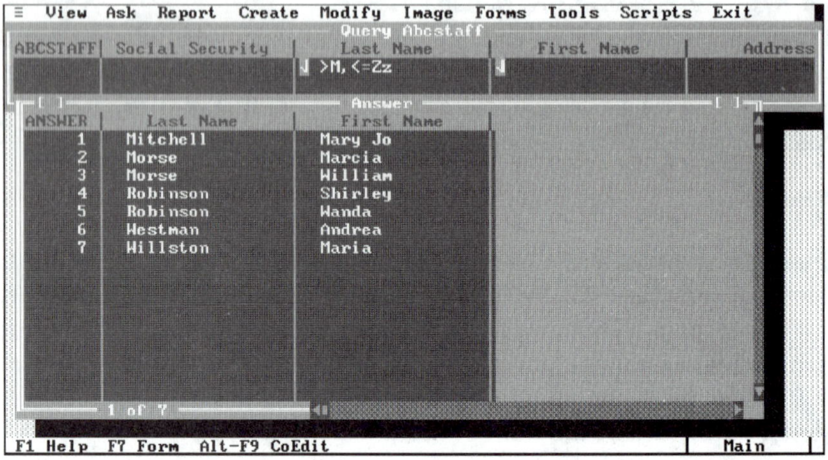

In this example, note that a comma is used to separate the two possibilities. Remember that whenever you want to enter more than one selection condition in a field, you must separate each with a comma.

Another example, this time performed with dates, illustrates this point. Suppose you need a report of all employees who were hired during 1987. Press (F3) to move up to the Last Name field of the Query Form, and press (CTRL)-(BACKSPACE) to delete the prior entry. Move the cursor to the Date Hired field, and enter the following expression:

```
>=1/1/87, <=12/31/87
```

Press (F2) to process the completed query. The results, shown in Figure 6-14, display the employees hired by ABC Temporaries in 1987. Yet another way to enter this expression would be **..87**, which would also indicate any date value falling in 1987.

You may have noticed another point while you were making this query. The limiting criterion for records was the date hired, yet the Date Hired field was not checked for inclusion in the resulting table. Paradox does not

Figure 6-14. Results of query asking for employees hired in 1987

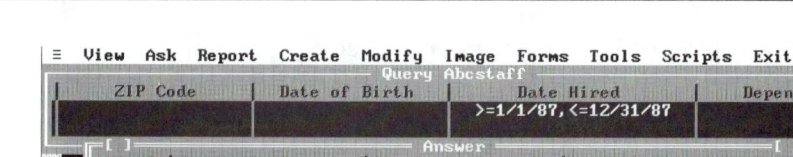
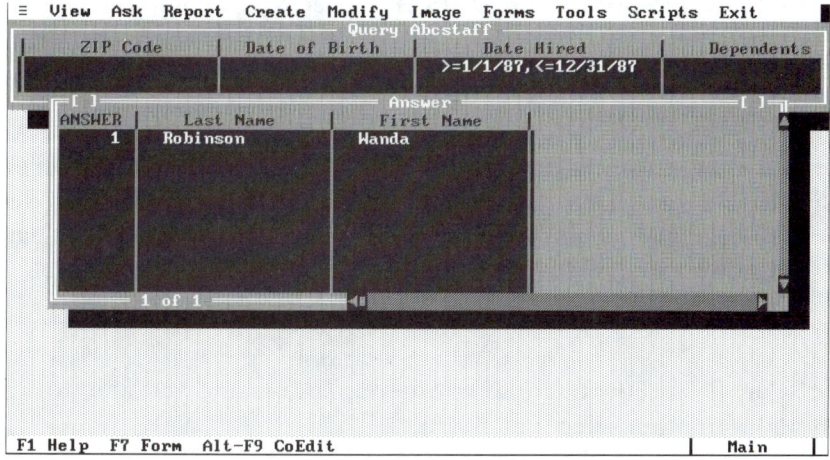

necessarily need to have the fields that are used to select the records included in the results, but it's usually a good idea to include fields containing the criteria at first so you can check the results.

You can also use the operators listed in Table 6-1 to build queries based on other types of ranges. Consider the common personnel problem of deciding who qualifies for vacation and who does not. At ABC Temporaries, every employee with one year or more of service qualifies for vacation. If you suddenly need a list of employees eligible for vacation, a simple query will do the task. Press (F3) to move back up to the Query Form and into the Date Hired field. Use (CTRL)-(BACKSPACE) to delete the previous query, and enter the following expression:

```
<= TODAY-365
```

This translates as "Less than or equal to today's date, minus 365 days." If you refer back to Table 6-1, you will note that Paradox uses the word "today" as a reserved word that indicates today's date (as measured by the computer's clock). Press (F2) to process the query, and you will see a list of employees who have been with the firm for a year or more. Depending on the date maintained by your PC's clock and the dates you entered for the employees, this list may or may not include every employee of the company.

The Not Operator

If you want to select a group of records that do not meet a specific condition, you can place the reserved word "not" ahead of your desired criteria. For example, if you wanted to see a list of all employees not earning $7.50 per hour, you could place the expression

```
not 7.50
```

in the Salary field of the query. Like other operators, the not operator can be combined with other selection criteria.

Matching Records Based on OR Criteria

The types of queries you have done so far will work fine for conditions in which a record must meet all of the specified criteria. Such cases of criteria are also referred to as *AND logic,* because you are qualifying a record where one condition is met, AND another condition is met.

Sometimes, however, you need a different sort of qualification. Suppose you want to find records that meet any one of multiple criteria, such as all employees who live in either Maryland or Virginia. This calls for a different type of logic, known as *OR logic.* You want to find records for employees in Maryland or in Virginia. Fashioning such queries in Paradox is simple. You just add as many lines to the Query Form as necessary; each line contains a separate condition, which the records must meet in order to qualify.

For an example, press (ALT)-(F8) to clear both tables, choose Ask from the main menu, and choose ABCSTAFF for the table. With the cursor in the first field of the Query Form, press (F6). Because the cursor is in the first field, this action will tell Paradox to place a checkmark in every field of the Query Form, so that every field will be included in the answer.

Move the cursor down one line by pressing (↓) once, and press (F6) again. You should now have two rows in the Query Form, each with checkmarks contained in every field. Next, place the cursor in the State field, and in the first row enter **MD**. Move the cursor down one line by pressing ⊕ once, and enter **VA**. Finally, choose DO-IT! to process the query. The results should show all of the employees who live in either Maryland or Virginia, as shown in Figure 6-15. (In the figure, the Address column has been rotated with (CTRL)(R) so the State column is visible.)

You can have up to 22 lines in a single Query Form. This gives you sufficient room to execute the most complex of queries by using OR logic.

Note that Paradox also lets you use the OR operator as an alternate way of composing queries based on OR criteria. If you use the OR operator, you place the query condition on a single line, with the reserved word OR between the desired conditions. For example, you could enter the expressions

```
Jones or Morse
```

in the last name field of a query, and the answer would provide records containing the last name of Jones or of Morse.

6

Figure 6-15. *Query and answer based on OR criteria*

Complex Matching

You can use Paradox's powerful query-by-example facility to define criteria for several fields, thereby setting up very complex searches. You can also combine AND and OR logic to isolate the results in precisely those records you will need. As an example, suppose that you wish to see all of the employees who live in Virginia or in Maryland, were hired in 1992, and are earning less than $10.00 an hour. If this sounds like overkill, rest assured that it is not; often, real-world management reports require more complex conditions than these before upper management is satisfied with the results.

In this example, what Paradox needs as selection criteria are a State equal to MD or VA; a Date Hired that is >=1/1/92 AND <=12/31/92; and a Salary value that is <=$10.00. To begin, press (ALT)-(F8) to get a fresh screen. Then choose Ask from the main menu, and enter **ABCSTAFF** as the desired table. Using the arrow keys or the mouse to position the cursor, enter the following matching criteria:

1. In the Last Name and First Name fields of *both* rows 1 and 2, enter a checkmark with (F6).

2. In the State, Date Hired, and Salary fields of *both* rows 1 and 2, enter a checkmark with (F6).

3. In the State field, on the first row, enter **VA**. On the second row of the same field, enter **MD**.

4. In the Date Hired field, on both the first and second rows, enter this expression:

   ```
   >=1/1/92, <=12/31/92
   ```

5. In the Salary field, on both rows 1 and 2, enter this expression:

   ```
   < 10.00
   ```

6. Finally, implement the query by choosing DO-IT!. The results should be similar to the example shown in Figure 6-16.

Figure 6-16. *Results of complex query*

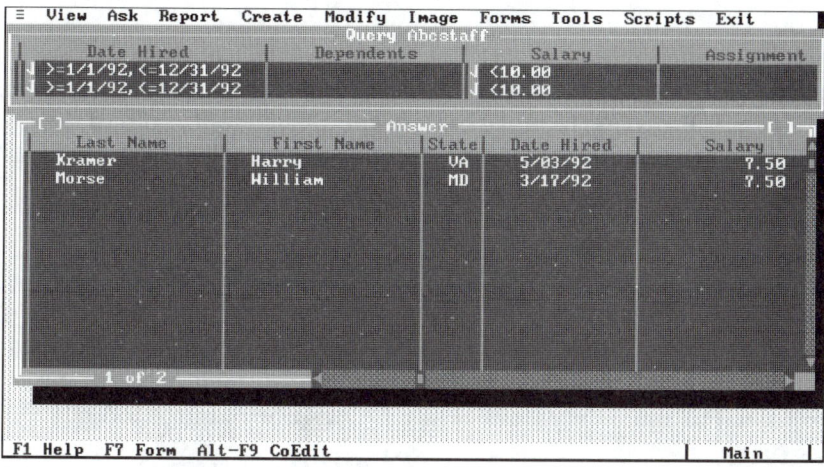

Using Calculations in Queries

6

You may find the reserved words that apply to numeric calculations to be of use in your own applications. These words can be used as a part of a query to find totals, minimum and maximum values, averages, or counts of occurrences. To see how these reserved words can be used, press (ALT)-(F8) to clear the screen, choose Ask from the main menu, and enter **ABCSTAFF** as the desired table.

For insurance purposes, perhaps you need to know the average number of dependents carried by the staff. Move the cursor to the Dependents field of the Query Form, and enter

CALC AVERAGE

in the field. Then press (F2) to process the query. The resulting answer shows the average number of dependents per employee of ABC Temporaries.

Press (F3) once to move back to the Query Form, and then change the expression to

CALC SUM

Press (F2). This time, Paradox displays the total number of dependents for the entire staff. Press (F3) to move back to the Dependents field of the Query Form, and press (CTRL)-(BACKSPACE) to delete the entry. Then move to the Salary field, enter the expression,

CALC MAX

and press (F2). The resulting answer shows the salary of the highest-paid employee of ABC Temporaries. If you had entered CALC MIN as the expression, the result would have been the minimum salary. If you press (F3) to move back to the Salary field of the Query Form, and then change the expression to

CALC SUM

and press (F2), Paradox will sum the salaries of all employees and display the total hourly payroll cost of the firm. Note that you can combine these statistical operators with your selection criteria. For example, you could average the salary for all employees on a particular assignment by placing the assignment name in the Assignment field and placing CALC AVERAGE in the Salary field.

A Reminder

The following information has been mentioned before, but it is of such importance that one more reminder may save you problems later. All of your queries are stored in a temporary table named ANSWER, which is erased or overwritten whenever you leave Paradox, change directories, or perform yet another query. If you want to save the results of any query, be sure to rename the ANSWER table by selecting Tools/Rename/Table from the main menu.

Using Query By Example

Another type of query, called *query by example,* makes use of *example elements*, instead of selection conditions, in the fields of the Query Form. The concept of query by example (QBE) is an important one to understand, because it adds flexibility to your use of the Ask command in Paradox. Think of example elements as a special type of query entry that lets you relate entries in one field of a table to entries in another field. You'll use example elements again in Chapter 9, to link multiple tables together. But you can also use query by example with a single table, whenever you want to base a query on a relationship between two fields.

Consider the Salary and Hourly Rate fields of the ABCSTAFF table. Perhaps you would like to know which employees have an hourly rate that is at least 1.5 times their salary. This is an ideal task for query by example, because you are asking a question that is based on a relationship between the two fields, Salary, and Hourly Rate. To build a query by example, you use the Example key ((F5)) to start an example in a column, and you then enter the example along with any expressions needed to define the desired data.

An example will help you understand this concept, so clear the desktop now with (ALT)-(F8). Then choose Ask from the main menu and enter **ABCSTAFF** as the desired table. With the cursor in the far-left column, press (F6) to add a checkmark to all columns. (Checking all columns is not required for the use of query by example, but is done for simplicity in this example.)

Next, move the cursor to the Salary field, and press Example ((F5)). Then, type the letters **ABC**. As you type, notice that the letters appear highlighted. This occurs because you pressed (F5); Paradox assumes you are entering an example element, and therefore highlights the letters used as an example.

Move the cursor to the Hourly Rate field, and a greater-than symbol (>). Press Example ((F5)), type the letters **ABC**, then type an asterisk, and then type the value 1.5. (As soon as you type the asterisk, the characters you type will no longer be highlighted, because Paradox allows only characters for example elements.) At this point, your Query Form will resemble the example shown in Figure 6-17.

Before processing this query, consider what the query is asking. All fields are checked, so all fields of the ABCSTAFF table will appear in the ANSWER table. What's different about this query is the way it will select the desired

Figure 6-17.   *Query Form using example elements*

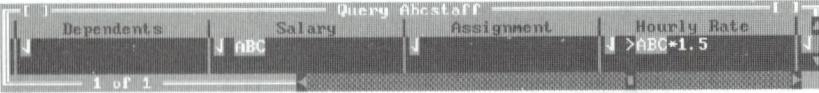

records. This time, an example (represented by the letters ABC) is used to draw a relationship between two fields of the table. The query is asking for all records where the amount in the Hourly Rate field is greater than 150 percent of the rate in the Salary field.

Go ahead and choose DO-IT! now to process the query. Your results will resemble those in Figure 6-18; only those records where the Hourly Rate value is more than 150 percent above the Salary value have been included in the ANSWER table.

For one more example of query by example, consider a more complex query that uses two lines on the Query Form. In this example, you want to

Figure 6-18.   *Results of a query by example*

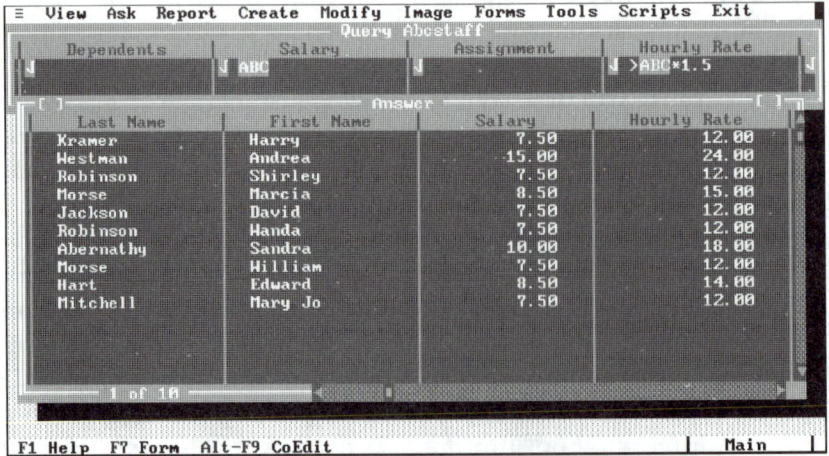

see which employees are earning more than Marcia Morse. You can draw an example between Marcia Morse's salary and the other salaries in the table.

First, press (ALT)-(F8) to clear the desktop. Choose Ask from the main menu, and enter **ABCSTAFF** as the desired table. First, move the cursor to the Last Name field of the first row, and enter **Morse**. Move to the First Name field of the first row, and enter **Marcia**. Move to the Salary field of that same row, and press Example ((F5)). Then type the word **MONEY**.

Next, press (CTRL)-(HOME) to get back to the far-left side of the Query Form, and press (↓) to move down by one row. With the cursor still at the far left, press Checkmark ((F6)) to add a checkmark to every field. Move the cursor over to the Salary field; you should be one row below the MONEY example element you entered earlier. Type a greater-than symbol (>), and then press Example ((F5)) to begin another example element; type the word **MONEY**. Press (F2) to process the query. Your results will resemble those shown in Figure 6-19; all employees who earn a salary greater than that of Marcia Morse are displayed in the ANSWER table. (In the figure, some columns have been rotated with (CTRL)-(R) so that the names and salaries can all be visible at the same time.)

6

Figure 6-19. *Results of second query by example*

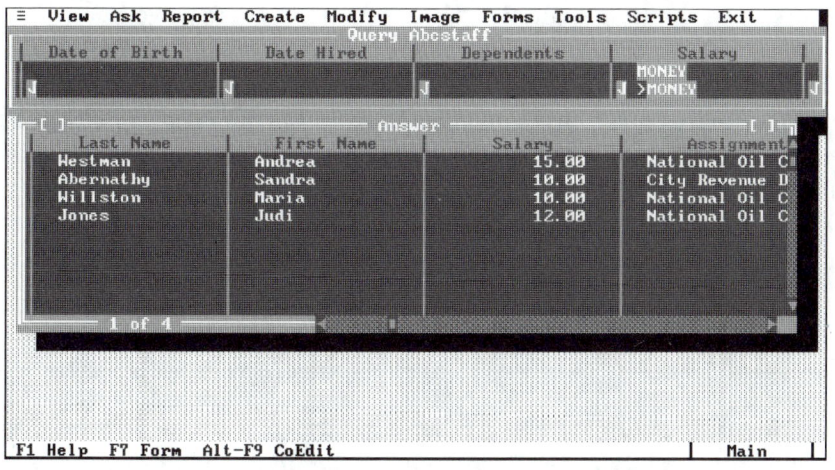

A special word of explanation about this query by example is in order. Whenever you use a two-line query and you use example elements, Paradox considers the first line of the query as a *definition of the example*. The second line of the query contains a selection condition that uses the example element as part of its expression. This process is different from the two-line queries shown earlier in this chapter; when example elements are not used, Paradox considers a two-line query to be using OR logic. In our first demonstration of query by example (Figure 6-18), only one row was needed in the Query Form, because the relationship was between two different fields of the table. In this second example, two rows are needed because the relationship drawn by the example uses the same field twice.

During the processing of the above query, you may have noticed the message, "Query may take a long time to process" in the lower-right corner of the screen. Whenever you process a query that Paradox thinks is unusually complex, it will display this message as a warning to you. In some cases (like this one), the query will not take an undue amout of time, but in other cases (particularly if your table has thousands of records), be prepared to wait for your results.

Chapter 9 will highlight additional queries by example. Until then, one point you should remember is this: The example element (such as the letters ABC) is not some arbitrary value that you must use. Paradox is only concerned with what the examples represent; in other words, when Paradox sees one example element in a query, it looks for a matching example element in the same query. In the first example, the letters ABC could have been XYZ, or the numbers 1234, or "nonsense." What is important is that Paradox must find at least two matching example elements in the query. Since query by example compares one field to another, it would make no sense to have only one example element in a query. Once Paradox finds the matching examples, it will perform whatever query operation is indicated by the expressions you enter in the Query Form.

Performing Operations

Besides using queries to extract data directly, you can use certain reserved words to cause a query to perform an *operation* on a table. Operations allow you to selectively add, delete, update, and find certain records. To perform such operations, you use special reserved words within certain columns of the Query Form. These reserved words and their purposes are shown here.

Word	Purpose
INSERT	Inserts new records with certain values into a table
DELETE	Deletes all records meeting certain criteria from a table
FIND	Finds records that meet certain criteria in a table
CHANGETO	Updates (changes) values in specified fields within all records that meet certain criteria in a table

Using INSERT

With INSERT, you can copy records from one table to another. Which records are added is determined by the structure of the query. Using INSERT within queries is a good way to move data selectively from one table to another when the structures do not precisely match.

The use of INSERT typically involves one or more *source tables* (from which data is copied), a *target table* (where the copied data is to be inserted), and example elements in Query Forms. In addition, you can also include specific criteria in the Query Forms, which will allow you to select records to be inserted into the target table.

Whenever a query involves more than one table, example elements are used. As mentioned earlier, example elements are common expressions you enter into the columns of the Query Form by pressing (F5) and entering the element. The element does not have to be any special word; it can consist of any characters, such as "ABC" or "test" or "Johnny5." All that matters is that the same example element be used in the fields being linked in the two tables.

First, fill out a Query Form for the source table or tables; place example elements in the fields you will want, and place any selection criteria you desire within the query. Next, fill out the Query Form for the target table. Place the reserved word **INSERT** in the far-left column of this form. Then place any expressions containing the example elements in the fields where you want the data inserted. Finally, use DO-IT! ((F2)) to process the query, and records will be inserted into the target table based on the query.

6

As an example, perhaps the national headquarters for ABC Temporaries wants a copy of the table from the local office, but they need just two fields: Social Security and Name (a combination of the Last Name and First Name fields). To supply the headquarters office with a table that contains the data in this format, you first create a new table, called HQDATA, with just two fields: Social Security and Name.

Creating the table is the easy part; how do you get the data into the table once it exists? The job can be done with INSERT, which will insert records from ABCSTAFF into the new HQDATA table. You would first build a query for the source table (ABCSTAFF), placing example elements in all of the fields that need to be inserted into the target table. In this case, example elements in the Social Security, Last Name, and First Name fields would be sufficient, as shown in Figure 6-20. Next, you would build a query for the target table (HQDATA) by first placing the reserved word **INSERT** in the far-left column of the Query Form and then placing the example elements in the fields that are to receive the inserted records. Since in this example the Last Name and First Name fields must be combined into a single Name field, you can use an expression (in this case, **last + ", " + first**) made up of the example elements to combine the names into one field. An example of the filled-in Query Form appears in Figure 6-21.

When the query is executed, the results will look like Figure 6-22. The records are inserted into the target table. Note that you will not see the target table on the screen unless you were viewing it when you performed the query that made the insertions. Also note that copies of the inserted records are stored in a temporary table named (appropriately enough) INSERTED. This temporary table is overwritten at the next INSERT operation, or it is discarded when you change directories or exit Paradox. It is also possible to make inserts to a table that already contains some records; simply specify the existing table as the target table.

Figure 6-20.   *Query of source table*

Figure 6-21. Query of target table

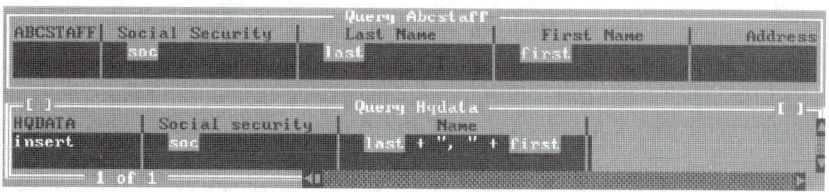

Using DELETE

With DELETE, you can delete records from a table, based on a query. This is particularly useful when you are performing the type of update that requires the removal of a large number of records, as in all students who graduated in a particular year.

6

Figure 6-22. Inserted records

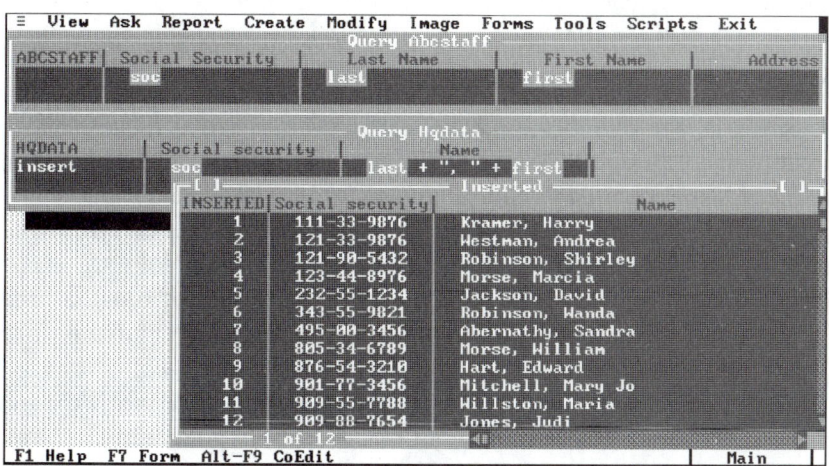

To use DELETE with a query, simply place the reserved word **DELETE** in the leftmost column of the Query Form. This tells Paradox that any records meeting the other conditions specified in the query are to be deleted from the table. After entering DELETE in the leftmost column, proceed to construct the remainder of the query as desired. (Note that if you do not enter any conditions in the Query Form, all records will be deleted.)

As an example, if (in a moment of temporary insanity) the manager of ABC Temporaries decides to give all clients a free week's worth of work with no billings, one way to do so after the hourly records had been entered into the existing HOURS table would be to delete all of the records in which the "week ending" date contained a value for the desired week. If that date were 5/23/92, the resulting query would resemble the following:

```
HOURS-----ASSIGNMENT----SOCIAL SEC----WEEKEND
DELETE                                 5/23/92
```

Once the Query Form is filled in and the query is executed, the records meeting the specified condition will be deleted from the table. The deleted records are stored in a temporary table named DELETED, so you can recover them with Tools/More/Add if you make an accidental, unwanted deletion. Keep in mind that the DELETED table is a temporary table, so if you change directories, exit Paradox, or overwrite the table by performing another deletion, the records will be gone forever.

Using FIND

With FIND, you can locate a specific record or a group of records based on the contents of a query. While you could use the Zoom ((CTRL)-(Z)) key to find a record, the Zoom key limits you to finding the record based on the value in a single field. With FIND as a part of a query, you can find records based on conditions specified for any number of fields.

To use FIND, enter the reserved word **FIND** in the leftmost column of the Query Form. Then proceed to construct the remainder of the query as desired. When you perform the query by choosing DO-IT!, Paradox will display the table that you queried—not the ANSWER table—with the cursor at the first record in the table that meets the conditions specified by the query. At the same time, Paradox will place all records meeting the specified criteria in an ANSWER table. In this case, the ANSWER table is not displayed automatically, but you can view it whenever you wish with the View option.

As an example, you might want to edit a record in the ABCSTAFF table for Marcia Morse. There is more than one person named Morse in the table, so using the Zoom key to find a last name of Morse might or might not result in the selection of the correct record. Instead, you can fill in a Query Form in a manner similar to this example:

```
ABCSTAFF--SOCIAL SEC---LAST NAME---------FIRST NAME----

FIND                    Morse           Marcia
```

When this is executed, the cursor will move to the record for Marcia Morse in the ABCSTAFF table. Keep in mind that FIND is unique in that the cursor appears in the table you are querying, and not in a temporary ANSWER table as with most queries. At this point, you can press Edit ((F9)) or CoEdit ((ALT)(F9)) to make any desired changes in the data. Also note that FIND finds only the first match. To check for additional matches, view the ANSWER table.

Using CHANGETO

With CHANGETO, you can update (change) a number of records, based on a query. This is very handy for global updates—for example, when you want to change the salary of every employee in a certain department by a given bonus amount, or when you want to change all telephone area codes for records of a certain city.

The operator CHANGETO is different from the other operator in that you can put CHANGETO in any column *except* the leftmost column of the Query Form; the other operator, when used in a query, *always* appear in the leftmost column of the query. The column in which you place CHANGETO will determine the field whose contents are changed by the query. You follow the operator with an expression, which tells Paradox how the data should be changed. As an example, the following combination of operator and expression changes the value shown, 212, to the new value, 718:

```
212, CHANGETO 718
```

6

In most cases, you will want some sort of selection criteria in one or more fields of the Query Form to determine when the change takes effect. Consider an example of a table containing names, cities, area codes, and telephone numbers, as illustrated here:

Name	City	Area Code	Phone
E. Smith	Brooklyn	212	555-4931
R. Jackson	New York	212	555-2387
L. Rodgers	Queens	212	555-4945
L. Fairfax	Brooklyn	212	555-9354

If the telephone company makes a change that results in all residents of Brooklyn and Queens being assigned a new area code of 718, you certainly do not want to manually update a few dozen (or hundred) records in a table like this one. Instead, the change can be performed with a single query and CHANGETO, as in the following example:

Name	City	Area Code	Phone
	Brooklyn	212, CHANGETO 718	
	Queens	212, CHANGETO 718	

In this example, the query translates to "For all records in which the city equals Brooklyn, change area code 212 to 718; and for all records in which the city equals Queens, change area code 212 to 718." When the query is executed, the records meeting the criteria (in this case, all those with either Brooklyn or Queens in the City field) will have the 212 area code replaced with 718.

Copies of the original records (before the changes) will be stored in a temporary table named CHANGED. You can examine this temporary table after executing the query to make sure that the correct records have been changed.

A Note About Repetitive Queries

As you use the power of Paradox queries to retrieve selected data, you may find yourself repeating the same queries over and over. To save time, you can save a query for later use, with the Scripts/QuerySave command from the main menu. With the Query Form visible on the screen, choose Scripts/QuerySave from the main menu. Enter a name for the query to be saved. When you want to reuse the query, choose Scripts/Play from the menu, and enter the name that you assigned to the query. Then, choose DO-IT! to process the query. Additional information about scripts can be found in Chapter 10.

Boosting Performance with QuerySpeed

To reduce the processing time needed by Paradox to perform often-used queries, you may want to make use of the QuerySpeed option of the Tools menu. (In earlier versions of Paradox, this was called Query Speedup.) For queries that you perform on a regular basis, this can be a very useful option. The QuerySpeed option, when selected while a particular query is visible on the screen, tells Paradox to build secondary index files for all non-key fields that contain a selection criterion. Once these index files have been built, Paradox uses them to quickly process your query. You do not need to do anything out of the ordinary to maintain these indexes; they are automatically updated each time you perform the query.

To use QuerySpeed, you must first have the Query Form you use regularly in the workspace. With the Query Form visible, from the main menu choose Tools/QuerySpeed. Paradox will display the message "Processing query speedup" as it creates the indexes. (Note that if there are no non-key fields used in the query, Paradox will instead display the message "No speedup possible," as key fields are already indexed.) Once the operation is complete, you can proceed to perform your query whenever you wish in the usual manner. The indexes are built through the query and are then available to accelerate zooms as well as other queries.

Although the QuerySpeed option can noticeably improve performance, there is a tradeoff involved: The building of the necessary index files will consume disk space. Keep in mind that you can use Tools/Delete to erase the index files created by QuerySpeed, so you may want to compare system performance versus available disk space with and without the advantages of this option.

6

Quick Summary

To build a query   From the main menu, choose Ask. Enter the name of the table to query, and the Query Form will appear. To include fields in the ANSWER table, move the cursor into the desired fields, and press the Check key ((F6)). To limit the records included in the ANSWER table, enter a matching expression in any desired field (omit this step if you want to see all records). Choose DO-IT! to process the query and display the ANSWER table.

To include duplicates in a query   Use the Check-Plus key ((ALT)-(F6)) instead of the Check key ((F6)) when indicating the desired fields.

To perform a calculation in a query   Use the reserved word CALC, followed by the reserved word for the type of calculation (AVERAGE, SUM, MIN, or MAX) in the desired numeric fields of the Query Form.

To save a query for later use   From the main menu, choose Scripts, then choose QuerySave. Enter a name for the query. To reuse the saved query, choose Scripts/Play from the menu and enter the name of the query.

To use query by example   Build your query using the steps outlined above. Use the Example key ((F5)) to start an example in the desired column, then enter the example. Repeat this process for each example needed.

To perform an operation in a query   Use one of the three reserved words INSERT, DELETE, or FIND in the leftmost column of the query, and fill in the desired conditions in the remaining columns. You can also use the reserved word CHANGETO in any column of the query (except the leftmost column), along with the desired conditions.

7

Introducing Reports

Creating reports is, for many users, what database management is all about. Although a Query Form is a powerful tool for gaining immediate answers to specific questions, much of your work with Paradox will probably involve generating reports. Detailed reports are easy to produce with Paradox, due in no small part to the program's philosophy of relying on visual examples to get the job done.

To select records for inclusion in a report, you design a query using the tools you have already learned about in Chapter 6. Once those records are contained in a table, you can print a report by using the standard report form provided with any table you create. For greater flexibility, you can use the report creation features of Paradox to design custom reports that meet your specific needs.

Paradox offers two types of reports: *standard* and *custom*. Standard reports are reports created automatically by Paradox when you need them. They contain all of the fields in a table, and the field names that you supplied during the table design are used as headings for the fields.

Custom reports, by comparison, are reports that you modify in some way to better fit your specific needs. A major advantage of Paradox over some older database managers is that it does not force you to design a custom report from scratch, starting with a blank screen. Paradox uses the standard report as the basis for all custom reports you design. You can add or remove fields from the standard report, change headings, lengthen or shorten columns, change formatting attributes, and save the modified design as a custom report. This approach saves much of the time it would usually take to design a custom report from a blank screen.

To design a custom report, you simply choose the Design option from the Report menu, and then choose a number to identify the custom report. Paradox then creates a report based on the standard report format, and you can choose to modify that report in any way you desire.

On the other hand, if a standard report will do fine, Paradox automatically creates a standard report for any table when you press the Instant Report (ALT-F7) key. The same report can also be chosen by selecting menu options from the Report choice on the main menu.

Both types of reports, standard and custom, are also available in two general formats: *tabular* and *free-form*. Tabular reports are columnar reports that contain any data you desire from the fields of the table. They can also include numeric information, such as totals or other calculations based on numeric fields. Tabular reports normally include headings that contain the specified title of the report, the date (determined by the PC's clock), and the page number for each page.

Free-form reports do not need to follow a columnar format. In a free-form report, fields can be placed in different locations on the screen. Figure 7-1 shows an example of a tabular report, and Figure 7-2 shows an example of a free-form report. Tabular reports will be discussed throughout this chapter, and free-form reports will be discussed in Chapter 12.

Generating a Standard Report

By far the fastest way to produce printed reports in Paradox is to use the standard report, because this report needs no designing in advance. To produce a standard report, simply view the desired table, turn on your printer, and press Instant Report ((ALT-F7)). You can also generate a standard report

Figure 7-1. **Tabular report produced by Paradox**

```
6/19/92                 Standard Report                  Page    1


Assignment          Social Security    Weekend date    Hours worked
----------          ---------------    ------------    ------------
National Oil Co.       909-88-7654       5/16/92            35
National Oil Co.       121-33-9876       5/16/92            30
National Oil Co.       121-90-5432       5/16/92            27
National Oil Co.       123-44-8976       5/16/92            32
City Revenue Dept.     343-55-9821       5/16/92            35
City Revenue Dept.     495-00-3456       5/16/92            28
City Revenue Dept.     232-55-1234       5/16/92            30
Smith Builders         876-54-3210       5/23/92            30
Smith Builders         901-77-3456       5/23/92            28
Smith Builders         805-34-6789       5/23/92            35
City Revenue Dept.     232-55-1234       5/23/92            30
City Revenue Dept.     495-00-3456       5/23/92            32
City Revenue Dept.     343-55-9821       5/23/92            32
National Oil Co.       121-33-9876       5/23/92            35
National Oil Co.       909-88-7654       5/23/92            33
```

7

Figure 7-2. **Free-form report produced by Paradox**

```
                         ABC Temporaries
6/19/92                  Free-Form Example Report       Page    1

Assignment: National Oil Co.
Social Security: 909-88-7654
Weekend date:  5/16/92
Hours worked:      35

Assignment: National Oil Co.
Social Security: 121-33-9876
Weekend date:  5/16/92
Hours worked:      30
```

Figure 7-2.   *Free-form report produced by Paradox* (continued)

```
Assignment: National Oil Co.
Social Security: 121-90-5432
Weekend date:   5/16/92
Hours worked:      27

Assignment: National Oil Co.
Social Security: 123-44-8976
Weekend date:   5/16/92
Hours worked:      32

Assignment: City Revenue Dept.
Social Security: 343-55-9821
Weekend date:   5/16/92
Hours worked:      35

Assignment: City Revenue Dept.
Social Security: 495-00-3456
Weekend date:   5/16/92
Hours worked:      28

Assignment: City Revenue Dept.
Social Security: 232-55-1234
Weekend date:   5/16/92
Hours worked:      30

Assignment: Smith Builders
Social Security: 876-54-3210
Weekend date:   5/23/92
Hours worked:      30

Assignment: Smith Builders
Social Security: 901-77-3456
Weekend date:   5/23/92
Hours worked:      28
```

by choosing Report from the main menu and then choosing Output, followed by the name of the table, then R, and then Printer.

The report shown in Figure 7-1 was produced from the HOURS table by means of the Instant Report key. Note that the report illustrates the design of a standard report. The date appears at the top left of each page; a report heading, "Standard Report," appears at the top center; and a page number appears at the top right. The names of the fields appear as column headings, and the data appears in single-spaced rows beneath the headings. For alphanumeric fields, Paradox uses the field width as defined in the table structure to determine the width of the column within the report. Numeric and short-number (integer) fields are assigned a default width of 6, currency fields a width of 14, and date fields a width of 9 (to allow for the possible dd-mon-yy format). If the name of the field is wider than the default width, Paradox will make the column as wide as the field name so that the entire heading will fit.

If you study the example in Figure 7-1 (or generate your own report by viewing the ABCSTAFF table and pressing (ALT)-(F7)), you will notice one trait of a standard report which may not be very appealing to you. Depending on the design of the structure, one or more columns may be divided by the right margin of the report, with part of the column appearing on one page and the remainder on the following page. You can quickly solve this problem by changing the width or moving the location of the columns in a custom report. If you are printing from a query, you can solve the problem by eliminating some fields from the ANSWER table.

If a report needs to be in a specific order, sort the table before producing the report.

Remember

Sending Reports to the Screen or to a File

Though reports created by pressing (ALT)-(F7) will go by default to the printer, you can choose to direct the output of any report to the screen or to a disk file as ASCII (American Standard Code for Information Interchange) text. To send a report to the screen or to a file, you cannot use the (ALT)-(F7) key combination; you must instead use the report choices from the Paradox menus.

A report sent to an ASCII file can be read by most word processors.

To send a report to the screen, choose Report/Output from the main menu and enter the name of the table that will be used to produce the report. From the next menu that appears, choose R for Standard Report; this may be the only menu choice shown unless you have created additional reports.

Next, you see a menu with three options:

```
Printer   Screen   File
```

This menu provides the options used for redirecting the output of the report. By choosing Screen from this menu, you can display the report on-screen instead of sending it to the printer. By selecting File, you can store the contents of the report in a disk file.

If you select Screen, the first page of the report appears in a Report Preview window, as shown in Figure 7-3. Also, note that the menu changes to reveal the options of the Report Preview mode.

Figure 7-3.   *The Report Preview window*

```
 ≡  Goto   Search   Cancel
[ ]                          Report Preview                          [ ]

    4/15/92                     Standard Report                     Page


 Assignment            Social Security  Weekend date   Hours worked
 -----------------     ---------------  ------------   ------------
 National Oil Co.      121-33-9876        5/16/92          30
 National Oil Co.      121-33-9876        5/23/92          35
 National Oil Co.      121-90-5432        5/16/92          37
 National Oil Co.      123-44-8976        5/16/92          32
 City Revenue Dept.    232-55-1234        5/16/92          30
 City Revenue Dept.    232-55-1234        5/23/92          30
 City Revenue Dept.    343-55-9821        5/16/92          35
 City Revenue Dept.    343-55-9821        5/23/92          32
 City Revenue Dept.    495-00-3456        5/16/92          28
 City Revenue Dept.    495-00-3456        5/23/92          32
 Smith Builders        805-34-6789        5/23/92          35

 F1 Help                                               Preview
```

In the Report Preview window, you can scroll through your reports and get a general idea of what they will look like when printed. Keyboard users can use ⬆, ⬇, (PGUP), and (PGDN) to scroll through a preview of a report; mouse users can use the scroll bars of the window.

The Report Preview menu contains three options: Goto, Search, and Cancel. Choose Goto when you want to see a particular page of a multipage report, or to the end of the report. The Search option lets you search through the data shown in the report for a particular item. To do this, choose Search and enter the search term in the dialog box that appears; Paradox will move the cursor to the first occurrence of that term within the report. The Cancel option, like all Cancel options in Paradox, exits the current operation (in this case, Report Preview). You can also exit Report Preview mode by closing the Report Preview window.

If you select File, Paradox will ask for a valid DOS filename. Enter any valid name, and the text of the report will be stored to the file. If you supply a filename that already exists, Paradox will warn you of this fact and will ask for confirmation before overwriting the existing file. Note that the ASCII text is stored in the file in the same format as it appears printed or on screen: with the headings, title, and page numbers, and large amounts of white space (or blank lines) between successive pages. This option of sending data to a disk file can be very useful for merging the contents of a report with a document; nearly all word processors for the IBM PC and compatibles can read in an ASCII file produced in this manner by Paradox. Consult your word processor's manual for details on how to do this.

7

Hands-On Practice: Producing Selective Reports with Ease

If you want maximum results in a minimum amount of time, keep in mind the flexibility that Paradox provides by storing the results of queries in the form of temporary tables. You can use these tables to generate your reports. And, in many cases, you can solve your formatting problems by including selected fields in the ANSWER table, while omitting unwanted fields.

For a fast, selective report, perform a query and then press (ALT)-(F7).

Take the instant report produced if you view the ABCSTAFF table, and press (ALT)-(F7) to print a report. In the resulting report the City field has been cut off unattractively. Perhaps all you are really interested in are the Last Name, Salary, Hourly Rate, and Assignment fields, and you know that these will comfortably fit on a single sheet of standard paper.

From the main menu, choose Ask. Then enter ABCSTAFF for the table name. Use the (F6) key to place checkmarks in the Last Name, Salary, Hourly Rate, and Assignment fields, and then choose DO-IT! to produce the result. The ANSWER table contains all of the records from the staff table, but with only the desired fields. Press (ALT)-(F7), and the instant report that is printed will resemble the one shown in Figure 7-4, with all of the desired data arranged within a single page width.

Figure 7-4.   *Instant report based on query with selected fields*

```
 6/19/92                 Standard Report                    Page   1


    Last Name        Salary      Assignment           Hourly Rate
    - - - - - - -    - - - - -   - - - - - - -        - - - - - - -
    Abernathy        10.00       City Revenue Dept.        18.00
    Hart              8.50       Smith Builders            14.00
    Jackson           7.50       City Revenue Dept.        12.00
    Kramer            7.50       Smith Builders            12.00
    Jones            12.00       National Oil Co.          17.50
    Mitchell          7.50       Smith Builders            12.00
    Morse             7.50       Smith Builders            12.00
    Morse             8.50       National Oil Co.          15.00
    Robinson          7.50       City Revenue Dept.        12.00
    Robinson          7.50       National Oil Co.          12.00
    Westman          15.00       National Oil Co.          24.00
    Willston         10.00       National Oil Co.          14.00
```

If you wanted specific records in the report, you could use the query-by-example methods detailed in the previous chapter to produce a subset of records in the ANSWER table. Also, if you wanted to see the instant report in some specific order, you could sort the ANSWER table and then produce the report. The built-in flexibility of Paradox lets you generate complex reports with little or no customizing.

One important point to remember about generating reports from an ANSWER table: Reports are stored as a part of the table. If you dispose of an ANSWER table without storing it under another name, the report will be disposed of as well. Since Paradox creates the standard report when you press (ALT)-(F7), this is not a problem. However, if you design a custom report for use along with an ANSWER table, be aware that you must rename the table by using the Tools/Rename/Table option if you want to keep and reuse the custom report (see "A Note About Reports" in Chapter 9).

Before proceeding, press (ALT)-(F8) to clear the tables and the Query Form from the desktop.

Designing a Custom Tabular Report

There will be times when you prefer the flexibility of customizing a report by placing fields, changing formatting attributes, adding custom headers and footers, and so on. Designing a custom report is the desired route when you need this kind of flexibility. A simplified list of the steps you must take to design such a report is shown here:

1. Choose the table for the report.

2. Choose a name (numeric designator) and description for the report.

3. Select a tabular or a free-form report.

4. Modify the Report Specification that appears on the screen, as desired.

5. Save the Report Specification.

Depending on how complex your needs are, the precise steps may vary in complexity. The basic process in designing a custom report, following the tabular format used by the standard report, will be presented here.

You first choose Report/Design from the main menu to begin the report's design process. After entering the name of the table to be used, select one of the available Report Specification numbers that appear in the form of a menu:

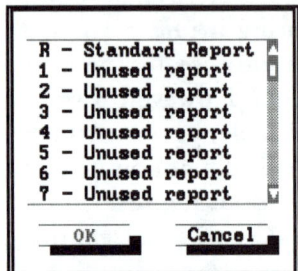

Paradox provides up to 14 possible designators for your custom reports. Once you have selected a number to assign to the report you are creating, Paradox will ask for a description. You can enter up to 40 characters, including spaces, to describe the report.

After you enter a description, Paradox displays a menu with two options, Tabular and Free-form. You can choose Tabular to design a report in the tabular, or columnar, style. (The other option, Free-form, is covered in Chapter 12.) Once you make the selection, Paradox displays the Report Designer in its own window, as shown in Figure 7-5. The contents of the window are derived from the standard report produced with the Instant Report key; in the process of designing a custom report, you can move fields, delete entire columns, and make other changes to the report. The design of a report, which you see within the Report Designer window, is referred to as the *Report Specification.*

Pressing (SHIFT)-(F5) *maximizes the currently active window; this is often helpful when designing a report.*

Tip

Figure 7-5.   *The Report Designer window*

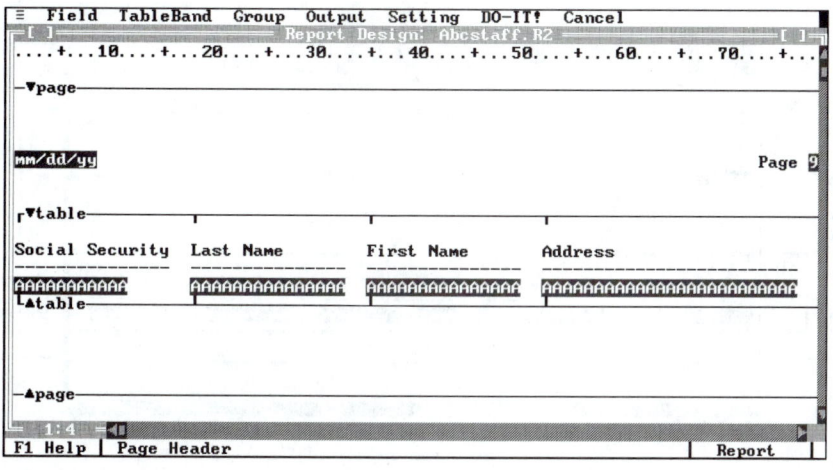

The Report Specification

The Report Specification is made up of several important parts, as illustrated in Figure 7-6. Paradox views each portion of the report as a horizontal area known as a *band*. There is a *report band*, a *page band*, a *group band*, and a *table band*, as shown in the illustration. These bands control what the report contains and how it will appear when printed.

The report band, which encompasses the overall screen, is printed once and contains everything that appears between the start and the end of the report. Inside of the report band is the page band, which appears once for each page of the report. At the start of the page band (or, the top of the page) will appear any page headers that you specify; the date, title, and page number in a standard report are default page headers. At the end of the page band (the bottom of the page) will appear any page footers that you include in the report's design.

Contained within the page bands are the group bands. Group bands, which are optional, are printed once for every group of records in a report.

Figure 7-6.   *Parts of a Report Specification*

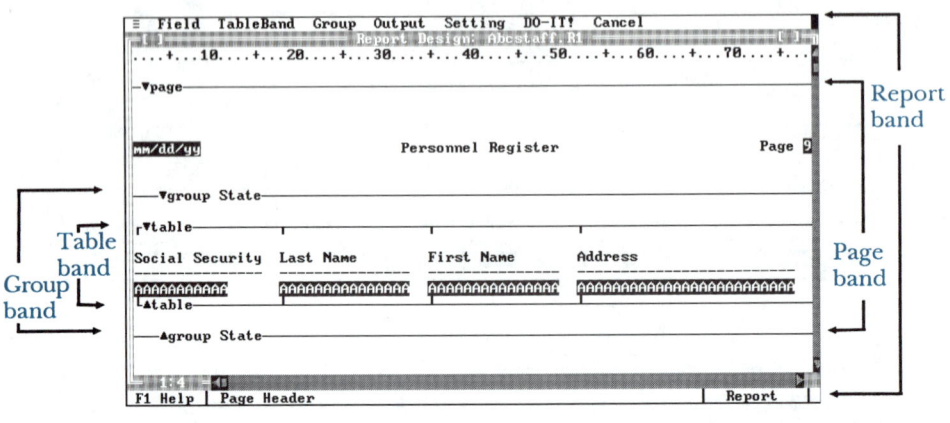

You may or may not want to group records in a report; as an example of grouping, you might decide to print a list of employees for ABC Temporaries by assignment. If you decide to include groups, Paradox lets you have up to 16 group bands in a single report.

    Finally, there are table bands. (In free-form reports, these are known as *form bands.*) Table bands indicate the actual information (usually fields) that will appear in the body of the report. The values in the table bands are represented by symbols called *field masks,* such as AAAAAAA for alphanumeric fields, 999999 for number fields, and mm/dd/yy for date fields. Table bands also contain the headings or field labels that appear at the top of the columns of printed data.

Making Changes to a Report Specification   Once the Report Specification appears in the Report Designer window, you can use various options of the Design menu to rearrange or remove fields and columns, set display formats, add bands for grouping, or make other desired changes. Whenever the Report Designer window is visible, you will see the Design menu, as shown at the top of Figure 7-7.

Figure 7-7. *The Design menu*

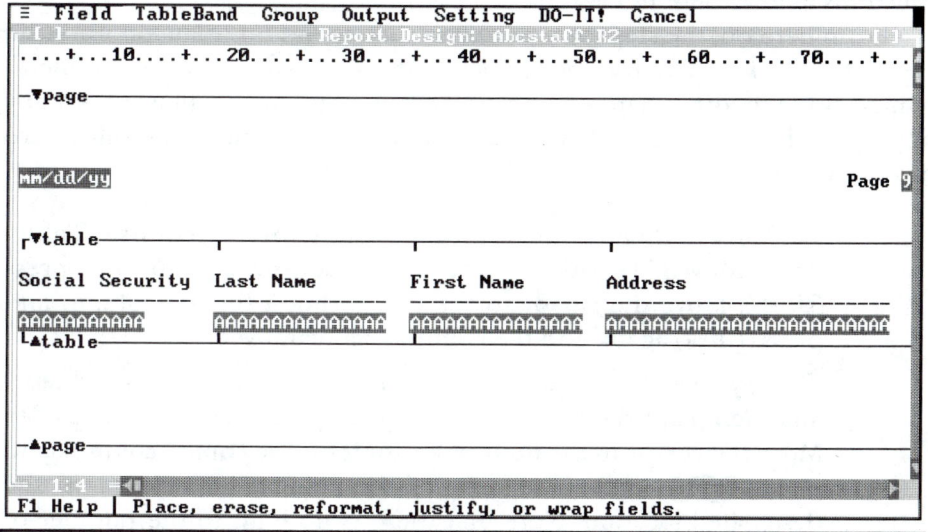

The Design Menu Options

The Field option controls general field placement and appearance; you can use this choice to place new fields in a report, remove existing fields from the report, change a field's format, set justification (left, center, and right), edit an expression used in a calculated field, or wordwrap a text field. The Field option also provides a Lookup choice that lets you include related tables in a report. This option is covered in detail in Chapter 9.

The TableBand option lets you insert or remove entire columns from the table band, resize columns, and move or copy columns to other locations. (The actual fields are placed inside the columns.) The Group option, designed for use with the optional groupings, lets you insert or delete groups, specify your group headings, change the sort order for a group, and change the types of groupings used. The Output option permits you to specify the printer, the screen, or a disk file as the default output device for the report.

The Setting option will be discussed in additional detail later. In a nutshell, this option lets you control a number of settings for the report, including page length and width, the left margin, setup strings for specialized font control of printers, and more. Finally, the DO-IT! option saves the modifications to the Report Specification, and the Cancel option performs the same functions as elsewhere in Paradox.

From here on, the steps you perform will depend on what you want the report to look like. You use the various options shown on the Design menu to modify the report. A hands-on practice session that further illustrates many of these options is provided later in the chapter. The features you will use are described here:

- *To Move Columns:* From the Design menu, choose Table-Band/Move. Place the cursor in the desired column and press (ENTER). Move the cursor to the new location for the column and press (ENTER) again, and the column will be moved.

- *To Copy Columns:* Choose TableBand/Copy from the Design menu, and then place the cursor in the desired column and press (ENTER). Move the cursor to the desired location for the copied column, and press (ENTER) again. The copy of the column will appear in the designated location. Note that there is no limit to the number of times you can copy a column containing the same field to different locations in a report. This can be very helpful with tabular reports that must display many fields; you can place common information, such as the name of an employee, in the first column of each page, while other fields appear in the remaining columns.

- *To Remove Columns:* From the Design menu, choose Table-Band/Erase. Then place the cursor in the desired column and press (ENTER) to erase the column.

- *To Resize Columns:* From the Design menu, choose Table-Band/Re-size. Then place the cursor at either edge of the desired column and press (ENTER). Use the cursor keys to contract or expand the size of the column to the desired width, and then press (ENTER) again to complete the resizing.

- *To Edit Headings or Footers in the Page Band:* Place the cursor in the desired portion of the page band, and enter the desired heading or edit existing headings. "Page Number" and "System Date" are fields, not literal text; these can be removed or added by choosing Fields from the Design menu and using Place to place the fields or Erase to erase them.

- *To Reformat Fields:* From the Design menu, choose Field/Reformat, and then place the cursor in the field you want to reformat. Press (ENTER) to select the field. Use arrow keys to change the width, or select from the menu the desired format for the field.

- *To Place New Fields:* From the Design menu, choose Field/Place and then choose the type of field desired (regular, summary, calculated, current date, current time, page number, or record number). If you chose a regular field, you will be prompted for the name of the field; if you choose a summary or calculated field, you can enter an expression that will calculate the field. The date and time fields will display a menu of varying formats, and you can select the format desired. Finally, place the field in the desired location and press (ENTER). You may need to add a column with TableBand/Insert to make room for the field.

- *To Remove Fields:* From the Design menu, choose Field/Erase. Then place the cursor on the desired field and press (ENTER).

Saving the Report

Once you have made the desired changes to the Report Specification, press DO-IT! ((F2)) or choose DO-IT! from the Design menu to save the report.

Note

To design a report that prints using compressed print, choose Setting/Setup/Predefined from the menu while designing the report. Then, select the compressed option that matches your type of printer.

Hands-On Practice: Designing a Custom Personnel Report

ABC Temporaries needs a personnel report with more to offer than the standard report. The report must include the Last Name, First Name, Phone, Date Hired, and Social Security fields as the first set of columns per page, and the Last Name, Salary, and Hourly Rate fields as the second set of columns per page. The date and time of the report should appear in the upper-right corner of the first page, and a report title should be centered at the top of the first page. Also, the Salary and Hourly Rate fields are to be totaled, producing figures that reflect the total hourly rate of income generated (assuming that all employees are working) and the total cost of salary for the entire staff.

To begin designing the report, choose Report/Design from the main menu. Enter ABCSTAFF as the table name, and choose 1 for the Report Specification. (If you have already used 1 for a different report, you can select a different number or replace the prior report.)

Paradox will prompt you for a description of the report; enter Personnel Register as the description. From the next menu that appears, choose Tabular to indicate that this will be a tabular report. In a moment, the Report Specification, based on the standard report for the ABCSTAFF table, will appear. Your screen now resembles the one shown in Figure 7-8.

Note that you can quickly move between the pages of a report that contains multiple fields (like this one) with the (CTRL)-(←) and (CTRL)-(→) key combinations. Try using (CTRL)-(→) repeatedly, and note the effect as the

Figure 7-8.   *A Report Specification*

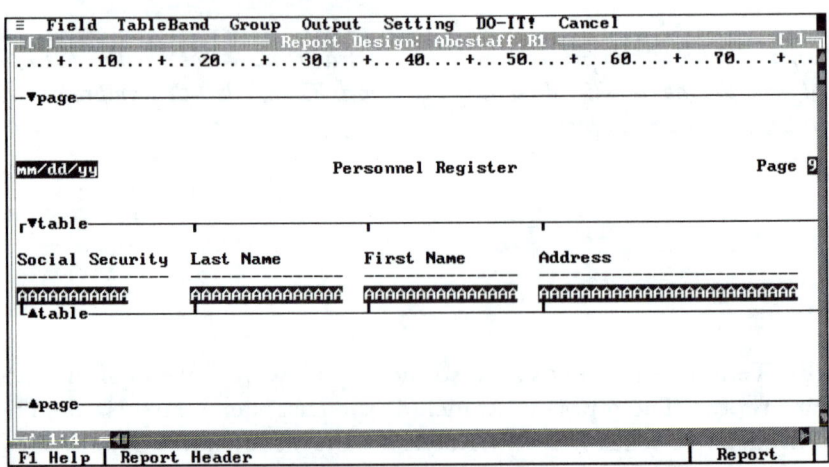

additional pages of the report come into view on the right. Use (CTRL)-(←) to get back to the far left edge of the report.

The headings need to be customized for this report; the page number, which currently appears at the top of the report, needs to be relocated to the bottom. The current date needs to be positioned at the right side of the top, rather than the left; and the custom heading needs to be amended to include the name of the company.

From the Design menu, choose Field/Erase, and then place the cursor anywhere in the "999" designation that indicates the page-number field. Press (ENTER) to erase the field, and then use the (BACKSPACE) key to erase the "Page" designation.

Move the cursor to the left slightly, roughly to position 70. The top of the screen provides a guide that indicates the relative column position of the cursor. To place the date and time fields in this area, choose Field/Place from the menu. Then select Date from the list of field types. Paradox will display a list of possible date formats; press (ENTER) to select the first format shown. Then, with the cursor at position 70, press (ENTER) to place the field.

Move the cursor down one line and back to position 70. Again, choose Field/Place from the menu. Then select Time from the list of field types. Paradox will display a list of possible time formats; select the second format shown in the menu. Then, with the cursor at position 70, press (ENTER) to place the field.

Use (CTRL)-(←) to quickly get back to the left side of the report. Directly above the "Personnel Register" title, add **ABC Temporaries**.

The date field at the left side of the report is no longer needed. So, from the menu choose Field/Erase, and place the cursor in the date field at the left side of the header. Then press (ENTER) to remove the field.

Deleting Unwanted Columns

To quickly rid the report of undesired fields and columns, you can use the Erase option from the TableBand choice on the Design menu. From the menu choose TableBand/Erase, and place the cursor anywhere in the Address field. Press (ENTER) to remove the column.

In a similar fashion, choose TableBand/Erase from the menu, and with the cursor positioned in the City field, press (ENTER) to delete the column.

7

Perform the same step for the State, ZIP Code, Date of Birth, Dependents, Assignment, and Comments fields.

Moving a Column

The column containing the Phone field needs to be relocated to the right of the First name field. Choose TableBand/Move from the menu. Place the cursor in the column containing the Phone field, and press (ENTER) to select the column. Paradox will prompt you to show the new location for the field.

Use (CTRL)-(←) to get back to the left side of the report. Place the cursor anywhere in the Date Hired field, and press (ENTER) to insert the column containing the Phone field into this location.

Next, choose TableBand/Move, place the cursor in the Social Security field, and press (ENTER) to select the field. Then move the cursor to the Date Hired field and press (ENTER) to move the field to its new location (now between the Date Hired and the Salary fields).

Duplicating a Column

The report now contains most of the desired fields on the first page, with the Salary and Hourly Rate fields occupying the second page. In this format, it would be difficult to tell which name belongs to which salary and hourly rate. Duplicating the last name in the second page of the report will make it easier to keep track of the fields.

From the menu, choose TableBand/Copy. Place the cursor anywhere in the column containing the Last Name field, and press (ENTER) to select the field. Place the cursor anywhere in the Salary field, and press (ENTER) to insert the Last Name field at this location.

Resizing a Column

As the report design now stands, the column containing the Last Name field on the second page is too close to the vertical bar that indicates the division between pages of a report. By widening the column containing the Last Name field on the second page, this can be corrected. From the menu, choose TableBand/Resize, place the cursor at the left edge of the Last Name field on the second page, and press (ENTER) to select the field. Press (→) three times to widen the column by three spaces, and press (ENTER) to set the new column width.

When resizing columns, the cursor cannot be inside the field within the column, as Paradox will not let you split a field in two.

Note

Adding Report Totals

All that is needed at this point are the totals of the Salary and Hourly Rate fields. From the menu, choose Field/Place to place a new field. Paradox next prompts you for the type of field desired; choose Summary/Regular, and then select Salary from the list of fields. Choose Sum and then Overall.

Paradox will then ask you to indicate the position for the summary total of the Salary values. Place the cursor in the footer section of the report band, just above the line at the bottom of the and directly underneath the location of the Salary field within the table band. Press (ENTER) to place the field, press (←) three times to shorten the width of the field, and press (ENTER) twice—once to set the number of decimal places, and once to complete the placement of the new field.

Again, choose Field/Place from the main menu to place a new field. From the next menu that appears, choose Summary/Regular, and then select Hourly Rate from the list of fields. From the next menu to appear, choose Sum. (The remaining choices on this menu are Count, Average, High, and Low. Average would provide an average value, Count would give the number of occurrences in the group, High would provide a maximum value, and Low would provide a minimum value.) After choosing Sum, select Overall from the next menu.

Paradox will then ask you to indicate the position for the summary total of the Hourly Rate values. Place the cursor in the footer section of the report band, just above the bottom of the Report Specification and directly underneath the location of the Hourly Rate field within the table band. Press (ENTER) to place the field, press (←) three times to shorten the width of the field, and press (ENTER) twice—once to set the number of decimal places, and once to complete the placement of the new field. Move the cursor eight characters to the left of the start of the Salary summary field you just placed, and enter **TOTALS:** as a label for this field.

To test the report before you save it, choose Output/Screen from the Design menu. The report will appear in a Report Preview window. If any errors exist, you can go back and correct them before saving the report.

When you are done previewing the report, first choose Cancel, or click on the Report Preview Close box, to close the Preview window. Then, choose DO-IT!. To see the results, choose Report/Output from the menu and enter **ABCSTAFF** as the desired table for the report. Select 1 from the menu for the desired Report Specification, and choose Printer (or Screen, if you prefer just to see the report on the screen). Within a moment, your custom report will be printed or displayed. It should look much like the report shown in Figure 7-9.

Remember

You can preview any report on screen before you save it, by choosing Output/Screen while designing the report.

Using the Group Menu Options

You can use the Group option of the Design menu to work with groupings of records within a report. Most likely, you will need to arrange reports broken down by groups. As an example, you might want to see all employees divided into groups by state of residence or by the name of the assignment. By utilizing the Group menu options, you can define up to 16 levels of groupings.

While 16 levels may seem like overkill, it is nice to know that Paradox will not limit you when you must base a complex report on a large number of subgroups. Multiple groupings can be quite common in many business applications. In something as simple as a national mailing list, for example, you might need to see records by groups of states, and within each state group by city, and within each city group by ZIP code. That alone represents three levels of grouping alone. Cut the data in the table more specifically, by other categories like income levels, and you will quickly come to appreciate Paradox's ability to perform groupings so effectively.

Figure 7-9. **Custom report**

```
                        ABC Temporaries
                        Personnel Register              6/19/92
                                                        8:16 pm


Last Name      First Name    Phone          Date Hired   Social Security
---------      ----------    -----------    ----------   --------------
Kramer         Harry         703-555-4323    5/03/92     111-33-9876
Westman        Andrea        301-555-5682    7/04/90     121-33-9876
Robinson       Shirley       301-555-4582   11/17/91     121-90-5432
Morse          Marcia        301-555-9802    7/25/85     123-44-8976
Jackson        David         703-555-2345    9/05/91     232-55-1234
Robinson       Wanda         202-555-9876    9/17/87     343-55-9821
Abernathy      Sandra        703-555-7337    2/17/88     495-00-3456
Morse          William       301-555-9802    3/15/92     805-34-6789
Hart           Edward        703-555-7834   10/19/86     876-54-3210
Mitchell       Mary Jo       703-555-7654   12/01/91     901-77-3456
Willston       Maria         301-555-2378    5/15/92     909-55-7788
Jones          Judi          703-555-2638    8/12/90     909-88-7654



Last Name      Salary        Hourly Rate
-----------    -----------   --------------
Kramer             7.50          12.00
Westman           15.00          24.00
Robinson           7.50          12.00
Morse              8.50          15.00
Jackson            7.50          12.00
Robinson           7.50          12.00
Abernathy         10.00          18.00
Morse              7.50          12.00
Hart               8.50          14.00
Mitchell           7.50          12.00
Willston          10.00          14.00
Jones             12.00          17.50

      TOTALS:    109.00         174.50
```

7

When you select Group from the Design menu while designing a report, the following menu will be displayed.

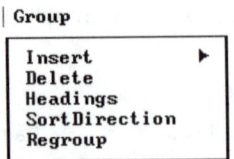

The Insert option lets you insert new groups into the report, and the Delete option lets you delete existing groups from the report. The Headings option is used to control where headings appear within the group. The SortDirection option is used to control whether groups should be sorted in ascending or descending order. Finally, using the Regroup option changes the ways existing groups are defined.

To add a new group to the report, choose Report/Design/Group/Insert. The next menu that appears will display three options: Field, Range, and NumberRecords. If you want to establish the group by field (for example, groups of records from the same state or with the same assignment), choose Field. You can also group records by a range of values in a field; choose Range if you desire this kind of grouping. Finally, Paradox lets you establish groups by a set number of records. You could set the report's design to isolate records into groups of 10, 15, or any set number of records per group. Choose NumberRecords to select grouping by such quantities as records.

When you have selected the desired type of grouping, Paradox will ask you to indicate the location for the group. You now move the cursor to the desired location, and press (ENTER) to place the new group band. Group bands must fall outside of table bands (or outside of form bands in the case of free-form reports) and inside the page band. (Refer back to Figure 7-6 to see a Report Specification that includes a group band for ABCSTAFF employees grouped by state.)

Once you have placed the desired group, you can check to see if the results are what you desire by choosing Output/Screen from the Design menu. The resulting report will be divided by group. When you are satisfied with the results, save the Report Specification by choosing DO-IT!.

You cannot add a group band inside a table band.

Hands-On Practice: Adding a Group by Assignment

Try adding a group by assignment name to the existing Personnel Register report you created earlier in the chapter. First, clear the desktop with (ALT)(F8). From the main menu, choose Report/Change, and enter **ABCSTAFF** as the table name. Select 1, Personnel Register, as the report to modify, and press (ENTER) to accept the prior description. The Report Specification for the report you designed earlier will appear.

To add the group to the report, from the Design menu choose Group and then Insert to insert a new group. The report is to be grouped by assignment name (which is a field), so choose Field. The next menu shows the fields available in the table; choose Assignment from the list.

Paradox next asks you to show where the group is to be inserted. Remember that group bands must appear between the table band and the page band. Since there is only one level of grouping in this report, things are simple. Move the cursor to the blank line just above the table band. Press (ENTER) to place the group. Your screen should now resemble the example shown in Figure 7-10.

Remember, you do not need to save and exit the report before seeing the results. Choose Output/Screen from the menu (or Output/Printer from the menu if you prefer to have the results printed). The report will be printed or will appear on your screen. It should resemble the one shown in Figure 7-11.

Note that the actual contents of the Assignment field do not appear with each group; to add the field, you will need to place it where you want it to appear. You can place the field used to control the group within the group band, and it will then print once for each occurrence of that group. To see how this works, choose the Field/Place/Regular option from the Design menu, and select Assignment from the menu of fields as the field to place in the report. Place the cursor in the blank line between the group band and the table band (directly underneath the designation, "Group Assignment"). Press (ENTER) to place the field, and again to set the width.

7

Figure 7-10.   *Report Specification with group (by assignment name) added*

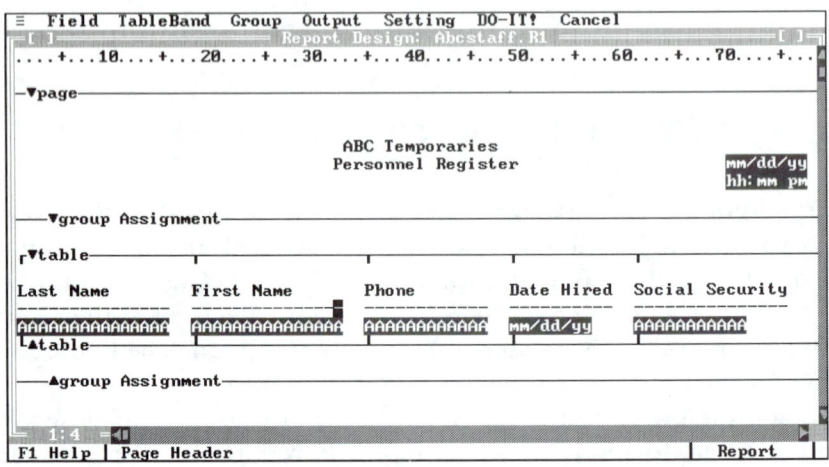

To see the results, from the Design menu choose Output/Screen or Output/Printer if you prefer having the results printed. The report will be printed or displayed, and this time the contents for the Assignment field will appear along with each group. If you previewed the report, choose Cancel, or click on the Close box to put away the Report Preview window. Save the report and return to the main menu by choosing DO-IT!.

Hands-On Practice: Creating a Report with Multiple Groups

You can add as many groups as are needed (up to the Paradox limit of 16) to further define your groups. As an example, consider the HOURS table, which contains records of the employee hours worked at different assignments. If what is needed is a report grouped by assignment and by "week ending" date within each assignment group, you must create a report containing more than one group.

Figure 7-11. **Example of report with grouping**

```
                         ABC Temporaries
                         Personnel Register                         6/19/92
                                                                    8:30 pm

Last Name      First Name     Phone            Date Hired    Social Security
- - - - - - -  - - - - - - -  - - - - - - - -  - - - - - -   - - - - - - - - -
Jackson        David          703-555-2345     9/05/91       232-55-1234
Robinson       Wanda          202-555-9876     9/17/87       343-55-9821
Abernathy      Sandra         703-555-7337     2/17/88       495-00-3456


Westman        Andrea         301-555-5682     7/04/90       121-33-9876
Robinson       Shirley        301-555-4582     11/17/91      121-90-5432
Morse          Marcia         301-555-9802     7/25/85       123-44-8976
Willston       Maria          301-555-2378     5/15/92       909-55-7788
Jones          Judi           703-555-2638     8/12/90       909-88-7654


Kramer         Harry          703-555-4323     5/03/92       111-33-9876
Morse          William        301-555-9802     3/15/92       805-34-6789
Hart           Edward         703-555-7834     10/19/86      876-54-3210
Mitchell       Mary Jo        703-555-7654     12/01/91      901-77-3456


    Last Name        Salary          Hourly Rate
    - - - - - - -    - - - - - - -   - - - - - - - -
    Jackson              7.50            12.00
    Robinson             7.50            12.00
    Abernathy           10.00            18.00


    Westman             15.00            24.00
    Robinson             7.50            12.00
    Morse                8.50            15.00
    Willston            10.00            14.00
    Jones               12.00            17.50

    Kramer               7.50            12.00
    Hart                 8.50            14.00
    Mitchell             7.50            12.00

         TOTALS:       109.00           174.50
```

7

From the main menu, choose Report/Design, and enter **HOURS** as the table name for this example. Choose 1 as the report name, and enter **HOURLY REPORT** as a description. Choose Tabular for the desired type of report, and the standard Report Specification for the HOURS table will appear.

In this case, you want a report grouped by assignment name, and within each assignment name, by groups of "week ending" dates. From the Design menu choose Group/Insert to insert a new group. Then choose Field to base the new group on a field.

From the list of field names, choose Assignment. Place the cursor just below the line in the page band containing the date, report heading, and page number. Press (ENTER) to place the group based on the Assignment field. To add the second group, choose Group/Insert from the Design menu, and then Field. From the list of fields, choose Weekend date. Place the cursor just underneath the Assignment group band and press (ENTER). Your screen should resemble the one shown in Figure 7-12.

Figure 7-12. *Report Specification containing multiple groups*

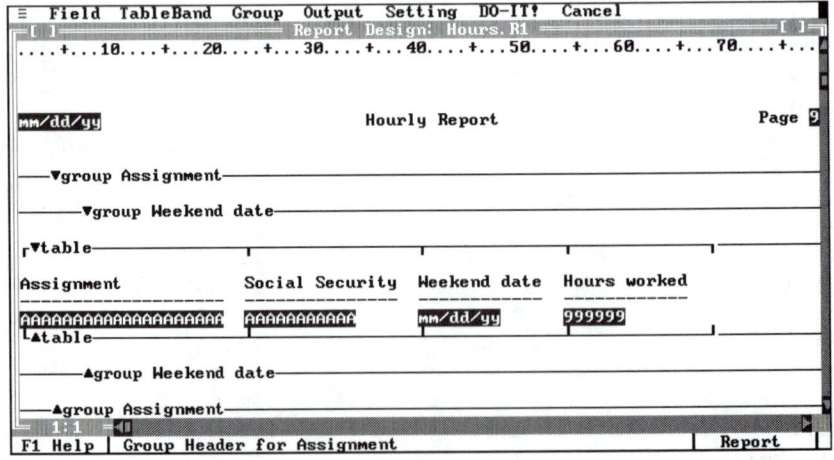

To test the results, from the menu choose Output/Screen. The results should be similar to those shown in Figure 7-13. Finally, choose DO-IT! to save the finished report, and return to the main menu.

Figure 7-13.   *Example of report with multiple groups*

6/19/92	Hourly Report		Page 1

Assignment	Social Security	Weekend date	Hours worked
City Revenue Dept.	232-55-1234	5/16/92	30
City Revenue Dept.	343-55-9821	5/16/92	35
City Revenue Dept.	495-00-3456	5/16/92	28
City Revenue Dept.	232-55-1234	5/23/92	30
City Revenue Dept.	343-55-9821	5/23/92	32
City Revenue Dept.	495-00-3456	5/23/92	32
National Oil Co.	121-33-9876	5/16/92	30
National Oil Co.	121-90-5432	5/16/92	37
National Oil Co.	123-44-8976	5/16/92	32
National Oil Co.	909-88-7654	5/16/92	35
National Oil Co.	121-33-9876	5/23/92	35
National Oil Co.	909-88-7654	5/23/92	33
Smith Builders	805-34-6789	5/23/92	35
Smith Builders	876-54-3210	5/23/92	30
Smith Builders	901-77-3456	5/23/92	28

7

The Delete and Headings Options of the Group Menu

You can delete unwanted groups with the Delete option of the Group menu. To delete an existing grouping, from the Design menu choose Group/Delete. Paradox will ask you to select the group that is to be removed. Place the cursor anywhere inside of the group band that is to be deleted, and press (ENTER). Paradox will require confirmation of the deletion by displaying the choices of Cancel and OK. You must choose OK to delete the group.

Remember

When you delete a group band, any fields or literal text contained within that group band will also be deleted.

To control where your headings appear, use the Headings option of the Group menu. Headings normally appear at the start of each group containing the heading, and at the start of "spillover" pages, in which a group that cannot fit on one page flows onto the next page. You can decide whether or not these headings will appear. From the Report Specification menu, choose Group/Headings. Place the cursor anywhere in the group band, and press (ENTER). Paradox will display a menu with two choices, Page and Group. If you choose the Page option, group headers will appear at the start of each group and at the top of every spillover page. If you choose the Group option, group headers will print at the start of each group but not at the top of the spillover pages.

In some cases, you may want to define groups solely to implement a particular sorting order. In such cases, you would just delete all the extra lines in the group band, so no lines appear between groups.

Changing the Sort Direction of a Report

On occasion, you may want to change the sort direction for a group of records. When you add a group band to a report, Paradox automatically handles the sorting necessary to generate the report, in the order of the groups you have specified. However, Paradox assumes that it should sort the data in *ascending* order to arrange the groups. If, for example, you group a report by a date field, the groups appear in the report by ascending order of dates, earliest to latest. If you want to change this to *descending* order (or change any other direction of any other group), you will need to use the SortDirection option of the Group menu.

To change the sort direction, choose Group/SortDirection from the Design menu. Paradox will ask you to select the desired group; move the cursor anywhere in the desired group, and press (ENTER). The next menu to appear displays two options: Ascending and Descending.

If you desire the group's sort direction to be ascending (letters alphabetically, numbers from least to greatest, and dates from earliest to latest), choose Ascending from this menu. If you want descending order (letters in reverse alphabetical order, numbers from greatest to least, and dates from latest to earliest), choose Descending from the menu. There will be no visible change in the Report Specification (other than the momentary appearance of the message "Settings changed"). But when the report is generated, any changes to the sort direction will take effect.

Note

If you reverse the sort direction within an inner group without changing the sort direction of the outer group, the outer group's sort order will override that of the inner group.

Using SetPrinter for Specialized Printing Needs

You can use the SetPrinter option of the Report/Design menu to select printer ports or to choose printer setup strings for taking advantage of your printer's specialized features. Selecting Setting/Setup from the Design menu reveals the Predefined and Custom options.

If you choose Predefined, Paradox lets you choose from among the following options for producing condensed or other specialized print on some of the most common types of printers:

STANDARDPRINTER
SMALL-IBMGRAPHICS
REG-IBMGRAPHICS
SMALL-EPSON-MX/FX

SMALL-OKI-92/93
SMALL-OKI-82/83
SMALL-OKI-192
HPLASERJET
HPLANDSCAPE-NORMAL
HP-PORTRAIT-66LINES
HP-COMPRESSED
HP-LANDSCAPE-COMPRESSED
INTL-IBM-COMPATIBLE
INTL-IBM-CONDENSED

Select the desired choice, and it will be recorded as a part of the report.

Note

If you choose Setting/Setup/Predefined, and Paradox displays a message indicating that no setup strings are currently defined, you need to install your printer drivers. Refer to the Installation Guide of your Paradox documentation.

By choosing Setting/Setup/Custom, you can enter custom setup strings or printer ports. The first menu to appear offers the following choice of printer ports:

```
LPT1   LPT2   LPT3   COM1   COM2   AUX
```

Select the desired printer port from the menu. (Most systems use the LPT1 as the printer port. Many serial printers, including earlier versions of the Hewlett-Packard LaserJet, use COM1 as the printer port.) The next prompt that appears is

```
Setup string:
```

Setup strings can be up to 175 characters in length. You can enter codes, such as the escape codes commonly used to select printer fonts, by entering a backslash (\ ) followed by the three-digit ASCII code representing that escape code. For example, to turn on compressed printing with an Epson MX/FX or Epson-compatible printer, you would enter \ 015 as a setup string. You should consult your printer manual for the list of escape codes appropriate to your printer. Before resorting to these, however, try the predefined list available from the Setting/Setup/Predefined option first to see if the desired mode of printing is available.

Keep in mind that the custom setup string that you enter will apply to the entire report. Save the completed report with DO-IT! ((F2)), and the setup string, along with any custom printer port settings you have chosen, will be automatically placed in effect when you print the report.

Note that the Custom Configuration Program (CCP) can be used to define printer setups globally and to add custom printer setups to the list. Refer to your Paradox documentation for details on this topic.

Hints for Report Design

Before you start to design your custom reports, you should plan the design of the report. This may mean asking the other users of the database what information will actually be needed from the report.

In many cases you will find it advantageous to outline the report contents and format on paper. Once the report has been designed on paper, your outline should resemble the actual report that is produced by Paradox. You may also find it helpful to print a list of fields from the table structure, particularly if you are designing a report that contains a large number of fields. This can be done by choosing Tools/Info/Structure from the main menu, entering the name of the table, and using (ALT)-(F7) to print the table.

Many additional types of reports, such as free-form styles and mailing labels, can be produced in Paradox. See Chapter 12 for a discussion of these reports.

Quick Summary

To generate an instant report   Display the desired table with View or by processing a query, and press Instant Report ((ALT-F7)).

To design a custom report   From the menu, choose Report/Design. Enter the name of the table on which the report will be based. Choose a number for the report from the next menu to appear, and enter a description for the report. Select a tabular or free-form report, then modify the report specification that appears on the screen, as desired. Finally, choose DO-IT! to save the report.

To add groups to a report   When designing the report, choose Group/Insert from the Design menu. Next, choose Field to establish the grouping based on a field, and then select the field to be used from the list of fields that appears. Place the cursor above the table band where the group is to be inserted, and press (ENTER) to place the new group.

To change the sort direction of a report   When designing the report, choose Group/SortDirection from the Design menu. Place the cursor anywhere within the desired group, and press (ENTER). Choose Ascending or Descending, as desired, from the next menu.

8

Presentation Graphics

Paradox offers powerful capabilities for displaying and printing graphs. Graphs can be prepared for data analysis or for presentation-quality reports. You can use the wide variety of styling features and options offered by Paradox to enhance the appearance of your graphs.

Typical Graphs

Some typical graphs you can create with Paradox are shown in Figure 8-1. Paradox lets you create any of the following types of graphs:

- Standard bar graph
- Stacked bar graph
- Rotated bar graph
- 3-D (three-dimensional) bar graph
- X-Y graph
- Area graph

- Line graph
- Pie chart
- Marker graph
- Combined lines and markers graph

The graphs consist primarily of elements representing the data contained within the table. The appearance of the elements varies, depending on the type of graph you select. In a bar or rotated bar graph, the data is illustrated with bars; in a line graph, the data appears as thin lines. An area graph combines a line graph with shadings underneath the lines to represent trends. In a marker graph, the data appears as small markers; and in a pie graph, data is represented as wedges of the pie. All graphs except for pie graphs have two axes: a horizontal axis, called the *x-axis* or *category axis,* and a vertical axis, called the *y-axis* or *value axis.*

Some graphs in Paradox are combinations or variations of the types just described. The stacked bar, rotated bar, and 3-D bar are all variations of a bar graph. An X-Y graph is a line graph that displays values along both the x- and the y-axes. X-Y graphs are used to show a corresponding relationship between two sets of numbers. Finally, a combined lines and markers graph combines a line graph with markers.

Making a Simple Graph

Paradox has some built-in features that make it very easy to produce a graph. The basic steps are as follows.

1. Use the View command to view the desired table.
2. Place the cursor in a numeric field of a table containing the data to be graphed.(The cursor can be on any record.)
3. Press the Graph key ((CTRL)-(F7)).

At first glance at this simple procedure, you might think that producing a graph must be more complicated, and it can be. The graphs themselves may be as simple or as complex as you care to make them. Thanks to the flexible

Figure 8-1. **Types of graphs created with Paradox**

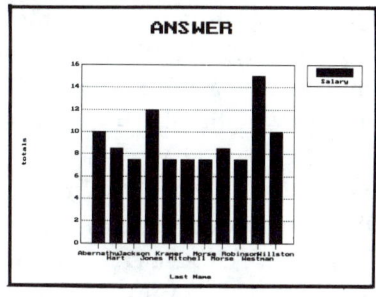

Standard bar graph

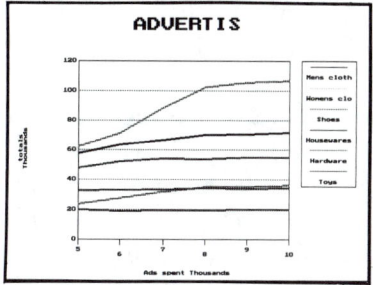

X-Y graph

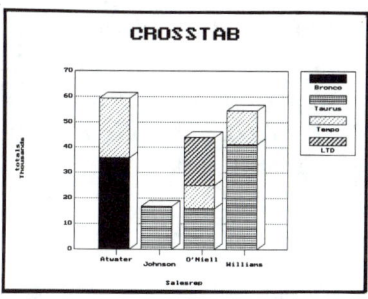

3-D bar graph (stacked)

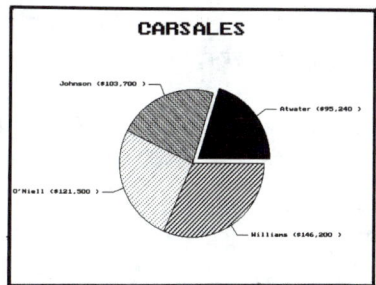

Pie chart

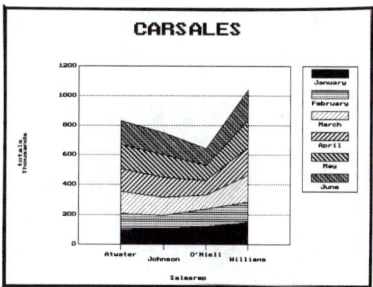

Area graph

8

options provided in Paradox, you can experiment with different types of graphs, customized text and legends, and fancy formatting. If all you need is a basic graph, however, the three steps just outlined will produce it.

Two points can help get the results you want when you use this quick technique. First, with unkeyed tables (or tables with only one field) Paradox uses the far left column of the table for names along the x-axis by default. With keyed tables, Paradox uses the rightmost key field. If the names you want to see along the x-axis are in a different field, you can perform a quick query-by-example operation and place the first checkmark in the column that contains the desired names. Include additional checkmarks in the column or columns containing the numeric data to be graphed, choose DO-IT!, and then use the resulting ANSWER table to draw the graph. The values shown in the first series in the graph are taken from the field containing the cursor. The next numeric field (if there are any more fields) provides the second series values, the third numeric field provides the third series values, and so on.

Second, you'll often want to graph just a subset of data from a particular database. Again, you may use the query-by-example techniques described in Chapter 6 to build an ANSWER table containing the desired subset of your data. Then draw the graph, based on the ANSWER table, by placing the cursor anywhere in the numeric field of the ANSWER table and pressing the Graph key (CTRL-F7).

You can use CTRL-R *to rotate the columns. In some cases, this can make queries unnecessary.*

Tip

Hands-On Practice: Creating an Instant Graph

You can try the techniques just described with the ABCSTAFF table created earlier in this text. As you will see, you can quickly create a bar graph showing the salaries of the employees. To get the names of the employees to appear as names along the x-axis of the graph, you'll need to have the employee names in the first column of the table. Since that is not the way the table was originally designed, you can perform a query that will extract the contents of the Last Name and Salary fields.

First, from the main menu, choose Ask, and enter **ABCSTAFF** as the table name. Use (F6) to place checkmarks in the Last name and Salary fields. Choose DO-IT! to process the query and display the ANSWER table. Next, move the cursor to the Salary field of the ANSWER table, and press Graph ((CTRL)-(F7)). The resultant bar graph shows the salaries represented by bars. If you see something other than a bar graph, the default settings in your version of Paradox have been changed. Don't be concerned, as you'll soon learn how to select different graph types for display.

The default type of graph created by Paradox is a stacked bar graph. Each of the patterns in the bar represent up to six numeric fields, starting from the field where the cursor is located. In the case of the ABCSTAFF table, there is only one numeric field, so Paradox displays a bar graph with only one bar pattern. Later in this chapter you will see examples of a table that supplies more numeric fields and the resulting default graphs displayed.

Changing the Graph Type

If the graph is still displayed, press any key to clear the graph and get back to the ANSWER table. While you still have the cursor placed in the Salary field of the table, you may wish to try creating other types of graphs. You can easily change the setting for the type of graph to be created with Image/Graph/Modify. Choose Image from the main menu, and then choose Graph. You will see the following menu:

```
Modify
Load
Save
Reset        ▶
CrossTab     ▶
ViewGraph    ▶
```

The Graph menu offers various options pertaining to graphs. You'll use Modify shortly to change the type of graph displayed. The Load and Save options are used to load or save the specifications for a graph. ("Save" in this case means the graph settings are saved, and not an image of the graph itself.) The Reset option resets the graph to the default display specifications.

CrossTab generates a crosstab of the current image, a topic covered in detail later in this chapter. Finally, ViewGraph reveals another menu with three choices: Screen (to display the graph on the screen), Printer (to print the graph), or File (to save the graph image as a disk file). Note that before you print a graph, your copy of Paradox should be configured to match your printer. If this has not been done, you'll find tips on selecting printers with the Custom Configuration Program in your Paradox documentation.

With the Graph menu still visible, select Modify. The Customize Graph Type screen shown in Figure 8-2 appears. This screen contains two areas. The upper area has one entry for Graph Type. In this box, you can enter a letter that represents the desired graph type. A help screen to the right shows the available graph types and the corresponding letters. For example, entering **S** causes "Stacked bar" to appear in the Graph Type entry, and entering **P** causes "Pie" to appear in the entry.

The bottom area of the screen contains entries for series override graph types. You use these entries to create a mixed graph, such as a stacked bar graph or a combination line and markers graph. The Series Override Graph Type options will be covered in a later section, "Using Series Override To Create Mixed Graphics."

Figure 8-2. *Customize Graph Type screen*

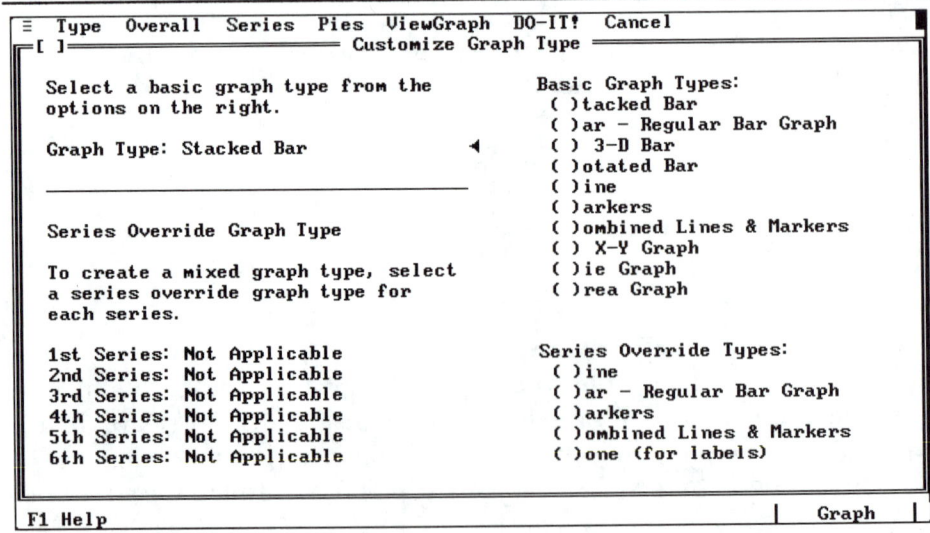

For now, you may want to try choosing one or two other graph types. After typing the letter of the desired graph type, choose DO-IT!, and then press Graph ((CTRL)-(F7)) to draw the corresponding graph. You can get back to the Customize Graph Type screen by pressing any key to clear the graph and choosing Image/Graph/Modify from the menu.

The default type of graph displayed or printed is a bar graph. To change the graph type, choose Image/Graph/Modify from the main menu.

Remember

Printing a Graph

To print a graph, with the cursor still in the desired field of the table and the desired graph-type settings chosen, choose Image/Graph/View Graph from the menu. You will see the following menu:

```
Screen
Printer
File
```

Choosing Screen option is equivalent to pressing the Graph key; it causes the graph to be displayed on the screen. The File option saves the image of the graph to a print file that is usable with other programs such as Lotus 1-2-3 or most desktop publishing software. Use the Printer choice to print the graph on your printer.

Make sure your printer is ready, and choose Printer now. The screen will clear, and in a moment you will see a message similar to this:

```
Graph Printer: HP Printers - HP LaserJet Plus (150 dpi)
   Mode: 150 x 150 dpi Med.
Press <<ESC>> to cancel printing
```

(Your message will probably differ, depending on the type of printer you have installed with your system.) Because graphs contain large amounts of graphic data, it will take some time for the graph to print. If you have a dot-matrix printer, the graph will probably print at slow to moderate speeds, line by line. With most laser printers, there will probably be no activity for a

8

minute or two, and then the graph will be printed. Laser printers must receive and compose the entire page in memory before any printing begins.

Parts of a Graph

Before considering the options that Paradox offers for creating graphs, you should know the parts of a graph, which are discussed here and shown in Figure 8-3.

Axes   The axes are the horizontal and vertical frames of reference, and they appear in all types of graphs except pie charts. The horizontal axis (or x-axis) is called the *category axis* because categories of data are normally plotted along this line. The vertical axis (or y-axis) is called the *value axis* because values are

Figure 8-3.   *Parts of a graph*

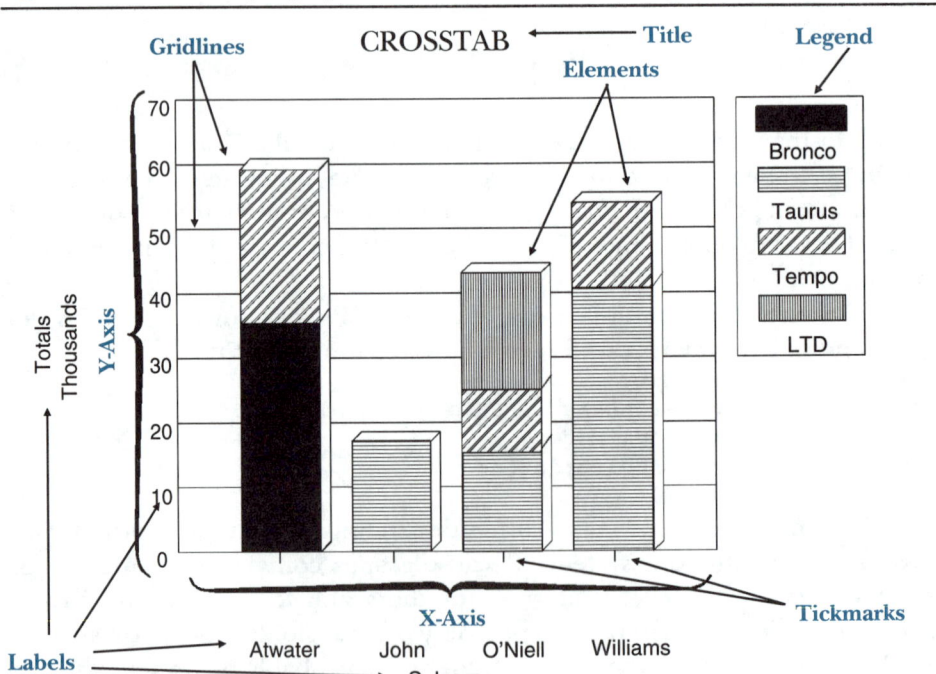

normally shown along this line. A variation on this rule is the rotated bar graph, where the axes are reversed, with the category axis vertical and the value axis horizontal. An exception to the rule is the X-Y graph, which shows values along both axes.

Tickmarks   Tickmarks are reference marks that designate the scale along the value axis and mark the categories of the category axis.

Labels   Labels describe the categories or values. By default, Paradox adds labels to the x-axis of a graph based on the contents of the leftmost column of the table. You can change these labels or omit them by using options described later in this chapter.

Gridlines   Gridlines are reference lines that extend across the entire area of the graph.

Elements   Elements are the bars, lines, markers, shaded areas, or pie wedges that represent the actual data in the graph. The form of the elements depends on the type of graph you choose. In a pie chart, the markers are wedges, or slices, of the pie. In a line graph, the markers are solid lines. (At some sharp angles, the lines in a line graph may appear jagged or broken; this is due to the limitations of the screen.) In a bar graph, the elements appear as bars. Each set of elements in a graph represents a field within the table. The field represented by the element is referred to as a *data series.* If a graph displays data from more than one data series, each data series will be represented by a different pattern or symbol. In Figure 8-4, for example, the January sales data make up one data series, and the February sales data comprise another data series. The data series are further differentiated by the pattern or shadings of the columns.

8

Legend   A legend defines the patterns (shadings) in the graph. The legend displays the pattern, followed by the label assigned to that pattern. Paradox uses the field names as default names within the legend, but this can also be changed, as described later in this chapter.

Title   The title normally appears at the top of the graph, although you can change the title position or omit the title entirely. If no title is assigned, Paradox uses the table name as a default for the title.

Figure 8-4.   *Stacked bar graph*

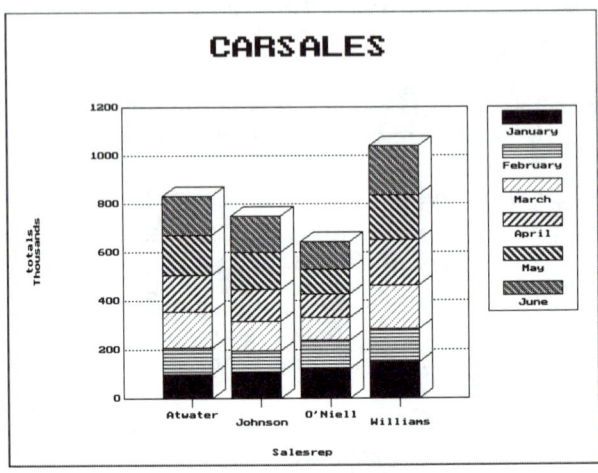

Hands-On Practice: Creating Different Graph Types

To try creating different graph types, you can quickly build a table of sales figures from four sales representatives. The table will contain data for the months of January through June.

To build the table, first use (ALT)-(F8) to clear all existing tables. Then choose Create from the main menu, and call the new table **CARSALES**. Give the following specifications for the fields:

Field Name	Field Type
SALESREP	A20
JANUARY	$
FEBRUARY	$
MARCH	$
APRIL	$
MAY	$
JUNE	$

Choose DO-IT! to save the new table, and use Modify/DataEntry to add the following records to the table. (Recall from Chapter 3 that when you enter values into currency fields of a table, **Paradox** will automatically add two decimal places, along with a comma to separate thousands; for instance, an entry of 95420 will appear on-screen as 95,420.00). When you're done, choose DO-IT! again to save the new records.

Salesrep: Atwater
January: 95240
February: 112350
March: 145410
April: 152800
May: 165400
June: 160390

Salesrep: Johnson
January: 103700
February: 89250
March: 121305
April: 134680
May: 152112
June: 148900

Salesrep: O'Niell
January: 121500
February: 114250
March: 97310
April: 96520
May: 101280
June: 112395

Salesrep: Williams
January: 146200
February: 138850
March: 179990
April: 187500
May: 184350
June: 201280

8

Once the table exists, place the cursor in the first currency column, which represents the sales figures for January. Choose Image/Graph/Modify from the main menu. For the graph type, enter **S** to choose Stacked Bar. (Unless your copy of Paradox has been modified, **S** will be the default choice.) Choose DO-IT!, then press the Graph key ((CTRL)-(F7)). You will see a stacked bar graph (Figure 8-4), with a different pattern representing each of the six months of sales figures. Because the Salesrep names are in the leftmost column of the table, Paradox automatically uses them as category names along the x-axis.

Press any key to exit the graph, and then press (F10) to activate the menu. Choose Image/Graph/Modify, and select Bar by entering **B** at the Customize Graph Type screen. Choose DO-IT! ((F2)), and then press Graph ((CTRL)-(F7)). The bar graph that appears should show a different bar for each of the sales months, as in Figure 8-5. (The 3-D bar graph provides a similar representation, but with a slight depth to the bars; you may want to try it to see the effect.)

Press any key to exit the graph, choose Image/Graph/Modify from the menu, and select Rotated Bar by entering **R** at the Customize Graph Type screen. Choose DO-IT!, and then press Graph ((CTRL)-(F7)). Notice that the graph now takes on a horizontal orientation, as shown in Figure 8-6.

Figure 8-5. *Multiple bar graph*

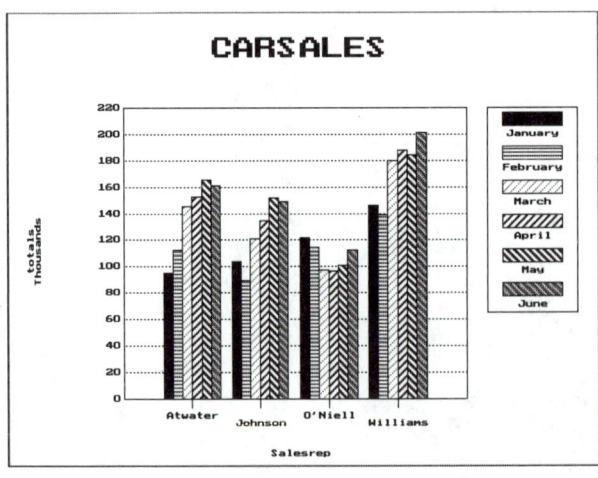

Figure 8-6. *Horizontal bar graph*

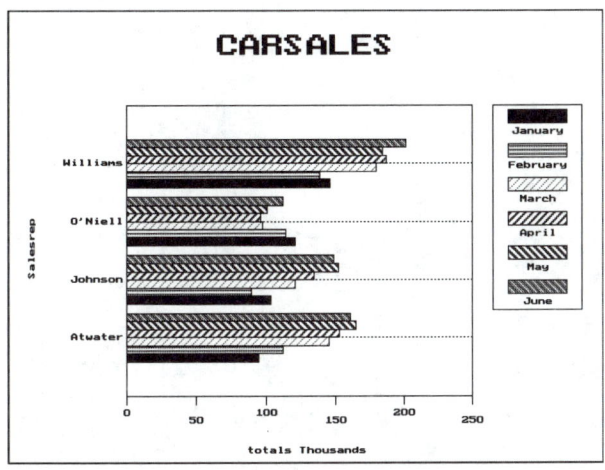

Press any key to exit the graph. Choose Image/Graph/Modify, and select Line by entering **L** at the Customize Graph Type screen. Choose DO-IT!, and then press Graph (CTRL-F7). The result shown in Figure 8-7 uses lines to represent the sales.

Try repeating the procedure outlined in the previous paragraph, displaying the table as a marker graph, a combined lines and markers graph, and an area graph. An area graph, illustrated in Figure 8-8, can be very useful when you want to show the combined effects of a group of numbers.

Using Series Override To Create Mixed Graphs

Paradox lets you present your data graphically in yet another manner—as mixed graphs, which combine one type of graph with another. As an example, you could highlight the sales for a particular month by showing those sales with a different indicator than for the other months. You can create mixed graphs by filling in the Series Override Graph Type options that appear when you choose Image/Graph/Modify.

8

Figure 8-7.   *Line graph*

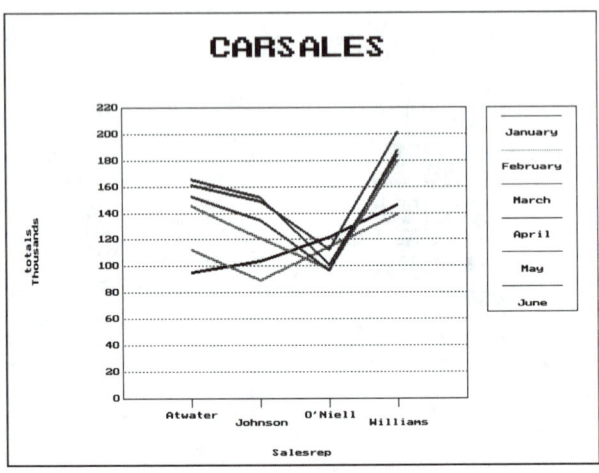

Figure 8-8.   *Area graph*

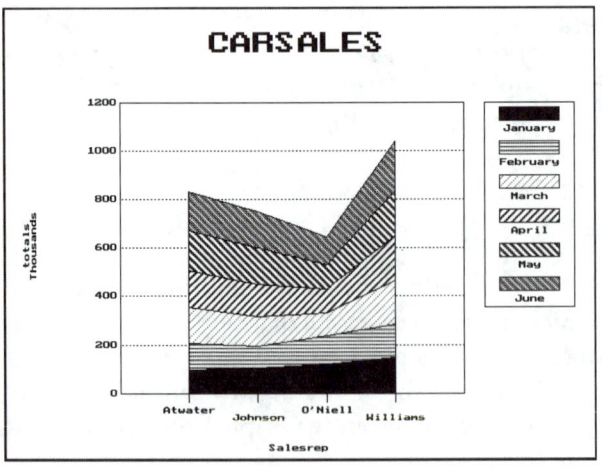

Whenever Image/Graph/Modify is selected from the menu, the Customize Graph Type screen that appears contains six entries at the bottom of the screen (Figure 8-9). These entries are for up to six possible series overrides; any entries you make here will tell Paradox to override the basic graph type (selected in the top half of the screen) for that particular data series. For example, if the chosen graph type was a bar graph and you wanted to represent the third numeric column with a line graph, you would change 3rd Series under Series Override Graph Type to Line.

To try this, with the cursor still in the first numeric field of the CARSALES table, press (F10) for the menu and choose Image/Graph/Modify. Select Bar as the graph type. Then press (ENTER) until the cursor moves down to 3rd Series in the Series Override Graph Type entry. Type **L** to change the third series to a line graph. Choose DO-IT!, and then press Graph ((CTRL)-(F7)). The results should resemble those shown in Figure 8-10; all months are represented with bars except for March, the third column or series, which is represented with a line.

When you create your graphs, you should examine your data to consider whether mixed graphs can be effectively used. Experimenting with the entries

Figure 8-9.   *Use the Series Override Graph Type entries to change how any data series is represented.*

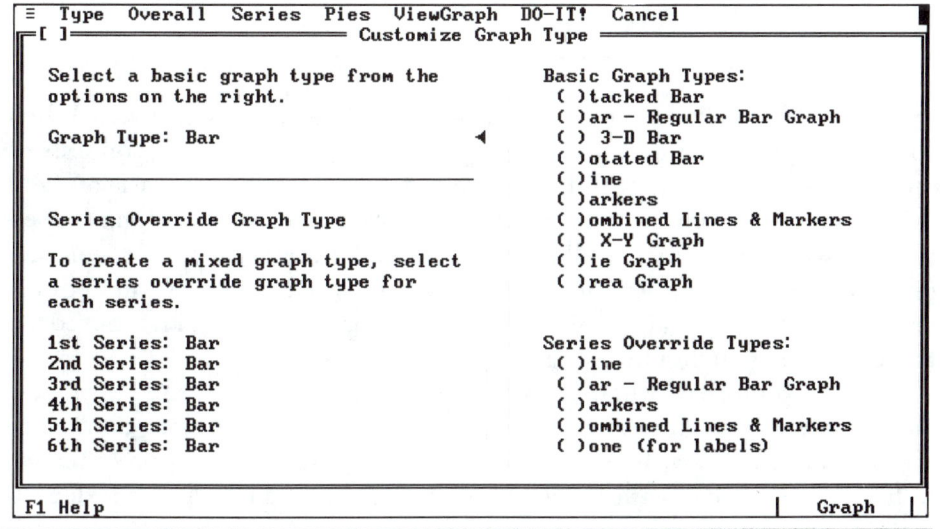

Figure 8-10.   *Mixed bar and line graph*

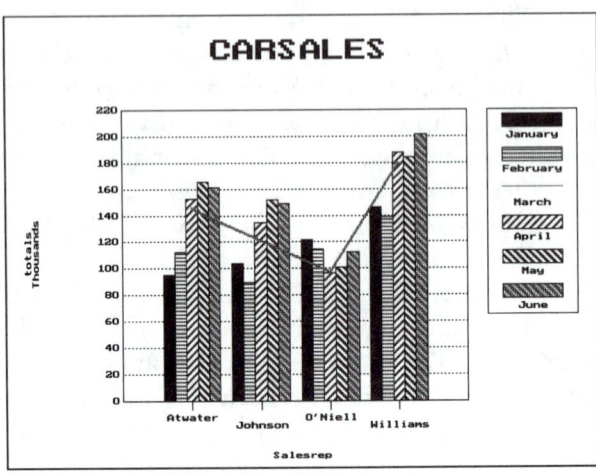

in the Series Override Graph Type box will provide you with some ideas as to how you can design your own mixed graphs.

Working with X-Y Graphs

X-Y graphs display sets of values along both the x-axis and the y-axis. When you select this type of graph as the graph type, Paradox uses the contents of the first numeric field within the table as the x-axis. The current field (wherever the cursor is located) and the next five fields in succession are used as the y-axis values. Since an X-Y graph shows the relationship between one set of values and another, the entire graph must be based on numeric or currency fields. Any alphanumeric fields containing text are ignored by Paradox when you plot an X-Y graph.

As an example of when an X-Y graph would prove useful, consider a department store manager's attempt to find out where advertising dollars are spent most effectively. Increases in advertising costs appear more effective with some items than with others. Storing sales figures for different departments in a table and creating an X-Y graph will clearly show the places in which increases in advertising are most effective. The table is shown here:

Ads spent	Men's clothes	Women's clothes	Shoes	House- wares	Hard- wares	Toys
5,000.00	57,800.00	62,650.00	23,700.00	48,000.00	32,600.00	19,700.00
6,000.00	63,800.00	71,350.00	27,850.00	52,220.00	33,100.00	18,950.00
7,000.00	66,750.00	88,570.00	31,780.00	54,200.00	33,520.00	19,400.00
8,000.00	70,450.00	102,300.00	34,900.00	53,950.00	34,200.00	19,550.00
9,000.00	70,600.00	105,560.00	35,250.00	55,100.00	33,980.00	19,700.00
10,000.00	71,700.00	106,600.00	36,120.00	54,980.00	34,150.00	19,650.00

The first column, Ads spent, indicates the amount of newspaper advertising purchased by the department store during a given week. The remaining columns show the sales figures for each department of the store during that week. If the cursor is placed in the second column of the table and the X-Y graph type is chosen using Image/Graph/Modify, the graph that appears when the Graph key is pressed resembles the one in Figure 8-11. On your monitor, the colors or shadings of the lines show that clothing and shoe sales

Figure 8-11. X-Y graph

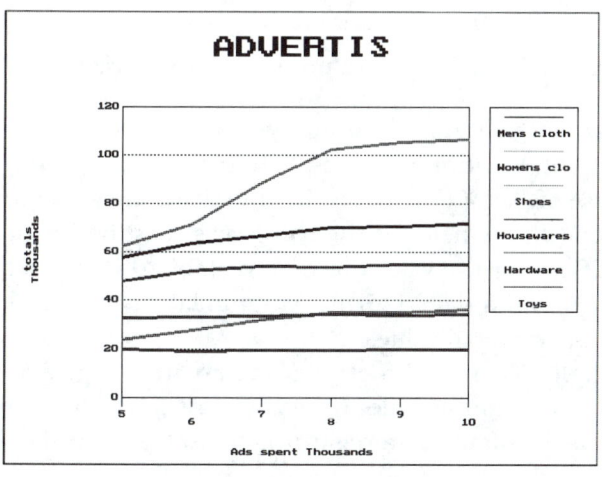

see noticeable increases when advertising costs increase, while the sales of hardware and toys remain relatively flat. Note that if the data in a table cannot be properly graphed as an X-Y graph (when the table has only one numeric field, for example), the graph will be blank.

Graphing Crosstabs

Paradox offers a CrossTab option on the Graph menu that allows you to create cross-tabulations of numeric data for graphing. A *cross-tabulation,* or *crosstab* for short, is another way of looking at your data. Crosstabs summarize the data in chosen categories. Using crosstabs, you can perform a spreadsheet-like numeric analysis on the data within a table.

Paradox lets you base a crosstab on one of four possible operations: sum, count, minimum, or maximum. If you choose Image/Graph/CrossTab from the main menu, Paradox presents these choices in a menu. Once you choose the desired type of cross-tabulation, Paradox asks you to identify the columns that contain the following three items:

- The data to be used as row labels in the crosstab (the data in this column will be used as x-axis labels when you generate a graph)
- The data to be used as column labels in the crosstab (the data in this column will define the series to be graphed)
- The crosstab values (the values to be summarized for the graph)

If you know that you want a summary type of crosstab, you can also use the (ALT)-(X) key combination in place of choosing Image/Graph/CrossTab. However, the use of (ALT)-(X) assumes that the fields are arranged in a certain order. With (ALT)-(X), the field for the row labels must be the one containing the cursor; the field for the values to be crosstabbed must be the rightmost field in the image; and the field for the column labels must be just to the left of the field for the crosstab values.

As an example of a use of a crosstab in creating a graph, consider the following table of automobile sales for a group of sales representatives. Each record in the table contains data regarding the sale of one automobile.

Salesrep	Model Name	Price	Date Sold
Atwater	Bronco	17,250.00	3/14/92
Johnson	Taurus	16,750.00	3/10/92
O'Niell	Tempo	9,085.00	3/15/92
Williams	Taurus	15,750.00	3/14/92
Atwater	Bronco	18,490.00	3/11/92
Atwater	Tempo	11,290.00	3/14/92
Atwater	Tempo	12,220.00	3/10/92
O'Niell	LTD	18,950.00	3/11/92
O'Niell	Taurus	15,990.00	3/12/92
Williams	Taurus	12,210.00	3/14/92
Williams	Tempo	13,212.00	3/11/92
Williams	Taurus	13,255.00	3/15/92

Perhaps what you need is a graph indicating the sales of each model for each sales representative. After you choose Image/Graph/CrossTab from the main menu and enter **1** to select Sum, Paradox asks for the cursor to be placed in the column containing the crosstab row labels. In this example, the Salesrep name is the desired column.

After the cursor has been placed and (ENTER) has been pressed, Paradox next asks for the cursor to be placed in the column containing the crosstab column labels. The cursor is moved to the Model name column in this example, and (ENTER) is pressed.

Paradox next asks that the cursor be moved to the column containing the values to be cross-tabulated. In this example, the cursor is placed in the Price column and (ENTER) is pressed. Paradox then creates the crosstab, as shown in Figure 8-12.

All that remains to create the graph is to press Graph ((CTRL)-(F7)). Since the cursor now resides in the crosstab table, the graph reflects the data contained in the crosstab. A stacked bar graph showing the crosstab is shown in Figure 8-13. Note that if the Date sold column did not exist in this example, the table could be crosstabbed with the (ALT)-(X) key combination.

Working with Pie Charts

Because of their design, pie charts are a different type of graph. Pie charts show the relationship between parts and a whole, so you can plot only a single

Figure 8-12.   *Tables with crosstabs*

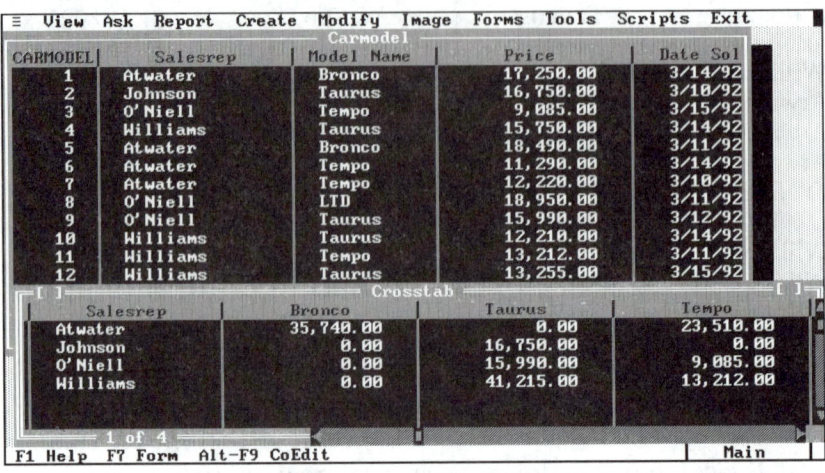

Figure 8-13.   *Stacked bar graph with crosstabs*

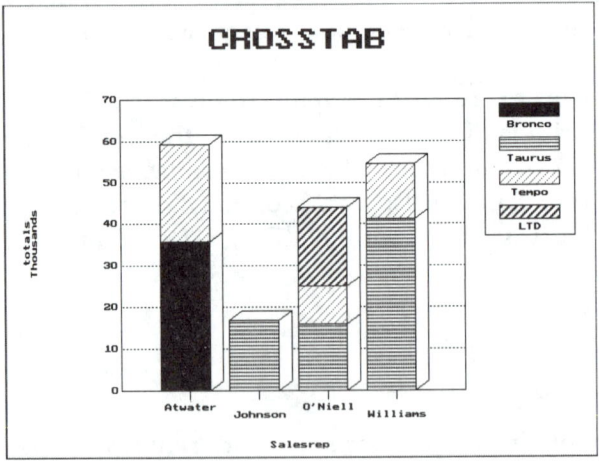

data series in a pie chart. When you select Pie as the graph type, Paradox uses the data in the column in which the cursor is located. Data in adjacent columns are ignored.

As an example, if you place the cursor in the March column of the CARSALES table, choose Image/Graph/Modify, select Pie as the graph type, press (F2), and then press (CTRL)-(F7), you will see a pie chart representing sales specifically for March. (The numbers may not be visible because the chart is not formatted for currency. You'll learn how to change the graph format settings in the next portion of this chapter.) Pie charts are generally used for illustrating any relationship between the component parts and the whole.

Changing the Graph Format Settings

Paradox also offers complete control over the colors, legends, markers, and similar graph elements with the Customize Graph Type menu. Get to the main menu and choose Image/Graph/Modify. When the Customize Graph Type screen appears, the Customize Graph Type menu appears at the top of the screen with the following options:

```
Type  Overall  Series  Pies  ViewGraph  DO-IT!  Cancel
```

The Type Option

Using the Type option is equivalent to filling in the desired type in the Graph Type option box of the same screen; when you are at the Customize Graph Type screen, you can select from among the ten valid types of Paradox graphs. Note that Paradox also displays the graph type as soon as you choose Image/Graph/Modify from the main menu.

The Overall Option

The Overall option provides a menu used to specify titles, colors, axis scale and format, gridlines, printer page layout, output device (printer or file),

8

and whether a waiting period should occur before the graph is displayed. If you select Overall, the following menu appears.

Choosing Titles displays a screen in which you can enter titles for a graph, as shown in Figure 8-14. (If you do not enter a title, Paradox defaults to the name of the table as the main title.) Note that when you choose Titles, options are also provided for changing font styles and font sizes. The possible font sizes are Small, Medium, Large, and Autosize; when you select Autosize, Paradox automatically selects a size for the fonts.

Choosing Colors reveals a menu with choices of Screen, Printer, and Copy. Use the Screen option to specify the colors to be used when the graph is displayed; use the Printer option to specify the colors to be used when the

Figure 8-14.   *Title Settings screen*

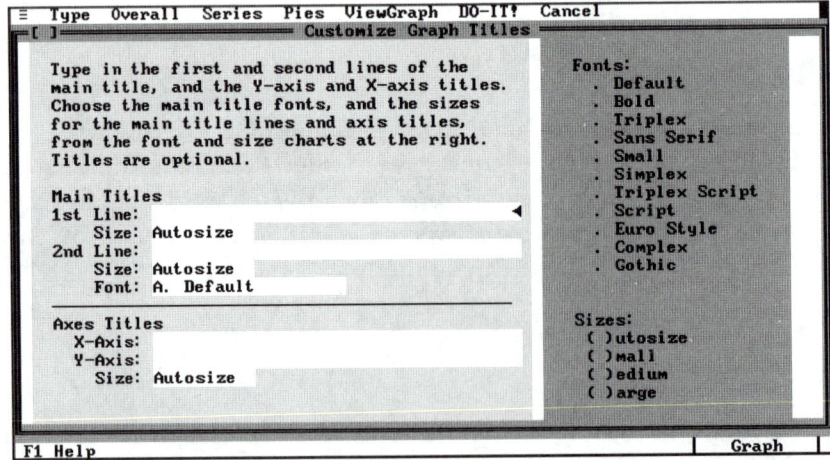

graph is printed. The Copy option lets you copy the screen colors to the printer settings, or copy the printer colors to the screen settings.

Selecting either the Screen option or the Printer option reveals the settings screen shown in Figure 8-15. Here, you can change the colors used for the background, frame, and grid of the graph; for the first and second title lines; for the x-axis and y-axis titles; and for each of the six possible data series. The colors on the screen that correspond to choices B through H can be chosen for the background color; any of the possible color choices on the screen can be used for the other elements of the graph. (Note that colors for pie charts are selected elsewhere, from the Pies option of the Customize Graph Type menu.)

Choosing Axes reveals the settings screen shown in Figure 8-16, which lets you change the scale used for the x-axis or the y-axis. In a graph, the *scale* is the incremental values (or the "range" of values) displayed along the axes. You can also change the format used to place the *tickmarks* (the short lines that cross the axis at regular intervals to denote a change in value). You can use Set Axis Scaling to choose Automatic or Manual. When you choose Automatic, Paradox starts the scale at zero and ends it at a value slightly above

Figure 8-15.   *Color Settings screen*

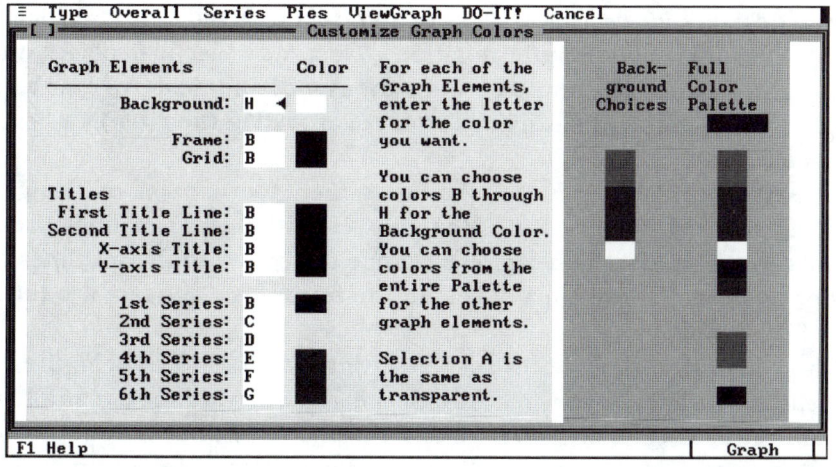

Figure 8-16.   *Axes Settings screen*

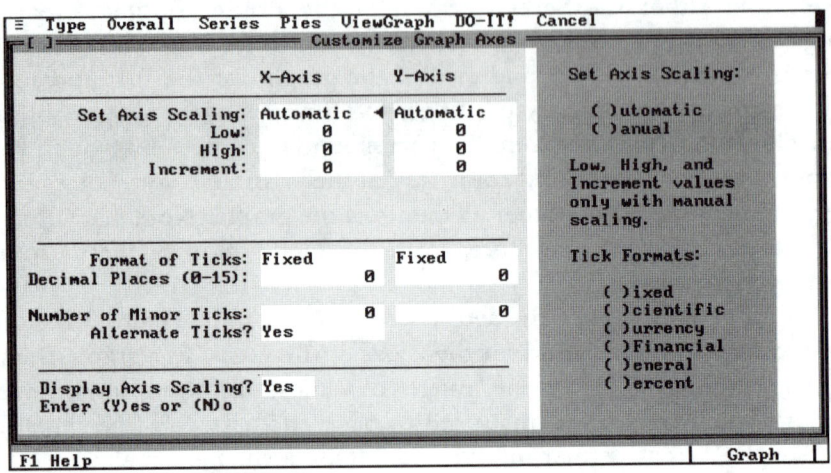

the highest value plotted on the graph. When you choose Manual, you can set the minimum and maximum values for the scale. For some applications, you may want to change the minimum and maximum scale, especially if all the values you are grouping fall within a small range. Tick Formats controls how the tickmark labels appear. These can be set to Fixed (with two decimal places), Scientific (as scientific notation), Currency (decimal places and a dollar sign), Financial (commas between thousands and negative numbers in parentheses), General (the original format displayed in the table), or Percent (as percentages).

Choosing Grids reveals the settings screen for control of the graph gridlines, shown in Figure 8-17. You can select the types of lines used as gridlines in the graphs. You can also change the colors of the gridlines with this option, and you can turn off or on the frame that appears around the edge of the graph.

Choosing PrinterLayout reveals the settings screen shown in Figure 8-18, with settings for left and top margins, the height and width of the graph, and orientation (landscape or portrait). Measurements with this option can be expressed in inches or in centimeters by changing the Measurement Units

Figure 8-17.   *Gridline Settings screen*

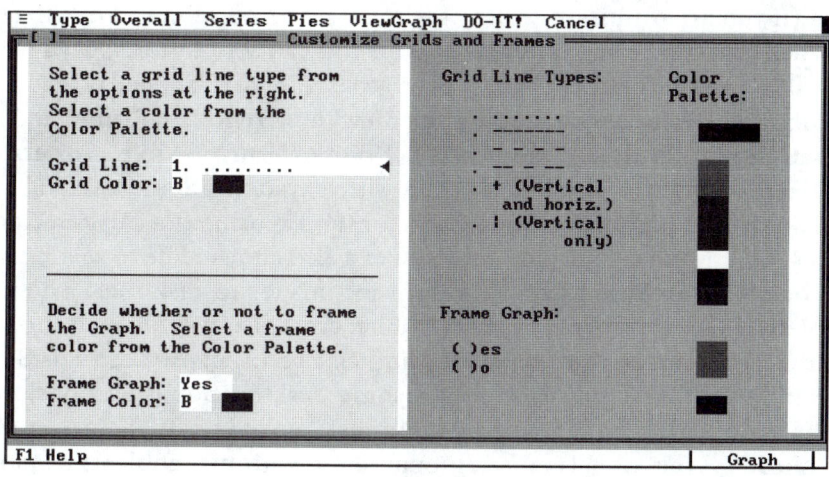

Figure 8-18.   *Printer Layout screen for graphs*

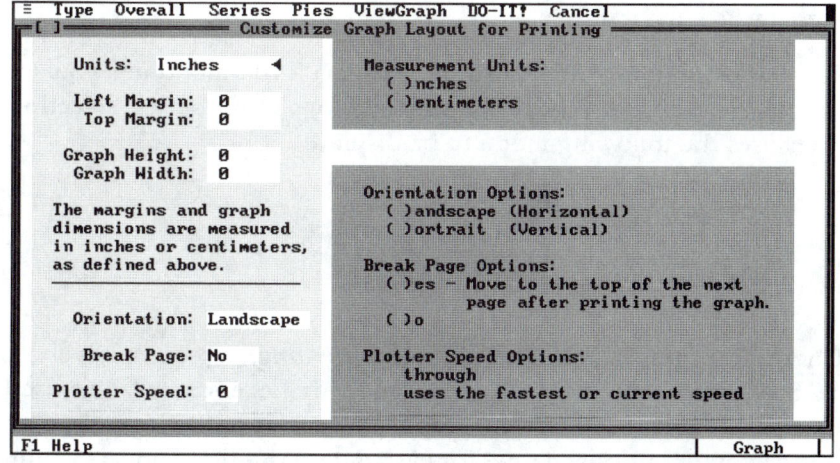

option while at this screen. You can also set the Break Page option to Yes, which tells Paradox to move to the top of the next page after printing the graph. (If you are printing a series of graphs, set this option to Yes when you want each graph on a separate page.) And you can set plotter speeds from a low of 0 (representing the slowest speed) to 9 (the fastest speed).

Choosing Device reveals another menu with two choices, Printer and File. You can use the Printer option to select one of four possible printers that have been previously installed for use with Paradox. (See the Installation section of your Paradox documentation for tips on using the Custom Configuration Program to install printers.) You can also choose File to select one of three possible file formats for storing print images to disk files. The three possible formats are Current Printer (which creates a disk file with the same print image format as your installed printer), EPS (Encapsulated PostScript, compatible with Borland's Sprint and some desktop publishing packages), and PIC (compatible with Lotus 1-2-3 graphs).

Choosing Wait reveals an additional menu with two choices: Keystroke and Duration. Selecting Keystroke tells Paradox to display each graph until any key is pressed. Selecting Duration lets you enter the length of time (in seconds) that Paradox will display the graph before clearing the screen. The Duration option can be useful for creating a slide show, where various graphs are displayed by a script you create.

The Series Option

The Series option of the Customize Graph Type menu lets you specify legends, labels, markers, fills, and colors used for a graph series. Selecting this option causes the following menu to be displayed.

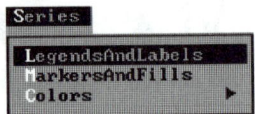

Choosing LegendsAndLabels reveals the settings screen that is shown in Figure 8-19. From this screen, you can select the legends or labels used for each series or data element of the graph. You can turn the legend on or off, and you can enter optional names for each data series that appears within the

Figure 8-19. *Legends and Labels screen*

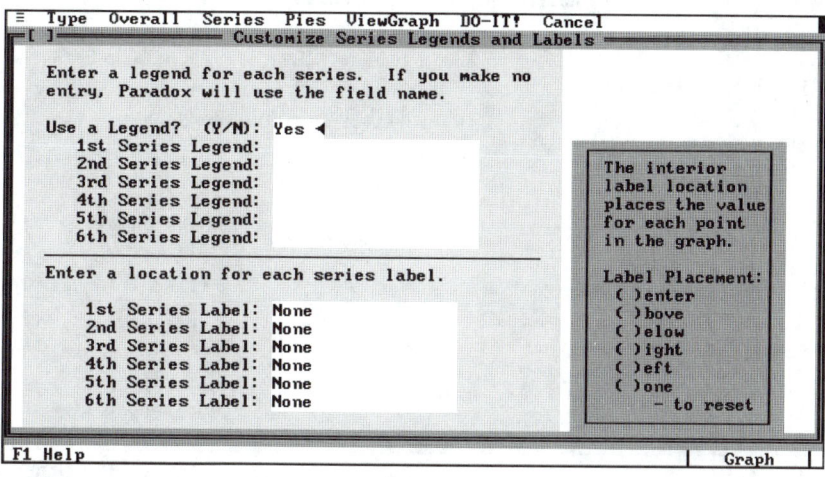

legend. (You'll often want to turn the legend off when graphing a single series of values.) If you enter no names for the legends, Paradox uses the field names as defaults for the legends. You are also provided with options for the placement of the labels; you can have labels centered (in the middle of the graph element), above the element, below the element, or to the right of the element. Finally, the None option of labels placement lets you tell Paradox to dispense with labels entirely.

Choosing MarkersAndFills reveals the settings screen shown in Figure 8-20. This screen provides the options needed to change the appearance of each of the data series in your graph. As the figure shows, you can choose from a wide variety of fill patterns and marker symbols. Marker symbols apply to marker graphs and combined graphs; fill patterns apply to area charts and bar charts. To change the patterns used in pie charts, you must use the Pies option of the Customize Graph Type menu.

Choosing Colors reveals another menu, with choices of Screen, Printer, and Copy. Use the Screen option to specify the colors used when the graph is displayed; use the Printer option to specify the colors used when the graph is printed. The Copy option lets you copy the screen colors to the printer

8

Figure 8-20.   *Fills and Markers screen*

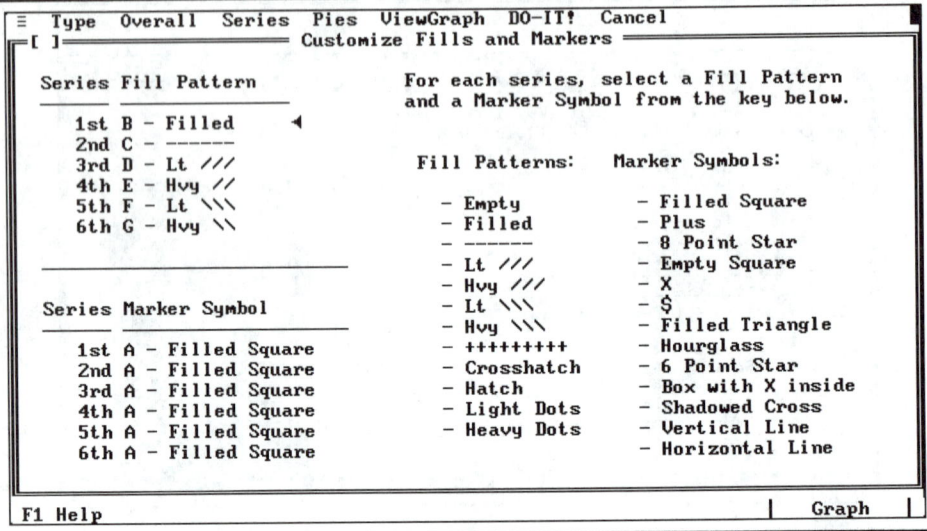

settings, or copy the printer colors to the screen settings. Selecting either the Screen option or the Printer option reveals the settings screen shown previously in Figure 8-15. In operation, this screen is identical to the Overall/Colors option described earlier.

The Pies Option

The Pies option pertains only to pie charts. When you select Pies, the settings screen shown in Figure 8-21 appears. From this screen you can explode pie slices (pull them out from other slices), choose fill patterns and colors for the slices, and choose a format for the labels. In the Label Format entry box, you can enter V (for value), P (for percent), C (for currency), or N (for no labels).

You can choose colors and fill patterns for up to nine slices of a pie chart. If a pie chart contains more than nine slices, the color and fill choices are repeated in order. In the Fill Pattern entry boxes, you can enter the letter that corresponds to your choice of fill type, as shown in the help screen on the

Figure 8-21. **Pie Settings screen**

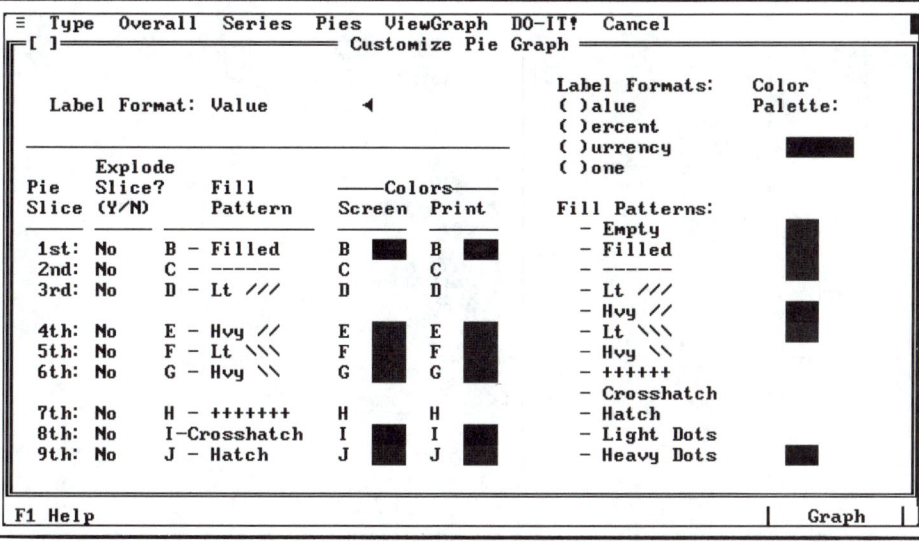

right. Note that under the Colors entries, you can choose colors for both screen display and for printing. Enter Yes or No in the Explode Slice? boxes to tell Paradox whether a particular pie slice should be exploded.

As an example of the use of the options that apply to pie charts, consider the problem of displaying the dollar values in the pie chart earlier. If the Customize Graph Type menu is not still displayed on your screen, choose Image/Graph/Modify from the main menu. Choose Pies from the menu. The next screen to appear, shown in Figure 8-21, offers options for customizing pie charts.

With the cursor in the Label Format entry box, enter C to select Currency. Press (ENTER) once to move to the 1st Pie Slice entry, and enter Y to change the Explode Pie Slice option from No to Yes. You may also want to experiment with changing some of the colors and fill patterns to suit your tastes; the help screen at the right shows the characters used to select the desired fill patterns or slice colors. When you are done, choose DO-IT! followed by Graph ((CTRL)-(F7)) to see the results. Figure 8-22 shows an example of a pie chart with an exploded slice.

8

Figure 8-22.    *Pie chart with one slice exploded*

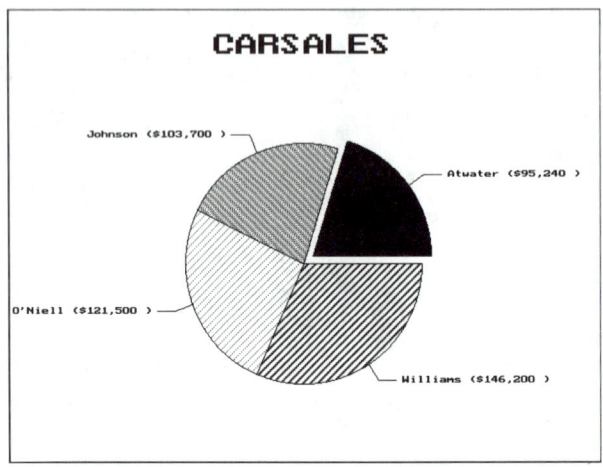

The ViewGraph Option

The ViewGraph option presents a menu that lets you display the graph on the screen, print the graph, or store a print image in a disk file. Note that all the ViewGraph options are also available from the main menu by choosing Image/Graph/ViewGraph. The options work in the same manner as described earlier in this text. Finally, the Help, DO-IT!, and Cancel options of the Customize Graph Type menu perform the same tasks as they do elsewhere in Paradox.

Experimenting with all of the graph options in Paradox will be time well spent. If you've examined the options described in the latter half of this chapter, it is probably evident that a detailed discussion of Paradox graphics could fill a book of its own. Try some of these options in combination with your own tables to become proficient at creating Paradox graphs.

Quick Summary

To create a graph   Place the cursor in the numeric field that is to be graphed, and press Graph ((CTRL)-(F7)).

To print a graph   Place the cursor in the numeric field that is to be graphed, and choose Image/Graph/ViewGraph from the main menu. Make sure your printer is ready, and then select Printer from the next menu to print the graph.

To change the graph type   Choose Image/Graph/Modify from the main menu. When the Customize Graph Type screen appears, make the desired changes to the graph type or to the series types. Choose DO-IT! to store the changes; then use Graph ((CTRL)-(F7)) to display the graph.

8

9

Using the Relational Powers of Paradox

As you learned in Chapter 1, Paradox is a relational database manager. Its relational capabilities allow you to define relationships between two or more tables. This chapter will describe a number of ways you can take advantage of the relational capabilities of Paradox. By using example elements within Query Forms, you can link multiple tables by means of a common field that exists in each table.

The hands-on practice examples in this chapter will make extensive use of the ABCSTAFF and HOURS tables that were created in Chapters 3 and 4. Therefore, if you did not create those tables as outlined earlier, you should do so now before proceeding.

Consider the ABCSTAFF and HOURS tables. The HOURS table contains records of the hours worked by each employee, and the client for whom (or assignment at which) the employee performed the work. However, the HOURS table does not contain the names of the employees. The ABCSTAFF table, on the other hand, contains the full names of each employee, but no record of the hours worked.

The payroll coordinator at ABC Temporaries now needs a report in the format outlined in Figure 9-1. This report will be used by the payroll department to handle check requests when the payroll is processed. A report with this kind of information is a relational report because it draws its information from more than one table. The ABCSTAFF table contains the Last Name and First Name fields. The HOURS table contains the Assignment and Hours worked fields. In order to produce a report based on these fields, you must design a query that will retrieve data from both tables and link them into a single table. That table can then be used to produce the desired report.

The key to retrieving data from a relational database is to link records on some sort of matching, or common, field. In this context, the term *common field* is used to indicate a field that is common to both tables. Consider an example of two tables containing records of computer parts and of purchasers who have ordered certain parts. These tables (called PARTS and ORDERS) are examples of tables that benefit from the use of relational commands. The PARTS table, which is shown by the table structure listed here, contains part numbers, descriptions, and the costs of each part.

Figure 9-1.   *Proposed relational report*

Last Name	First Name	Assignment	Hours worked
Westman	Andrea	National Oil Co.	37
Smith	William	Smith Builders	40
Jones	Judi	City Revenue Dept.	35
Abernathy	Frank	City Revenue Dept.	35
∿∿∿∿∿	∿∿∿	∿∿∿ ∿∿∿ ∿∿∿	∿
∿∿∿ ∿∿∿∿	∿∿∿∿∿	∿∿∿∿∿ ∿∿∿ ∿∿∿∿	∿
∿∿∿∿∿ ∿∿∿	∿∿∿∿	∿∿∿∿∿ ∿∿∿ ∿∿∿∿	∿
∿∿∿∿ ∿∿∿∿∿∿	∿∿∿∿∿ ∿∿∿	∿∿ ∿∿∿∿∿ ∿∿ ∿∿∿∿∿	∿

Name of Field	Type
PARTNO	numeric
DESCRIPT	alphanumeric
COST	dollar

The ORDERS table, on the other hand, contains the names and customer numbers of the customers who order computer parts, as well as the part numbers and quantities of the parts that have been ordered.

Name of Field	Type
CUSTNO	numeric
CUSTNAME	alphanumeric
PARTNO	numeric
QUANTITY	numeric

Using two separate tables is a better solution than using a single table in this case, because a single table would require unneeded duplication of information. If you had a single table with all of the fields present in these two tables, each time one customer ordered a part number that had been previously ordered by another customer, you would have to duplicate the part description and part cost. To avoid such duplication, you can use two tables and link the tables together based on the contents of the common part number field, PARTNO, as illustrated in Figure 9-2. With all relational databases, you can establish a link between common fields to match a particular record in one table with a corresponding record in another table.

Take ABC Temporaries' problem of the payroll again. If you needed to know how many hours Andrea Westman worked, you could find out by looking at the data from the two tables, as shown in Figure 9-3. You would first look at the listing from the ABCSTAFF table and find the social security number for Ms. Westman, which is 121-33-9876. You would then refer to the listing of the HOURS table and look for all of the records with a matching social security number. The Hours worked fields from these records could be used to calculate the salary for Ms. Westman. The process of matching social security numbers between the tables could be repeated for every employee in the company.

An important point to realize is that without a field that contains matching data in each of the tables, such a relational link is not possible. This is one

Figure 9-2.   *Concept of relational database*

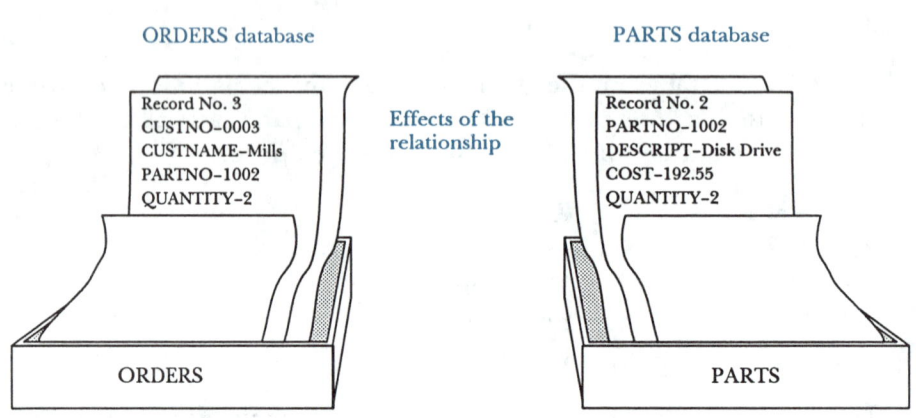

Figure 9-3.   *HOURS and ABCSTAFF tables*

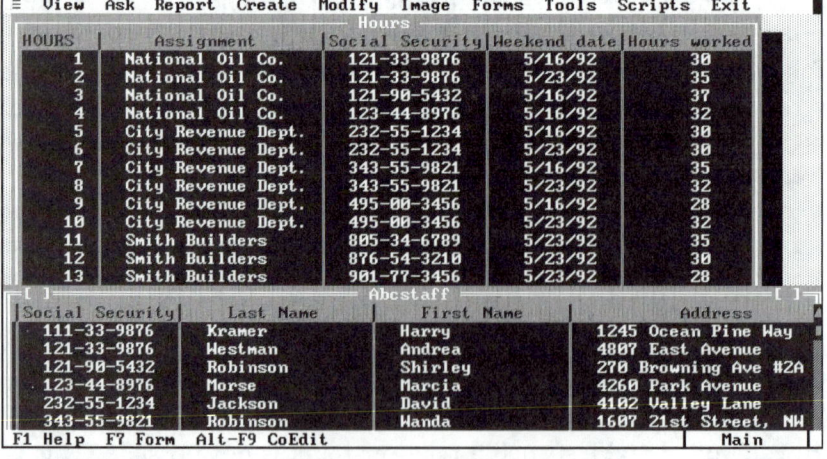

reason that the design of complex, relational databases is not a process to be taken lightly. If an important field is not included in a table, you may find it difficult or impossible to access multiple tables in the desired manner. As Figure 9-3 illustrates, the Social Security field makes it possible to access data simultaneously from both tables.

To link multiple tables in Paradox, you use a Query Form in a manner similar to that for nonrelational queries, which you performed in Chapter 6. The one notable difference is that you use example elements in the common fields of the Query Forms. These example elements tell Paradox which fields are used to provide the links between tables.

Querying from Two Tables

To query from two tables, use Clear All ((ALT)-(F8)) if necessary to clear the desktop. From the main menu, choose Ask, enter the name for the first table, and choose the fields for inclusion in the answer in the normal manner, by using (F6) to place checkmarks in those fields. You can also set any selection criteria that the records must meet by entering these criteria in the fields of the Query Form, as described in Chapter 6.

When the first Query Form contains the desired checkmarks and criteria, choose Ask from the main menu and enter the name for the second table. Paradox places a Query Form for the second table below the first. You can again proceed to choose the fields to be included in the answer and enter any desired selection criteria. Figure 9-4 shows a workspace containing two Query Forms from the ABCSTAFF and HOURS tables, with selected fields of Last Name and First Name from the ABCSTAFF table and Weekend date and Hours worked from the HOURS table.

Finally, enter the example element that is used to link the tables that have the common field. To enter an example element, place the cursor in the common field, press Example ((F5)), and enter an example element.

An example element is not some arbitrary value that you must always use. Paradox is only concerned about what the examples represent—that is, the same value in two separate tables. As you can see in Figure 9-5, the "identical" in both Social Security fields could have been entered as "12345", or as the word "nonsense." You can enter any set of letters or numbers (but no spaces

9

Figure 9-4.   *Fields selected for querying two tables*

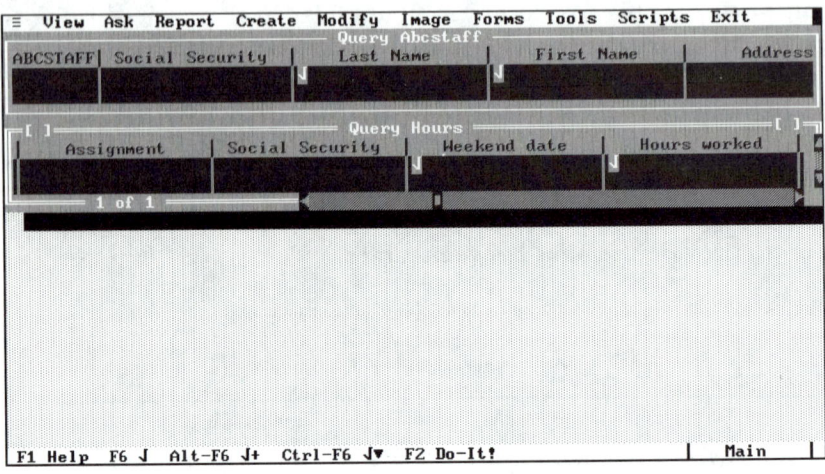

Figure 9-5.   *The example element that links two tables*

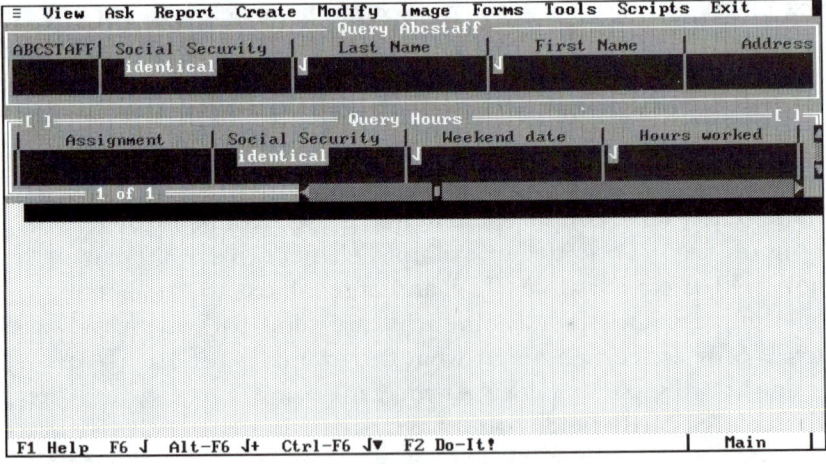

or punctuation marks) as an example element; what is important is that the example elements entered into the fields of the two tables are the same.

The example element appears highlighted as you enter it, which visually identifies it as an example element and not just criteria for the field. Next, move the cursor to the common field in the second table, press Example ((F5)) again, and fill in the same example element used in the common field of the first table. Figure 9-5 shows the queries with the same example element entered into the Social Security fields of both tables.

Performing the Query

Once you have entered the example elements, chosen the desired fields, and supplied any record selection criteria, you are ready to perform the query. Choose DO-IT!, and an answer based on the query will appear, as shown in Figure 9-6.

Figure 9-6. *Answer to relational query*

```
≡  View   Ask   Report   Create   Modify   Image   Forms   Tools   Scripts   Exit
                                    Query Abcstaff
 ABCSTAFF │ Social Security  │    Last Name    │    First Name    │    Address
          │ identical        │                 │                 │
                                     Query Hours
 │   Assignment   │ Social Security │  Weekend date  │  Hours worked │
 │                │ identical       │                │               │
 [ ]                                Answer                         [ ]
 ANSWER  │   Last Name  │  First Name  │ Weekend date │ Hours worked
     1   │ Abernathy    │ Sandra       │  5/16/92     │     28
     2   │ Abernathy    │ Sandra       │  5/23/92     │     32
     3   │ Hart         │ Edward       │  5/23/92     │     30
     4   │ Jackson      │ David        │  5/16/92     │     30
     5   │ Jackson      │ David        │  5/23/92     │     30
     6   │ Jones        │ Judi         │  5/16/92     │     35
     7   │ Jones        │ Judi         │  5/23/92     │     33
     8   │ Mitchell     │ Mary Jo      │  5/23/92     │     28
     9   │ Morse        │ Marcia       │  5/16/92     │     32
    10   │ Morse        │ William      │  5/23/92     │     35
    11   │ Robinson     │ Shirley      │  5/16/92     │     37
    12   │ Robinson     │ Wanda        │  5/16/92     │     35
    13   │ Robinson     │ Wanda        │  5/23/92     │     32
    14   │ Westman      │ Andrea       │  5/16/92     │     30
    15   │ Westman      │ Andrea       │  5/23/92     │     35
 F1 Help   F7 Form   Alt-F9 CoEdit                              Main
```

One important point to remember is that the order you follow in supplying the data does not matter. You could first fill in the example elements, then pick the fields to be included in the answer, and then provide any record selection criteria. Or you could perform all of the necessary steps for one table, proceed to perform all of the steps for the second table, and then choose DO-IT! to process the query. Regardless of the order, once you process the query, the answer appears. (Note that the order of the fields in the query will determine the order that fields appear in the answer.) If you need a printed report at this point, the easiest way to get one would be to press (ALT)-(F7) for an instant report.

Hands-On Practice: Querying from Two Tables

To get a listing containing the employee's last name, assignment, "week ending" date, and the number of hours worked, using both tables linked through the common (Social Security) field, try the following steps. Press Clear All ((ALT)-(F8)) to clear the desktop. From the main menu, choose Ask and enter **ABCSTAFF** as the table name. Use (F6) to mark the Social Security and Last Name fields for inclusion in the answer. Move the cursor to the Social Security field and press (F5) to start an example element. Enter

ABCD

as the example element. From the menu, choose Ask, and this time enter **HOURS** as the name of the table. When the Query Form for the second table appears, use the (F6) key to place checkmarks in the Assignment, Weekend date, and Hours worked fields. Then move the cursor to the Social Security field, press (F5) to start an example element, and enter

ABCD

as the example element. Finally, choose DO-IT!. The result of the relational query should appear on the screen, as shown in Figure 9-7.

Selection criteria can be used in either table to limit the records available in a relational query. As an example, perhaps you only want to see records for National Oil so that you can bill that particular client for services rendered

Figure 9-7. *Results of first practice query*

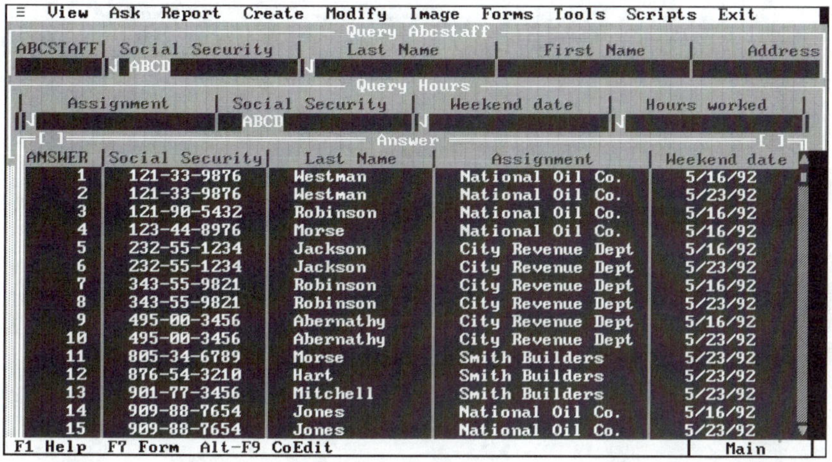

```
≡  View  Ask  Report  Create  Modify  Image  Forms  Tools  Scripts  Exit
                          Query Abcstaff
ABCSTAFF│ Social Security  │    Last Name    │   First  Name    │     Address
        │  ABCD           │                 │                  │
                          Query Hours
│   Assignment   │  Social Security │   Weekend date  │  Hours worked  │
│                │  ABCD           │                 │                │
┌─[ ]─                         Answer                        ─[ ]─┐
│ ANSWER │Social Security│  Last Name  │   Assignment     │ Weekend date  ▲
│      1 │ 121-33-9876   │ Westman     │ National Oil Co. │ 5/16/92  ▓
│      2 │ 121-33-9876   │ Westman     │ National Oil Co. │ 5/23/92
│      3 │ 121-90-5432   │ Robinson    │ National Oil Co. │ 5/16/92
│      4 │ 123-44-8976   │ Morse       │ National Oil Co. │ 5/16/92
│      5 │ 232-55-1234   │ Jackson     │ City Revenue Dept│ 5/16/92
│      6 │ 232-55-1234   │ Jackson     │ City Revenue Dept│ 5/23/92
│      7 │ 343-55-9821   │ Robinson    │ City Revenue Dept│ 5/16/92
│      8 │ 343-55-9821   │ Robinson    │ City Revenue Dept│ 5/23/92
│      9 │ 495-00-3456   │ Abernathy   │ City Revenue Dept│ 5/16/92
│     10 │ 495-00-3456   │ Abernathy   │ City Revenue Dept│ 5/23/92
│     11 │ 805-34-6789   │ Morse       │ Smith Builders   │ 5/23/92
│     12 │ 876-54-3210   │ Hart        │ Smith Builders   │ 5/23/92
│     13 │ 901-77-3456   │ Mitchell    │ Smith Builders   │ 5/23/92
│     14 │ 909-88-7654   │ Jones       │ National Oil Co. │ 5/16/92
│     15 │ 909-88-7654   │ Jones       │ National Oil Co. │ 5/23/92  ▼
F1 Help  F7 Form  Alt-F9 CoEdit                              │   Main
```

by the staff of ABC Temporaries. Press (F3) once to move the cursor from the ANSWER table back up to the Query Form for the HOURS table. Then move the cursor to the Assignment field, and enter

```
National Oil Co.
```

as the selection criteria. Choose DO-IT!. The old ANSWER table will be rewritten, and the ANSWER table (Figure 9-8) will display only those employees who put in time for National Oil.

Paradox allows you to add a selection criterion in the same query field as the example element; just use a comma to separate the example element and the selection criterion. As an example, perhaps you wish to retrieve records using the fields you have already checked for inclusion in the answer, but you only want to see records for Ms. Andrea Westman. Press (F3) to move the cursor back up to the Assignment field of the second Query Form, and use (CTRL)-(BACKSPACE) to delete the selection criterion from the field.

Move the cursor to the Social Security field, add a comma after the example element, and then enter

```
121-33-9876
```

Figure 9-8.   *Results of practice query for National Oil Co.*

```
☰  View  Ask  Report  Create  Modify  Image  Forms  Tools  Scripts  Exit
                              Query Abcstaff
ABCSTAFF│ Social Security │    Last Name    │   First Name   │     Address
         ↓ ABCD                            ↓
                              Query Hours
       Assignment        │ Social Security │ Weekend date  │ Hours worked
    ↓ National Oil Co.       ABCD              ↓               ↓
  [ ]                          Answer                               [ ]
  │Social Security│  Last Name  │    Assignment    │ Weekend date │ Hours w▲
    121-33-9876      Westman      National Oil Co.     5/16/92        30
    121-33-9876      Westman      National Oil Co.     5/23/92        35
    121-90-5432      Robinson     National Oil Co.     5/16/92        37
    123-44-8976      Morse        National Oil Co.     5/16/92        32
    909-88-7654      Jones        National Oil Co.     5/16/92        35
    909-88-7654      Jones        National Oil Co.     5/23/92        33



      ═ 1 of 6 ═            ◄                    ►

 F1 Help  F7 Form  Alt-F9 CoEdit                          │  Main
```

Press (F2) to process the query. The results will show the records for Ms. Westman, as shown in Figure 9-9.

If you often use the same query to link multiple tables, save the Query Form with Scripts/QuerySave. See Chapter 10 for more details on scripts.

Using the Inclusion Operator

Paradox offers an *inclusion operator* (the exclamation mark), which can be used to force Paradox to include all records from one or more tables in the answer, whether they have matching links or not. For instance, consider the query illustrated in Figure 9-6. In the ANSWER table, you do not see any records for Mr. Kramer or for Ms. Willston, two late entries to the ABCSTAFF table. The reason no records appear for these individuals is that there are no entries for them in the HOURS tables. Since Paradox cannot find any matching records in the HOURS table to link by example to the ABCSTAFF table, it does not show any entries for these individuals in the ANSWER.

Figure 9-9. *Relational query for a single name*

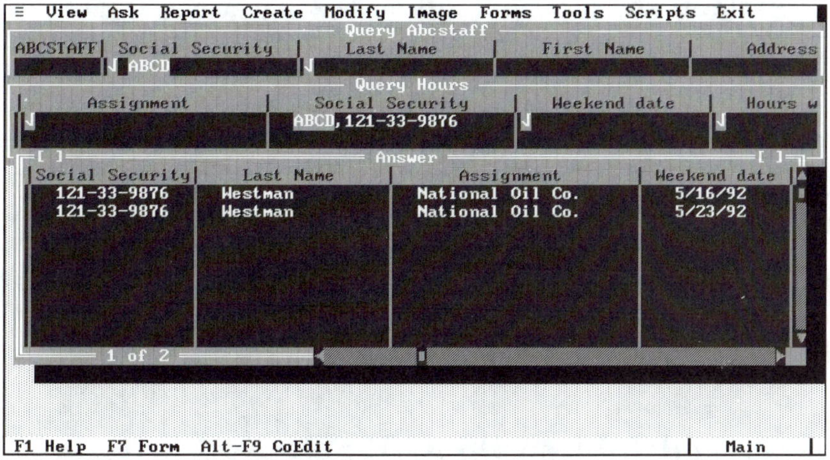

But what if you want to see all records in the ABCSTAFF table included in the query result, regardless of whether there are matching records or not? This is where the use of the inclusion operator comes in. By adding an inclusion operator (the exclamation mark) in a particular field of a Query Form, you tell Paradox to include all entries in that field (of the original table) within the ANSWER table. So, if you place an exclamation mark in the Social Security field of the Abcstaff Query Form, Paradox will include all Social Security field entries in the Answer table. To try using the inclusion operator, perform the following steps:

1. Press (F3) to move the cursor back up to the Social Security field of the Hours Query Form. Use (BACKSPACE) to delete the comma and the social security number for Ms. Westman; leave the example element intact.

2. Press (F3) again to move the cursor up to the Abcstaff Query Form. With the cursor in the Social Security column beside the example element, type ! .

9

3. Press (F2) to process the query. The results, shown in Figure 9-10, show Social Security numbers for Mr. Kramer and Ms. Willston, but there are no matching entries in the Assignment and Week ending fields.

The inclusion operator can be quite useful, as it often causes information to appear that would otherwise be overlooked. It provides an excellent way of highlighting possible data-entry errors. For example, suppose a record entered into the HOURS table contained a nonexistent social security number. Using an inclusion operator in the Social Security field of the Hours Query Form would cause that record to appear in the ANSWER table; the lack of a matching last name would make it obvious that an error had occurred.

Using Linked Tables with AND Selection Criteria

Paradox does not limit the way you use selection criteria: you have the same flexibility as you do in queries performed on a single table. Perhaps you

Figure 9-10.   *Results of inclusive query*

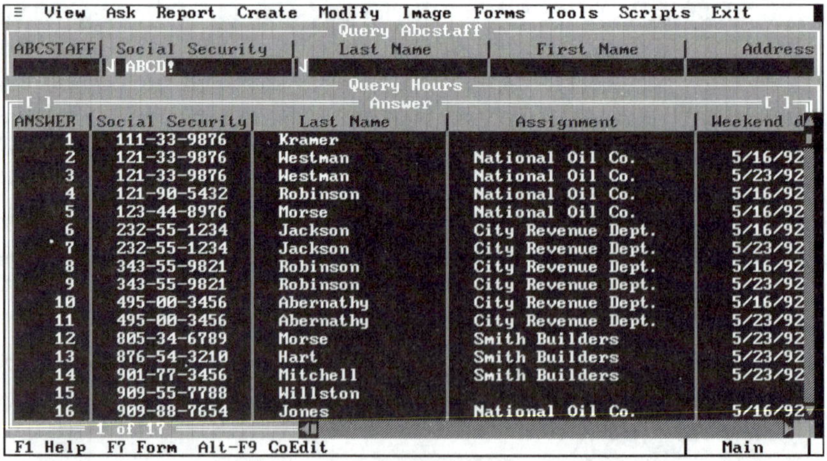

need a listing of employees who worked for the City Revenue Department during the week ending 5/23/92.

Press (F3) twice, to move back to the Abcstaff Query Form. Press the (BACKSPACE) key once, to delete the inclusion operator (but leave the example element intact). Then, press (F4) once to move to the HOURS Query Form. Move the cursor into the Weekend date field, and enter:

5/23/92

Next, move the cursor to the Assignment field and enter

City Revenue Dept.

Press (F2) to process the query. The results, shown in Figure 9-11, show all employees who worked for the City Revenue Department *and* worked on the "week ending" date of 5/23/92.

The Selection conditions do not need to be in the same table. For example, you might need a listing of all employees assigned to National Oil who are earning more than $10.00 an hour. The fields you are using to limit the records, Salary and Assignment, are in two different tables.

Figure 9-11.   *Query of linked tables using the AND condition*

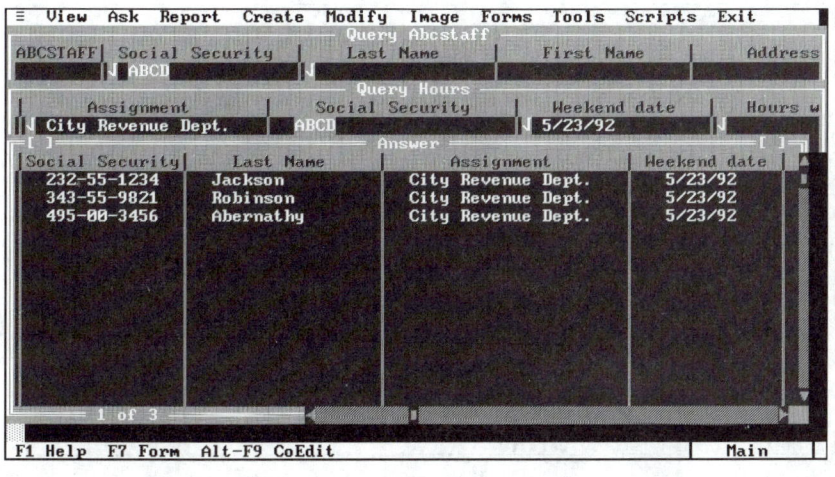

Press (F3) twice to get back to the Query Form for the ABCSTAFF table. In the Salary field of this form, enter

`>10`

Then move to the second Query Form with (F4). In the Assignment field, use (CTRL)-(BACKSPACE) to delete the "City Revenue Dept." entry. Enter

`National Oil Co.`

as the condition. Move to the Weekend date field and use (CTRL)-(BACKSPACE) to delete the prior entry in this field. Finally, press (F2) to process the query. The result, as shown in Figure 9-12, shows that four records meet the two conditions.

Using Linked Tables with OR Selection Criteria

You can enter additional criteria in the additional rows of the Query Forms to specify OR conditions, in which records are selected when one *or*

Figure 9-12.   *Query of linked tables with selection conditions in both tables*

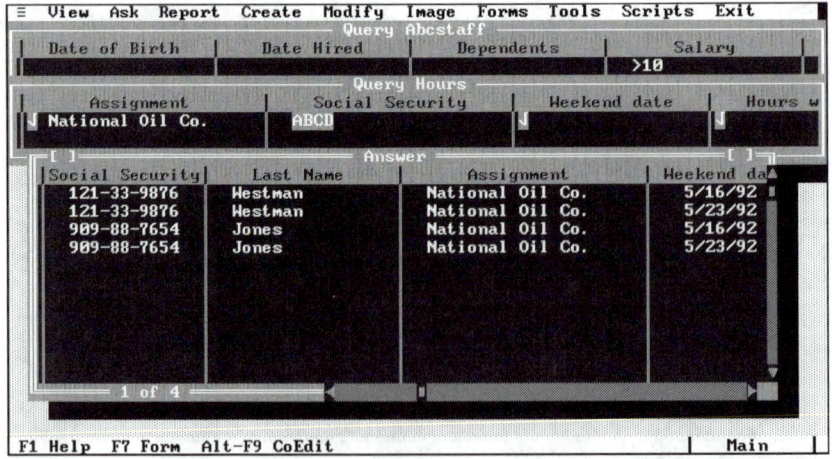

another condition is met. As an example, perhaps you want to see all of the employees who are assigned to National Oil or to Smith Builders.

First press (ALT)-(F8) to clear the desktop. You will need to use something a little different for queries of multiple tables using OR conditions. You must enter example elements that will link either of the conditions on each line of the Query Form.

From the main menu, choose Ask, and enter **ABCSTAFF** for the table name. Place checkmarks in the Social Security and Last Name fields with (F6). Move to the Social Security field, press (F5) to begin the example, and enter

```
FIRST
```

as the example element. Move the cursor down one line, and press (F6) to add a checkmark. Then press (F5) to begin another example. Enter

```
SECOND
```

as the name for the second example. Move the cursor over to the Last Name field, and press (F6) to add a checkmark in the field on the second row of the Query Form.

From the main menu, choose Ask, and enter **HOURS** as the name for the second table to be queried. Move to the Assignment field, enter a checkmark with (F6), and enter

```
National Oil Co.
```

as the selection criterion. Place the cursor in the Social Security field and press (F5) to begin the example element. Then enter

```
FIRST
```

as the matching example element for linking the tables. To complete this line of the query, move the cursor to the Weekend date and Hours worked fields, and press (F6) while in those fields to include them in the ANSWER table.

Move the cursor down one line and back to the Assignment field. Add a checkmark with (F6), and then enter

```
City Revenue Dept.
```

9

as the selection criterion for this row of the query. Move the cursor over to the Social Security field. Press (F5) to begin the example element, and enter

SECOND

as the matching example element for linking the tables. Finally, move the cursor to the Weekend date and Hours worked fields, and press (F6) while in those fields to include them in the ANSWER table. At this point, your query should resemble the example illustrated in Figure 9-13.

Before you process this query, take a moment to think about how it is structured. The first line of the Query Form for HOURS, which will select records that contain National Oil Co. in the Assignment field, is linked to the ABCSTAFF table through the example element called FIRST. The second line of the Query Form for HOURS, which selects records with City Revenue Dept. in the Assignment field, is linked to the ABCSTAFF table through the example element called SECOND. In the case of an OR condition like this one, Paradox is performing two separate queries at the same time: one to link records having National Oil Co. in a field, and the other to link records having City Revenue Dept. in the field. To see the results, press (F2), and the ANSWER table will appear, as shown in Figure 9-14.

Note that you can also use the OR operator in a field, to specify OR conditions. For example, you could enter National Oil Co. OR Smith Builders on a single line of a query in the Assignment field.

Figure 9-13.   *Query of linked tables using OR logic*

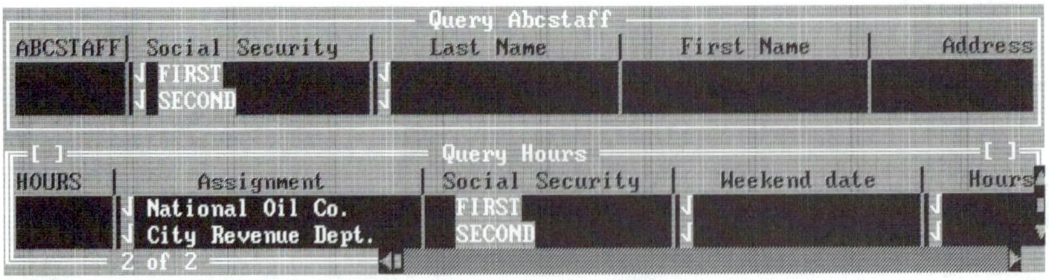

Figure 9-14.   *Answer from the OR query based on two tables*

```
 ≡  View  Ask  Report  Create  Modify  Image  Forms  Tools  Scripts  Exit
                            Query Abcstaff
 ABCSTAFF│ Social Security  │    Last Name    │   First Name   │   Address
         │√ FIRST           │                 │                │
         │√ SECOND          │                 │                │
                               Query Hours
 HOURS │       Assignment      │ Social Security │  Weekend date  │  Hours
       │√ National Oil Co.     │  FIRST          │                │
       │√ City Revenue Dept.   │  SECOND         │                │
  [ ]                            Answer                          [ ]
  │Social Security│   Last Name    │     Assignment     │ Weekend date │
  │  121-33-9876  │ Westman        │ National Oil Co.   │   5/16/92    │
  │  121-33-9876  │ Westman        │ National Oil Co.   │   5/23/92    │
  │  121-90-5432  │ Robinson       │ National Oil Co.   │   5/16/92    │
  │  123-44-8976  │ Morse          │ National Oil Co.   │   5/16/92    │
  │  232-55-1234  │ Jackson        │ City Revenue Dept. │   5/16/92    │
  │  232-55-1234  │ Jackson        │ City Revenue Dept. │   5/23/92    │
  │  343-55-9821  │ Robinson       │ City Revenue Dept. │   5/16/92    │
  │  343-55-9821  │ Robinson       │ City Revenue Dept. │   5/23/92    │
  │  495-00-3456  │ Abernathy      │ City Revenue Dept. │   5/16/92    │
  │  495-00-3456  │ Abernathy      │ City Revenue Dept. │   5/23/92    │
  │  909-88-7654  │ Jones          │ National Oil Co.   │   5/16/92    │
  │  909-88-7654  │ Jones          │ National Oil Co.   │   5/23/92    │
 F1 Help   F7 Form   Alt-F9 CoEdit                            │   Main
```

Linking More than Two Tables

In theory, you can link as many tables as you need (up to the number of open files that your operating system can handle at one time) to provide you with the answers you need while you are using Paradox. (In practice, more than six linked tables may cause an out-of-memory condition.) You can see an example of linked tables by creating one more table, CLIENTS, which will contain the addresses of the clients served by ABC Temporaries.

Use (ALT)-(F8) to clear the desktop. From the main menu, choose Create. Call the new table CLIENTS. Define the following fields:

Field Name	Field Type
Client name	A25
Address	A25
City	A15
State	A2
ZIP Code	A5

9

After defining the structure, save the table by pressing (F2). Then choose Modify/DataEntry from the main menu, enter **CLIENTS** for the table name, and add the three records shown here to the new table:

```
Client name: National Oil Co.
Address: 1201 Germantown Road
City: Fairfax
State: VA
ZIP: 22025

Client name: City Revenue Dept.
Address: 2000 Town Hall Square
City: Alexandria
State: VA
ZIP: 22305

Client name: Smith Builders
Address: 2370 Rockville Pike
City: Rockville
State: MD
ZIP: 20852
```

Choose DO-IT! to save the edits, and then clear the workspace with (ALT)-(F8).

Perhaps you need a listing of assignments, the city of each assignment, the name of each employee, and "week ending" dates so that you can track the validity of expense reports handed in by your staff for car mileage. The fields you need are in three different tables, so you will need to fill in three Query Forms to get the answer you need.

From the main menu, choose Ask and enter **ABCSTAFF** for the table name. When the Query Form appears, move the cursor to the Social Security field and press (F5) to begin an example. Enter **1234** as the example. Then move the cursor to the Last Name field and place a checkmark with (F6) to include this field in the answer.

From the main menu, choose Ask, and enter **HOURS** for the table name. When the Query Form appears, move the cursor to the Social Security field and press (F5) to begin an example. Enter **1234** as the example. Then move the cursor to the Weekend date field and press (F6) to include this field in the answer.

Move the cursor to the Assignment field, and press (F5) to begin the example element that will provide the link to the third table. Enter **5678** as the example. Then from the menu choose Ask, and enter **CLIENTS** as the desired table to display another Query Form. Move the cursor to the Client name field, press (F5) to begin the example, and enter **5678** as the example element that tells Paradox to match the data found in the Assignment field of the HOURS table.

To complete the query, first press (F6) so that a checkmark will tell Paradox to include the name of the client in the answer. Then move to the City field and press (F6) again to add a checkmark in this field. Press (F2) to process the query. The result, shown in Figure 9-15, includes the desired fields selected from the ABCSTAFF, HOURS, and CLIENTS tables.

One additional point can be noted from this example. The example element used to link the second and third tables was placed in two fields that had different field names. (The HOURS table stored the name of the client in a field called Assignment, while the CLIENTS table stored the name of the clients in a field called Client name.) Unlike some relational database managers, Paradox does not require you to name the fields with identical field names before you can draw links between different tables, nor must the fields have

Figure 9-15. *Results of the query based on three tables*

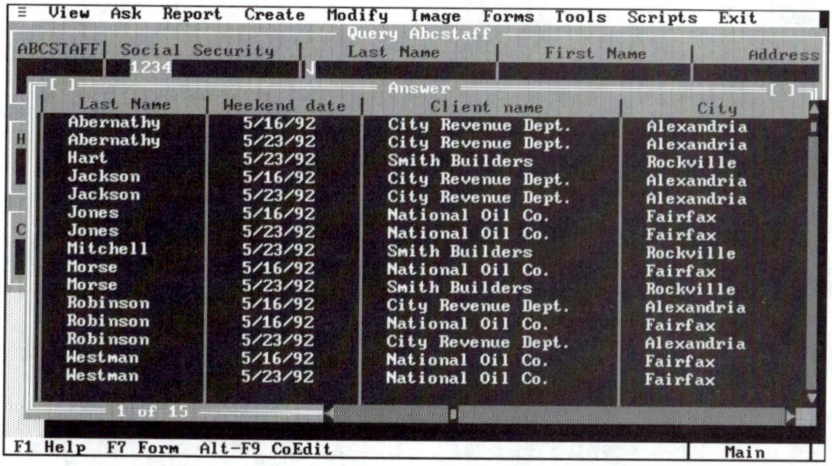

Last Name	Weekend date	Client name	City
Abernathy	5/16/92	City Revenue Dept.	Alexandria
Abernathy	5/23/92	City Revenue Dept.	Alexandria
Hart	5/23/92	Smith Builders	Rockville
Jackson	5/16/92	City Revenue Dept.	Alexandria
Jackson	5/23/92	City Revenue Dept.	Alexandria
Jones	5/16/92	National Oil Co.	Fairfax
Jones	5/23/92	National Oil Co.	Fairfax
Mitchell	5/23/92	Smith Builders	Rockville
Morse	5/16/92	National Oil Co.	Fairfax
Morse	5/23/92	Smith Builders	Rockville
Robinson	5/16/92	City Revenue Dept.	Alexandria
Robinson	5/16/92	National Oil Co.	Fairfax
Robinson	5/23/92	City Revenue Dept.	Alexandria
Westman	5/16/92	National Oil Co.	Fairfax
Westman	5/23/92	National Oil Co.	Fairfax

identical widths. The only requirement is that the *data* contained in the linked fields can be matched. It would make no sense, for example, to try to draw a link between two fields containing dissimilar data, such as a phone-number field and a date-of-birth field.

Creating and Using Multitable Forms

Paradox lets you create multitable forms, which let you view or edit data from more than one table at a time. Multitable forms can be very useful with sales or billing applications, where you often want to display a number of records (such as those for purchases) that are linked to a single record (such as that of a customer). This section will show how a multitable form can be used for the personnel needs of ABC Temporaries. The form in the following example will use the ABCSTAFF table to show data for any employee of ABC Temporaries and will use the HOURS table to show all hours worked for that employee.

You can use multitable forms any time you want to display data from two or more tables at the same time. While a relational link between the tables is common, such a link is *not* a requirement. You can have multitable forms with linked tables, or you can have multitable forms with unlinked tables. When the tables are unlinked, each table on the form is accessed independently of the others; think of it as moving between tables, but in a form view instead of the usual table view. On the other hand, if the tables are linked, then the records on one table will depend on the records in another. In our example, the records that appear in the hours portion of the form will be linked to a particular employee.

In sales applications, multitable forms are very useful for displaying orders associated with a given customer.

Note

Whenever you design a multitable form, you are actually placing several forms (one for each table) on the screen. One form must be the *master form*; the remaining forms are *embedded forms*. When tables are linked, the master form controls what records appear in the embedded forms; in effect, the master form "owns" any embedded forms. When tables are unlinked, it does not matter which table is used as the basis of the master form. In these cases, you may want to use the table that logically should be at the top of the form as the master form. In our example, each employee will own a series of one or more records for hours worked during a week. Therefore, the form based on the employees' table (ABCSTAFF) becomes the master form, and the form based on the hours worked (HOURS) becomes the embedded form.

Keep in mind that if the tables are linked, both tables must have a matching key field. If the relationship is a "one-to-many" relationship (as in this example, with one employee having many records of hours worked), then the detail table (in this case, HOURS) must have a secondary key. To meet this requirement in the example, you will later use Modify/Restructure to add keys to the Social Security and Weekend date fields of the HOURS table.

The basic steps involved in creating a multitable form are to first decide which table is to be the basis of the master form, and then design and save the forms to be used as embedded forms by using the usual methods of form design covered in Chapter 5. Finally, you begin designing the form for the master table, and choose Multi/Tables from the Forms menu. You use this menu option to place the embedded form or forms onto the master form and to specify the link (if any) between your master form and the embedded forms.

Note the following limitations regarding multitable forms:

- A master form can be a multipage form, but it cannot be a multi-record form.

- An embedded form can be a multirecord form, but it cannot be a multipage form.

- Nesting of embedded forms is not permitted; that is, you cannot embed a form within another embedded form.

- A maximum of nine embedded tables is permitted.

Hands-On Practice: Creating a Multitable Form

You've already determined that the ABCSTAFF table is to be the basis of the master form for the form you wish to create for ABC Temporaries. The next step is to design and save the form that will serve as the embedded form. The managers at ABC Temporaries have suggested a form with a listing of the "week ending" date, hours worked, and assignment name for each employee. The conceptual design of such a form is shown in Figure 9-16.

Clear the desktop by pressing (ALT)-(F8). From the main menu, choose Modify/Restructure. For the table name, enter **HOURS**. When the table structure appears, move the cursor to the first field, Assignment. Because key fields must be at the top of a table, you'll move this field's location in the structure, by deleting it from its present location and then adding it back at the bottom of the table.

With the cursor in the Assignment field, press (DEL) to delete the field. Then, move the cursor down three rows to a new, blank row. Enter **Assignment** as the field name, press (ENTER), and then enter **A20** for the field type and width. Next, move the cursor back up to the first row of the structure, and add an asterisk after the A11 field designation beside the Social Security field. Also, add an asterisk after the D field designation beside the Weekend

Figure 9-16.   *Proposed multitable form*

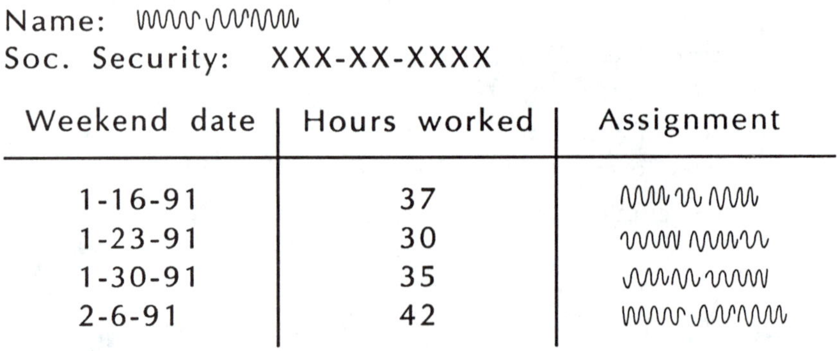

Name: ⌇⌇⌇⌇ ⌇⌇⌇⌇⌇⌇
Soc. Security: XXX-XX-XXXX

Weekend date	Hours worked	Assignment
1-16-91	37	⌇⌇⌇ ⌇⌇ ⌇⌇⌇
1-23-91	30	⌇⌇⌇ ⌇⌇⌇⌇
1-30-91	35	⌇⌇⌇⌇ ⌇⌇⌇
2-6-91	42	⌇⌇⌇ ⌇⌇⌇⌇⌇

date field. Then choose DO-IT! to save the changes. (Adding the asterisks will make these fields into key fields so they can be properly linked within the multitable form.)

If any tables are on the desktop, clear them with (ALT)-(F8). From the menu, choose Forms/Design. Enter **HOURS** as the name for the table. Select 1 from the menu of form names, and enter **Multirecord of Hours Worked** as a form description.

With the cursor at row 1, column 1, choose Multi/Records from the menu to place the multirecord region on the new form. From the next menu, choose Define. Next, press (ENTER) to begin the selection at the upper-left corner.

Move the cursor 50 spaces to the right, and press (ENTER) to define the region. Paradox will now ask you to add (or delete) the repeating rows for the additional records. Press (↓) nine times, and then press (ENTER). (This will allow for a total of ten hourly records visible in the form at a time.)

Move the cursor back to row 1, column 1. Choose Field/Place/Regular from the menu. Select Weekend date from the list of fields, and press (ENTER) twice to place the field.

Move the cursor two spaces to the right. Choose Field/Place/Regular from the menu. Select Hours worked from the list of fields and press (ENTER); then press (←) ten times to narrow the field's width, and press (ENTER) again to place the field.

Move the cursor two spaces to the right. Choose Field/Place/Regular from the menu. Select Assignment from the list of fields, and press (ENTER) twice to place the field.

This is all you need for the hourly portion of the multitable form. You can add headings later, after embedding this form onto the master form. First, however, you must save this form. Choose DO-IT! to save the form and return to the menu.

The final step in the process is to design the master form and to use the Multi/Tables option to place the embedded form and to specify the link. From the menu, choose Forms/Design, and enter **ABCSTAFF** as the name of the table. Select 3 as the name for the new form, and enter **Multitable with Hours** as a description.

Move the cursor to row 5, column 10, and enter

Name :

9

as a label. Add one space, and choose Field/Place/Regular from the menu. Select First Name from the list of available fields, and press (ENTER) twice to place the field.

Press the (SPACEBAR) once, choose Field/Place/Regular from the menu. Select Last Name from the list of available fields, and press (ENTER) twice to place the field.

Move the cursor to row 7, column 10, and enter

```
Soc. Security:
```

as a label. Add one space, and choose Field/Place/Regular from the menu. Select Social Security from the list of available fields, and press (ENTER) twice to place the field. This is all the data that will be needed for the master form, so you are ready to embed the other form and establish the link between the two tables.

Choose Multi from the menu. (You use this option whenever you want to design or remove a multitable form.) The next menu to appear offers two choices: Tables and Records. In this case, Tables is the proper choice because it is used to place, remove, or move a form from another table. (The other choice, Records, is used with multirecord forms as described in Chapter 5.)

Choose Tables from the menu. When you do so, the following menu appears.

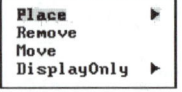

The Place option is used to embed another form. The Remove option removes an existing embedded form. The Move option lets you move an existing embedded form to another location, and the DisplayOnly option lets you specify whether a form will be used only for display or for editing. Since you wish to place the hourly form, choose Place. The next menu to appear offers the choice of Linked or Unlinked. Since the records in the HOURS table will be linked to each respective employee when displayed in this form, choose Linked.

Paradox will now ask you for the name of the table to link. Enter HOURS as the table name. The list of forms available for the HOURS table will next appear; choose 1, which corresponds to the multirecord form you created earlier. Next, this menu appears.

Choose Social Security from the menu, which tells Paradox to match records in the HOURS table with a record in the ABCSTAFF table based on matching Social Security numbers. A shaded box, representing the multirecord form for HOURS you created earlier, will appear on the screen.

Use the arrow keys to roughly center the shaded box in the lower portion of the screen, and then press (ENTER) to place the box. Move the cursor until it is immediately above the upper-left corner of the shaded box. Enter **Weekend Date** and then press (→) four times. Enter **Hours worked** and then press (→) ten times. Finally, enter **Assignment**

With the hourly form embedded on the master form and the labels added, the form is complete. Choose DO-IT! to save the form and return to the menu. Choose View, and enter **ABCSTAFF** as the table to view. The form can be chosen like any other form with the Image/PickForm option. Once you are viewing the table, choose Image/PickForm from the menu. From the menu of available forms, choose number 3, Multitable with Hours. You should see a record displayed in the multitable form, as shown in Figure 9-17. (Note that if you see a record for Mr. Kramer, you won't see any records for the weeks worked, because there are no records in the HOURS table for this employee.) Try using the (PGUP) and (PGDN) keys to move around the ABCSTAFF table. Note that as you move from employee to employee, the appropriate hourly records appear in the lower portion of the form. Also, try using the (F3) and (F4) keys to move between the master and embedded portions of the form.

Referential Integrity: A Note and a Warning

When you link tables while designing a multitable form, Paradox automatically establishes certain rules regarding *referential integrity*. This means

Figure 9-17.   *Record displayed in the multitable form*

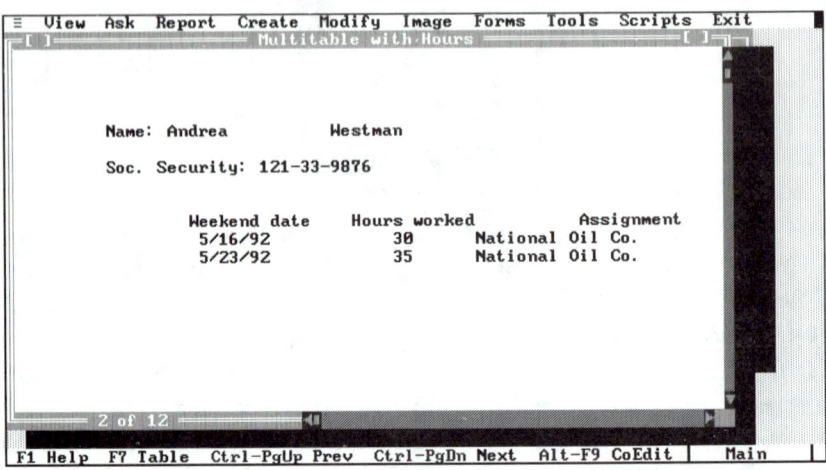

that Paradox protects you by imposing certain rules on what kinds of edits and deletions can be made when you use the form. For example, Paradox would not let you change a social security number or delete an employee in the ABCSTAFF table as long as there were records for that social security number in the HOURS table. To make such an edit or a deletion would break the logical link between the tables. You could, on the other hand, delete all the records for a given social security number in the HOURS table, and then delete the employee from the ABCSTAFF table.

Paradox provides the benefit of referential integrity only as long as you are adding or editing through the multitable form that establishes the link. Once this link has been established, Paradox won't let you edit the tables on an individual basis in that editing session. But once you leave the current editing session, you are unprotected if you decide not to use the form. If you design and use linked multitable forms, it is a wise idea to avoid any editing of the tables on an individual basis. Sticking with the forms will maintain the referential integrity provided by Paradox.

A Note About Reports

Generating reports from a relational database is no different than generating reports from a nonrelational database. You design your reports in the same manner as with other tables, as outlined in Chapter 7. One way is to simply base the report on the relational table (which is the one created as an ANSWER table as the result of your queries). Remember that if you are going to design a custom report to be used with an ANSWER table and you want to keep the report, save the ANSWER table under a different name. To do so, choose Tools/Rename/Table/Answer from the main menu, and give the table a new name. The associated custom reports that you create for use along with the ANSWER table will be saved under the new name. Another method that gets around the limitation of using the ANSWER table is described in more detail shortly.

Of course, as your primary tables change with the addition and editing of data, you will find that each time you need an up-to-date report of a relational nature, you must perform a query to get the most recent data from the related tables into an ANSWER table to produce the report. If you are using custom reports, this creates a new problem: each time you generate an answer and rename that ANSWER table to a new name, it overwrites the old name if you use the same name. In the process, your custom report also gets overwritten, since it was associated with the old ANSWER table that you named earlier.

One way around this is to copy the structure from the ANSWER table to a "dummy" table and create the custom report while using the dummy table. You can then empty the dummy table of any records, transfer the results of your most recent queries into the dummy table, and then generate the desired custom report.

To create a dummy table based on the structure of the ANSWER table, go to the main menu and choose Tools/Copy/Table. When prompted for the name of the table to copy, enter **ANSWER.** Paradox will ask for a new table; enter any name you desire for the new dummy table. Once you supply the name, Paradox will copy the ANSWER table into the new table under your assigned name. If you have not yet created the desired report, you can design it while you are using the dummy table and save it (by pressing (F2)

9

when you are finished with the Report Specification) along with the dummy table.

Next, empty all records from the dummy table. To do this, choose Tools/More/Empty from the main menu, and enter the name of your dummy table. Confirm the action by selecting OK from the next menu that appears, and the dummy table will be emptied of records.

Whenever you need to generate the report based on the relational data, structure your queries to provide the answer you want; then, from the main menu, choose Tools/More/Add to add records to the dummy table. When Paradox prompts you for the source table name, use ANSWER for the target table, use the name of your dummy table. Paradox will copy the records to the dummy table, and you can generate the report. Remember to empty all records from the dummy table after each use with Tools/More/Empty from the main menu, or you may accidentally generate a report with more records in the dummy table than you actually want.

Another way to create multitable reports is to use Field/Lookup when designing the report and to create calculated fields within the report's design, which will access the fields in the other tables. This method has the advantage of not using the ANSWER table, so you need not worry about copying the records in the ANSWER table to another file. The basic steps in this method are as follows.

1. Begin designing the report, using the table that is the primary source of your data. (For example, if you wanted a listing of hours worked, you would design the report around the HOURS table.) The table with the most key fields is normally the master table.

2. From the menu, choose Field/Lookup. This option lets you set, remove, or change links to the records in another table.

3. From the next menu, choose Link. Then enter the name of the table to be linked.

4. From the next menu, select the field by name that will provide the match.

5. Use Field/Place/Calculated to place the calculated fields that will provide the data from the other tables. Use a format like

        [ABCSTAFF->LAST NAME]

with the calculated field enclosed in brackets and the field name preceded by the other table name, a hyphen, and a greater-than symbol. This tells Paradox where to find the matching data.

Follow the normal methods of report design (detailed in Chapter 7 and Chapter 12) to place the fields where desired. When you generate the report, Paradox will automatically establish the link between tables and produce the desired data.

Hands-On Practice: Creating a Multitable Report

To try the method just described, choose Report/Design from the menu. This example will provide a report of hours worked that includes "week ending" dates and the last name of the employee. For the table name, enter **HOURS**. Then select 2 as a report name (or some other number if you have alre ly used 2 as a name). For a description, enter **Multitable sample**. For the type of report, choose Tabular.

The Report Specification will appear, with fields automatically inserted for the fields in the HOURS table. From the Design menu, choose Field/Erase. Move the cursor to the Social Security field and press (ENTER) to remove the field.

Choose Field/Lookup/Link. Enter **ABCSTAFF** as the table to be linked to this report. You will now see this menu:

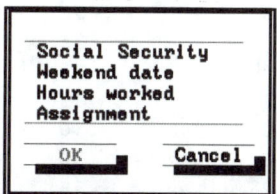

The Social Security field should be highlighted. This is the field that will provide the link, so press (ENTER) to select it.

Now that you've linked this report to the other table, you can add calculated fields that refer to the other table. With the cursor still at the start of the old location of the Social Security field, choose Field/Place/Calculated from the menu. For the expression, enter

9

```
[ABCSTAFF->LAST NAME]
```

Be sure to include the surrounding brackets, and the hyphen and greater-than symbol between the table name and the field name. Then press (ENTER) twice to place the field.

Replace the heading above the field, "Social Security," with **Last Name**. For simplicity's sake, this will be the only field referenced from the other table. In practice, you could add other fields by using the same type of expression in additional calculated fields.

To see the results, from the Design menu choose Output/Screen (or choose Output/Printer if you prefer a printed copy). The report should resemble the sample shown in Figure 9-18. Close the Report Preview window by choosing Cancel or clicking on the Close button. Then choose DO-IT!. The report will be saved, and you will be returned to the main menu.

When you have created a multitable report with this method, you can use the report at any time along with the existing tables; there is no need to perform a relational query beforehand, since the relational link is designed

Figure 9-18.   *Sample multitable report*

```
6/12/92              Multitable Sample      Page   1

Last Name        Weekend date    Hours worked    Assignment
- - - - - - - -  - - - - - - - - -  - - - - - - - -  - - - - - - - - - -
Westman          5/16/92               30         National Oil Co.
Westman          5/23/92               35         National Oil Co.
Robinson         5/16/92               27         National Oil Co.
Morse            5/16/92               32         National Oil Co.
Jackson          5/16/92               30         City Revenue Dept.
Jackson          5/23/92               30         City Revenue Dept.
Robinson         5/16/92               35         City Revenue Dept.
Robinson         5/23/92               32         City Revenue Dept.
Abernathy        5/16/92               28         City Revenue Dept.
Abernathy        5/23/92               32         City Revenue Dept.
Morse            5/23/92               35         Smith Builders
Hart             5/23/92               30         Smith Builders
Mitchell         5/23/92               28         Smith Builders
Jones            5/16/92               35         National Oil Co.
Jones            5/23/92               33         National Oil Co.
```

into the report. This type of report takes a little longer to design, but once stored you can produce reports very quickly.

Quick Summary

To query from two tables   Clear the workspace if necessary, with Clear All ((ALT)-(F8)). From the menu, choose Ask. Enter the name for the first table, and choose the fields for inclusion with the Check ((F6)) key. Place any desired selection criteria in the fields of the Query Form. When the first query form is filled in, choose Ask from the menu, and enter the name of the second table. Again, choose fields for inclusion with the Check ((F6)) key, and place any desired selection criteria in the fields of the Query Form. Finally, enter the example element used to link the common field, by moving the cursor to the common field in each query form, pressing Example ((F5)), and entering an example element. Choose DO-IT! to process the query.

To use linked tables with AND selection criteria   Add as many conditions as are needed, in the different fields of either of the query forms.

To use linked tables with OR selection criteria   In each query form, use the (↓) key as necessary, to add additional lines for more criteria to the Query Form, or include the OR operator between multiple query criteria.

To generate relational reports   Build and process a query that performs the relational link. Then design (if necessary) and generate the report based on the ANSWER table provided by the relational query.

9

10

The Power of Scripts

Paradox allows you to define combinations of keystrokes called *scripts* that can automate many of the tasks you normally perform when you are using Paradox. The script capability is similar in function to the macro capabilities presented in some other popular software. Scripts let you record a sequence of characters in a single key combination or as a named file. You can save the script and later use it to play back those keystrokes by pressing the same single key combination, or you can use a menu option to retrieve the script file by name. When the script is played back, Paradox works as if you had manually performed the operations contained within the script.

You can use a feature of Paradox called *instant scripts* to quickly assign a sequence of operations to a key combination. By using scripts, you can save literally hundreds of keystrokes you must use regularly to print daily reports, fill in complex Query Forms, or perform similar repetitive tasks.

If you use commercially available keyboard enhancers like SuperKey and ProKey, you are familiar with the advantages of automating your work with scripts. Other keyboard-enhancer users may wonder whether they should simply continue to use such products instead of using Paradox's script capability. The advantage of using the script capability within Paradox is

279

twofold. First, you will not need to access the additional memory that a memory-resident keyboard enhancer would consume. Second, you will avoid possible conflicts between Paradox operations and the memory-resident keyboard enhancer. Memory-resident programs have, in the past, been known to conflict with other software packages. Borland's SideKick and SuperKey are both compatible with Paradox; however, there is no guarantee that you will not encounter any problems using other memory-resident packages with Paradox. Another advantage of scripts is that they can be incorporated into larger PAL scripts; keyboard macros cannot.

Note

Scripts are ideal for automating repetitive tasks otherwise performed through the Paradox menus.

The easiest way to use a script is to record and/or play back an instant script. With the (ALT)(F3) (Instant Script Record) key combination, you can start and end the recording of an instant script. You can play back that script at any time with (ALT)(F4) (Instant Script Play). When you record an instant script, it is saved to disk automatically before you exit Paradox. You can replay the script at any time, and the script will remain available until you create another instant script. Each instant script you record overwrites the previous instant script.

Note

Paradox will not let you record mouse actions within a script. Whenever you begin recording a script, Paradox turns off the mouse pointer, and the mouse remains inactive until you finish recording the script.

To create an instant script, perform the following steps:

1. Press (ALT)(F3). The message "Beginning recording of Instant" will momentarily appear at the bottom of the screen.

2. Perform whatever Paradox operations you wish recorded in the script. (Remember—don't use the mouse.)

3. Press (ALT)(F3). The message "Ending recording of Instant" will momentarily appear at the bottom of the screen.

To play back the instant script, press (ALT)-(F4). The Paradox operations that were performed when the script was recorded will be carried out as if those menu options had been entered by hand.

Instant scripts are always saved under the name INSTANT.SC. This means that any instant script you record will overwrite the existing one.

Hands-On Practice: Recording and Playing an Instant Script

Perhaps you regularly need to print a report of employees' hours worked, including the names of the employees. In the case of ABC Temporaries, this requires the use of the relational database based on two tables, ABCSTAFF and HOURS, so you need to fill out a Query Form with example elements each week when you need the report. This is a perfect task for a script.

Press (ALT)-(F3) to start recording the instant script. Clear the workspace with (ALT)-(F8). Then, from the main menu, choose Ask and enter **ABCSTAFF** as the name of the table. Move the cursor to in the Social Security field, press (F5) to begin an example, and enter **SAME**. Then use (F6) to place checkmarks in the Last Name and First Name fields.

Press (F10) for the menu, choose Ask, and enter **HOURS** as the table name. Move to the Social Security field, press (F5) to begin an example, and enter **SAME**. Then use the (F6) key to place checkmarks in the Weekend date and the Hours worked fields. Finally, choose DO-IT! to process the query. If you have a printer attached, turn it on and press (ALT)-(F7) for an instant report.

Finally, press (ALT)-(F3) to end the recording of the script. Now that the script exists, you can use a single key combination to ask about the tables, fill in the Query Form, and generate the report. To see how this is done, first clear the workspace with (ALT)-(F8). Then press (ALT)-(F4) to play the instant script. Depending on your PC's speed, it may take a few moments to see the results, but Paradox is performing the work in the background.

When Paradox is done performing the steps recorded within the script, the ANSWER table based on the query will appear along with the Query

10

Forms, resembling the example shown in Figure 10-1. If you chose to print
an instant report while you were recording the script, that report would again
be printed.

Saving an Instant Script Under Another Name

Any instant script you create is stored as a script with the name INSTANT.
If you want to keep that script and not overwrite it the next time you create
an instant script, you can do so by changing the script's name. Simply go to
the main menu with (F10) and choose Tools/Rename/Script. Paradox will ask
you for the name of the script; enter **INSTANT**. You will then be asked to
enter a new name for the script. Enter any valid DOS name of eight characters
or less (and no spaces), and the script will be renamed.

Once you have renamed the script, you cannot replay it with (ALT)-(F4),
but you can replay it at any time by choosing the script by name through the
Script menu. This is discussed in the following section.

Figure 10-1.   *Results of the instant script*

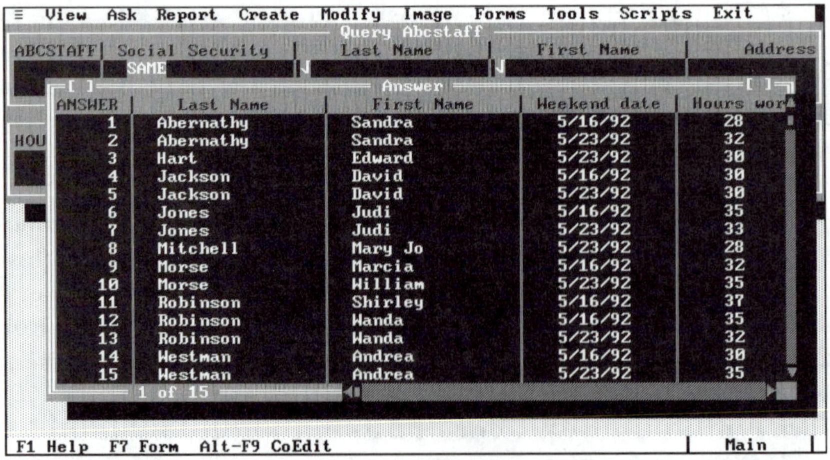

Recording and Playing Scripts

If you use scripts regularly, you will need to be able to store and play more than a single script. Paradox allows you to create a virtually unlimited number of scripts by letting you store *custom scripts*. Each custom script is assigned a name, which must again follow the standards of DOS files (eight characters or less, with no spaces).

When you first record a script, Paradox saves the script file with an .SC extension. When you play back a recorded script for the first time, Paradox compresses the original script file, and saves a compressed version of the same file, using an extension of .SC2. Thereafter, the file with the .SC2 extension is used when you play the script. You should not however, erase the original .SC file, because it contains the program code of the script (and it can be edited, or integrated into a PAL program). Paradox does not allow you to add any extension of your own when providing names for your scripts; Paradox assigns the .SC and .SC2 extensions automatically.

The basic steps for creating a custom script are as follows.

1. From the main menu, choose Scripts/BeginRecord.
2. Enter a name for the new script.
3. Perform the operations that are to be recorded in the script. (Remember—don't use the mouse.)
4. From the main menu, choose Scripts/End-Record.

Once the script has been recorded, you can play it at any time by choosing Scripts/Play from the main menu and entering the name for that script.

Hands-On Practice: Creating a Custom Script

Perhaps you need a script that will isolate all employees assigned to the National Oil Company and produce the custom report you designed earlier showing those employees. The first step is to begin recording the script. Clear the workspace with (ALT)-(F8). Then choose Scripts from the main menu.

The next menu to appear shows the following options:

```
Scripts

Play
BeginRecord
QuerySave
ShowPlay
RepeatPlay
Editor              ▶
```

The BeginRecord option is used to start recording the script, and the Play option is used to play an existing script. The remaining options will be discussed shortly.

Choose BeginRecord from the menu. Paradox will now display a prompt asking for a name for the script. For this example, enter **MYFIRST** as the name. Paradox will momentarily display a message in the lower-right corner, indicating it is beginning a script called MYFIRST, and then the main menu will reappear. You are now ready to perform the options that will be recorded within the script.

Since you want only the employees for National Oil, you will need a query. Press (F10) for the menu. Although the menu should be active, it's a good idea to get into the habit of starting menu tasks within scripts with (F10) (or with (ALT)-(F8)). That way, whenever you play back the script, you'll start from a common point (the menu). Choose Ask from the menu and enter **ABCSTAFF** as the table name. With the cursor still at the far left side of the table, press (F6) to place checkmarks in all fields. Then move the cursor to the Assignment field and enter this criterion:

```
National Oil Co.
```

Choose DO-IT! to process the query. The ANSWER table that appears will contain only those employees assigned to National Oil.

Press (F10) to activate the main menu, and choose Report/Output. For the name of the table, enter **ANSWER** From the next menu of possible reports to choose, select R for standard report. Then select Printer (or, if you do not have a printer attached or simply prefer not to use paper, choose Screen). Finally, clear the desktop with (ALT)-(F8). This is not a requirement, but it is done in this case for aesthetic reasons.

Choose Scripts from the main menu. You will notice that the Scripts menu now has some other choices than it did when you began. It now shows the following options:

```
Scripts

Cancel
End-Record
Play
QuerySave
RepeatPlay
```

The Cancel option lets you cancel the recording of the script, and the End-Record option will stop recording and save the script. (The remaining options will be discussed later in this chapter.)

Choose End-Record to end the recording of your script. The script will be stored under the name MYFIRST, which you assigned earlier, and the main menu will reappear.

Playing the Custom Script

To play the script, choose Scripts from the main menu, and then choose Play. Paradox will ask for the name of the script; enter **MYFIRST**, and the script will be played. The resulting report will appear on the screen or will be printed.

Using Play and QuerySave

Once you begin recording a script, two new options appear in the Scripts menu: Play and QuerySave. These are options that you may find useful as you begin working regularly with scripts.

The Play option lets you play an existing script while you are in the midst of recording a new script. In this manner, you can combine existing scripts to perform more complex tasks.

The QuerySave option can also be useful. Though you could store the steps necessary for a query in any script, just as you did in the example earlier, the QuerySave option of the Scripts menu offers the advantage of storing only the query. To save a query, while the Query Form is present in the workspace, choose Scripts/QuerySave from the menu. Paradox will ask you for a name for the script. Enter the desired name, and Paradox will save the present Query Form in that script. Whenever you wish to reuse that query,

10

simply choose Scripts/Play from the menu and enter the name of the script that contains the query. The query will reappear, and you can then choose DO-IT! ((F2)) to process it and obtain up-to-date results.

The advantage of saving a query as a script in itself, using the QuerySave option, is that when the script is played, the query appears but is not immediately executed (as may be the case with a query you save with BeginRecord). With this method, you can make changes to the query if you wish before pressing (F2) to process the query.

Using ShowPlay

Another way to play a script, but at a speed sufficiently slow to observe the results, is with the ShowPlay option of the Scripts menu. To use this option, choose Scripts/ShowPlay from the main menu, and enter the name of the script to be played. Paradox will then offer the choice of Fast or Slow as the playback speeds for the script. You select your desired choice of speeds, and the script is played at that speed.

To see an example, choose Scripts/ShowPlay from the main menu. For the name of the script, enter **MYFIRST**. Paradox will display a menu with two choices: Fast and Slow. Choose Slow from the menu. The script will be replayed at a slow speed. When it has finished, you may want to repeat this process, choosing Fast from the menu to observe the difference in playback speeds.

Using RepeatPlay

You can repeat a script a selected number of times with the RepeatPlay option of the Scripts menu. To use this option, choose Scripts/RepeatPlay from the main menu, and then enter the name of the script to be played. Paradox next asks for the number of times you want the script played. You can enter a number up to 99,999, or you can enter the letter C, in which case the script gets played continuously. If you need to interrupt a script while it is repeating, press (CTRL)-(BREAK) and select Cancel from the menu that appears.

The INIT Script

If there is a set of tasks that you normally perform each time you start using Paradox, you can record the tasks in a script and assign the script the name INIT. If a script named INIT is found, it will be run by Paradox as soon as the program is started. Note that the INIT script must be stored in the default directory unless you are on a network, in which case the INIT script must be stored in a private directory. (Use the Custom Configuration Program, described in your Paradox documentation, to change the default directory.)

Managing Your Scripts

Because scripts can save so much time, they tend to collect quickly in your subdirectory. Before you know it, you will have dozens of scripts for various tasks, some of which you may no longer be using. You can keep things organized with the various options of the Tools menu for deleting scripts, renaming scripts, or displaying lists of scripts.

To delete unwanted scripts, choose Tools/Delete/Script from the main menu. Paradox will ask you for the name of the script to delete; if you are unsure of the spelling, you can press (ENTER) alone to see a menu of all available scripts. Enter the script name or choose it by name from the menu, and Paradox will ask for confirmation by displaying a menu with two choices, Cancel and OK. You must choose OK to delete the script.

You can use a similar menu choice to rename a script. From the main menu, choose Tools/Rename/Script, enter the current name, and then enter the new name for the script.

To see a list of your scripts, choose Tools/Info/Inventory/Scripts from the main menu. Press (ENTER) to choose the default directory (or enter an optional directory name), and the scripts contained in that directory will appear in a temporary table called LIST, similar to the example in Figure 10-2. The dates displayed indicate the date each script was created or last modified.

10

Figure 10-2.   *A list of scripts*

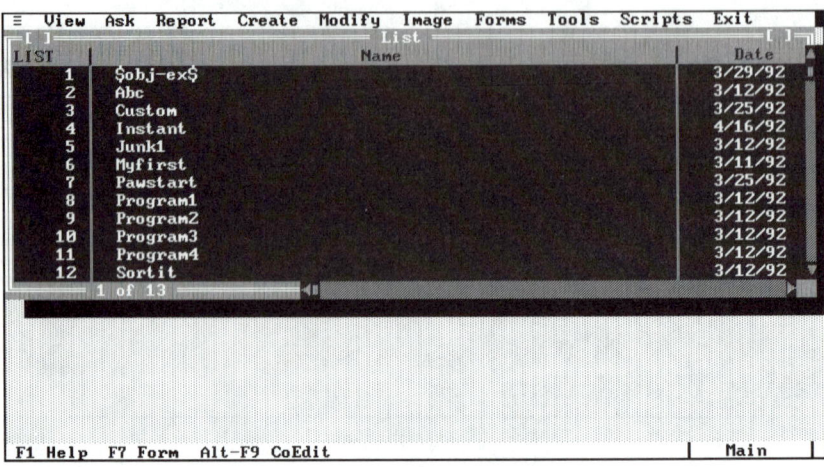

Quick Summary

To record an instant script   Press (ALT)-(F3), then perform the desired actions to be recorded. When done, press (ALT)-(F3) again.

To play an instant script   Press (ALT)-(F4).

To record a custom script   From the menu, choose Scripts/BeginRecord. Enter a name for the script. Perform the desired actions to be recorded. From the menu, choose Scripts/EndRecord.

To play a custom script   From the menu, choose Scripts/Play. Enter the name of the desired script.

To save a query as a script   With the query form(s) visible on the screen, choose Scripts/QuerySave from the menu. Enter the desired name for the script.

To delete unwanted scripts   From the menu, choose Tools/Delete/Script. Enter the name of the script to delete, or press (ENTER) and choose the desired script from the list that appears.

11

Managing Files

Once you have created a table, you will probably need to make changes to the design of it. Despite your best-laid plans, the need for additional fields or for changes to existing fields will arise. With Paradox, no database design is cast in stone. You can readily add new fields or change the design of an existing field.

In addition to helping you manage the characteristics of your tables, Paradox also lets you manage files by doing tasks usually achieved through DOS—tasks such as erasing and renaming files. Modifications to the structure of a table are performed through the Modify option of the main menu. Tasks such as erasing and renaming files can be performed from the Tools option of the main menu.

Paradox Objects

To effectively manage your files, you will need to know how Paradox stores those files. To handle database work, Paradox stores your records in tables. The table is a separate disk file with a default extension of .DB. A table, however, is just one of many types of *objects* in Paradox. Paradox objects include tables and various family members associated with tables, including forms and reports. Reports are saved with a default extension of .R; forms are saved with an .F extension.

The custom forms and reports that you create have numbers added to the .F or .R extensions. For example, a custom report given the name of 2 from the menu would be stored with the same name as the table, but with an extension of .R2; a form assigned the number 5 for its name would be stored with the same name as the table, but with an .F5 extension. Also included as objects within Paradox are any temporary tables, such as ANSWER or LIST. Of course, since these are temporary, they are overwritten by successive operations.

You can view the members of a Paradox family at any time. Just choose Tools/Info/Family from the main menu, and enter the name of the desired table.

Remember

When you delete a table, the associated family members (such as custom forms and reports) are also deleted.

Changing the Table Design

To change the design (or structure) of a table, go to the main menu, and choose Modify and then Restructure. Paradox will prompt you for the name of the table to be changed, so enter the table name. The table structure will then appear, as shown in Figure 11-1.

Make the desired changes to the field names and field types. Remember—you can press (INS) to insert a new, blank row within the structure. And you can delete an existing row by placing the cursor anywhere within the row, and pressing (DEL).

Once you have completed the changes to the structure, choose DO-IT! from the menu to complete the redesign of the table. (If you change your mind, you can choose Cancel from the menu, and any changes made to the table will not be saved.)

Figure 11-1. *Table structure for existing table*

```
 ≡  Borrow   Justfamily   FileFormat   DO-IT!   Cancel
[≡]                        Restructure: Abcstaff                            [▪]
     1   Social Security          A11*              ═══════ FIELD TYPES ═══════
     2   Last Name                A15          A_:  Alphanumeric.
     3   First Name               A15          All characters up to
     4   Address                  A25          max of 255 (ex: A9).
     5   City                     A15
     6   State                    A2           M_:  Memo. Alphanumeric
     7   ZIP Code                 A10          characters, 240 maximum
     8   Date of Birth            D            display in table view.
     9   Date Hired               D
    10   Dependents               N            N:  Numbers with or
    11   Salary                   $            without decimal digits.
    12   Assignment               A20
    13   Hourly Rate              $            $:  Currency amounts.
    14   Phone                    A12
    15   Comments                 M25          D:  Dates in the form
                                               mm/dd/yy, dd-mon-yy,
                                               or dd.mm.yy.

                                               Use * for key fields
                                               (ex: N*). Not memos.
  F1 Help                                                        Restructure
```

Renaming Files

You can rename Paradox objects from within Paradox by using the Tools/Rename command. Paradox lets you rename tables and associated objects, or just the forms, reports, or scripts. To rename a Paradox object, go to the main menu and choose Tools. From the Tools menu, which appears next, choose Rename.

The next menu displays these choices:

```
Table
Form
Report
Script
Graph
```

This menu provides you with the options of renaming a table, a form, a report, a Paradox script, or a graph. You can also rename the forms and reports associated with a table. Choose the desired item to rename, and Paradox will prompt you for the stored name of the item. Enter or select the item, and

Paradox will ask you for a new name. Supply the name of your choice, and Paradox will rename the object.

Use the Rename option from the Paradox menu to rename tables, so the associated family objects will also be renamed. If you use the DOS RENAME command to rename tables, the associated objects won't be renamed automatically.

Deleting Files

The Delete option of the Tools menu also aids in the maintenance of Paradox objects. It can be used to delete tables, reports, forms, scripts, query speedups (which are explained later in this chapter), KeepSets, and graphs. Also on this menu is a ValCheck option, which lets you delete ValCheck files (created with the Modify/ValCheck option).

To delete a Paradox object, select Tools from the main menu, and then choose Delete from the next menu that appears. Select the object to be deleted, and Paradox will prompt you for the name of the object. Choose the object, and Paradox will next display a menu offering the choices of Cancel and OK. You must confirm the deletion by selecting OK before Paradox will delete the object. Remember that if you delete a table, its family of associated objects is also deleted.

Changing a Directory

Although you should never need to change directories if you leave all of your data in a single Paradox subdirectory, some PC users use so many subdirectories that the ability to switch directories from within a program becomes critical. The Directory option, available from the More selection on the Tools menu, can perform this important task. To change a directory, choose Tools from the main menu, and choose More from the next menu that appears. You will see additional choices that would not comfortably fit on the first menu.

Once you select More, another menu appears. The Directory choice from this menu is used to change directories. Choose this command, and Paradox will prompt you for a directory name. Enter the name of a valid subdirectory, and Paradox will switch to that subdirectory. Note that Paradox will always clear its workspace when you change directories; any unsaved work and temporary tables will be lost. You can permanently reset your directory with the Defaults/SetDirectory option of the Custom Configuration Program. See your Paradox documentation for details.

Remember

When you change directories, Paradox clears its workspace.

Accessing DOS

When you need to erase, rename, or copy files that are not Paradox files or objects, you can resort to the use of such DOS commands as ERASE, RENAME, and COPY to perform basic housekeeping. But Paradox's ToDOS option, available from the More choice of the Tools menu, lets you perform such DOS functions as formatting or copying a disk without leaving Paradox. Selecting Tools/More/ToDOS results in the appearance of a DOS prompt. (The (CTRL)-(O) key combination can be used for the same purpose.) Perform the desired DOS functions, or run another program (see the warning that follows). When you are done, type **EXIT** at the DOS prompt to return to Paradox.

To see how this works, get to the main menu and choose Tools/More. Choose ToDOS from the next menu that appears, and you will see something similar to the following on the screen:

```
Warning! Do not delete or edit Paradox objects
or load RAM-resident programs.
To return to Paradox, type EXIT

The IBM Personal Computer DOS
Version 3.30 (C)Copyright International Business Machines Corp
1981, 1987
Copyright Microsoft Corp. 1981, 1987
```

You are now back in DOS, but Paradox remains in a portion of your computer's memory. Try entering the following command:

```
COPY ABCSTAFF.R TEST.TMP
```

The message "(1) files copied" shows that the file has been copied with the DOS COPY command. If you prefer, try running another program, but be forewarned that the program must be very small to run in a standard (640K RAM) computer along with Paradox. Do *not* try to load memory-resident programs. (A later section, "A Warning About Accessing DOS" will explain why.) Note also that you should *not* use the DOS PRINT and MODE commands through the Paradox ToDOS option, because these commands may alter memory, causing problems when Paradox is reloaded.

The fact that Paradox remains in memory while you use the ToDOS option severely limits what programs you can run. Paradox requires 640K of memory. Subtract this figure from the amount of your computer's *available* memory (what is left after DOS has loaded), and then subtract the amount of memory consumed by any memory-resident software that you may be using. The figure that remains is the amount of memory currently available for use by other programs.

Most desktop computers will not be able to load and run additional programs of significant size, but you can use most DOS functions, such as COPY and FORMAT, because these functions use very little memory.

To return to Paradox, at the DOS prompt type **EXIT** and press (ENTER). In a moment, the Paradox workspace appears, and you are again ready to work in Paradox.

Using Big-DOS Instead of ToDOS

If you are desperate for additional memory, you can use the special (ALT)-(O) key combination within Paradox to access DOS. The (ALT)-(O) key combination (as opposed to (CTRL)-(O)) is referred to as the *Big-DOS key,* and it accesses DOS just as (CTRL)-(O) or the ToDOS menu option does. However, with (ALT)-(O), Paradox saves much more of its own environment to disk. The end result is that it takes longer to get to DOS with (ALT)-(O), but you are left with roughly 500K of available memory on a 640K machine.

A Warning About Accessing DOS

Do *not* use the ToDOS option to load any software that is memory resident. These programs are also known as TSRs, which stands for *terminate and stay resident*. Memory-resident programs are those that "pop up" at the touch of a key combination that contains (SHIFT), (CTRL), or (ALT). If you load a memory-resident program from ToDOS, the TSR will probably overwrite portions of Paradox that are temporarily stored in the memory of your computer. When you try to return to Paradox by typing **EXIT**, you may be in for an unpleasant surprise. Your computer will probably freeze, requiring a complete reboot of the system.

If you do not know whether a program is a TSR, do not try to load the program through the DOS window supplied by ToDOS. Instead, save your changes with DO-IT!, and exit from Paradox before trying to load the program in question.

Also, while at DOS you should not copy Paradox objects for other uses in Paradox, because corruption of files may occur. Use the Tools menu options to make copies of Paradox objects.

Exporting and Importing Data

No PC is an island. You may need to use other programs along with Paradox, or other people in your office may use such popular programs as Lotus 1-2-3 or Microsoft Word with its MergePrint option. The ExportImport option, located on the Tools menu, allows you to import files from other programs into Paradox, and to export data from Paradox tables for use by the other programs.

If you wish to export or import files, go to the main menu and choose Tools/ExportImport. The next menu that appears provides two choices: Export, which is used to move data from Paradox to other programs, and Import, which is used to move data from other programs into Paradox.

Exporting Data

When you choose Export, Paradox will display the following menu:

You can export from Paradox to one of eight possible formats, as indicated by the choices in this menu. The choices are Quattro or Quattro Pro worksheet format (.WKQ or .WQ1), 1-2-3 worksheet format (.WKS or .WK1), Symphony worksheet format (.WRK or .WR1), dBASE format (.DBF), PFS:File format (no extension), Reflex format (.RXD or .R2D), VisiCalc format (DIF), and ASCII text format. As a general rule, most word processors will read information stored as ASCII text. Many spreadsheets will transfer data that follows the Lotus 1-2-3 file format, and most database managers will transfer files using the popular dBASE file format. If it is not obvious which format your software package uses, check your user's manual.

If you choose dBASE from the available menu options, Paradox will ask which version of dBASE you are using (dBASE II, dBASE III, or dBASE IV). If you select Reflex, Quattro, 1-2-3, or Symphony, Paradox will ask which version of the program you are using. If you select ASCII, Paradox will ask whether or not the data should be delimited with some type of field marker (such as quotation marks). The ASCII format, with a quotation mark as a delimiter, is often used with merge files (such as WordStar/MailMerge). When exporting to a word processor, in some cases you get better results using Report/Output/File from the menu. You may want to try both methods to see which works best for you.

After you have selected the type of file format, Paradox will display a dialog box asking for the name of the table to export. Enter the name of the table that will supply the records. Paradox will next ask for a valid filename for the exported file. You can add an extension, if desired, to the exported file. (Note that if you choose Quattro, Reflex, 1-2-3, or dBASE and omit the extension, Paradox will supply the proper extension automatically.)

11

Once you have entered a valid filename, Paradox will export the table you chose into the new file. If a file with the same name you selected for the exported file exists, Paradox will not automatically overwrite the existing file; it will present you with a menu with Cancel and Replace options, and you must choose Replace to overwrite the file.

Importing Data

To import data from Paradox, select Tools/ExportImport from the main menu and then choose Import from the next menu that appears. Paradox will display the following menu:

As you can see, Paradox imports data from foreign files using the same eight possible formats used for exporting files. The choices are Quattro or Quattro Pro worksheet format (.WKQ or .WQ1), 1-2-3 worksheet format (.WKS or .WK1), Symphony worksheet format (.WR1), dBASE format (.DBF), PFS:File format (no extension), Reflex format (.RXD or .R2D), VisiCalc format (DIF), and ASCII text format.

If you select Quattro, 1-2-3, Reflex, or Symphony, Paradox will ask which version of the program you are using. If you select ASCII, Paradox will ask whether or not the data is delimited with some type of field marker (such as quotation marks). Imported dBASE files are analyzed by Paradox automatically, and the program determines which version of dBASE was used to create the file.

After you have selected the type of file to be imported, Paradox will display a display box asking for the name of the file to import. Enter the name of the foreign file that will supply the records. Paradox will next ask for a name for the new table into which the records will be imported. Enter a table name of your choice, and Paradox will perform the conversion. During this process, it will display a progress report on the screen.

Some Notes on Importing Data

Paradox makes certain assumptions as it imports data from other programs into a Paradox table. When importing ASCII text that is delimited, Paradox assumes that the delimiters used are the double quotation marks around the fields and the comma as a separator between fields. If the delimiters are any other characters, you must use the Custom Configuration Program to change the default delimiters.

Paradox must convert the data in different fields to its own field formats. Depending on the other program, the results will usually be what you want, but you may in rare cases need to do some fine-tuning. Paradox tries to determine the precise field names and best field types to use, based on the contents of the foreign file you are importing.

If Paradox cannot determine the field name, it will name the new field as FIELD-n, where n represents the number of the field in the order of the structure. Paradox also maintains a temporary table called PROBLEMS. If any records cannot be successfully converted during the conversion process, they will be stored in the PROBLEMS table. Finally, note that field types may or may not come across as the exact type of field you would prefer in Paradox. Table 11-1 shows how types of data from various program files will be imported into Paradox.

Paradox and Quattro Pro

If you must work with both databases and spreadsheets, the most effective way to use Paradox along with a spreadsheet is to make use of Borland's Quattro Pro. Paradox and Quattro Pro are designed to work well together. In addition to Quattro Pro's being fully compatible with the Lotus 1-2-3 file format (up to version 2.2), Quattro Pro and Paradox can reside concurrently in memory. This is possible with a feature called Paradox Access. With Paradox Access, you can run Quattro Pro from within Paradox, automatically load a table into a Quattro Pro spreadsheet, work with the table while in Quattro Pro, and return to Paradox at the touch of a single key combination.

To use Paradox Access, you must have Quattro Pro version 2.0 or above. You must also have two megabytes or more of installed memory. If you want to access data stored on an SQL Server on a network, you will also need to have

Table 11-1. *How Types of Fields Are Imported into Paradox*

Field Type	Type Within Paradox
dBASE character	Alphanumeric
dBASE number	Number
dBASE number with 2 decimal places	Currency
dBASE logical	Alphanumeric with 1-character width
dBASE date	Date
dBASE memo	Memo
PFS field, nonnumeric	Alphanumeric
PFS field, numbers	Number
PFS field, numbers with 2 decimal places	Currency
PFS field, using dd/mm/yy format	Date
DIF field, text	Alphanumeric
DIF field, numbers	Number
DIF field, numbers with 2 decimal places	Currency
DIF field, text in a dd/mm/yy format	Date
1-2-3 labels	Alphanumeric
1-2-3 numbers	Numeric
1-2-3 numbers with 2 decimal places	Currency
1-2-3 numbers, formatted as mm/dd/yy	Date
Symphony	See 1-2-3 above

Paradox SQL Link installed (Paradox SQL Link is available separately from Borland). If you do not have sufficient memory to use Paradox Access, you can still share files between Paradox and Quattro Pro; you can also use the menu options in Quattro Pro to directly view, query, or edit Paradox tables.

Before you can use Paradox Access, you must do the following:

1. Run the SHARE command from DOS. (You may need to change to your DOS subdirectory to run the SHARE command.) If you get a "Bad command or filename" error message when trying to run SHARE, copy the program SHARE.EXE from your DOS Supplemental Diskette into your Paradox directory, or into a directory named in your PATH statement.

2. Use the PXACCESS batch file to start Paradox. PXACCESS.BAT can be found on your Quattro Pro disks. This is a batch file that will start Paradox with various memory options that optimize it for simultaneous use with Quattro Pro.

3. Make sure that your Paradox working directory and your private directory are different directories. While in Paradox, choose Tools/Net/SetPrivate, and change your private directory to something other than the directory that holds your working database files.

Once you have started Paradox with the PXACCESS batch file, you can use the (CTRL)-(F10) key combination to switch back and forth between Paradox and Quattro Pro. Whenever you switch to Quattro Pro, Quattro Pro loads the ANSWER table by default. While in Quattro Pro, you can load any Paradox table (memory permitting) with Quattro Pro's Load File command.

When you have finished working in Quattro Pro, press (CTRL)-(F10) again, and you will be back in Paradox. With Paradox Access, there is no need to close spreadsheet files, or exit Quattro Pro as you normally would. You can later go from Paradox back to Quattro Pro again with (CTRL)-(F10), and the workspace in Quattro Pro will be intact.

Protecting Tables

To ensure security, Paradox lets you protect your tables from unauthorized access. Perhaps you are storing salary records, medical histories, or something else that contains sensitive information, and you do not want any savvy computer user to be able to browse through your files at will. Paradox provides tools for protecting your files with passwords. These tools are available from the More option of the Tools menu.

To protect a table, choose Tools/More/Protect from the main menu. The next menu that appears will provide three options: Password, ClearPasswords, and Write-protect.

Tip

*The passwords that you assign to tables or scripts should be written down in a safe place. If you assign a password to a table and later forget the password, **there is no way to access that table without the password**. In short, do not lose your passwords. Also, it might be wise to store unprotected copies of your tables in a secure place, such as a locked file cabinet.*

To protect a table from unauthorized access, choose Password from the menu. Paradox will next ask you whether you wish to protect a table or a script. Choose Table, and enter the name of the table that is to be protected.

Remember

Passwords are case sensitive.

Once you have supplied the name, Paradox will display a dialog box, asking you to supply a password. Enter the desired password, which can be up to 15 characters long. For your protection, Paradox will ask you to repeat the password. Once you have entered it twice identically, Paradox will display a table for the addition of any optional auxiliary passwords.

If you are not using Paradox on a network, you can omit the addition of any auxiliary passwords. Just choose DO-IT! ((F2)), and Paradox will assign the password to the table. From then on, any attempts to view or manipulate the table will require the entry of the password. Paradox automatically prompts the user for the password as he or she chooses commands that would require access to the protected table.

Removing a Password

To remove password protection from a table, follow the same steps you use to add a password. When Paradox prompts you for the master password, press (ENTER) without entering any name, and Paradox will "decrypt" the table, removing the password protection.

Using ClearPasswords

Also available from the Protect menu is the ClearPasswords option. This choice does not remove password protection (to do that, see the previous paragraph), but it can be useful in maintaining security. When you access a table with a password, Paradox remembers that you have been granted access, and the program will let you manipulate the data in that table for the remainder of the session. However, in some cases you might want Paradox to reinstate the protection of your tables—for example, when you leave for lunch but want to leave your computer turned on and in Paradox.

You can use the ClearPasswords option to restore the protection of your password-protected tables after you have entered a password. In effect, this command negates the effect of your previous action of supplying the passwords, so any access of protected tables will again require the entry of the passwords.

To clear your passwords, choose Tools/More/Protect from the main menu. From the next menu that appears, choose ClearPasswords. Paradox will request confirmation of this action by displaying a menu with Cancel and OK as choices. Select OK to proceed, and Paradox will clear its memory of any passwords you have entered since you started your session.

Quick Summary

To restructure a table   From the menu, choose Modify/Restructure. Make the desired changes to the table structure, and choose DO-IT! ((F2)).

To rename a Paradox object   From the menu, choose Tools/Rename, and then choose the desired object (a table, form, report, script, or graph). Enter the name of the object and then enter the new name desired.

To delete a Paradox object   From the menu, choose Tools/Delete, and then choose the desired object (a table, form, report, script, QuerySpeed, KeepSet,

ValCheck, or graph). Enter the name of the object, and then confirm your choice by choosing OK.

To access DOS from within Paradox   From the menu, you should choose Tools/ More/ToDos (or press (CTRL)-(O)). When done with DOS, enter EXIT at the DOS prompt to return to Paradox. To access DOS with a maximum amount of free memory while at DOS, press (ALT)-(O).

To export a Paradox table for use with other software   From the Tools menu, choose ExportImport, then Export. From the next menu, select the desired file format (Quattro, 1-2-3, Symphony, dBASE, PFS, Reflex, VisiCalc, or ASCII). If asked, choose a version for the file format. Enter the name of the table to export when asked, and then the name for the new file. (Remember, you can include a drive identifier and/or pathname along with the new filename.)

To import files created by other software programs for use in Paradox   From the Tools menu, choose ExportImport, then Import. From the next menu, select the desired file format (Quattro, 1-2-3, Symphony, dBASE, PFS, Reflex, VisiCalc, or ASCII). If asked, choose a version for the file format. Enter the name of the file to import when asked. (Remember, you can include a drive identifier and/or pathname along with the filename.) Finally, enter the name for the new table into which the records will be imported.

To password-protect a table   From the menu, choose Tools/More/Protect and Password. From the next menu, choose Table, and enter the name of the table to be protected. Finally, enter the desired password twice, and choose DO-IT! ((F2)).

12

Advanced Report Topics

Chapter 7 began the process of describing how Paradox can meet your reporting needs through standard and custom reports. This chapter continues with that topic, describing the use of free-form reports in detail.

You can create free-form reports in Paradox from the Report Designer window. Unlike tabular reports, free-form reports are not limited to a columnar format. In a free-form report, you can place the fields wherever they need to appear. Perhaps the most well known example of a free-form report is a sheet of mailing labels. Mailing labels do not appear in columnar (or tabular) form; instead, the name, address, city, state, and ZIP code fields are placed in a desired location to fit a printed label. Besides mailing labels, free-form reports can also be used for common tasks like printing checks, generating invoices, and creating reports that contain large amounts of textual material.

Although you cannot create a free-form report as quickly as you can generate a tabular report with the Instant Report key, a default free-form report can be created almost as quickly by choosing the appropriate options and saving the report immediately. To quickly create a free-form report that uses the default format, simply perform these steps:

1. Choose Report/Design from the main menu, and enter the name for the table.

2. Choose a name and enter a description for the report.

3. Select Free-Form from the next menu that appears. The default Report Specification for a free-form report will appear on the screen.

4. Choose DO-IT! ((F2)) to store the default free-form report.

Once you have created a default free-form report, you can generate the report by choosing Report from the main menu, and then choosing Output followed by the name of the table. Then choose the stored report by name from the menu that appears, and select Printer, Screen, or File as desired. Figure 12-1 shows a portion of the report produced from the ABCSTAFF table, using the steps just outlined.

Note that the report illustrates the design of a default free-form report. The date appears at the top-left of each page, and a report heading, which uses the description you entered when you named the report, appears at the top-center of the page. A page number appears at the top-right of the page. The names of the fields appear as field headings, and the contents of each field appear to the right of the field name. Each record in the table used to print the report appears with all of the fields in the record.

If you would like to use a free-form report as the default report, you can replace the Standard Report (called R) with a free-form report that you design for the appropriate table. Then, pressing (ALT)-(F7) will print that report.

Hands-On Practice: Producing a Selective Free-Form Report

As with tabular reports, you can use temporary tables to generate free-form reports that meet your precise needs. You can often save time by limiting the fields produced in an ANSWER table and basing a free-form report that uses the default Report Specification on that temporary (ANSWER) table. As an example, perhaps you need a quick mailing list. You only need the names

Figure 12-1. *Example of default free-form report*

```
6/20/92                    Test1                    Page   1

Social Security: 111-33-9876
Last Name: Kramer
First Name: Harry
Address: 1245 Ocean Pine Way
City: McLean
State: VA
ZIP Code: 22304-1234
Date of Birth:  5/12/72
Date Hired:  5/03/92
Dependents:        0
Salary:              7.50
Assignment: Smith Builders
Hourly Rate:             12.00
Phone: 703-555-4323
Comments: Too new to evaluate.

Social Security: 121-33-9876
Last Name: Westman
First Name: Andrea
Address: 4807 East Avenue
City: Silver Spring
State: MD
ZIP Code: 20910-0124
Date of Birth:  5/29/61
Date Hired:  7/04/90
Dependents:        2
Salary:             15.00
Assignment: National Oil Co.
Hourly Rate:             24.00
Phone: 301-555-5682
Comments: Did well on last two assi

Social Security: 121-90-5432
Last Name: Robinson
First Name: Shirley
Address: 270 Browning Ave #2A
City: Takoma Park
State: MD
ZIP Code: 20912
```

Figure 12-1.   *Example of default free-form report* (continued)

```
Date of Birth: 11/02/64
Date Hired: 11/17/91
Dependents:        1
Salary:               7.50
Assignment: National Oil Co.
Hourly Rate:         12.00
Phone: 301-555-4582
Comments: Too new to evaluate.
```

and addresses of the employees, and for this example, you only need those employees who live in Maryland.

First clear the desktop, if necessary with (ALT)-(F8). From the main menu, choose Ask, and enter **ABCSTAFF** for the table name. Use the (F6) key to place checkmarks in the Last Name, First Name, Address, City, State, and ZIP Code fields. In the State field, enter **MD**. Then choose DO-IT! to process the query. The fields you selected with checkmarks in the ANSWER table should appear, along with only those records that have MD in the State field.

From the main menu, choose Report/Design, and enter **ANSWER** for the table name. From the next menu that appears, choose 1 as a name and enter **TEST1** as a description for the report. Select Free-Form from the next menu that appears, press (ENTER) and then choose DO-IT! to store the default free-form report.

From the main menu, choose Report/Output, and enter **ANSWER** as the table name. Choose 1 for the name of the report from the menu that appears, and select Printer or Screen as desired. The report should resemble the one shown in Figure 12-2.

This technique of using default free-form reports along with ANSWER tables can prove quite useful when you need free-form listings such as address or telephone directories, or similar listings based on selective data. Keep in mind that if you want to save one of these reports so you can generate it again, rename the ANSWER table so that the report will not be erased the next time you perform a query.

Before proceeding, press (ALT)-(F8) to clear the desktop.

Figure 12-2. *Example of a report based on the ANSWER table*

```
6/20/92                    Test1                    Page 1

Last name: Morse
First name: Marcia
Address: 4260 Park Avenue
City: Chevy Chase
State: MD
ZIP Code: 20815-0988

Last name: Morse
First name: William
Address: 4260 Park Avenue
City: Chevy Chase
State: MD
ZIP Code: 20815-0988

Last name: Robinson
First name: Shirley
Address: 267 Browning Ave #2A
City: Takoma Park
State: MD
ZIP Code: 20912

Last name: Westman
First name: Andrea
Address: 4807 East Avenue
City: Silver Spring
State: MD
ZIP Code: 20910-0124
```

Designing a Custom Free-Form Report

You will probably want to change the default design of the free-form report to meet your own needs. As with tabular reports, Paradox provides extreme flexibility for free-form report design. You can rearrange the location of fields, delete unwanted fields, or add calculated or summary fields. You can also change margins and use grouping options to generate free-form reports with records divided into specific groups.

The basic steps involved in designing a custom free-form report are as follows.

1. Choose a table for the report.

2. Select a name (numeric designator) and enter a report description.

3. From the next menu that appears, you should choose Free-Form as the report type.

4. Modify the Report Specification that appears on the screen. By pressing (F10), you can choose any of the available options that apply to free-form reports from the Design menu.

5. Choose DO-IT! to save the report.

The Report Specification

The Report Specification is made up of several parts, as illustrated in Figure 12-3. The most significant part of a free-form report is the form band, which contains most fields that appear in the report. (Fields can appear in other bands, as in group bands, to identify the group.) Form bands are used in free-form reports; table bands are used in columnar reports.

All items (table fields, calculated or summary fields, or literal text) that are placed within the form band appear once for each record in the table. Within the form band, you include the information (usually fields) that is needed in the body of the report. Since free-form reports do not limit you to placing the fields within specific columns, you can place them anywhere on the screen that they are needed. The values in the form band appear as *field masks,* with letters (such as AAAAA) indicating alphanumeric fields, numbers (such as 999999) representing number fields, and mm/dd/yy designations representing date fields. Literal text can be placed anywhere to describe field contents or to provide other information within the report.

Free-form reports bear some similarities to tabular reports. Both make use of a page band, which appears once for each page of the report. Page bands can contain any page headers or footers you specify, along with dates, times, or page-number fields. Free-form reports can also contain group bands,

12

Figure 12-3. *Parts of a Report Specification for free-form reports*

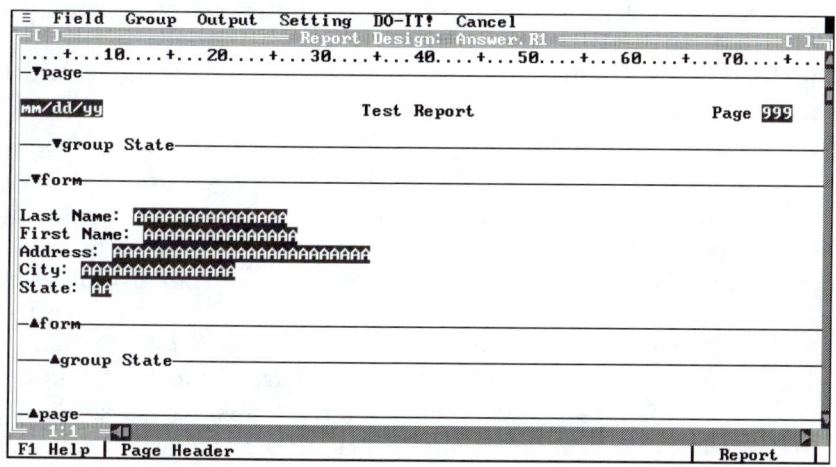

which serve the same purpose as they do with tabular reports. Group bands are optional and are printed once for each group of records in the report. As an example of a group, you might prefer to print a free-form report of employees divided into groups by assignment. A single report can contain up to 16 group bands.

To modify the report, you will need the various options provided by the menu that appears while you are designing a free-form report. The menu provides the following options:

- *Field*   Use the Field option to place fields, change the format of fields, justify or wordwrap fields, include fields from linked tables (as detailed in Chapter 9), and delete unwanted fields.

- *Group*   Use the Group option to add, remove, sort, or change the format for groupings within the report.

- *Output*   Use the Output option to generate a report (to the printer, screen, or file) while you are in the process of designing the report. This can be very helpful when you want to see if a report's format is satisfactory before you save the report.

- *Setting* Use the Setting option to trim unwanted blank lines or spaces, change page layout dimensions, set margins, format for mailing labels, enter setup strings, or configure your printer port.

The DO-IT! and Cancel options perform the same tasks as they do elsewhere in Paradox.

The precise options that you choose from the menus while designing a free-form report will, of course, vary with your desired final design. The hands-on practice sessions in this chapter will demonstrate the more commonly used options that Paradox provides. For your reference, the common tasks you can perform while designing free-form reports are listed here:

- To place new fields, choose Field/Place from the Design menu, and then choose the type of field desired from the next menu that appears. If you select Regular as the field type, Paradox will display a menu of the available fields. If you select Summary or Calculated, you can enter an expression that will calculate the field. If you select the Date or Time field, you can choose from among the available date or time formats.

- To remove fields, choose Field/Erase from the Design menu. Then place the cursor on the desired field and press (ENTER) to erase it. You can use (CTRL)-(Y) to delete an entire line.

- To edit a header or footer in the page band, place the cursor in the desired portion of the page band. Enter the desired heading or edit the existing heading. The page number and system date are fields, not literal text. You can remove or add these by selecting Field from the Design menu and using the Place option to place the fields or the Erase option to erase unwanted fields.

- To reformat fields, choose Field/Reformat from the Design menu. Then place the cursor in the field you want to reformat, and press (ENTER) to select the field. Enter a width, or select from the menu the desired format for the field.

- To add literal text (such as field titles), place the cursor at the desired location and type the desired text.

- To link the report to another table, choose Field/Lookup/Link. Enter the name of the other table, and then choose the key field

12

from the list of fields that appears. (See Chapter 9 for more details on multitable reports.)

Saving the Report

After the desired changes have been made to the Report Specification, choose DO-IT! to save the report.

Hands-On Practice: Creating a Custom Personnel List

In the case of ABC Temporaries, the managers want a custom personnel list that will resemble the format shown here:

```
(date)            Personnel List           (page no.)

Name: XXXXXXXXXX XXXXXXXXXX   Soc. Sec: 999-99-9999
Address: XXXXXXXXXXXXXXXXXXXXXXXXXX
City: XXXXXXXXXXXXXX   State:XX   Zip Code: 99999

Date Born: MM/DD/YY     Date Hired: MM/DD/YY

Comments:  XXXXXXXXXXXXXXXXXXXXXXXXXXXXXX
           XXXXXXXXXXXXXXXXXXXXXXXXXXXXXX
           XXXXXXXXXXXXXXXXXXXXXXXXXXXXXX
```

Press (F10), if necessary, for the main menu, and choose Report/Design. Enter **ABCSTAFF** as the table name. For the name of the report, choose 3 (or select another unused name if you have already used 3 for a different report). For a description, enter **PERSONNEL LIST**. Paradox now displays a menu listing two choices, Tabular and Free-form. Select Free-Form, and the Report Specification will appear.

Use the (DEL) key to delete the word "Last" from the Last Name heading. Also delete the entire First Name heading. Place the cursor at the start of the Social Security heading. Press (CTRL)-(Y) to delete the line containing the Social Security field. Next, place the cursor at the start of the first name field, press the (INS) key to get into Insert mode (the cursor takes on the shape of a thin line), and then press (BACKSPACE) (to pull the field up onto the prior line). Add a space between the last name and first name fields.

Move the cursor three spaces to the right of the first name field, and enter the following:

```
Soc. Sec:
```

Then choose Field/Place/Regular from the menu. Choose Social Security from the list of fields, and then press (ENTER) twice, once to place the field and once to set the field width.

Place the cursor two spaces to the right of the City field, and enter the following:

```
State:
```

Then choose Field/Place/Regular from the menu, and select State. Press (ENTER) twice, once to place the field and once to set the field width.

Place the cursor two spaces to the right of the State field, and enter the following:

```
Zip Code:
```

Then choose Field/Place/Regular from the menu, and select ZIP Code. Press (ENTER) twice, once to place the field and once to set the field width.

Place the cursor at the start of the now unneeded State heading on the line below. Press (CTRL)-(Y) twice to delete the next two lines, and then press (ENTER) once to add an extra blank line. Move the cursor four spaces to the right of the end of the Date of Birth field. Enter the following:

```
Date Hired:
```

From the menu, choose Field/Place/Regular, and select Date Hired. Choose the first date format from the next menu that appears. Press (ENTER) to place

12

the field. Place the cursor at the start of the next line. Use the (CTRL)-(Y) key combination to delete the lines containing the extra unneeded Date hired field, along with the Dependents, Salary, Assignment, Hourly Rate, and Phone fields. Press (ENTER) again to add another blank line in the form band. Then move the cursor down one line (below the Comments line), and press (ENTER) three times to add three more blank lines below the Comments line.

One last step that remains is to increase the size of the Comments field in the report, and to add wordwrap to the field. Whenever you include long fields (such as memo fields) in a report, you will often want to use the WordWrap option of the Field menu. This option lets you force the contents of a field to appear on multiple lines (you specify how many lines are allowed in the report).

First, since there is sufficient room, let's widen the Comments field. From the menu, choose Field/Reformat. Place the cursor anywhere in the Comments field, and press (ENTER). Next, press (→) ten times (to widen the field by ten characters), and press (ENTER) to set the new width.

Next, choose Field/WordWrap from the menu. If the cursor is not still in the Comments field, place it anywhere in the field now, and press (ENTER). Paradox next displays this dialog box asking for the number of lines:

With this dialog box, you have two choices. You can enter a numeric value indicating a set number of lines, and Paradox will always limit the information shown or printed in the report to that number of lines. Or, you can enter the letter **V** (for *variable length*), and Paradox will use as many lines as are necessary to accommodate the contents of the field.

For this example, enter **3**. Paradox will confirm your entry by displaying the message "Word wrap value recorded" in the lower-right corner of the screen. When you are done, your Report Specification will resemble the example shown in Figure 12-4.

To test the design before saving the report, choose Output/Screen from the menu. When you have finished previewing the report, close the Report Preview window by clicking on the Close box, or by choosing Cancel from

Figure 12-4.   *Report Specification for the custom personnel list*

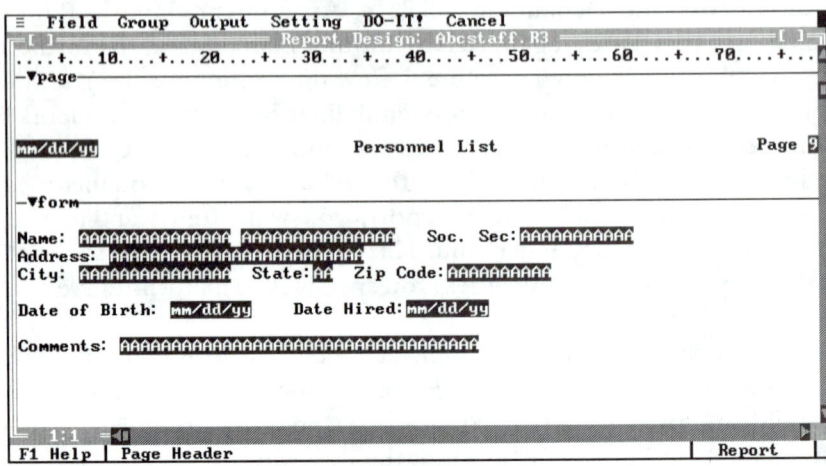

the menu. Finally, choose DO-IT! to save the report and return to the workspace.

Designing Mailing Labels

You can use the free-form reports available within Paradox to generate mailing labels. The basic steps in this process involve designing a form band of the report to contain the fields desired in the label; removing all extra lines from the report bands and page bands; setting the page length to Continuous to avoid the usual page breaks that occur with normal printer paper; and using the LineSqueeze and FieldSqueeze options of the RemoveBlanks menu to suppress blank lines and unwanted spaces. To generate more than one label per row of the page, simply add as many page widths as you need, and choose Labels from the Design menu to continue the printing.

12

Consider the example of creating mailing labels for ABC Temporaries in the "two-across" format. From the main menu, choose Report/Design, and choose ABCSTAFF as the table name. Select 4 as the report name, and enter **MAILING LABELS** as the description. Then choose Free-Form from the next menu, and the Report Specification will be displayed.

Place the cursor just below the page-band border, and press the Report Delete Line key ((CTRL)-(Y)) six times to remove the lines in the page heading. Move the cursor to the blank line above the Social Security field and press (CTRL)-(Y) twice, once to delete the blank line and once to delete the line containing the Social Security field.

Use the (DEL) key to delete the Last Name heading. Move the cursor to the start of the First Name heading. Go into Insert mode by pressing the (INS) key until the cursor appears as a thin line. Then press (BACKSPACE) once to delete the existing carriage return and move the first name field onto the same line as the last name. Press the (SPACEBAR) once to add a space, and then use the (DEL) key to delete the First Name heading. Also use the (DEL) key to delete the headings for the Address and City fields, leaving the fields intact.

Move the cursor down to the start of the State heading, and press (CTRL)-(Y) ten times to delete all of the remaining fields. Then press (ENTER) four times to add four extra blank lines. These will serve as spacing between the labels. In your own applications, you can add as many lines as are necessary to fit your particular labels.

Place the cursor two spaces to the right of the City field, and choose Field/Place/Regular from the menu. Select State from the list of fields, and press (ENTER) twice to place the field and set the width.

Next, move the cursor two spaces to the right of the end of the state field, and choose Field/Place/Regular from the menu. Select ZIP Code from the list of fields, and press (ENTER) twice to place the field and set the width.

Move the cursor below the form band and into the page band, and place the cursor at the left edge. Then press (CTRL)-(Y) four times to remove the extra blank lines. (Since this report will be used with mailing labels, no extra space, header, or footer are necessary.)

At this point, your screen should resemble the example shown in Figure 12-5. You can visually check the results while still designing the report; to do this, choose the Output option of the Design menu.

Figure 12-5.   *Report Specification for mailing labels*

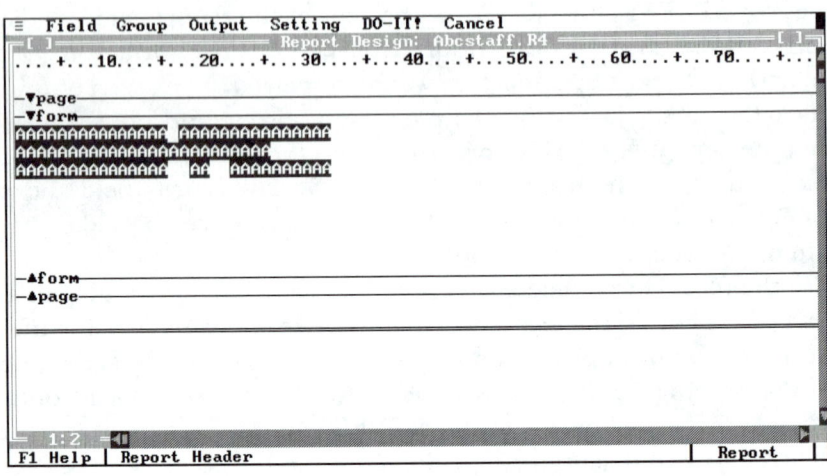

Select Screen from the next menu that appears, and you should see a report that resembles this:

```
Kramer          Harry
1245 Ocean Pine Way
McLean,   VA                         22304-1234



Westman         Andrea
4807 East Avenue
Silver Spring    MD                  20910-0124



Robinson        Shirley
267 Browning Ave #2A
Takoma Park      MD       20912
```

This report approximates the appearance of mailing labels, but there are obviously a few problems. The names have too much space between them, as do the city and state fields. This is because Paradox is using the default lengths of the fields.

12

The RemoveBlanks menu option can be used to solve this problem. Close the Report Preview window, and choose Setting from the menu. The following menu options will appear.

```
Setting

RemoveBlanks    ▶
PageLayout      ▶
Margin
Setup           ▶
Wait            ▶
Labels          ▶
```

The RemoveBlanks option lets you tell Paradox to trim extra leading or trailing blank spaces, or to suppress the printing of blank lines when a field is empty.

Choose RemoveBlanks from the menu. The next menu offers two options: LineSqueeze and FieldSqueeze. The LineSqueeze option tells Paradox to suppress the printing of lines when all of the fields in that line are blank. The FieldSqueeze option suppresses extra spaces between fields. Choose FieldSqueeze from the menu, and then choose Yes from the next menu to confirm the action.

This will put the names closer together, but the labels will still print last name first. A more pleasant appearance would be to show the first name followed by the last name. To accomplish this, the name fields must be moved. Place the cursor at the start of the last name field, and make sure you are in Insert mode (press the (INS) key until the cursor assumes a thin flat shape). Press the (SPACEBAR) once to push the last name field to the right one space.

From the menu, choose Field/Erase. Place the cursor within the first name field, and press (ENTER) to remove the field. Then move the cursor back to the far left, to the space you inserted beside the last name field. From the menu, choose Field/Place/Regular, and choose First Name from the list of fields that appears. Then, press (ENTER) twice to complete the placement of the field.

For one last aesthetic touch, move the cursor to the space immediately following the city field, and insert a comma. This will cause a comma to appear between each city and state when the report is printed.

You can immediately see the results by selecting the Output option of the Design menu. Select Screen from the next menu that appears, and this time you should see a report with names and addresses in a format resembling this one:

```
Harry Kramer
1245 Ocean Pine Way
McLean, VA 22304-1234


Andrea Westman
4807 East Avenue
Silver Spring, MD 20910-0124


Shirley Robinson
267 Browning Ave #2A
Takoma Park, MD 20912
```

All that remains is to provide the labels in the "two-across" format, which prints two labels across the page. To perform this task, you will add a page width for each additional label you need across the page, and you will use the Labels option of the menu to tell Paradox to use a "print-across" format.

You will need to adjust the width of the pages, since labels are not normally 80 characters wide each. From the menu, choose Setting/ PageLayout/Width. Backspace through the default width of 80, and enter **40** as the new width for the mailing labels. Choose Setting from the menu. From the next menu that appears, select PageLayout. Choose Insert to add the second page width.

Finally, choose Setting/Labels from the menu. Then select Yes to confirm the use of the mailing-label format. This time, test your design by turning on your printer, and choosing Output/Printer (the two-across label format is not visible in the Report Preview window on screen). You should see an example similar in format to the one shown here (although your employee names may be in a different order):

```
Harry Kramer                        Andrea Westman
1245 Ocean Pine Way                 4807 East Avenue
McLean, VA  22304-1234              Silver Spring, MD  20910-0124



Marcia Morse                        David Jackson
4260 Park Avenue                    4102 Valley Lane
Chevy Chase, MD  20815-0988         Falls Church, VA  22044
```

```
Sandra Abernathy                    William Morse
1512 Redskins Park Drive            4260 Park Avenue
Herndon, VA  22071                  Chevy Chase, MD  20815-0988
```

This looks fine on the screen, but when you print the labels you'll also want the page length set to Continuous to match continuous-form labels. From the menu, choose Setting/PageLayout/Length. Backspace over the existing value, and enter **C** to set the page length to Continuous.

Note

If you use sheet labels with a laser printer, leave the Setting/PageLayout/Length value at 66 or less. With Hewlett-Packard LaserJet printers, a value of 60 often works well.

Finally, choose DO-IT! to save the report. You can generate the report at any time with the usual menu options of Report/Output followed by the name of the table and of the report, and then the choice of output destinations (Printer, Screen, or File).

When dealing with mailing labels, remember that they can be difficult to align in the printer. You may want to experiment with sheets of ordinary paper first, before trying to print on the actual labels.

You can make changes as needed to fit your preferred size of labels. For example, if less space is desired between labels, remove blank lines with CTRL-Y; if more space is needed, make sure you are in Insert mode (press the INS key until the cursor takes on the shape of a thin line). Then press ENTER where you want to add new blank lines. You can use the various options displayed when you choose Setting/PageLayout to change your page widths, lengths, or the number of labels that appear across a page. Be sure to choose the Labels option from the menu when you are designing a report that will provide mailing labels, so Paradox will print across in the proper format.

Form Letters

You can also generate form letters with a free-form report. Since literal text can be entered anywhere you wish within the form band of the free-form report, you can simply type the text of the form letter into the report's form band. Insert the fields at the desired locations; use the FieldSqueeze option (from the menu, you choose Setting/RemoveBlanks/FieldSqueeze) to close up any excess space between the contents of fields and the literal text that makes up the letter. An example of a free-form report designed as a form letter appears in Figure 12-6.

Note the presence of the reserved word PAGEBREAK in this report form. Use this reserved word to tell Paradox to start a new page. The word PAGEBREAK must appear on a line by itself, flush at the left margin, and it must be in uppercase letters.

Depending on where you place PAGEBREAK, you will get different results. For example, if you place the word at the header or footer of a group, Paradox will start a new page for each group. If you place it at the start of a form band, each record will occupy a separate page.

Creating Invoices

You can generate invoices by designing free-form reports to contain calculated fields or summary fields. Consider the ABC Temporaries billing

Figure 12-6.   *Example of form letter*

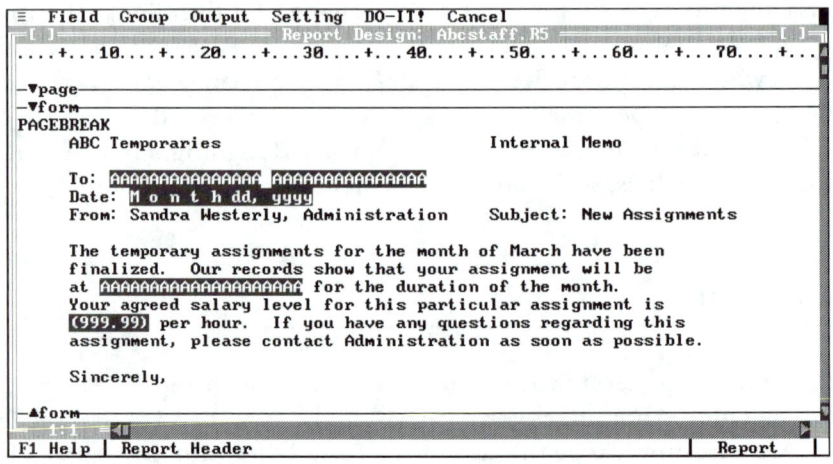

task. Each client needs an invoice that shows the hours worked and a total amount due for the employees who worked for that client. The Report Specification shown in Figure 12-7 could handle this need.

This particular report is based on an ANSWER table that draws data from the ABCSTAFF and HOURS tables. The tables are linked through an example element in the Social Security field. The Assignment, Weekend date, and Hours worked fields from the HOURS table are selected for inclusion in the ANSWER table, as are the Last Name, First Name, and Hourly Rate fields from the ABCSTAFF table. The calculated field shown next to the Total heading for each employee is a result of the expression

[Hours worked] * [Hourly Rate]

and the summary field shown next to the Total Due for Services Rendered heading is a summary field based upon a calculated field (with the same expression).

To create the summary field, select Field/Place/Summary/Calculated. Then the expression just given is entered. The Sum option is chosen from the next menu that appears, and PerGroup is selected to indicate that the

Figure 12-7. *Report Specification for invoices*

```
≡  Field  Group  Output  Setting  DO-IT!  Cancel
═[ ]══════════════ Report Design: Answer.R1 ══════════════[ ]═
....+...10....+...20....+...30....+...40....+...50....+...60....+...70....+...
─▼page
──▼group Assignment─────────────────────────────────────
                                          ABC Temporaries
   For client: AAAAAAAAAAAAAAAAAAAAA     47 Summer Valley Way
                                          Herndon, VA 22070
─▼form
Employee: A. AAAAAAAAAAAAAAA   Wk Ending:mm/dd/yy Hours:9999 Total:99999
─▲form

                    Total Due for Services Rendered: (999,999.99)
PAGEBREAK
──▲group Assignment─────────────────────────────────────
─▲page

═ 1:1  ═◀▌
F1 Help │ Report Header                              │ Report │
```

field will show a summary total for each group (or client). Finally, the field is placed in the desired location. The results of a report following this design are shown in Figure 12-8.

Without the addition of the reserved word PAGEBREAK in the Report Specification shown in Figure 12-7, the billings would print in a continuous format. The PAGEBREAK notation causes each assignment group to print on a separate page.

Figure 12-8.   *Example of an invoice*

```
                                                         ABC Temporaries
For client: City Revenue Dept.                        47 Summer Valley Way
                                                        Herndon, VA 22071


Employee: S. Abernathy     Wk Ending:   5/16/92  Hours:   28  Total: 504.00
Employee: S. Abernathy     Wk Ending:   5/23/92  Hours:   32  Total: 576.00
Employee: D. Jackson       Wk Ending:   5/16/92  Hours:   30  Total: 360.00
Employee: D. Jackson       Wk Ending:   5/23/92  Hours:   30  Total: 360.00
Employee: W. Robinson      Wk Ending:   5/16/92  Hours:   35  Total: 420.00
Employee: W. Robinson      Wk Ending:   5/23/92  Hours:   32  Total: 384.00

Total Due for Services Rendered:    2,604.00


                                                         ABC Temporaries
For client: National Oil Co.                          47 Summer Valley Way
                                                        Herndon, VA 22071

Employee: J. Jones         Wk Ending:   5/16/92  Hours:   35  Total: 612.50
Employee: J. Jones         Wk Ending:   5/23/92  Hours:   33  Total: 577.50
Employee: M. Morse         Wk Ending:   5/16/92  Hours:   32  Total: 480.00
Employee: S. Robinson      Wk Ending:   5/16/92  Hours:   27  Total: 324.00
Employee: A. Westman       Wk Ending:   5/16/92  Hours:   30  Total: 720.00
Employee: A. Westman       Wk Ending:   5/23/92  Hours:   35  Total: 840.00


Total Due for Services Rendered:    3,554.00


                                                         ABC Temporaries
For client: Smith Builders                            47 Summer Valley Way
                                                        Herndon, VA 22071

Employee: E. Hart          Wk Ending:   5/23/92  Hours:   30  Total: 420.00
Employee: M. Mitchell      Wk Ending:   5/23/92  Hours:   28  Total: 336.00
Employee: W. Morse         Wk Ending:   5/23/92  Hours:   35  Total: 420.00

Total Due for Services Rendered:    1,176.00
```

Final Advice

The majority of operations you will perform when designing reports are the same with tabular reports as with free-form reports. The main differences are that with tabular reports, the Setting menu includes the Formats and GroupRepeats options. With free-form reports, however, these options are not available. Instead, two new options are offered, Labels and RemoveBlanks. All other options are the same between the two types of reports, and you can perform similar steps to design your tabular or free-form reports. See Chapter 7 (if you have not already read it) for additional important details on report design.

Quick Summary

To quickly create a default free-form report   Choose Report/Design from the menu. Enter the name for the table on which to base the report. Choose a name and enter a description for the report when prompted. Select Free-Form from the next menu, then choose DO-IT! ((F2)) to store the default report.

To create a custom free-form report   From the menu, you should choose Report/Design. Enter the name for the table on which to base the report. Choose a name and enter a description for the report when prompted. Select Free-Form from the next menu. Modify the Report Specification that appears on the screen. Use the available menu options for placing and moving fields, adding group bands, and changing settings.) When done with the report's design, choose DO-IT! to store the report.

13

Using the Paradox Application Workshop

If you've closely followed this text, you should already have a basic knowledge of how to put Paradox to work in your word environment. You have created various tables, used the menu options for getting information from those tables, designed custom reports, and used scripts to automate your work. But what is for many users the most advanced feature of Paradox has been saved for this chapter: the Paradox Application Workshop (called the Personal Programmer in previous versions of Paradox). The Application Workshop is an applications development tool; you can use it to create complete applications—including custom menus and help screens—for users of your tables, reports, and forms. And you need not learn to program to create these applications; all you need to do is choose from a series of menu selections.

The Application Workshop has been significantly enhanced over the Personal Programmer utility found in previous versions of Paradox. The large number of options available throughout the Application Workshop make it possible to design and implement complex applications; at the same time, this level of flexibility may overwhelm the new user of the Application

Workshop. This chapter does not attempt to cover all possible options of the Application Workshop; to do so would require a book in itself. But the examples herein will provide a basic idea of how simple applications can be designed with this utility. If you wish to delve further into the Application Workshop's capabilities, you will find explanations of all its features and options in your Paradox documentation.

An Application Defined

First let's examine why applications are so important to database users. In a nutshell, an *application* makes things easier on the average user, by combining a series of "building blocks" such as tables, forms, reports, and scripts into a complete system. An application is what makes, for example, an accounts receivable database different from an accounts payable database. Both systems may deal with the same kinds of information—dollar amounts, and documents addressed to recipients that contain breakdowns of those amounts. But the accounts receivable database is designed to deal with debtors' payments to the company using the database, and the accounts payable database handles the company's payments to its creditors. The fields used in the tables in both systems might be quite similar in form, but the operations handled by the two systems would be notably different. In both cases, Paradox provides the tools necessary to handle the tasks involved, but it is the application that makes the two systems perform differently.

Besides helping you meet the requirements of specific tasks, an application is the glue that binds together the building blocks of a database—one or more tables, the forms, and the reports—into a complete operating unit. Applications are nothing new in the computer world, and there is a good chance that you have already used several types of specialized applications based around a database of some sort. Programs to handle mailing lists, manage inventory, track sales, and do accounting are all specialized applications that use databases, with which you may have had some experience.

Unfortunately, to gain the benefits of these applications, you had to buy a software package designed for the application (or pay a programmer to write it), and then you were often stuck with something that did most, but not all of what you wanted. With the Paradox Application Workshop, however, you can build custom applications designed to do precisely what you want, without learning programming, and without hiring a programmer.

The Design of a Typical Application

13

To further illustrate how an application can make things easier, consider the work you've done in the examples throughout this book to create a database system for ABC Temporaries. You have made tables for tracking data for employees and time worked for clients, and you have designed custom forms and custom reports. Now that you are familiar with Paradox, whenever you need to add or edit data in your database, or generate reports from it, you can load Paradox and use its various menu options to accomplish the desired results.

But what happens when you want to show someone else in the office how to add or edit data, or how to produce reports? That person must go through the same learning curve, getting sufficiently familiar with the Paradox menus to be able to accomplish the same kind of results that you can manage. If your office has the usual moderate-to-high staff turnover common in today's business world, you could be faced with frequently having to show others how to use Paradox for the same applications, year in and year out.

The answer to this sort of dilemma, repeatedly proven by thousands of human programmers, is to build *custom applications*. Such applications have menu choices so specific that casual users need no specialized training to use the applications. The Paradox Application Workshop lets you design an application to communicate in the terms that your office staff will understand.

For example, the employees of ABC Temporaries commonly need to perform the following tasks:

- Add new employees to the ABCSTAFF table
- Edit or delete employees in the ABCSTAFF table
- Add client time to the HOURS table
- Edit client time in the HOURS table
- Add new clients to the CLIENTS table
- Edit or delete clients in the CLIENTS table

- Print lists of employees, client time records, client names and addresses, and so forth

You can automate all of these tasks by using the Application Workshop to create an application that provides one or more simple menu choices for each of the operations. If you were to try to sketch out the design of such an application on paper, it might resemble that in Figure 13-1.

This example design makes use of some common application components: a *main menu*, and multiple secondary *submenus*. As you design your own applications, you may find the use of submenus for specific areas, such as working with a particular table or generating reports, to be a wise idea. If you try to place too many menu choices on a single menu, the application can become visually confusing. When designing any application, it is usually helpful to sketch out on paper a preliminary design like the above example, before you start to use the Application Workshop. Having the design outlined

Figure 13-1.   *Design of the application for ABC Temporaries*

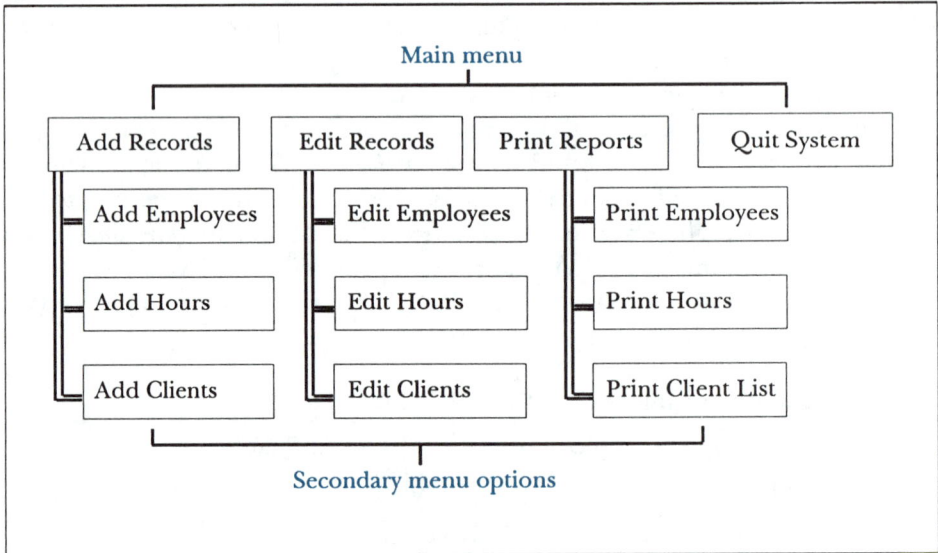

in this manner gives you a visual point of reference as you are actually building the application with the program.

Installing the Paradox Application Workshop

Before using the Paradox Application Workshop, you must install it. The Workshop program is *not* automatically installed as a part of the normal Paradox installation procedure. The installation process differs depending on what Paradox version you are using, so in all cases you should refer to the Installation chapter in the *Paradox Application Workshop Guide* (included with your Paradox documentation).

Hardware Requirements for the Workshop

To operate, the Paradox Application Workshop requires a hard disk with at least 2MB of free disk space, 640K of base memory, and at least 1.5MB of total memory. You can run applications developed with the Application Workshop on a 640K machine, but you must have some extended or expanded memory installed in your machine to use the Application Workshop itself.

The Installation Process

Assuming you are using Paradox for DOS, switch to the \PDOX40 subdirectory, insert the Application Workshop Disk #1 in drive A, and enter the following:

```
A:INSTALL
```

to begin the installation of the Workshop program. Refer to your Paradox documentation for additional details on the installation, and follow the prompts that appear on the screen to complete the process.

Updating Your AUTOEXEC.BAT File PATH Statement

Note

As indicated in the Installation chapter of the Paradox Application Workshop Guide, in order for the Application Workshop to operate while you use other subdirectories, you must update the DOS PATH statement in your AUTOEXEC.BAT file.

The Application Workshop installation process normally places the Workshop files in a subdirectory named \PDOX40\WORKSHOP, and the PATH statement should include the path to this subdirectory. You can update your AUTOEXEC.BAT file with any word processor that can load and save files as ASCII text, or with the DOS COPY command (see your DOS manual for details). A typical AUTOEXEC.BAT file that provides a path to both the PDOX40 and the WORKSHOP subdirectories might resemble the following:

```
date
path=c:\perfect;c:\;c:\lotus;c:\pdox40;c:\pdox40\workshop
cls
type menu
```

If you prefer not to change your AUTOEXEC.BAT file, you can execute a PATH command just before starting the Paradox Application Workshop, by typing the command at the DOS prompt. For example, assuming your hard disk is drive C, you could enter

```
PATH=C:\PDOX40;C:\PDOX40\PAW
```

at the DOS prompt to set the needed path.

Using a PATH statement, either in the AUTOEXEC.BAT file or directly at the DOS prompt, allows you to store your applications in subdirectories of your choosing, while running the Paradox Application Workshop from any of those subdirectories.

Using the Application Workshop: An Overview

You already know much of what you need to use the Application Workshop, if you've worked through the preceding chapters of this book.

The Application Workshop uses the same kinds of menus and dialog boxes that appear throughout Paradox. And a series of thorough help screens are visible the entire time you are in the Workshop, explaining your options each step of the way.

Creating any application with the Application Workshop involves the following steps:

1. Choose a directory to store the application, by selecting Application/Directory from the Application Workshop menu. If you have already created the Paradox tables, forms, reports, and scripts that will be used by the application, they should be copied into this directory.

2. Select Application/New from the menu. In the dialog box that appears, enter a name and other relevant information for the new application.

3. Design the menu structure for the application.

4. Define the desired action (called Action Objects) for each menu option.

5. Attach the Action Objects to menu options, if you did not do so when you designed the actions.

6. If desired, use Application/Edit to create a Startup Screen (this step is optional).

7. Choose Application/Finish to cause the scripts for the application to be generated and stored in the current directory.

8. Choose Exit/To Paradox or Exit/To DOS to leave the Application Workshop.

Once you complete an application, you can run it just as you would run any Paradox script.

The exercise that you will do through the remainder of this chapter demonstrates how you can build a complete application, using the above steps. To build the application you will need the following tables, forms, and reports:

- The ABCSTAFF table created in Chapter 3
- The HOURS table created in Chapter 4

- The custom form for the ABCSTAFF table created in Chapter 5
- The custom report for the ABCSTAFF and HOURS tables created in Chapter 7

If you have not yet created any of these items, refer back to the appropriate chapters and do so before proceeding. Also, if you have not yet installed the Paradox Application Workshop, do so now.

An Exercise Using the Paradox Application Workshop

If you have not yet altered your AUTOEXEC.BAT file's PATH statement as instructed previously, do so now. Then, before starting the Paradox Application Workshop, restart your PC so that the AUTOEXEC.BAT file will set the proper path. (Or, if you prefer, enter the suggested PATH command directly at the DOS prompt.) Then switch to the subdirectory that contains the tables, reports, and forms you will use in the example application. (You can create the tables, forms, and reports from within the Paradox Application Workshop, but building the application will take far less time if the necessary building blocks already exist when you start the Application Workshop.)

Start Paradox now in the usual manner. Then start the Paradox Application Workshop, by choosing Utilities from the System menu (use the mouse or (ALT)-(SPACEBAR)). Then select Workshop from the menu that appears. As the Paradox Application Workshop loads, you will briefly see an introductory screen. (If you have recently installed Paradox, you may also be prompted to indicate what type of monitor you are using.) Then the main menu for the Paradox Application Workshop appears, as shown in Figure 13-2. At the top of the screen are the Application Workshop menu options, described here:

- *Application*   This menu lets you open existing applications, create new applications, change directories, and finish the building of applications.

- *ActionEdit*   This menu lets you create or modify Action Objects, which are actions that you assign to the various menu choices of an application.

Figure 13-2. The Application Workshop main menu

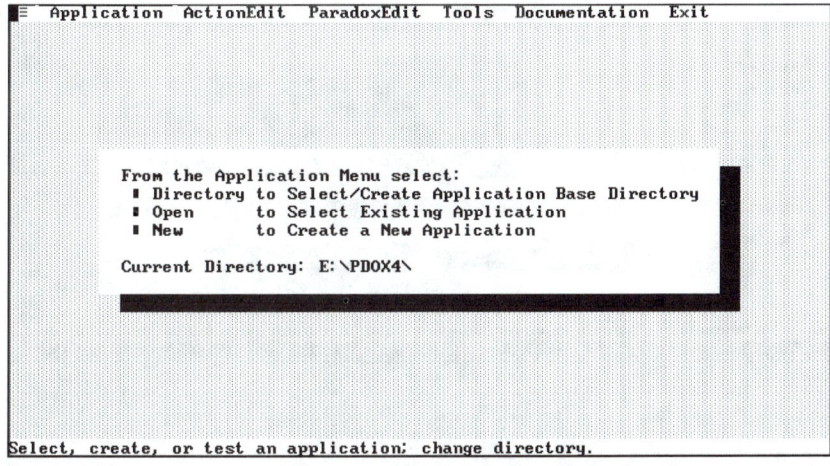

```
≡  Application  ActionEdit  ParadoxEdit  Tools  Documentation  Exit




        From the Application Menu select:
          ▪ Directory to Select/Create Application Base Directory
          ▪ Open      to Select Existing Application
          ▪ New       to Create a New Application

        Current Directory: E:\PDOX4\




Select, create, or test an application; change directory.
```

- *ParadoxEdit* This menu contains the options for designing and changing Paradox objects (tables, forms, reports, or scripts).

- *Tools* This menu contains the options for copying, renaming, and deleting objects.

- *Documentation* This menu lets you generate documentation describing your application.

- *Exit* Use this option to exit the Application Workshop and return to Paradox or to DOS.

In this exercise, you want to create a new application for ABC Temporaries, so choose New from the Application menu. If you are asked whether you want to create a new application table, answer Yes. In a moment, you will see the New Application dialog box shown in Figure 13-3.

The cursor is flashing in the Application ID field. Here you must enter an eight-character ID for the application; this will be used by the Workshop program as a filename for the script. Follow the DOS file-naming conventions when making this entry; you can use any combination of characters that is

Figure 13-3.   *The New Application dialog box*

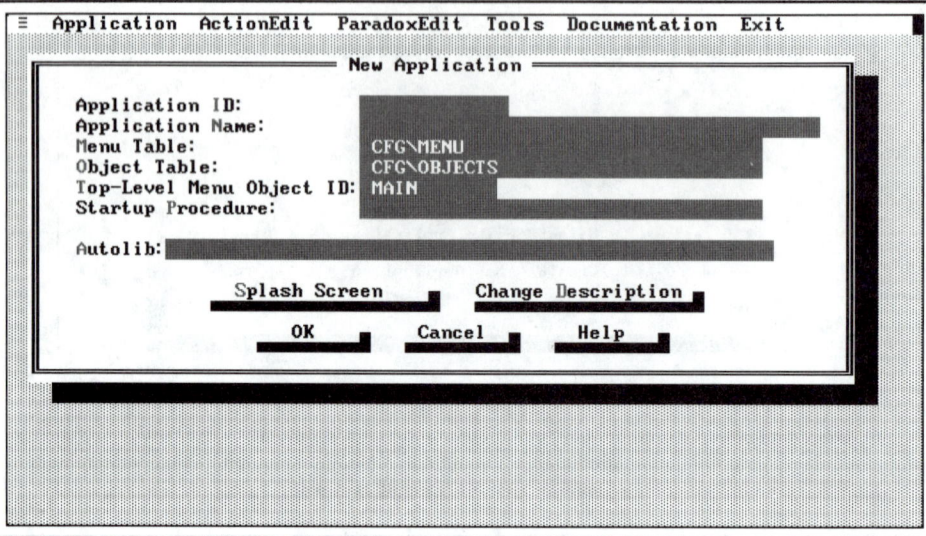

acceptable as a DOS filename. For this example, enter **STAFF** and press the
(TAB) key to move to the next field.

In the Application Name field, enter

```
ABC Temporaries Tracking System
```

These are the only two entries that are required in the New Application
dialog box, but the remaining options, described below, may be of interest as
you build more complex applications.

- The Menu Table entry, which reads CFG\MENU by default, lets you
  specify where the Application Workshop will store a special menu
  table that it uses to keep track of your application's menu structure.
  (A subdirectory by this name is automatically created by the Application Workshop.)

- In similar fashion, the Object Table field lets you specify where a
  special table describing Action Objects will be stored; the default
  location is CFG\OBJECTS.

- The entry you make in the Top-Level Menu Object ID field appears as the name of your application's menu bar; the default for this choice is MAIN.

- The Startup Procedure and Autolib fields are used by advanced PAL programmers; see your Application Workshop documentation for details on these entries.

- The Splash Screen command button can be used to design an introductory screen that is displayed when the application is first started, and the Change Description button can be used to enter a detailed written description of the application.

Next, (TAB) to the OK button and press (ENTER), or click on the OK button. In a few moments, a blank application menu bar appears on the desktop, as shown in Figure 13-4. This menu bar is where you will place the menu choices for the main menu of your application. In this exercise, you will first place the main menu options needed; then, using the ActionEdit menu, you will specify what action should result from each menu choice. (When designing your own applications, you have the flexibility of either designing the menu first and then assigning actions, or designing the Action Objects first and later assigning them to menu choices.)

Double-click on the <New> menu choice of the Application menu bar, or highlight it and press (ENTER) to select it. The following menu appears.

```
┌Menu Insert─┐
│SubMenu     │
│Action      │
└────────────┘
```

This menu lets you insert another menu (using the SubMenu choice), or insert an action (using the Action choice). If you want this menu option to lead directly to an action, such as editing a table or printing a report, you would choose Action. However, we want the first three menu options of our application to lead to other menus, so choose SubMenu now. A Menu Definition dialog box appears, as shown in Figure 13-5.

In the Menu Definition box, you need to enter a keyword and a description. The keyword you enter names the menu option that will appear when the application runs. The description will appear at the bottom of the screen whenever the menu option is highlighted. Enter the word **Add** in the Keyword

Figure 13-4.   *A blank application menu bar*

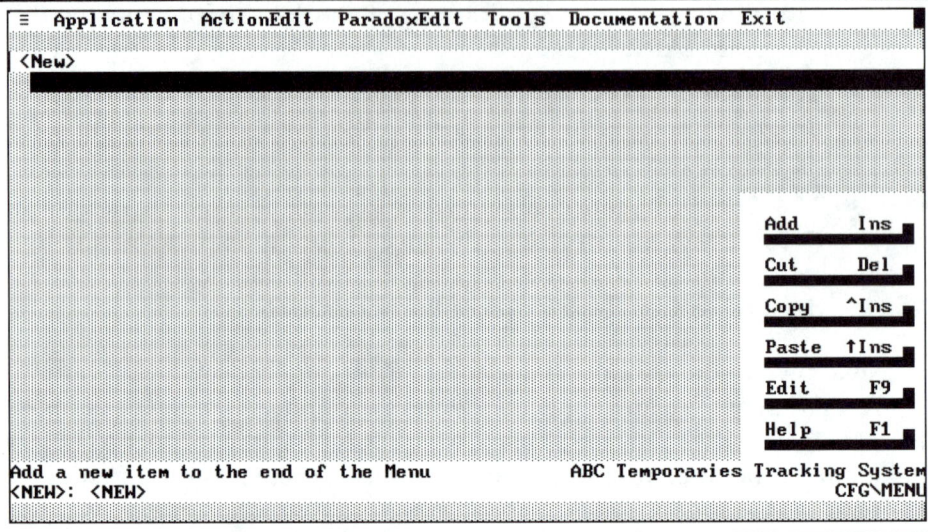

Figure 13-5.   *The Menu Definition dialog box*

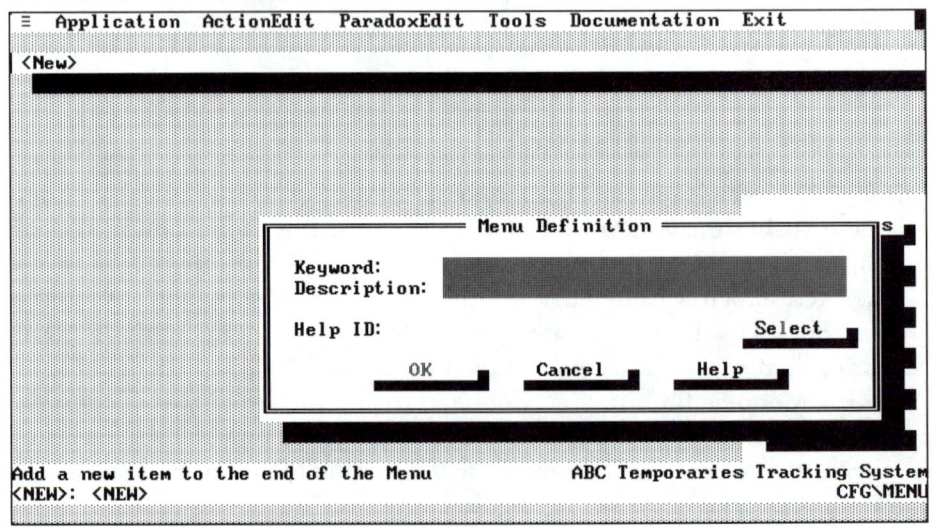

field, and press (TAB) to move to the Description field. Enter the following in the Description field:

```
Add records to STAFF, HOURS, CLIENTS.
```

Then, (TAB) to the OK button and press (ENTER), or click on OK. In a moment, the new Add menu appears on the menu bar, and another <New> menu option appears beside it.

Note

Hereafter in this exercise, an instruction to "choose" a button or option in a dialog box, or an item in a list box, means to click it with the mouse or to highlight it and press the (ENTER) key.

Double-click on the <New> option, or highlight it with the (→) key and press (ENTER). The Menu Insert menu again appears, asking if you want to insert another menu, or an action. Choose SubMenu again. This time, when the Menu Definition dialog box appears, enter the word **Edit** in the Keyword field. Then press (TAB) and enter the following in the Description field:

```
Edit or delete records in STAFF, HOURS, CLIENTS.
```

(TAB) to the OK button and press (ENTER), or click on OK. In a moment, the new Edit menu appears on the menu bar, and another <New> menu option appears beside it.

Double-click on the <New> option, or highlight it with the (→) key and press (ENTER). In the Menu Insert menu, choose SubMenu again. In the Menu Definition dialog box, enter **Print** for the keyword, and enter the following for the description:

```
Print reports.
```

Choose the OK button. In a moment, the new Add menu appears on the menu bar, and another <New> menu option appears beside it.

Double-click on the <New> option, or highlight it with the (→) key and press (ENTER). When the Menu Insert menu again appears, this time choose Action. You'll see an expanded Menu Definition dialog box, as shown in Figure 13-6. The additional options in this dialog box will let you assign an action to the menu choice.

Figure 13-6.   *Expanded Menu Definition dialog box*

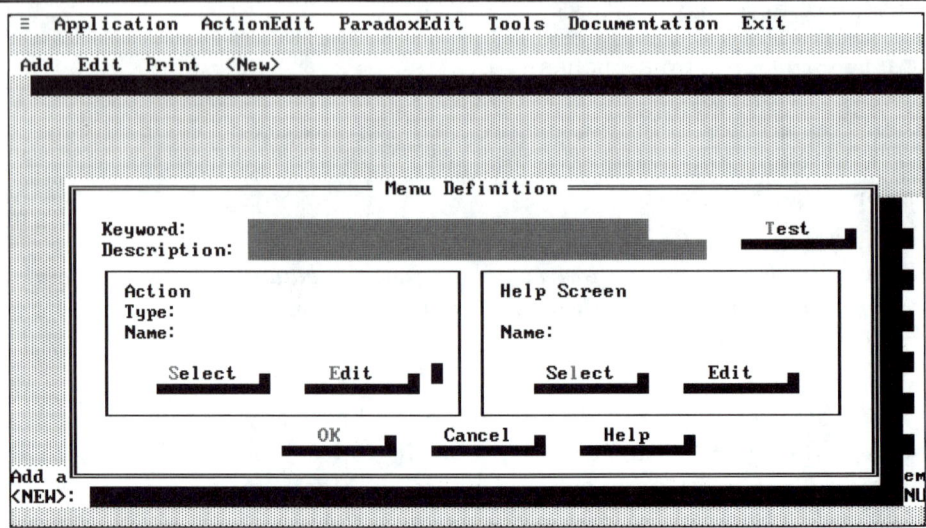

In the Keyword field, enter **Quit**, and enter the following description in the Description field:

```
Leave system and return to Paradox.
```

Next, find the Select button, located in the Action portion of the dialog box. Click on the Select button, or (TAB) to the Select button and press (ENTER). In a moment, the Object Type list box appears, as shown in Figure 13-7. From this list box, you can select the desired action that you want to occur when the menu option is selected.

Since you are selecting an action for the Quit option, choose Quit To Paradox from the list box (highlight the option and press (ENTER), or double-click on it). The list box disappears to again reveal the expanded Menu Definition dialog box. (You will notice that Quit to Paradox is now shown as an action in the Action portion of this dialog box.) Choose the OK button to complete the definition of this menu.

With the main menu options for your STAFF application defined, you are ready to define the submenus. Use the (←) key to highlight the Add option

Figure 13-7. **The Object Type list box**

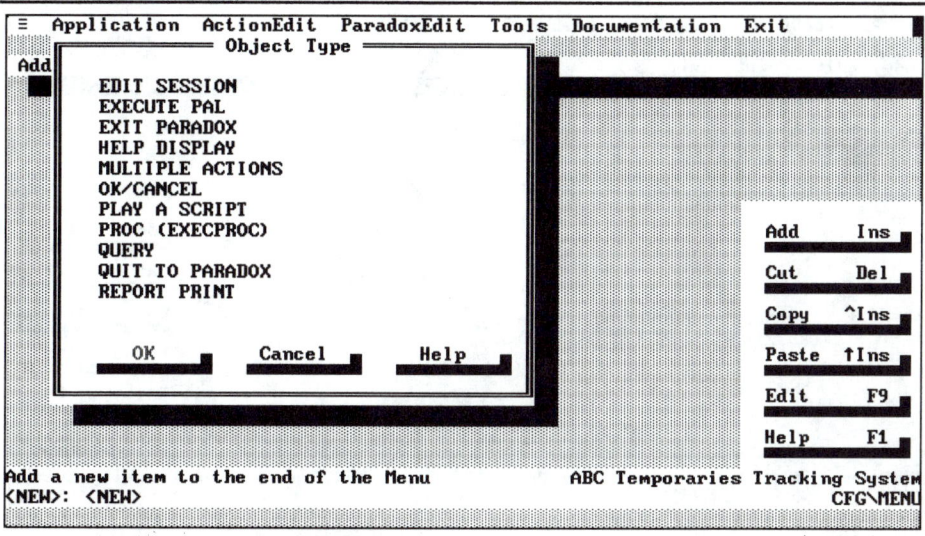

and press (ENTER), or click on the Add option. When you do so, a submenu with a single option, <New>, appears beneath the Add menu option, as shown in Figure 13-8.

With the <New> submenu open, press (ENTER), or double-click on <New>. The following Menu Insert menu appears.

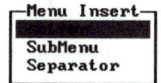

Here you have a choice of placing an action, a submenu, or a separator line at the current location in your submenu. Recall from our design of the original application that this menu is to have three options for adding records to all three tables. So choose Action, and the expanded Menu Definition dialog box again appears.

In the Keyword field, enter **Employees**. In the Description field, enter

```
Add records to the ABCSTAFF table.
```

Figure 13-8.   *Submenu for the Add option*

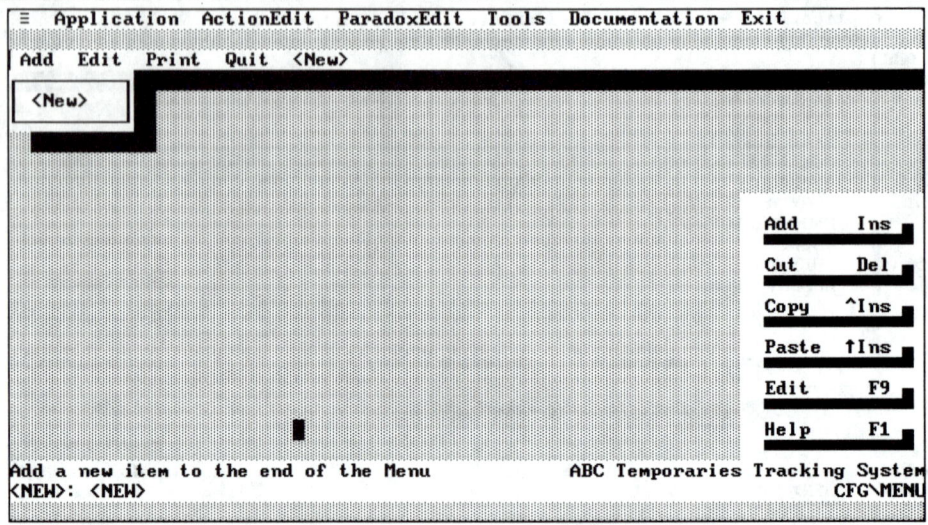

Choose the Select button in the Action portion of the dialog box. When the Object Type list box appears, choose Edit Session from the list. You'll next see the dialog box that is shown in Figure 13-9.

Choose the New button. When the prompt for a new Edit Session name appears, enter **ADD EMPLOYEES,** and press (ENTER) or click on OK. In a moment, an Edit Session dialog box appears, as shown in Figure 13-10.

In an Edit Session dialog box like this one, you can specify which tables your users will be able to edit. The Tables on Workspace area, which occupies most of the dialog box, will display tables that are available for editing. Additional options near the bottom of the dialog box let you specify whether passwords will be needed for editing, what modes will be used for editing, and any prompts that appear when the user edits the table. Many of the options in this dialog box are beyond the scope of this chapter, but you can refer to your *Application Workshop Guide* for details on the more advanced options that appear here, and elsewhere in the Application Workshop screens.

Figure 13-9. *The Select: Edit Session dialog box*

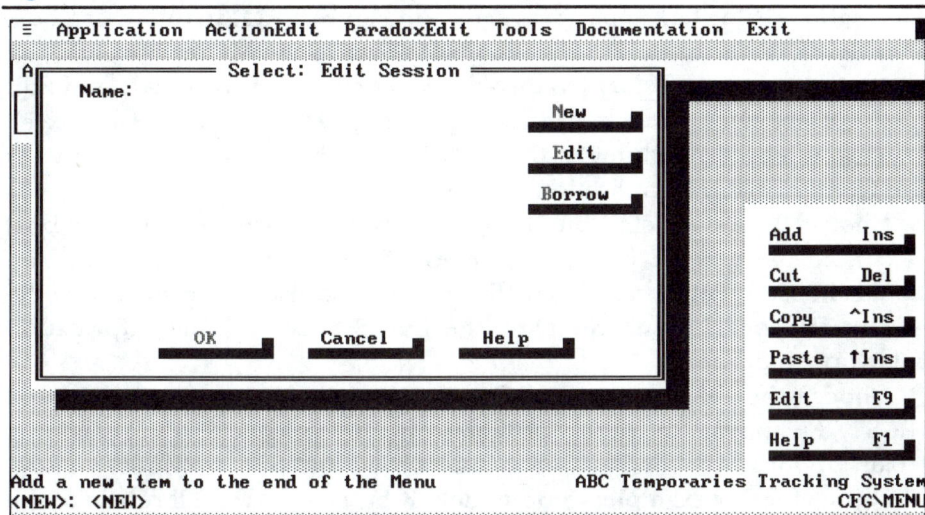

Figure 13-10. *The Edit Session dialog box for the Add Employees option*

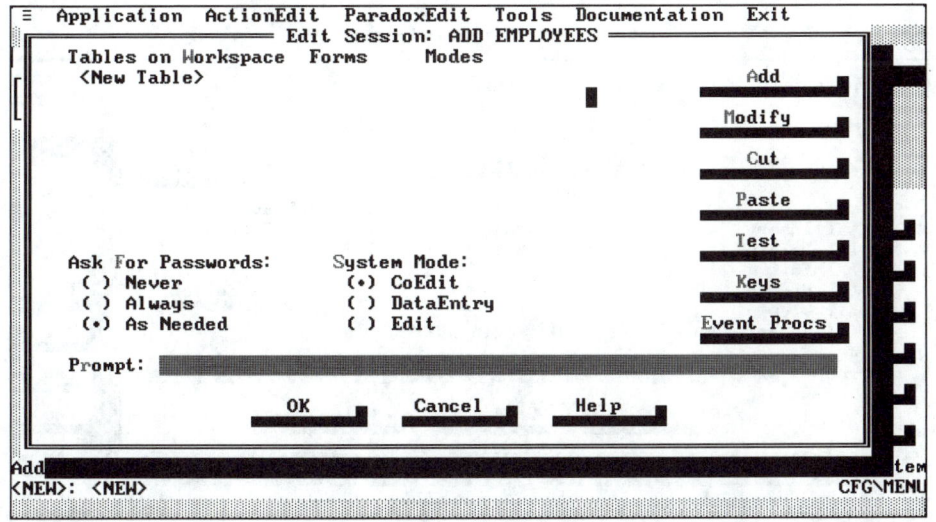

Choose the Add button to add a new table. The Edit Session – Table Information dialog box appears, as shown in Figure 13-11. In this dialog box, enter **ABCSTAFF** in the Table field. (TAB) down to the Modes box, and use (↑) and (↓) and the (SPACEBAR) to turn off the check boxes for Delete and Edit (mouse users can just click on these options to unmark the check boxes). Doing so will prevent editing of the ABCSTAFF table when the user chooses Add from the STAFF application's menu.

Choose the Form Select button. In a moment, a Form Selection list box, containing the existing forms for the ABCSTAFF table, will appear. You should choose 1, Personnel Update Form, from this list. When you do so, the list box disappears, again revealing the Edit Session – Table Information dialog box underneath.

Choose the OK button. The Edit Session dialog box reappears, and ABCSTAFF appears in the list of tables on the workspace. The remaining default options, Ask for Passwords/As Needed and System Mode/CoEdit, will suffice for this example. Choose the OK button, and you'll return to the Menu Definition dialog box.

Figure 13-11.   *The Edit Session – Table Information dialog box*

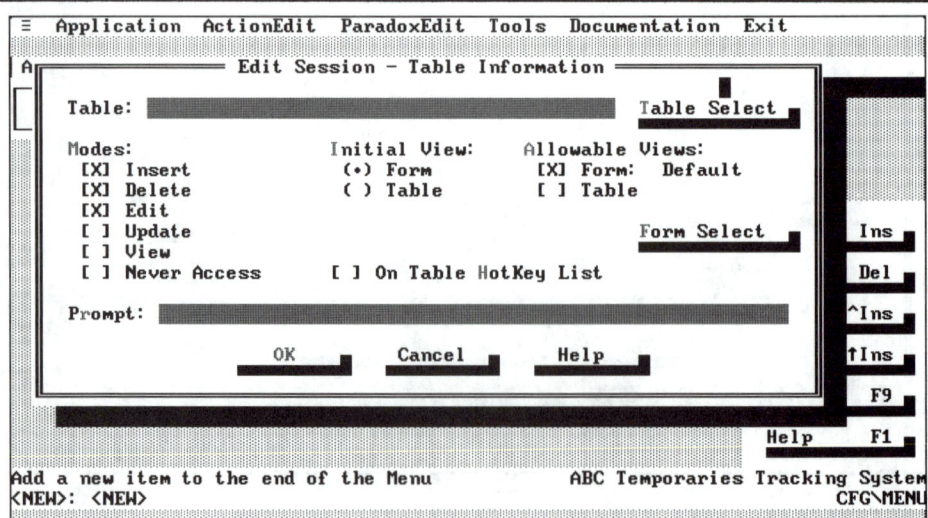

Choose OK from the Menu Definition dialog box. The dialog box closes, and the Employees choice is added to the submenu.

Highlight the <New> choice in the Add submenu, and press (ENTER) or click on <New>. From the Menu Insert menu that appears, choose Action; you'll then see the familiar expanded Menu Definition dialog box. In the Keyword field, enter **Hours**. In the Description field, enter

```
Add records to the HOURS table.
```

13

Choose the Select button. When the Object Type list box appears, choose Edit Session. In a moment, the Select: Edit Session dialog box appears. Choose the New button. When the prompt for a new Edit Session name appears, enter **ADD HOURS**, and then press (ENTER) or click on OK. In a moment, an Edit Session dialog box appears.

Choose the Add button to add a new table. When the Edit Session – Table Information dialog box appears, enter **HOURS** in the Table field. (TAB) down to the Modes box, and use the arrow keys and the (SPACEBAR) to turn off the check boxes for Delete and Edit (mouse users can just click on these options boxes to unmark the check boxes). Doing so will prevent editing of the Hours table when the user chooses Add from the STAFF application's menu.

Choose the OK button. The Edit Session dialog box reappears, with HOURS in the Tables on Workspace list. Choose the OK button to return to the Menu Definition dialog box. Choose OK from the dialog box; the Menu Definition dialog box closes, and the Hours choice is added to the submenu.

Highlight the <New> menu choice of the Add SubMenu and press (ENTER), or click on <New>. From the Menu Insert menu, choose Action; this causes the expanded Menu Definition dialog box to appear. In the Keyword field, enter **Clients**. In the Description field, enter

```
Add records to the CLIENTS table.
```

Choose the Select button. When the Object Type list box appears, choose Edit Session from the list). In a moment, the Select: Edit Session dialog box appears.

Choose the New button. When you see the prompt for a new Edit Session name, enter **ADD CLIENTS** and press (ENTER) or click on OK. In a moment, an Edit Session dialog box appears. Choose the Add button to add a new table. In the Edit Session – Table Information dialog box, enter **CLIENTS** in the Table field. (TAB) to the Modes box, and turn off the check boxes for Delete and Edit.

Choose the OK button. The Edit Session dialog box now returns, with CLIENTS in the Tables on Workspace list. Choose OK, and the dialog box vanishes to reveal the Menu Definition dialog box underneath. Choose OK from the dialog box; it closes, and the Clients choice is added to the submenu.

The next step is to define the actions for the options of the Edit submenu. Use the (→) key to highlight the Edit option, or click on the Edit option. When you do so, another submenu with a single option, <New>, appears beneath the Edit menu option.

With the <New> submenu open, press (ENTER), or double-click on <New>. You'll see the Menu Insert menu, from which you can place an action, a submenu, or a separator line at the current location in your submenu. Choose Action from the menu, and the expanded Menu Definition dialog box again appears. For Keyword, enter **Employees**; for Description, enter

```
Edit or delete records in the ABCSTAFF table.
```

Choose the Select button. When the Object Type list box appears, choose Edit Session from the list to bring up the Select: Edit Session dialog box.

Highlight the <New> choice in the dialog box and press (ENTER), or click on <New>. As the new Edit Session name, enter **EDIT EMPLOYEES**, and press (ENTER) or click on OK. In a moment, an Edit Session dialog box appears.

Choose the Add button to add a new table. In the Edit Session - Table Information dialog box, enter **ABCSTAFF** in the Table field. (TAB) to the Modes box, and turn off the check box for Insert. Doing so will prevent adding of records to the ABCSTAFF table when the user chooses Edit from the STAFF application's menu.

Choose the Form Select button. In a moment, a Form Selection list box, containing the existing forms for the ABCSTAFF table, appears. Choose 1, Personnel Update Form, from this list, and the Edit Session – Table Information dialog box reappears.

Choose the OK button, and the Edit Session dialog box reappears, with ABCSTAFF in the list of tables on the workspace. Tab to or click in the Prompt field, and enter the following:

```
Ctrl-Z to search a field, Alt-Z to search again.
```

When the application runs, the user will see this prompt as a reminder of which keys can be used to search in a field for a specific value.

Finally, choose OK, and the dialog box vanishes to reveal the Menu Definition dialog box underneath. Choose OK to close the Menu Definition dialog box and add the Employees choice to the Edit submenu.

Highlight the <New> menu choice and press (ENTER), or click on <New>. From the Menu Insert menu, choose Action; you'll again see the expanded Menu Definition dialog box. For the Keyword, enter **Hours**; in the Description field, enter

```
Edit or delete records in the HOURS table.
```

Choose the Select button. When the Object Type list box appears, choose Edit Session from the list. In a moment, the Select: Edit Session dialog box appears.

Choose <New>. When the prompt for a new Edit Session name appears, enter **EDIT HOURS** and press (ENTER) or click on OK. In a moment, an Edit Session dialog box appears.

Choose the Add button to add a new table. When the Edit Session – Table Information dialog box appears, enter **HOURS** in the Table field. In the Modes box, turn off the check box for Insert. Doing so will prevent the addition of records to the HOURS table when the user chooses Edit from the STAFF application's menu.

Choose OK, and the Edit Session dialog box reappears, with HOURS in the list of tables on the workspace. (TAB) to or click in the Prompt field, and enter the following:

```
Ctrl-Z to search a field, Alt-Z to search again.
```

Finally, choose OK, and the dialog box vanishes to reveal the Menu Definition dialog box underneath. Choose OK from this dialog box to close it, and the Hours choice is added to the submenu.

Highlight the <New> menu choice and press (ENTER), or click on <New>. From the Menu Insert menu, choose Action. In the expanded Menu Definition dialog box, enter **Clients** as the keyword. In the Description field, enter

```
Edit or delete records in the CLIENTS table.
```

13

Choose the Select button. When the Object Type list box appears, choose Edit Session from the list. In a moment, the familiar Select: Edit Session dialog box appears. Choose the New button. When the prompt for a new Edit Session name appears, enter **EDIT CLIENTS**, and press (ENTER) or click on OK. In a moment, an Edit Session dialog box appears.

Choose the Add button. When the Edit Session – Table Information dialog box appears, enter **CLIENTS** in the Table field. In the Modes box, turn off the check box for Insert. Choose OK, and the Edit Session dialog box reappears, with CLIENTS in the list of tables on the workspace. (TAB) to or click in the Prompt field, and enter the following:

```
Ctrl-Z to search a field, Alt-Z to search again.
```

Choose OK, and the dialog box vanishes to reveal the Menu Definition dialog box underneath. Choose OK to close the Menu Definition dialog box, and the Clients choice is added to the submenu.

The next step is to define the actions for the options of the Print submenu. Use (→) to highlight the Print option, or click on the Print option. When you do so, another submenu with a single option, <New>, appears beneath the Print menu option.

With the <New> submenu open, press (ENTER) or double-click on <New>. On the Menu Insert menu, choose Action, and the expanded Menu Definition dialog box reappears. Enter **Employees** as the keyword, and enter the following as the description:

```
Print employee report.
```

Choose the Select button. When the Object Type list box appears, choose Report Print from the list to bring up the Select: Report Print dialog box.

Highlight the <New> choice in the dialog box and press (ENTER), or click on <New>. When prompted, enter **PRINT EMPLOYEES** for the new Report Print name; then press (ENTER) or click on OK. In a moment, a Report Print dialog box appears, as shown in Figure 13-12.

In this dialog box, you can specify how a report will be generated when a user chooses the menu option for printing a report. Various options in the dialog box let you choose a table, and a stored report to use (you can also use the default standard report for any table). You can use the check boxes to

Figure 13-12. *The Report Print dialog box for Print Employees option*

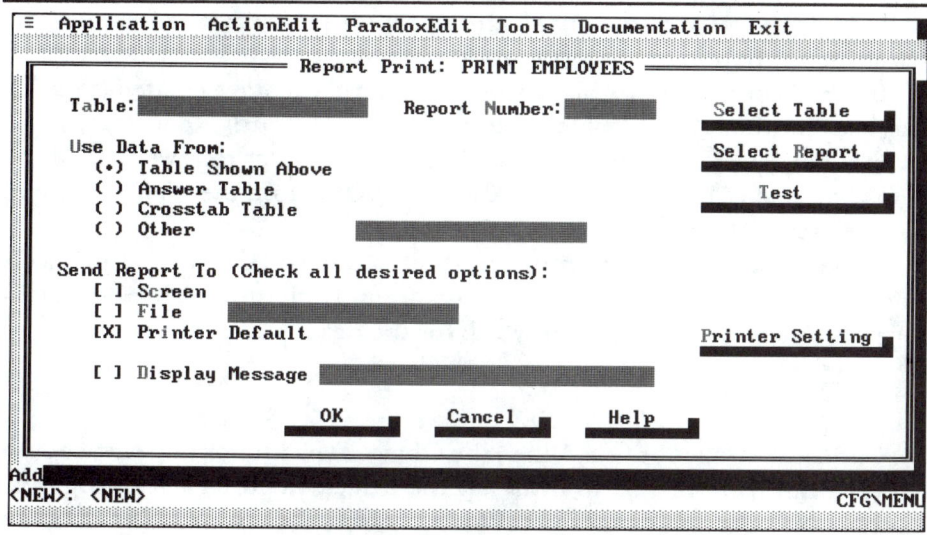

determine whether a report is sent to the screen, to a file, or to the printer, and whether a message will be displayed while the report is printing.

In the Table field, enter **ABCSTAFF** as the name of the table on which the report is based. Then choose the Select Report button to select a report. In a moment, a list box appears displaying the reports available for the ABCSTAFF table. Choose 1, Personnel Register, from the list box.

Finally, choose the OK button of the Report Print dialog box; the dialog box vanishes to reveal the Menu Definition dialog box underneath. Choose OK to close the Menu Definition dialog box; the Employees choice is added to the Print submenu.

Choose the <New> option of the Print submenu. The Menu Insert menu is displayed. Choose Action, and the expanded Menu Definition dialog box again appears. For the keyword, enter **Hours**; for the description, enter

```
Print report of hours worked.
```

Choose the Select button. When the Object Type list box appears, choose Report Print from the list to bring up the Select: Print Report dialog box.

Choose <New> in the dialog box. When you are prompted for a new Report Print name, enter **PRINT HOURS**, and press (ENTER) or click on OK.

In a moment, a Report Print dialog box appears. In the Table field, enter **HOURS** as the table name on which the report is based. Then choose the Select Report button to choose a report.

In a moment, a list box displaying the reports you have created (in prior chapters) for the HOURS table appears. Choose 1, Hourly Report, from the list box. Finally, choose OK, and the dialog box vanishes to reveal the Menu Definition dialog box underneath. Choose OK to close the dialog box and add the Hours choice to the Print submenu.

Choose the <New> option of the Print submenu. On the Menu Insert menu, choose Action, and the expanded Menu Definition dialog box again appears. Enter **Clients** as the keyword; for the description, enter

```
Print client list.
```

Choose the Select button. When the Object Type list box appears, choose Report Print from the list to bring up the Select: Report Print dialog box. Choose <New> in the dialog box. When prompted for a new Report Print name, enter **PRINT CLIENTS**, and press (ENTER) or click on OK. In a moment, a Report Print dialog box appears. In the Table field, enter **CLIENTS** as the name of the table on which the report is based. Then choose the Select Report button to choose a report.

In a moment, you'll see the same list box displaying the reports you have previously created for the HOURS table. Choose R, Standard Report, from the list box. Finally, choose OK in the Print Report dialog box. The dialog box vanishes to reveal the Menu Definition dialog box underneath.

Choose OK from the Menu Definition dialog box; it will close, and the Clients choice is added to the Print submenu.

At this point, all the necessary menu options have been added to the application, and all menu actions have been defined. You now need only to generate the application. Open the Application menu (press (F10), and highlight Application and then press (ENTER), or just click on the Application menu). Choose Finish from the Application menu.

The Application Workshop program will flash various messages on the screen as it builds the application. When it is done, choose Exit/To Paradox from the main menu, to leave the Application Workshop and return to Paradox.

Running the Application

From the Paradox main menu, choose Scripts/Play, enter **STAFF** as the name of the script to play, and the application will run. Try the various menu options now, to get a feel for the application. When done, you can choose Quit from the application's main menu, to return to Paradox.

Users of your application do not need to enter the Paradox Application Workshop to run the application; there are a number of ways in which an application created with the Paradox Application Workshop can be run. Probably the most familiar method for other Paradox users is to run the application from within Paradox. Because the application is a series of sophisticated PAL scripts, it can also be run with the Scripts command on the Paradox main menu.

If you choose to store your applications in separate subdirectories (a good hard-disk management technique), you'll need to first change to that subdirectory after starting Paradox. Choose Tools/More/Directory from the main menu, and enter the name of the directory. Once in the directory, choose Scripts/Play, and enter the name of the application to run it.

You can also run an application from DOS by starting Paradox with the program name, followed by the name of the application. For example, get to the subdirectory containing the STAFF application with the DOS CD\ command. Then enter **PARADOX STAFF** to load Paradox and run the application.

Modifying an Application

"Nothing is constant except change," so the saying goes. To modify an application, you follow these general steps:

1. Start the Application Workshop (open the System menu with the mouse or with (ALT)-(SPACEBAR), and choose Utilities/Workshop).

2. Choose Open from the Application menu to open an existing application.

3. Make the desired changes.

13

4. Choose Finish from the Application menu to save the changes. The Application Workshop then rewrites the PAL code behind the application; during this time, various messages will appear on the screen.

5. When this rewrite process is complete, use the Exit menu option to leave the Application Workshop.

Assuming you followed the steps earlier in this chapter to create the sample STAFF application, you can practice changing an application by performing the steps outlined in the following paragraphs. You'll see how to make use of a Query Form within the application, and use the results of that query to print a report.

Get into the Application Workshop (if you are not already there) by choosing Utilities/Workshop from the System menu. If the ABC Temporaries application is not already on the desktop, you will need to load it now. To do so, select Open from the Application menu. In a moment, a list box of applications appears (the list may contain just the one application you have created so far). With the STAFF application highlighted, choose OK from this dialog box to begin making changes to the application. You'll see the menu bar for the application appear on the desktop.

For this example, you will change the Hours option under the Print menu, so that a query is performed first, and a report is then printed based on the results of the query. Since an existing action is already assigned to the Hours choice of the Print menu, you will need to edit that action. Open the Print menu of the application, and choose Hours (highlight Hours and press (ENTER), or double-click on Hours). The Menu Definition dialog box then appears, as shown in Figure 13-13.

Currently, Report Print is specified as an action for this menu choice; this is what you want to change. What you want now is this series of actions: execute a query, and then print a report based on the query. The Application Workshop lets you assign multiple actions to any menu choice, using the Multiple Actions option.

Click on the Select button in the Action area of the dialog box, or (TAB) to the Select button and press (ENTER). In a moment, the Object Type dialog box appears, with a list of available actions that you can assign to menus. Choose Multiple Actions from this list; you'll then see the Select: Multiple Actions list box.

Figure 13-13. *The Menu Definition dialog box for the existing application*

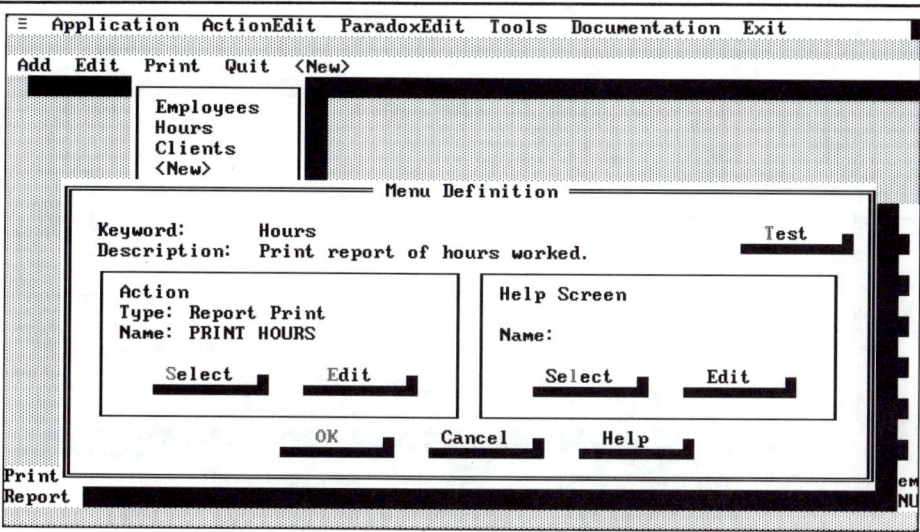

In the Select: Multiple Actions list box, choose the New button. (As usual, you can either click on the New button, or (TAB) to it and press (ENTER); the remainder of this exercise assumes you are familiar with these options.) You are prompted for the name of the Multiple Action. Type **RELATIONAL REPORT** and press (ENTER). You next see a Multi-Action dialog box, as shown in Figure 13-14.

Here you will specify all of the actions that you want to occur in response to a menu choice. Choose the Add button now, to add the first of the multiple actions. From the Object Type list box that appears, choose Query, and then OK. In a moment, a Select: Query dialog box appears, where you can enter a query name or create a new query.

Choose New from the Select: Query dialog box. When the prompt for a query name appears, type **HOURS WORKED** and press (ENTER). In a moment, a Query By Example dialog box appears, as shown in Figure 13-15. In this dialog box, you can specify the queries to be used, and you can create new queries. Choose the QBE button now, and in a moment the Application Workshop main menu is replaced by a Query-By-Example menu, with choices of Add, Remove, Help, Done, and Cancel. Choose Add from the menu, to add a Query Form to the workspace. When the Select Table dialog box

Figure 13-14.   *The Multi-Action dialog box*

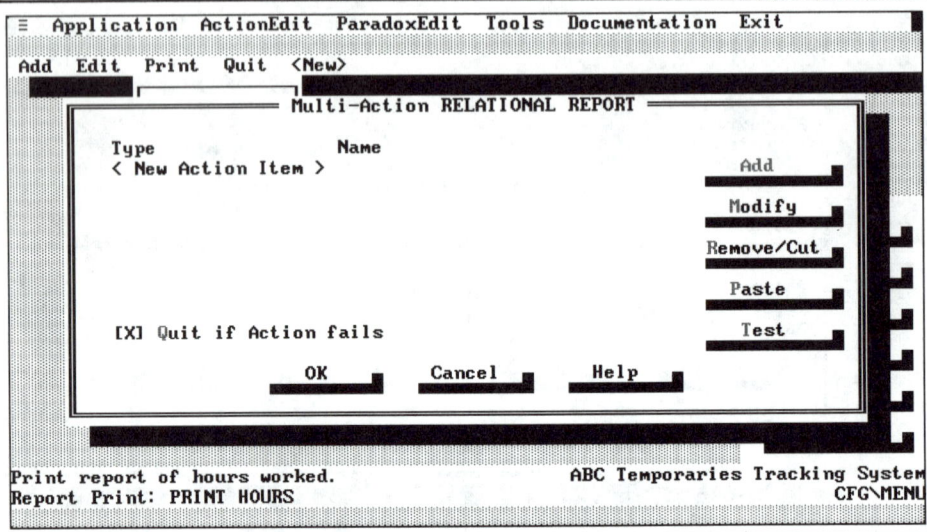

appears, enter **ABCSTAFF** as a table name. When the Query Form appears for the ABCSTAFF table, (TAB) over to the Social Security field. Press (F5) to begin an example element, and type the following:

ABCD

Then use the (TAB) and (F6) keys (or the mouse) to place checkmarks in the Last Name and First Name fields.

Choose Add from the main menu again, to add another Query Form to the workspace. When the Select Table dialog box appears, enter **HOURS** as a table name. When the Query Form appears for the HOURS table, (TAB) to the Social Security field. Press (F5) to begin an example element, and again type

ABCD

Then use the (TAB) and (F6) keys (or the mouse) to place checkmarks in the Weekend date and Hours worked fields. Finally, choose Done/Save from the main menu to complete this query; the Query By Example dialog box will reappear.

Figure 13-15. *The Query By Example dialog box*

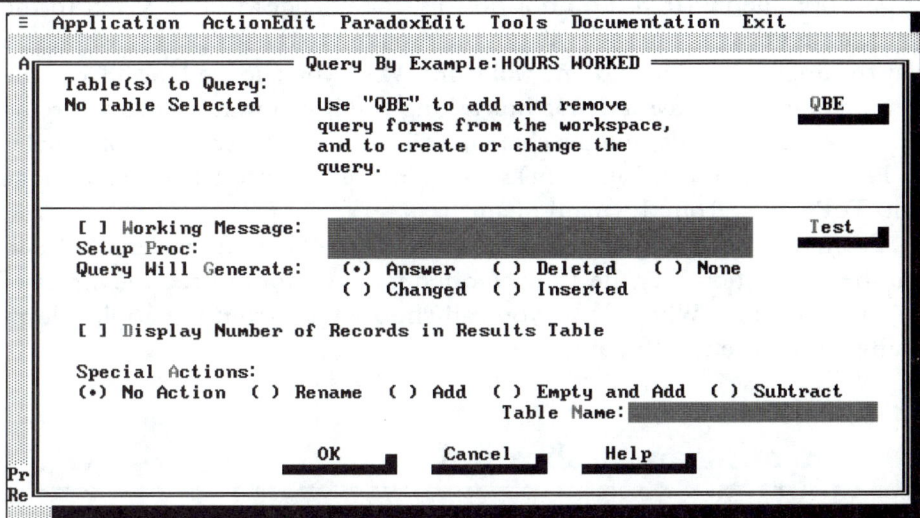

The remaining options in the dialog box can be left unchanged; choose OK, and the Application Workshop main menu will reappear, followed in a moment by the Multi-Action dialog box.

One more action item is needed, since a report must be printed after the query is executed. Choose Add from the dialog box; when the Object Type list box appears, choose Report Print, and then OK.

When the Select: Report Print dialog box appears, choose New. When the prompt for a new report name appears, type **RELATIONAL REPORT** and press (ENTER). In a moment, a Report Print dialog box appears. For the table name, enter **ANSWER.** (TAB) over to (or click on) the Report Number field, and type **R.** (This selects a standard report to be used with the ANSWER table that the query will generate.) Finally, choose OK from the Report Print dialog box. In a moment, the Multi-Action dialog box reappears; choose OK from this dialog box.

Finally, the Menu Definition dialog box reappears, and Multiple Actions now appears as the chosen action in the Action portion of this dialog box. Choose OK, and the Application menu reappears on the desktop.

With the changes complete, you must now choose Finish from the Application menu. (If you do not do this, the changes will be saved to the application's design, but they will not be rewritten to the script, and when you play the application, the old one will run.) When you choose Finish from the menu, Paradox displays a dialog box asking you if you want to overwrite the old scripts. Choose OK, and the changes will be written to a new script. Finally, to leave the Application Workshop and return to Paradox, choose Exit/ToParadox from the main menu.

From the Paradox main menu, choose Scripts/Play, and enter **STAFF** to run the application. Try the Print/Hours menu option, to see the effect of the modifications. When done, you can choose Quit from the application's main menu, to return to Paradox.

Documenting an Application

Open the Documentation menu of the Application Workshop, and you will see three options: Menu Tree, Action Detail, and Cross Reference. Each menu option lets you direct the output to the screen, a file, or the default printer.

Choose the Menu Tree option to generate a printout (or screen display or file) of the menu structure of your application, in a tree format. Use the Action Detail option to produce a list that shows complete definitions for each action object assigned in your application. Use Cross Reference to generate a cross-reference report. This report shows which Paradox objects or actions are referenced by action objects in your application.

Just the Beginning...

Hopefully, this chapter has given you an idea of the power and ease of use that can be provided by a professional application written with the help of the Paradox Application Workshop. Chapter 16, Sample Applications, provides additional examples of how the Application Workshop can be used to aid in the design and implementation of complete applications. If your job can be made easier through the use of custom applications, take the time to explore more of Application Workshop's features. You'll be glad you did.

14

Introduction to PAL Programming

While you may not have purchased Paradox with the intention of becoming a computer programmer, you will find that programming with Paradox is not as difficult as you might expect. As you will see in this chapter, you program in Paradox through the use of PAL commands. PAL is an abbreviation for Paradox Application Language, the programming language that is built into Paradox. Having programs that automate the way Paradox works for you is well worth the effort it takes to design and write these programs. You can create applications with the Paradox Application Workshop, as detailed in the previous chapter, but a knowledge of PAL programming adds flexibility to what you can do with Paradox. Armed with such knowledge, you can create applications based on your own program designs. It is not recommended that you attempt to modify applications built by the Application Workshop, because they are highly modular in nature. However, you can learn much about good programming style by studying the applications created by the Application Workshop.

Any computer program is simply a series of instructions. These instructions are commands that cause the computer to perform specific tasks. The commands are written in a file contained on a disk, and they are performed each time the file is retrieved from the disk.

In a way, you are already familiar with PAL programs, because scripts (detailed in Chapter 10) are stored in PAL. To create your PAL programs, you will probably use a combination of the keystrokes stored in scripts and various commands that are a part of PAL.

Creating and Maintaining a PAL Program

You can create PAL programs with the Editor built into Paradox or with any word processor that can save text as ASCII files. The Paradox Editor normally assigns a file extension of .SC to all programs you write; if you use a word processor outside of Paradox to write programs, you should add an .SC extension to the program when you save it.

To create a program in the Paradox Editor, choose Scripts/Editor/New from the Paradox menu. Next, you enter the filename for the script when prompted, and the PAL Editor appears within a blank window. At this point, you can type the desired lines of the program. You can correct mistakes with the (BACKSPACE) or (DEL) key and with the usual cursor keys. One handy shortcut key to remember for major modifications is the (CTRL)-(Y) key combination, which deletes the line that the cursor is on. Once the program is completed, choose DO-IT! ((F2)) to save the program.

Running any PAL program is the same as running any script recorded in PAL; from the Paradox main menu, choose Scripts/Play, and enter the name of the program. If there are no errors in your program, the program performs as planned. If there are any bugs in the program, Paradox stops running and presents you with a menu with two options: Cancel and Debug. Selecting Cancel returns you to the main menu; selecting Debug displays the line where the error was detected, along with a description of the problem.

To edit an existing PAL program, choose Scripts/Editor/Open from the main menu and enter the name of the program. The existing program appears within the Editor. Make the desired changes and choose DO-IT! to save the edited program.

Your First PAL Program

You can try creating and running a simple program in PAL now. Choose Scripts/Editor/New from the menu; when prompted, enter **PROGRAM1** as the name for the script. In a moment, the Editor appears in a window, as shown in Figure 14-1.

Note that the filename, PROGRAM1, automatically appears in the window's title bar, with an .SC extension assigned by Paradox. In the Editor window, type the following lines, pressing (ENTER) at the end of each line:

```
? "Enter your name:"
ACCEPT "A15" TO TheName
? "The name that you entered was: "
?? TheName
SLEEP 5000
```

Once you've entered these lines, choose DO-IT! to save the completed program. From the menu, choose Scripts/Play, and enter **PROGRAM1** when

14

Figure 14-1.   *Editor window*

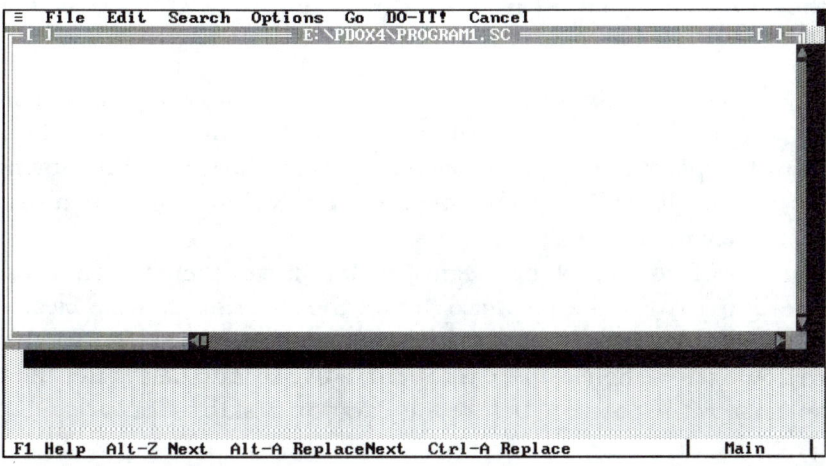

prompted for the name of the script. You should see the prompt "Enter your name" appear on the screen. Type your name and press (ENTER), and you'll see the response provided by the program.

Some common commands used in PAL will be explained later in this chapter. For now, here's an explanation of the program you just created. The ? command on the first line displays the "Enter your name" message on the screen. Whenever Paradox sees the question mark as a starting command, it places whatever follows the question mark on the screen at the current cursor location.

The second line of the program reads

```
ACCEPT "A15" TO TheName
```

In this line, the ACCEPT command tells Paradox to accept a value typed at the keyboard, and to store that value to an area in memory. Such areas in memory are called *memory variables,* and each memory variable must have its own name so that it can be identified by the different parts of your program. In this case, "TheName" is the name of the memory variable. The designation "A15" indicates that the variable will contain alphanumeric data, and will store a maximum of 15 characters. (You can use the same type designations for memory variables that you use when naming fields of a table.)

The third and fourth lines of the program,

```
? "The name that you entered was: "
?? TheName
```

use the ? and ?? commands to display the response. The ?? command is similar to the ? command explained earlier. The only difference is that the ?? command displays the information on the same line, without moving the cursor to a new line. The ? command always moves the cursor to a new line before displaying the information.

The SLEEP command that begins the last line of the program is used to provide time to view the response before the Paradox desktop clears. The number indicates approximately the number of milliseconds that the program should pause; hence, there is roughly a five-second delay after the name is displayed by the program before the Paradox desktop clears.

Using PAL Scripts in Larger Applications

One of the most useful traits of Paradox programming is that scripts in Paradox are normally stored in PAL. As a result, it is a simple matter to store a series of actions in Paradox to a script, and use the text of that script as part of a more complex PAL program. This is commonly done for such tasks as placing a particular table in use, choosing a sort order, and printing stored reports.

For example, the ABCSTAFF table contains the names and addresses of the employees for ABC Temporaries. On a monthly basis, a report sorted by last name is required. The report is a default Paradox report. To first sort the table, you can choose Modify/Sort from the main menu, and enter the name of the table (in this example, ABCSTAFF) at the prompt. Next, you enter a new name for the sorted table. When the Sort Questionaire appears, you place a 1 for first sort field beside the desired field name (in this example, Last Name). You then choose DO-IT!, and the sorted table appears. To print the table, you press (F10) to activate the main menu, and choose Report/Output, followed by the name of the table. You choose the default report form from the next menu, and then choose either Printer or Screen, and the desired report is produced. If you've followed the exercises in this book, these actions are already familiar to you.

With PAL programming, before beginning the actions described above to sort the table and print the report, you press (ALT)-(F3) to begin recording an instant script. Once the last action is completed, you press (ALT)-(F3) again, and recording of the script stops. As noted in Chapter 10, instant scripts are stored under the name INSTANT.SC in the default directory. The contents of the script just described would resemble the following:

```
{Modify} {Sort} {ABCSTAFF} {Same} Down "1" Do_It!
Menu {Report} {Output} {Newfile} {R} {Screen}
```

The Paradox Editor has a File/InsertFile option for reading other script files into an existing file. Hence, the easiest way to write portions of programs for selecting tables, printing reports, and so on is to perform the actions while recording a script, then use the File/InsertFile menu option when in the Editor to read the contents of the script into the larger program. You can tie

14

together the various tasks by means of menu choices implemented with the SHOWPOPUP...TO command, described later in this chapter.

Remember that menu choices in PAL always appear within braces. In the prior example, {Sort}, {Report}, and {Output} were menu selections chosen during the recording of the script. Paradox function keys are always spelled out, as are cursor keys and the (ENTER) key. In the example, DO-IT! and Menu represent the DO-IT! ((F2)) and Menu ((F10)) keys, and Down and Up represent the (↓) and (↑) keys. Any text entered in response to a Paradox prompt will be surrounded by quotation marks.

Interacting with Users

Much of PAL programming involves interaction with the user of the program. Various commands are provided for displaying information on the screen and for getting replies from the user. For example, the ? and ?? commands display data on the screen, the @ command places the cursor at a specific position, and the ACCEPT command gets a value from the user. Here is a brief list explaining some of the more common PAL commands:

Command	Explanation
? *<expression>*	Writes the contents of *expression* at the beginning of a line below the current cursor position.
?? *<expression>*	Writes the contents of *expression* at the current location of the cursor.
@ *<row>,<col>*	Positions the cursor at the selected row and column location.
ACCEPT *<data type>* TO *<variable name>*	Accepts a value from the keyboard and stores it to the named memory variable.
BEEP	Sounds a beep.
CLEAR	Clears the Paradox desktop.
MESSAGE *<expression>*	Displays a message at the lower-right corner of the screen.

Command	Explanation
MOVE TO [*field name*]	Moves the cursor to the named field of the active table.
PRINT <*expression*>	Sends values to the printer.
PRINTER ON/OFF	Turns on (or off) echoing of screen output to the printer.
SHOWPOPUP <*menu item list*> TO <*variable name*>	Creates and displays a Pop-up menu. The item selected is stored as <*variable name*>. (This command is one of several available for creating menus.)
STYLE ATTRIBUTE *n*	Sets the display attributes for text shown on the screen.
SLEEP *n*	Pauses the program for *n* milliseconds.
TEXT <*text to be shown*> ENDTEXT	Displays all text between TEXT and ENDTEXT on the screen.
VIEW <*table name*>	Displays a table in the Paradox workspace; equivalent to choosing View from the menu.

14

Note that this list is a brief introduction; there are many additional commands you can use to manipulate data when programming in PAL. Refer to your *PAL Programmer's Guide* for a complete list of commands and functions.

As an example that includes more of the commands just described, you can write a simple program in PAL to ask for the name and age of a user, and then display that information on the screen using a different screen color. The program is shown below; to create it, choose Scripts/Editor/New from the main menu, and call the program PROGRAM2. As the first line of the program demonstrates, you can add comments to a PAL program by starting the line with a semicolon. Whenever a line begins with a semicolon, PAL does not act on what is contained in the line. Hence, you can include programming comments, which are usually notes that help you understand parts of the program, by writing text after a semicolon.

```
 ; -This is a simple test of PAL programming
CLEAR
STYLE ATTRIBUTE 20
```

```
@ 5,15
?? "Type your name, and press RETURN: "
ACCEPT "A20" TO TheName
STYLE ATTRIBUTE 45
@ 8,15
?? "Enter your age: "
ACCEPT "N" PICTURE "##" TO TheAge
STYLE ATTRIBUTE 12
@ 12,10
?? "Your name is ", TheName, " and you are ", TheAge, " years
  old."
SLEEP 5000
BEEP BEEP BEEP
```

When you are done, save the program with DO-IT!, and run it by choosing Scripts/Play from the main menu and entering **PROGRAM2** as the name of the script to be played. The program prompts for a name and age (using red characters on blue background for the name prompt and magenta characters on green background for the age). Finally, the response containing the name and age is displayed, using red characters on a black background.

Since much of your work in Paradox involves working with tables, you will need to access those tables and their fields, within a PAL application. As mentioned in the list of commands earlier, you can use the VIEW <*table name*> command to display a table on the screen, and you can use the MOVETO [*field name*] command to move to a particular field. In scripts, you can use field names from the currently active table by placing square brackets around the name of the field. In the following script, the VIEW "Abcstaff" statement places the ABCSTAFF table on the workspace, the MOVETO [SALARY] statement moves the cursor to the SALARY field of the table, and the EDITKEY command, equivalent to pressing Edit ((F9)) places the user in an editing mode. The next three statements, WAIT TABLE, MESSAGE, and UNTIL, cause the table to remain visible until editing is completed; the WAIT TABLE and UNTIL commands are described in detail near the end of this chapter.

```
VIEW "Abcstaff"
MOVETO [SALARY]
EDITKEY
WAIT TABLE
      MESSAGE "Press F2 when done."
UNTIL "F2"
DO_IT!
```

Decision Making Within a Program

In many PAL programs, Paradox will need to perform different operations depending on the user's response to a menu option or depending on different values encountered in a table. For example, if the user has a choice of editing or printing a record based on choices shown in a main menu, the program must be able to perform the chosen operation. Paradox uses the IF, ELSE, and ENDIF commands to branch to the part of the program where the chosen operation is performed. The IF and ENDIF commands are used as a matched pair enclosing a number of other PAL commands. The ELSE command is optional and is used within the body of IF...ENDIF as another decision step. The IF...ENDIF command set can be used to decide between actions in a program. The format of the commands are as follows.

```
IF <condition exists> THEN
    <desired commands here>
ELSE
    <more desired commands here>
ENDIF
```

This decision-making command sequence must always start with IF and end with ENDIF. The commands that you place between the IF and ENDIF commands determine exactly what will occur if the condition is true, unless an ELSE is encountered. If an ELSE is encountered and the condition specified by ELSE is true, the commands that follow ELSE are carried out. A good way to write these commands is to write them in "pseudocode" first and then compare them.

Pseudocode	PAL

If last name is Cooke, then display last name.	IF LASTNAME = "Cooke" THEN
	    ? LASTNAME
	ENDIF

If monthly rent is less than $300, then display "Reasonably priced."	IF RENT < 300 THEN
	    ? "Reasonably priced"
	ENDIF

14

Using IF...ENDIF alone will work fine for making a single decision, but if you wish to add an alternative choice, you'll need the ELSE statement.

Pseudocode	PAL

If last name is Cooke, then print last name; or else print "There is no one by that name in this database."	```IF LASTNAME = "Cooke" THEN```
	 `    ? LASTNAME`
	 `ELSE`
	 `    ? "There is no one by that`
	 `      name in this database."`
	 `ENDIF`

Paradox will evaluate the condition following the IF command to see if any action should be taken. If no action is necessary, Paradox will simply move on to the next command after the ENDIF command. As an example of the use of the IF and ENDIF commands, the following PAL program asks a user for his or her age, and then displays an appropriate message depending on the response.

```
CLEAR
@ 5,10
?? "Enter your age. "
ACCEPT "N" TO TheAge
;---act on the response.
IF TheAge > 20 THEN
     @ 10,10
     ?? "Of legal drinking age."
ELSE
     @ 10,10
     ?? "Sorry. No alcohol served to minors."
ENDIF
SLEEP 5000
```

In this simple example, the program displays one of two messages depending upon the response given. The SLEEP 5000 command is added after the IF...ENDIF command to provide time for the user to view the response before the Paradox menu reappears.

Evaluating Multiple Choices with Switch, Case, and ENDSWITCH

Your program may need to make more than two or three decisions from a single user response. A series of IF...ENDIF statements could do the job, but using more than three IF...ENDIFs to test the value of one field or memory variable is unwieldy. An easier way is to use the SWITCH, CASE, and ENDSWITCH commands. With the CASE statement, the IF...ENDIF tests are made into cases, and Paradox then chooses the first case, second case, or another case. These cases are grouped between a SWITCH command and an ENDSWITCH command. The OTHERWISE command works exactly like the ELSE in an IF...ENDIF statement. The basic syntax for these commands is as follows.

```
SWITCH
    CASE <first condition>:
        <perform these commands>
    CASE <second condition>:
        <perform these commands>
    CASE <third condition>:
        <perform these commands>
    OTHERWISE:
        <perform these commands>
ENDSWITCH
```

Note that the OTHERWISE statement (and any commands that follow it) is optional. Note also that there is no limit to the number of CASE statements. This example shows three, but you could have ten, twenty, or more CASE statements within a SWITCH...ENDSWITCH statement.

With the SWITCH...ENDSWITCH statement, the first CASE statement that meets a specified condition will be acted on, and the rest will be ignored. If no condition for any of the CASE statements is met and an OTHERWISE statement is included, the commands following the OTHERWISE statement are carried out. If no condition for any of the CASE statements is met and an OTHERWISE statement is not included, control of the program proceeds to

14

the next statement after the **ENDSWITCH** command. The following program demonstrates the use of the **SWITCH...ENDSWITCH** statement:

```
CLEAR
TEXT
   Enter 1 to view the ABCSTAFF table.
   Enter 2 to view the HOURS table.
   Enter 3 to view the CLIENTS table.
ENDTEXT
ACCEPT "N" PICTURE "#" TO Choosy
;---respond to the answer.
SWITCH
    CASE Choosy = 1:
     ClearAll {View} {ABCSTAFF}
    CASE Choosy = 2:
     ClearAll {View} {HOURS}
    CASE Choosy = 3:
     ClearAll {View} {CLIENTS}
    OTHERWISE:
     @ 5,5
     ?? "Invalid choice!  Enter a number from 1 to 3."
     BEEP BEEP BEEP
     SLEEP 5000
ENDSWITCH
```

In this program, a series of options is displayed using the **TEXT...ENDTEXT** statement. The **TEXT** and **ENDTEXT** commands cause everything between them to appear on the screen. Next, the **ACCEPT** statement is used to get the response, in the form of a single-digit numeric value, from the user. Finally, the **CASE** statements between **SWITCH** and **ENDSWITCH** take the appropriate action, depending on the response; if the user enters 1, the ABCSTAFF table appears; if the user enters 2, the HOURS table appears; and, if the user enters 3, the CLIENTS table appears.

Caution

Remember that every CASE and OTHERWISE command must end with a colon, or the program will crash with a "colon expected" error message.

Going in Circles

There will be many times when your program will need to perform the same task repeatedly. Paradox has two commands, WHILE and ENDWHILE, that are used as a matched pair to repeat a series of commands for as long as is necessary. You enclose the commands that you wish to repeat between the WHILE and the ENDWHILE commands. The WHILE command always begins the loop, and the ENDWHILE command normally ends the loop. The series of commands contained within the WHILE loop will continue to execute until the condition, specified immediately next to the WHILE command, is no longer true. You determine when the loop should stop by specifying the condition; otherwise, the loop could go on indefinitely. The WHILE...ENDWHILE statement uses the following syntax:

WHILE *<condition exists>*
 <commands to be repeated>
ENDWHILE

The following program demonstrates the use of WHILE...ENDWHILE statement by counting to 10, and displaying the value after each increase in a memory variable called CountIt:

```
CLEAR
CountIt = 0
WHILE CountIt < 11
       ? "The value of CountIt is now ", CountIt
       SLEEP 500
       CountIt = CountIt + 1
ENDWHILE
SLEEP 1000
```

In this program, after the desktop is erased with the CLEAR command, a memory variable called CountIt is created, and a numeric value of zero is stored to that variable. The next line,

```
WHILE CountIt < 11
```

indicates the start of the WHILE...ENDWHILE loop. The specified condition is CountIt < 11, so the loop will repeat for as long as the value of the memory variable, CountIt, is less than 11. The lines between the WHILE and the ENDWHILE commands display the value of the variable, pause the program (giving the user time to read the screen), and increase the value of the variable by one. Once the value of CountIt reaches 11, control of the program passes beyond the ENDWHILE command to the command that follows.

Creating Menus in PAL Programs

You can create menu options that tie together various portions of a PAL program, using the SHOWPOPUP and TO commands. This command sequence lets you display menu options complete with help text in a style that imitates the Paradox menus. The syntax for the SHOWPOPUP...TO statement is as follows.

```
SHOWPOPUP <title>  CENTERED/@ <row>,<col>
  <first option>   : <help text>:tag,
  <second option>  : <help text>:tag,
  <last option>    : <help text>:tag
ENDMENU TO <variable name>
```

When the program runs, Paradox automatically places the named options in a pop-up menu. If you include the CENTERED clause, the menu is placed in the center of the screen. If you use the @ <row>,<col> clause, the upper-left corner of the menu is placed at the row and column coordinates you specify. For example, this command

```
SHOWPOPUP "My Menu" @ 10, 12
```

would cause the menu to appear with its upper-left corner placed at row 10, column 12. (Again, there is no limit to the number of options you can include; although for readability, you should design your systems so that all the options for a menu will comfortably fit on the screen.)

As each item is highlighted, the help text appears beneath the menu items. Once a choice is made, a text string identified as the "tag" is stored to the memory variable. Your program can then act on that variable as desired, usually through the use of the SWITCH...ENDSWITCH sequence. The following example demonstrates the use of SHOWPOPUP...TO in a rewrite of the program shown earlier to view different tables. Instead of using TEXT and ENDTEXT to display choices, this program uses SHOWPOPUP...TO to provide the options as menu choices.

```
CLEAR
SHOWPOPUP "ABC Temporaries" CENTERED
     "View ABCSTAFF" : "View the ABCSTAFF table in a window." :
            "ABC",
     "View HOURS" : "View the HOURS table in a window." :
            "HOURS",
     "View CLIENTS" : "View the CLIENTS table in a window." :
            "CLIENTS"
ENDMENU TO Choosy
;---respond to the answer.
SWITCH
     CASE Choosy = "ABC":
          ClearAll{View}{ABCSTAFF}
     CASE Choosy = "HOURS":
          ClearAll{View}{HOURS}
     CASE Choosy = "CLIENTS":
          ClearAll{View}{CLIENTS}
ENDSWITCH
```

Notice that in this example the CASE statements test for text strings that are the names supplied in the *tag* portion of the command, such as "ABC" and "HOURS." You must enclose these items in quotes, and you must add commas at the end of all but the last statement in a group of SHOWPOPUP statements. Omission of the commas is a common cause of program bugs when developing PAL applications.

Putting It All Together in a Complete PAL Application

You can use any or all of the techniques discussed in this chapter to develop a complete application in PAL. The following simple application provides options for adding new records to the ABCSTAFF table, editing the table, sorting the table, and printing the default report for the table.

The application consists of two programs; both can be created and saved separately using the Editor. The first program, named ABC.SC, displays the menu, acts on the appropriate choices, and includes the necessary commands or Paradox keystrokes to add and edit data, and to print a default report. The second program, named SortIt.SC, is a routine for sorting the table. Note that the fourth option of the application's main menu calls the sorting routine by using the PLAY "SortIt" statement. In PAL, the PLAY command calls another program. When the second program completes its execution, control returns to the main program. You can use the PLAY command to easily implement *modular programming techniques* (the use of many small programs to build a large application) as your PAL programs grow more complex.

Two commands in the program that have not yet been described are the WAIT TABLE...UNTIL statement and the SORT command. You use WAIT TABLE...UNTIL *<condition>* to cause a table to remain on the screen until the user does something (specified by the condition) to clear the table. The SORT command lets you sort a table, and it uses the syntax SORT "*table-name*" ON "*field1*",..."*field2*",..."*fieldN*". The same sort could be stored in a program by recording an instant script and choosing the sort options from the Paradox menu, but the SORT command is faster to include in a program once you know the syntax of the command.

```
;---ABC.SC is ABCSTAFF table application.
Choosy = " "
WHILE Choosy <> "EXIT"
     CLEAR
     SHOWPOPUP "ABC Temporaries" CENTERED
     "Add records" : "Add new records to ABCSTAFF table." :
          "ADDER",
     "Edit records" : "Edit records in ABCSTAFF table." :
          "EDITOR",
     "Sort records" : "Sort the ABCSTAFF table by last name or
          ZIP." : "SORTER",
     "Print records" : "Print records in ABCSTAFF." : "PRINTER",
     "Quit System" : "Return to Paradox main menu." : "EXIT"
     ENDMENU TO Choosy
;---respond to the answer.
SWITCH
     CASE Choosy = "ADDER":
```

```
              ClearAll {Modify}{DataEntry}{abcstaff}
              Menu {Image}{PickForm}{F}
              ;---in data entry mode until user hits DO-IT key.
              WAIT TABLE
                    MESSAGE "—Press DO-IT! (F2) when finished."
              UNTIL "F2"
              DO_IT!
              ClearAll
        CASE Choosy = "EDITOR":
              ClearAll {Modify}{Edit}{abcstaff}
              ;---in table mode until user completes edits.
              WAIT TABLE
                    MESSAGE "—Press DO-IT! (F2) when finished."
              UNTIL "F2"
              DO_IT!
              ClearAll
        CASE Choosy = "SORTER":
              ClearAll
              PLAY "SortIt"
        CASE Choosy = "PRINTER":
              ClearAll Menu {Report}{Output}{abcstaff}{R}{Printer}
ENDSWITCH
ENDWHILE
CLEARALL
CLEAR


;---This program is stored as SortIt.SC---
CLEAR
TEXT
  This option sorts the ABCSTAFF file to a new file.
  The new file will be stored under the name "SORTFILE."
  Enter 1 to sort by last name.
  Enter 2 to sort by ZIP code.
ENDTEXT
ACCEPT "N" PICTURE "#" TO WHICHWAY
;---respond to answer.
IF WHICHWAY = 1 THEN
      SORT "abcstaff" ON "Last Name" TO "sortfile"
ELSE
      SORT "abcstaff" ON "ZIP Code" TO "sortfile"
ENDIF
CLEAR
```

14

Because PAL is such a rich programming language, not all of its commands and functions can be covered in this brief introduction. The *PAL Programmer's Guide* provided with your Paradox documentation includes more detail on all the commands and functions in PAL. Other references, such as *PAL Made Easy* (Cary Jensen and Loy Anderson, Osborne/McGraw-Hill, 1991) can teach you the specifics of programming in PAL. Also, keep in mind that you can learn a great deal about programming in PAL by studying the programs created by the Paradox Application Workshop, which is detailed in Chapter 13.

15

Networking with Paradox

This chapter provides information that you will find useful if you intend to use the network version of Paradox. Included in this chapter are an overview of local area networks, requirements and instructions for using Paradox on a network, and general hints for effective network use.

The complexity of local area networks requires this chapter to be a bit more technical than most other chapters in this book. It is assumed that the reader is already familiar with the use of Paradox, fundamental DOS commands (including the use of DOS subdirectories), and the network commands for the particular network on which Paradox is installed. Refer to the appropriate manuals for network operation to answer any questions you have about the use of your network's operating system commands.

Paradox and Networks

A *local area network,* or *LAN,* is a system of computer communications that links together a number of personal computers, usually within a single building, for the transfer of information between computer users. In its minimal configuration, a local area network consists of two PCs connected by some type of wire that allows information to be transferred between the two machines. A local area network allows the sharing of printers, modems, hard disks, and other devices that may be attached to computers on the network. Files (such as Paradox tables) and commonly used software can also be shared. Figure 15-1 illustrates how computers can be linked together by means of a local area network.

There are different designs for local area networks, but all LANs are made up of the same basic components: servers, workstations, and the physical cable that links the components together. *Servers* are computers that provide devices that can be used by all users of the network. Most servers are one of three types: file servers, which provide shared hard disks; print servers, which provide shared printers; and communications servers, which provide shared modems. Servers can simultaneously provide more than one of these functions; a single server, for example, may have a hard disk and a printer attached, making that server both a file server and a print server.

Workstations are the computers attached to a network that do not normally provide shared resources for other users. These stations are used by the individual users of the network to run software that may be present on a workstation or on the file server. Some types of networks allow the simultaneous use of the same computer as a file server and a workstation, although this practice is not recommended—network performance suffers as a result. Paradox version 4 can be installed on a network's file servers, workstations, or both. The Paradox LAN Pack must be installed on a file server.

Under the terms of the license agreement, network users are limited to one active user of Paradox per copy of Paradox 4 and five users per copy of the Paradox LAN Pack. It is possible to have a mix of Paradox versions on a single network. As an example, you could have three copies of Paradox version 4 (two installed on a file server and one installed on a workstation) along with one Paradox LAN Pack (installed on the file server). Such a combination would allow up to eight users to access Paradox at the same time. It is also possible to have different versions of Paradox on the same LAN, but this is not recommended. It's best to upgrade all copies of Paradox on the network to version 4. If you mix Paradox 4 with installed copied of older versions, network users running the different versions won't be able to access the same file (or the same directory) simultaneously.

Figure 15-1. *Local area networks*

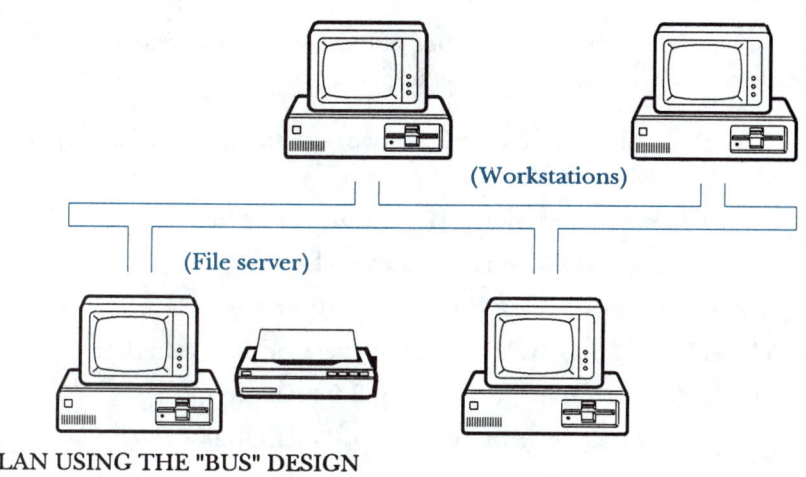

(Workstations)

(File server)

LAN USING THE "BUS" DESIGN

15

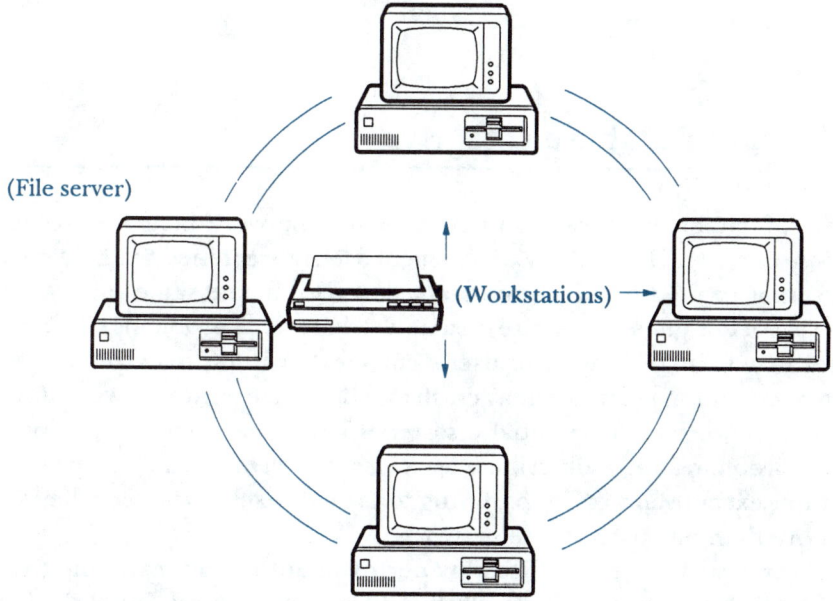

(File server)

(Workstations)

LAN USING THE "TOKEN-RING" DESIGN

Paradox and Compatible Networks

At the time of this writing, a number of local area networks are compatible with Paradox. They include the following:

- The IBM Token Ring or PC Network with IBM PC LAN program, version 1.12 or higher
- The 3COM 3+ share network version 1.5 or higher
- The Novell network, version 2.0A or higher
- A Banyan Vines network, version 2.10 or higher
- The AT&T Star GROUP for DOS, version 3.1 or higher
- Microsoft LAN Manager, version 2.0 or higher
- DEC Pathworks network, version 1.0 or higher

In addition, any network that is completely compatible with any of these networks can use Paradox. The network must use DOS 3.1 or above, or OS/2 version 1.0 or above.

Paradox and Database Integrity

Users of database software on any local area network face the problem of *database integrity*. The stability of the database is threatened whenever two users attempt to modify the same database record at the same time. If the software is not designed to operate on a network, serious problems can occur. One user may write over another user's changes, or in more extreme cases, the network operating software may crash and bring the entire network down. In network lingo, such a potential disaster is known as a *collision*. Another common problem, aptly described as a *deadly embrace*, can occur when applications execute endless loops, trying to provide exclusive use of the same file to more than one user on the network.

To prevent such problems, Paradox performs automatic *family* and *record locking*, and it also lets users specifically lock files when desired. Family locking causes a table and its associated objects in use by one user to be restricted or made unavailable to other users on the network. Record locking performs the same type of safeguard, but does so for an individual record within a file.

Paradox will automatically perform the most advantageous type of locking on any table that you use. In addition to the locking that is set automatically by Paradox, you can use specific menu options to designate files as locked or as available, by means of a "prevent-lock" menu option.

Requirements for Network Use

To run Paradox on a network, you will need certain minimum hardware configurations in your file servers and workstations. The computers can be any IBM PC, XT, AT, or PS/2 models, or completely IBM-compatible PCs, with any combination of disk drives. The computers must be equipped with 640K of memory and with DOS 3.1 or above (DOS 3.2 or above if you are using the IBM Token Ring network).

Some network operating systems use relatively large amounts of conventional memory. As a result, Paradox cannot be loaded into conventional memory while you are working in such a network. In these cases, you must use an expanded memory board that meets the EMS or EEMS specification. The expanded memory board must contain a minimum 512K of RAM.

Note

Network requirements for Paradox with SQL Link are different than those stated here. Refer to your SQL Link Users' Guide *for additional information.*

A Note on Installation

The actual process of installing Paradox on your network will not be detailed in this book, as the process varies greatly according to the brand of network hardware and software you are using. If you are faced with the task of installing Paradox on a network, you should thoroughly study the *Network Installation Guide* provided with your Paradox documentation.

15

The remainder of this chapter assumes that your network administrator (the person who manages the network) has already installed Paradox on your network for your use.

Hints on Getting Started with a Network

The precise method used to start Paradox varies from network to network. Some networks use their own custom menus, which will display Paradox, along with other available programs on the network, as a series of menu choices. Other networks use batch files to start programs. In any case, do not start Paradox from the shared data directory or from the Paradox system directory.

If the copy of Paradox you will use is installed on the file server, you want to be sure you are linked to the file server directory in order to access those files. You should contact your network administrator to determine the proper command or menu choice to start Paradox on your network.

If you attempt to load Paradox on a network and you are unsuccessful, the reason could be indicated by one of the following four common error messages:

- *Can't start Paradox: total number of authorized users has been reached.* This message means that the limit for the number of authorized users on your network has been reached. You must wait for someone who is currently using Paradox on the network to quit using Paradox before you can use the program. To avoid this kind of problem on a long-term basis, you may want to purchase an additional copy of Paradox, or an additional LAN Pack. If you install a single copy of Paradox on your workstation, you will have access to it at all times. (Other network users will not be able to use your copy of Paradox, even when you are not using it.)

- *Can't start Paradox: can't get private directory.* This message means that Paradox was unable to reserve the private directory that is used for your temporary tables. This message usually indicates a problem

with the way Paradox was installed on the network. Contact your
network administrator for assistance with this problem.

- *Can't start Paradox: invalid PARADOX.CFG file.*   This message indicates a problem with the way Paradox was installed, a problem with
  your DOS path, the presence of more than one configuration file
  on the same physical drive, or a problem with the path set by the
  network operating system software. Contact your network administrator for assistance with this problem.

- *Unable to record lock/unlock Paradox net file.*   This message can occur
  for a number of reasons. Either the map to the logical drive specified
  for the PARADOX.NET file is not properly set up, or you do not
  have proper access rights to the PDOXDATA directory, or there are
  garbage PARADOX.LCK files left behind because of an abnormal
  exit from Paradox (in which case you can delete the files and restart
  Paradox). Contact your network administrator, if necessary, for
  assistance.

15

Using Paradox on a Network

Paradox's built-in sophistication lets you use it on a network much as you
would on a computer not attached to a network. As mentioned earlier,
Paradox will automatically lock (prevent other users from having full access
to) tables, reports, and forms when necessary. To share tables, forms, and
reports with other users, no special precautions need to be taken, other than
storing the tables and associated objects in a shared directory on the network.

As you use Paradox on the network, certain operations that you perform
will cause Paradox to place limitations, in the form of locks, on what other
users can simultaneously do with the data that you are using. This prevents
damage to a table or an associated object when two or more users are working
with the same data. As an example, if you restructure a table, Paradox
automatically places a *full lock* on that table so that no other user can add or
edit data while you are changing the table's structure. Also, if another user is
viewing a table, Paradox will not let you restructure that table until that user
finishes with the table. If a table that you want to use is restricted in some way

by some type of lock, Paradox will display a message telling you which network user is using that table.

Network Locks

To prevent the damage that could result from concurrent access, Paradox places restrictions on your data when necessary. These restrictions are described here.

Full Lock   This is the most restrictive type of lock that can be placed on a table or object. A full lock prevents another user from accessing that table or object for any reason. Operations that involve major changes to the data, such as sorting to the same table, restructuring a table, emptying a table, and protecting (encrypting) a table, often require full locks. If you place a full lock on a table, the table's family is also locked.

Dir Lock   The directory lock is equivalent to having full locks on all tables in a directory.

Write Lock   This type of lock lets other users access a table or object, but they cannot make any changes to it while the write lock remains in place.

Prevent Write Lock   This restriction prevents other users from placing a write lock on a table or object while you are using it.

Prevent Full Lock   This restriction prevents other users from placing a full lock on a table or an object. Other users will be able to perform any operation with the object simultaneously, except for an operation that requires a full lock. In Paradox, this is the least restrictive type of lock you can place on an object or a table.

While Paradox handles locking in the background to protect your data, you will find it helpful to know which menu options result in certain types of locks. This may help you plan your own operations so as to minimize inconvenience for fellow users. Table 15-1 shows the types of locks Paradox places on tables and associated objects automatically as a result of your choosing menu options. The table includes the most commonly used Paradox options; for a full list of all menu options, see your Paradox documentation.

Table 15-1. *Automatic Locks Resulting from Commonly Used Menu Options*

Command/Option	Type of Lock
Ask	Prevent full lock.
Create	Full lock on table being created.
Forms/Design	Full lock on form; prevent full lock on table.
Forms/Change	Full lock on form; prevent full lock on table.
Modify/Edit	Full lock.
Modify/CoEdit	Prevent full lock; prevent write lock while a record is locked.
Modify/DataEntry	Prevent full lock on source table; prevent write lock on source when DO-IT! is used to add entries to source.
Modify/Restructure	Full lock.
Modify/Sort	Full lock if sort is to same table; write lock on source; full lock on target if sort is to new table.
Report/Output	Prevent full lock.
Report/RangeOutput	Prevent full lock.
Report/Design	Prevent full lock on table; full lock on report.
Report/Change	Prevent full lock on table; full lock on report.
Tools/Rename	Full lock on source and target.
Tools/ExportImport/ Export	Write lock on source.
Tools/ExportImport/ Import	Full lock on target.
Tools/Copy/Table	Write lock on source; full lock on target.
Tools/Copy/Form	Write lock on source form; full lock on target form, prevent lock on table.
Tools/Copy/Report	Write lock on source report, full lock on target report, prevent lock on table.
Tools/Copy/Script	Write lock on source script, full lock on target script, prevent lock on table.
Tools/Copy/Just- Family	Full lock on target table and objects; write lock on source table objects prevent full lock on source table.

15

Table 15-1.   *Automatic Locks Resulting from Commonly Used Menu Options*
(continued)

Command/Option	Type of Lock
Tools/Delete/Table	Full lock on table.
Tools/Delete/Form	Full lock on form; prevent full lock on table.
Tools/Delete/Report	Full lock on report; prevent full lock on table.
Tools/Delete/KeepSet	Full lock on both table and object.
Tools/Delete/ValCheck	Full lock on both table and object.
Tools/More/Add	Write lock on source, prevent write lock on target.
Tools/More/Empty	Full lock.
Tools/More/Protect	Full lock.
View	Prevent full lock.
ValCheck/Define	Full lock on table during editing or data-entry session.
ValCheck/Clear	Full lock on table during editing or data-entry session.

Placing Explicit Locks

Although Paradox does an excellent job of placing locks automatically, there may be times when you prefer to place a certain type of lock manually, to ensure that you will be able to access an object when you need to. As an example, imagine you have a request on your desk to restructure a table as soon as possible, and you are on your way out the door to lunch. Past habit tells you that it is difficult (or impossible) to get full control over that shared table in the busy hours following lunch. You may decide to place a full lock on the table now so that you can restructure it when you return from lunch.

To place explicit locks, use Tools/Net/Lock from the main menu. To place explicit prevent locks, choose Tools/Net/PreventLock from the menu. When you choose either of these options, Paradox will ask if you wish to place (or prevent) a full lock or a write lock. Choose FullLock or WriteLock from the menu to place or prevent the desired type of lock.

Using CoEdit

Paradox offers a special editing mode that allows multiple users maximum access to a shared table. When you want to edit a shared table on the network, use the Modify/CoEdit option rather than the Modify/Edit option. The important difference between these two options is that CoEdit is designed to allow concurrent access to the table. In comparison, Edit will force a full lock on the table, making it impossible for anyone else to use the table while you are editing records.

To use the CoEdit option, simply choose Modify/CoEdit from the main menu, and then enter the name of the table to edit. This option will place a prevent full lock on the table being edited. It will also place a prevent write lock whenever you lock a single record (see the next section).

Record Locking on Demand with (ALT)-(L)

You can lock a single record, allowing other users to modify other records while preventing your locked record from being modified by anyone else. This can be very useful if you know in advance that you are going to edit a series of records, and you want to lock the records so that they remain available.

Paradox automatically locks a record whenever you are in CoEdit mode and you begin to change a record. You can also lock a record explicitly by placing the cursor anywhere in the record and pressing (ALT)-(L). (The (ALT)-(L) key is a toggle, so pressing it repeatedly locks and unlocks the current record.)

When you press (ALT)-(L) or when you begin changing a record while in CoEdit mode, the message at the bottom of the screen will indicate that the record has been locked. Other users will be able to view the record, but they will not be able to modify or delete the record until you unlock it by pressing (ALT)-(L) again or by moving the cursor away from the record.

Who Has the Lock?

On a busy network, you may try to gain exclusive access to a particular table, and see an error message similar to "Table has been locked by Mary

15

and 2 others." To find out who is responsible for tying up the table in this kind of situation, use the Lock option of the Tools/Info menu.

From the main menu, choose Tools/Info/Lock, and then enter the name of the table you are attempting to use. Paradox will respond with the names of the users who have placed locks on the table. Unfortunately, Paradox cannot kick those users off the network for you; you will have to solve this problem yourself.

Dealing with the "Lockout-After-DataEntry Syndrome"

When adding data into a shared table on a busy network, you may often find yourself locked out of a table at the end of a data-entry process. What happens is this: You choose Modify/DataEntry to begin adding records, and Paradox places a prevent full lock on the table. The new records get placed in the temporary ENTRY table, where Paradox normally puts the new records you add while using the DataEntry mode of operation. An hour later, you are done adding data and you press DO-IT! (F2), which normally causes Paradox to place a prevent write lock on the original table, and you proceed to add the records to that table. In the last two minutes, however, someone else on the network has begun sorting the table to another table, so that person now has a write lock on the original table. You are prevented from completing your data entry process until the write lock is released. The table being sorted contains 40 fields and 39,000 records, which means it will be locked for a while yet.

There are two ways to deal with this type of problem. One method is to place an explicit lock on the table with Tools/Net/Lock from the menu before starting the data entry. This will ensure that the table remains available for your use, although it will not win you any friends on the network. A second method, less obtrusive to other users, is to proceed with the data entry without placing any explicit locks beforehand. If you find the table locked upon completion of the data entry, while you are still in DataEntry mode choose KeepEntry from the menu, to save the table under the temporary table name ENTRY. Later, when the original table is available, you can use Tools/Add to add the new records in the ENTRY table to another table. A recommended alternative is to use CoEdit for data entry on a network, as CoEdit is designed to allow simultaneous data entry by multiple users.

Be sure to either add the records to the original table or rename the
ENTRY table before you exit from Paradox. Since ENTRY is a temporary
table, it will be lost if you exit without renaming it.

Changing Your Private Directory or User Name

While running on a network, Paradox maintains a private directory and
user name for you. The private directory is where your temporary tables are
stored. You can change the private directory with the SetDirectory option,
available from the Net menu.

To change your private directory, choose Tools/Net/SetPrivate from the
main menu, and then enter the new directory (including the drive identifier
and the path, if desired). To change your user name, choose
Tools/Net/Username from the main menu, and enter the desired new user
name. Note that selecting either of these options will cause Paradox to clear
the workspace and to delete any temporary tables.

15

Refreshing Your Screen

Whenever you are working with shared tables, your screen image may
not necessarily reflect reality at a given instant. It is possible that you will view
a table and someone will modify a record five seconds after you have used
the View option to bring the table onto your screen. Until your screen is
"refreshed" (updated) with the most current information in the table, you will
be viewing slightly inaccurate data. You can change the interval of time at
which Paradox automatically refreshes your screen image by choosing
Tools/Net/AutoRefresh and entering a desired value (in seconds) for the
refresh time. You can also manually refresh the screen image at any time by
pressing (ALT)-(R).

Listing Users

You can obtain a list of the users who are currently running Paradox on
the network at any time. From the main menu, choose Tools/Info/Who, and
a table appears, listing all network users currently running Paradox.

If You Have SQL Link...

Network users of Paradox can take advantage of Paradox SQL Link, an optional product from Borland that allows Paradox to access SQL (Structured Query Language) databases stored on SQL servers. Paradox works with Paradox SQL Link to let users access remote SQL data without learning complex SQL commands. SQL is an industry-standard data language for relational databases residing on minicomputers, mainframes, and PC database servers. If Paradox SQL Link is installed on your network, the following menu commands offer the additional options described. Note that all of the commands may not provide all the options shown, depending on the type of server used and your access rights to the SQL tables on the network.

- *Ask*   You can use Ask to query a remote table stored on the SQL Server. Note that not all Paradox query options are available when querying remote SQL tables.

- *Report*   You can use Report to design and print reports based on the remote tables.

- *Create*   You can use Create to create remote tables. When you choose this option, Paradox will ask whether you want to create a local table or a table on the SQL Server.

- *Modify/Dataentry*   You can use Modify/DataEntry to add new records to a table on the SQL Server.

- *Forms*   You can use Forms to create a data entry form for a table on the SQL Server.

- *Tools/Delete*   You can use Tools/Delete to delete a table on the SQL Server.

- *Tools/More/Add*   You can use this option to specify the name of a table on the SQL Server as a source or destination table for adding records.

- *Tools/More/Empty*   You can use this option to specify the name of a table on the SQL Server to empty.

Also, note that when Paradox SQL Link has been installed, the Tools menu displays the additional SQL command. When you choose SQL from the Tools menu, another menu provides you with options related specifically to SQL: Connection, Transaction, ReplicaTools, SQLSave, and Preferences. You can gain additional information about these commands from the SQL Link *Users Guide* supplied with Paradox SQL Link.

General Network Hints

To make the most effective use of Paradox on a network, you should keep a few points in mind. In any multiuser environment, large numbers of files tend to clutter the working space on the file servers. To hold such clutter to a minimum, heavy users who do not need to share table access should be provided with individual subdirectories on each file server or on local hard disks if available. If some users will be creating smaller files that will not be used by other network users, encourage them to store such files at their workstations rather than on the file server. This will leave the server more available for its intended purpose: providing shared files.

Back up all tables and associated objects regularly to floppy disks or a tape backup. Create new applications at a workstation, and thoroughly test those applications before placing the files in shared space on the file server. A multiuser environment is not the best place to finalize an application's design.

Improving Performance Through Workstation Use

You can significantly increase the performance of Paradox on a network by using the hard disk installed at the workstation, if the workstation has one. The best way to improve performance is to install a separate copy of Paradox on the workstation's hard disk. Other network users will not be able to access that copy, but the workstation itself will benefit from a significant performance increase, because the Paradox program will not have to be pulled across the network from the file server's hard disk. By installing Paradox on your local hard disk, you eliminate the delays that occur when Paradox has to access the server for the program files, yet you can still work with tables stored in shared directories on the server.

15

If economics don't permit the purchase of a separate copy of Paradox for your workstation, but you do have a local hard disk, you can still improve performance by copying certain Paradox program files to your workstation's disk. Use the usual DOS commands (see your DOS manual for details) to copy the following files from the Paradox program directory on the server to your local hard disk:

    PARADOX.EXE
    PARADOX.IDX
    PARADOX.AUX
    PARADOX.OV1
    PARADOX.OV2
    PARADOX.HLP
    PARADOX.MSG

Tip

If you use either of the above suggestions (installing a seperate copy of Paradox on the workstation or copying the selected program files to the workstation), you should make sure that your search path will search your local hard disk directory before it searches the server's hard disk.

Improving Performance Through Memory Designation

Another way to gain significant improvement in performance when using Paradox is by making more memory available. Paradox uses VROOM technology (VROOM is Borland's Virtual Runtime Object-Oriented Memory Manager). Because VROOM automatically manages extended and expanded memory when they exist, the addition of either type of memory to your workstation will benefit Paradox.

Caution

If either expanded or extended memory is installed in your workstation, do NOT reconfigure that memory to act as a fast virtual disk (or RAM disk). Paradox, with its VROOM technology, automatically makes the best use of expanded or extended memory. If you devote part of the expanded or extended memory as a RAM disk, Paradox won't be able to make use of it, and performance may actually be degraded as a result.

Quick Summary

To list users on the network   From the main menu, choose Tools/Info/Who.

To list locks placed on a table   From the main menu, choose Tools/Info/Lock; then enter the name of the desired table.

To place a lock on a table   From the main menu, choose Tools/Net/Lock. From the next menu, choose FullLock to place a full lock on the table, or choose WriteLock to place a write lock on the table.

To prevent a lock on a table   Choose Tools/Net/PreventLock from the main menu. From the next menu, choose FullLock to prevent others from setting a full lock on the table, or choose WriteLock to prevent others from setting a write lock on the table.

To edit a table while allowing shared access   From the main menu, choose Modify/CoEdit (or press (ALT)-(F9)).

To lock or unlock a single record while in CoEdit mode   Press the (ALT)-(L) key combination.

To change your private directory or your user name   From the main menu, choose Tools/Net/SetPrivate (to change your private directory), or choose Tools/Net/User-Name (to change your user name). Enter the desired new directory name or user name.

15

16

Sample Applications

This chapter contains step-by-step details for building two sample Paradox applications. You will want to try these applications as written, and then modify and expand them to fill your own needs.

Note

To greatly accelerate the development process, you will use the Paradox Application Workshop for the applications in this chapter. If you have not yet installed the Paradox Application Workshop on your system, do so now, as detailed in Chapter 13, before beginning your work in this chapter.

The instructions for building the applications in this chapter are complete, but slightly abbreviated. The do not contain the same level of detail that was presented in Chapter 13's stepped procedures for using the Paradox Application Workshop. If you have not yet examined Chapter 13, you should do so now before using the Paradox Application Workshop to build these applications.

Tip

If you do not want to spend the time involved in building these applications yourself, they are available on disk, along with other sample Paradox tables, forms, and reports used throughout this book. See the coupon at the front of this book for details on obtaining this disk.

Building a Mailing List

The Mailer application maintains a mailing list. The application offers menu options for adding names to the list, editing existing names, and deleting names that are no longer needed. Printer options allow the printing of names in the form of a registry.

Before starting, you may want to create a new directory to store the tables, forms, reports, and application files needed by the application. You can do this by choosing Tools/More/ToDOS from the Paradox menus to get to DOS; then from the DOS prompt enter the MD command to create a subdirectory. For example, this command

MD MAILER

will create a subdirectory called \MAILER. Then enter EXIT to return to Paradox, and use Tools/More/Directory to switch to the new directory you just created.

Your first step is to create a table for the application. Choose Create from the main menu and call the table MAILLIST, and specify the fields and their characteristics as listed in Table 16-1.

When you're done, save the table with (F2).

Now load the Paradox Application Workshop, by choosing Utilities/Workshop from the System menu. Choose Application/New from the Appli-

Table 16-1. *Structure for MAILLIST Table*

Field Name	Field Type
Lastname	A20
Firstname	A20
Company	A20
Address	A30
City	A20
State	A2
Zip Code	A10

cation Workshop's main menu. If asked whether you want to create a new application table, choose OK. In a moment, the New Application dialog box appears, as shown in Figure 16-1.

For the Application Name, enter **Mailing List**. For the Application ID, enter **MAILER**. Choose OK from the dialog box, and in a moment you'll see a new menu bar for the application.

Select <New> from the application's menu bar (highlight <New> and press (ENTER), or double-click on <New>). From the Menu Insert menu that appears, choose Action. This causes a Menu Definition dialog box to appear.

In the Keyword field of the dialog box, enter

```
Add Names
```

For the Description, enter **Add new names to the mailing list**. Next, choose Select from the Action portion of the dialog box. When the Object Type list box appears, make sure Edit Session is highlighted, and then choose OK. In the Select: Edit Session dialog box that appears, choose New.

Figure 16-1.   *The New Application dialog box*

16

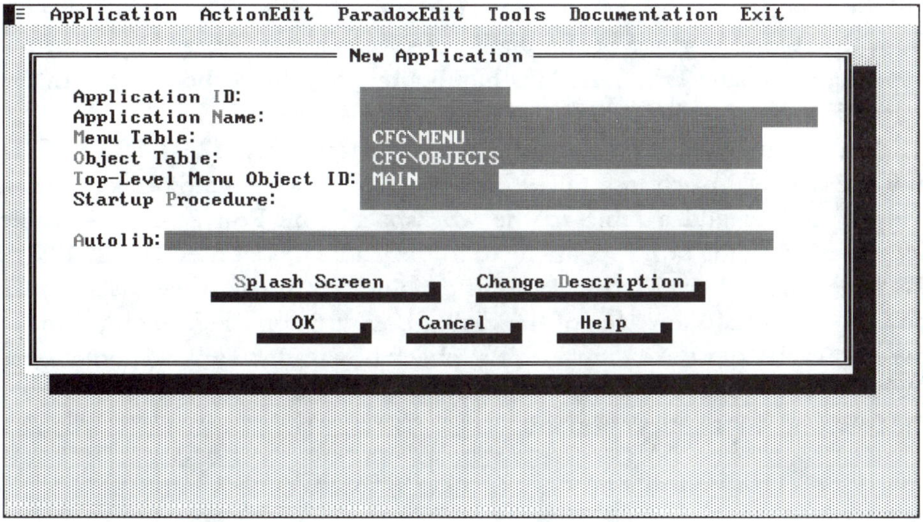

When prompted for a new edit session name, enter **ADD RECORDS**, and press (ENTER) or choose OK. When the Edit Session dialog box appears, choose Add to add a table to the workspace. The Edit Session – Table Information dialog box appears next; in the Table field, enter **MAILLIST** as the table name. In the Modes area of the dialog box, turn off the Delete and Edit check boxes; then choose OK to close the dialog box. When the Edit Session dialog box reappears, turn on the DataEntry option in the System Mode area. In the Prompt field, type the following:

```
Add new records, press F2 when done.
```

Then, choose OK twice to close the Edit Session dialog box and then the Menu Definition dialog box underneath. Your first option, Add Names, is now added to the menu.

For the next menu choice, choose <New> from the menu bar. From the Menu Insert menu that appears, choose Action; the Menu Definition dialog box again appears.

In the Keyword field, enter

```
Edit Names
```

For the Description, enter **Edit names in the mailing list**. Next, choose Select from the Action portion of the dialog box. When the Object Type list box appears, make sure Edit Session is highlighted, and then choose OK. In the Select: Edit Session dialog box that appears, choose New.

When prompted for a New Edit Session name, enter **EDIT RECORDS**, and press (ENTER) or choose OK. When the Edit Session dialog box appears, choose Add to add a table to the workspace. The Edit Session – Table Information dialog box appears next; in the Table field, enter **MAILLIST** as the table name. In the Modes area of the dialog box, turn off the Insert check box. In the Initial View area of the dialog box, turn on the Table option. In the Allowable Views area, turn on the check box under Table. Then choose OK to close the dialog box. When the Edit Session dialog box reappears, enter the following in the Prompt field:

```
Use Ctrl-Z to search any field, Alt-Z to search again.
```

Choose OK twice to close the Edit Session dialog box and then the Menu
Definition dialog box underneath. The Edit Names option is now added to
the menu.

Before proceeding further, you will need to create a report for use with
the table; you can create reports and other Paradox objects from within the
Paradox Application Workshop with the ParadoxEdit menu.

Open the ParadoxEdit menu, and choose Reports. In the Report Selection dialog box that appears, enter **MAILLIST** as the table name, and then
press (TAB). Because no reports yet exist for the new table, in a moment you'll
see the list showing the standard report and all unused reports, as shown in
Figure 16-2.

Highlight 1, Unused Report, and choose the Design button. In a moment,
a Report Title dialog box appears. Enter **Registry of Names** for the report
title, and choose FreeForm. In a moment, a default free-form report appears,
based on the MAILLIST table. The free-form report style is fine to use as is
for the report that's needed by this application, but if you wish, you can make
any "cosmetic" changes desired, using the techniques outlined in Chapters 7
and 12. Then choose DO-IT! to save the report.

16

Figure 16-2.   *The Report Selection dialog box*

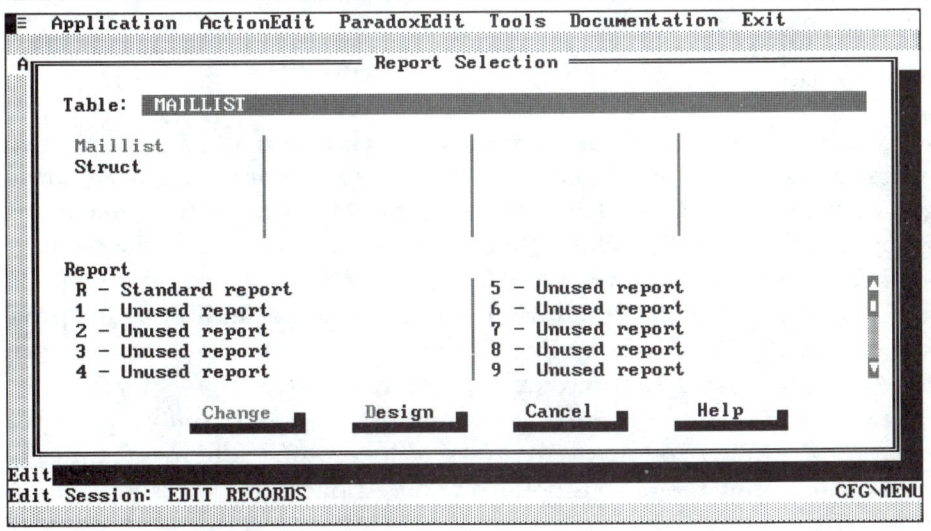

For the next menu choice, choose <New> from the menu bar. From the Menu Insert menu, choose Action, and you'll again see the Menu Definition dialog box.

In the Keyword field of the dialog box, enter

```
Print Registry
```

For the Description, enter **Print registry of names**. Choose Select from the Action area of the dialog box. When the Object Type list box appears, highlight Report Print, and choose OK. In the Select: Report Print dialog box, choose New.

When prompted for a new Report Print name, enter **PRINT NAMES**, and press (ENTER) or choose OK. This causes the Report Print dialog box to appear. In the Table Name field, enter **MAILLIST**. Then choose Select Report. When the Report Selection list box appears, choose 1, Registry of Names, from the list, and then choose OK.

In the Send To portion of the dialog box, turn on the Screen and File check boxes, and turn on the Display Message check box. Then choose OK to close the dialog box. When the Menu Definition dialog box reappears, choose OK to close it and add the Print Registry option to the menu.

For the last menu choice, choose <New> from the menu bar. From the Menu Insert menu, choose Action. When the Menu Definition dialog box appears, in the Keyword field enter

```
Quit System
```

For the description, enter **Leave application and return to Paradox**. Then choose Select. From the Object Type list box that appears, choose Quit to Paradox. Press (ENTER) to choose OK, and the Menu Definition dialog box reappears. Choose OK, and the Quit System choice is added to the menu.

Now complete the application, by opening the Application menu and choosing Finish. Watch as the various messages appear, indicating the progress of the script. Then choose Exit/ToParadox from the main menu, to exit the Application Workshop and return to Paradox. Use Scripts/Play from the Paradox main menu to run the application. (Remember, you assigned it a name of MAILER.) You may want to try adding some additional features of your choice, using the various options of the Application Workshop.

A Database for Tracking Inventory and Sales

For an example of a more complex (and fully relational) application, consider the problems involved in tracking sales of items. The transactions themselves must be recorded, in a transactions table; listings of customers who purchase the items are maintained in a customers table; and lists of saleable items (the inventory) are kept in an inventory table. The application must be able to query all the related tables as necessary, to produce the necessary reports.

Creating the Directory and the Tables

Before starting, you may want to create a new directory from DOS, to store all of the sales files used in the application. You can use the Tools/More/ToDOS command to get to the DOS prompt, then enter the appropriate DOS commands. For example, these commands

CD\PDOX40

MD\SALES

create a new subdirectory called SALES in the Paradox directory. Return to Paradox by typing **EXIT** at the DOS prompt. Then use Tools/More/Directory to change to the SALES directory.

Choose Create from the main menu, and call the table TRANSACT (for transactions). Enter the structure shown in Table 16-2.

16

Table 16-2. *Structure for TRANSACT Table*

Field Name	Field Type
Customer Code	A4
Product Code	A4
Quantity Sold	N
Date of Sale	D

Choose DO-IT! to save the structure. Select Create again, and call the next table CUSTOM (for customers). Enter the table structure shown in Table 16-3.

Choose DO-IT! to save the structure. Select Create again, and call the next table PRODUCTS. Enter the table structure shown in Table 16-4.

Save the table's structure by choosing DO-IT!.

Designing the Application's Menu Structure

Start the Paradox Application Workshop; choose Utilities/Workshop from the System menu. Choose Application/New from the Application Workshop's main menu. If asked whether you want to create a new application table, choose OK. In a moment, the New Application dialog box appears, as shown earlier in Figure 16-1.

For an Application ID, enter **SALES**; for Application Name, enter **Sales Management System**. Choose OK from the dialog box, and in a moment a new menu bar for the application will appear.

Choose <New> from the application's menu bar. From the Menu Insert menu that appears, choose SubMenu. You'll next see the Menu Definition dialog box.

In the Keyword field of the dialog box, enter

```
Sales Transactions
```

For the description, enter **Add or edit sales transactions**. Then press (ENTER) or choose OK from the dialog box, to place the first menu option, Sales Transactions, on the menu.

Table 16-3.   *Structure for CUSTOM Table*

Field Name	Field Type
Customer Code	A4
Customer Name	A30
Address	A30
City	A15
State	A2
Zip Code	A10

Table 16-4. *Structure for PRODUCTS Table*

Field Name	Field Type
Product Code	A4
Description	A30
Cost	$
Supplier	A30

Choose <New> from the application's menu bar. From the Menu Insert menu that appears, choose SubMenu. When the Menu Definition dialog box appears, in the Keyword field enter

```
Maintain Customers
```

For the description, enter **Add, edit, or delete customers**. Then press (ENTER) or choose OK to place the next option, Maintain Customers, on the menu.

Once again, choose <New> from the application's menu bar. From the Menu Insert menu that appears, choose SubMenu. When the Menu Definition dialog box appears, in the Keyword field enter

```
Inventory
```

For the Description, enter **Add, edit, or delete items in stock**. Then press (ENTER) or choose OK to place the next menu option, Inventory, on the menu.

Again choose <New> from the application's menu bar. From the Menu Insert menu, choose SubMenu. In the Keyword field of the Menu Definition dialog box, enter

```
Print Reports
```

For the description, enter **Print reports of sales, inventory, or customers**. Press (ENTER) or choose OK to place the next menu option, Print Reports, on the menu.

For the last menu choice, again choose <New> from the menu bar. From the Menu Insert menu, choose Action. In the Keyword field of the Menu Definition dialog box, enter

```
Quit
```

16

For the Description, enter **Leave application and return to Paradox**. Then choose Select from the dialog box. From the Object Type list box that appears, choose Quit to Paradox. After pressing (ENTER) to choose OK, the Menu Definition dialog box reappears. Choose OK, and the Quit choice is added to the menu.

Now that the main menu options are complete, you can proceed to define the submenu choices and their respective actions for the application. Click on the Sales Transactions menu choice, or highlight it and press (ENTER). When the <New> menu opens below it, double-click on it or press (ENTER); the Menu Insert menu appears.

Choose Action from the Menu Insert menu, and an expanded Menu Definition dialog box appears. Enter the following for a keyword:

```
Add Sales
```

and for a description, enter **Enter new sales transactions**. Next, choose Select from the Action portion of the dialog box. When the Object Type list box appears, make sure Edit Session is highlighted, and choose OK. In the Select: Edit Session dialog box that appears, choose New.

When prompted for a New Edit Session name, enter **ADD SALES** and press (ENTER) or choose OK. In the Edit Session dialog box, choose Add to add a table to the workspace. In the Table field of the Edit Session – Table Information dialog box that next appears, enter **TRANSACT** as the table name. In the Modes area, turn off the Delete and Edit check boxes; choose OK to close the dialog box. When the Edit Session dialog box reappears, turn on the DataEntry option in the System Mode area. In the Prompt field, enter the following:

```
Add new records, press F2 when done.
```

Then, choose OK twice to close the Edit Session and then the Menu Definition dialog box, and add the Add Sales choice to the submenu.

Choose <New> in the submenu, and choose Action from the Menu Insert menu that appears. In the expanded Menu Definition dialog box, enter the following for a keyword:

```
Edit/Delete Sales
```

For a description, enter **Edit or delete sales transactions**. Next, choose Select from the Action portion of the dialog box. When the Object Type list box appears, make sure Edit Session is highlighted, and choose OK. In the Select: Edit Session dialog box, choose New.

When prompted for a New Edit Session name, enter **EDIT SALES** and press (ENTER) or choose OK. When the Edit Session dialog box appears, choose Add to add a table to the workspace. In the Table field of the Edit Session – Table Information dialog box, enter **TRANSACT** as the table name. In the Modes area of the dialog box, turn off the Insert check box. In the Initial View area, turn on the Table option. In the Allowable Views area, turn on the Table check box. Choose OK to close the dialog box. When the Edit Session dialog box reappears, enter the following in the Prompt field:

```
Use Ctrl-Z to search a field, Alt-Z to search again.
```

Choose OK twice to close the Edit Session and then the Menu Definition dialog box, and add the Edit/Delete Sales choice to the submenu.

Next, you will need to define the menu options for the Maintain Customers menu. Click on the Maintain Customers menu choice, or highlight it and press (ENTER). When the <New> menu opens below it, double-click on it, or press (ENTER); the Menu Insert menu appears.

Choose Action from the Menu Insert menu. In the expanded Menu Definition dialog box that next appears, enter the following for a keyword:

```
Add Customers
```

For a description, enter **Enter new customers**. Choose Select from the Action portion of the dialog box. When the Object Type list box appears, make sure Edit Session is highlighted, and then choose OK. In the Select: Edit Session dialog box, choose New.

When prompted for a New Edit Session name, enter **ADD CUSTOMERS** and press (ENTER) or choose OK. When the Edit Session dialog box appears, choose Add to add a table to the workspace. In the Table field of the Edit Session – Table Information dialog box that next appears, enter **CUSTOM** as the table name. In the Modes area of the dialog box, turn off the Delete and Edit check boxes, and then choose OK to close the dialog box. When the

16

Edit Session dialog box reappears, turn on the DataEntry option in the System Mode area of the dialog box. In the Prompt field, enter the following:

```
Add new records, press F2 when done.
```

Then, choose OK twice to close first the Edit Session and then the Menu Definition dialog box, and place the Add Customers choice in the submenu.

Choose <New> in the submenu. Next, choose Action from the Menu Insert menu. In the expanded Menu Definition dialog box that appears, enter the following for a keyword:

```
Edit/Delete Customers
```

and for a description, enter **Edit or delete customers**. Next, choose Select from the Action portion of the dialog box. When the Object Type list box appears, make sure Edit Session is highlighted, and choose OK. In the Select: Edit Session dialog box, choose New.

When prompted for a New Edit Session name, enter **EDIT CUSTOMERS** and press (ENTER) or choose OK. When the Edit Session dialog box appears, choose Add to add a table to the workspace. In the Table field of the Edit Session – Table Information dialog box, enter **CUSTOM** as the table name. In the Modes area of the dialog box, turn off the Insert check box. In the Initial View area, turn on the Table option. In the Allowable Views area, turn on the Table check box; then choose OK to close the dialog box. When the Edit Session dialog box reappears, enter the following in the Prompt field:

```
Use Ctrl-Z to search a field, Alt-Z to search again.
```

Then choose OK twice to close the Edit Session and then the Menu Definition dialog box, and add the Edit/Delete Customers choice to the submenu.

Next, you will need to define the menu options for the Inventory menu. Click on the Inventory menu choice, or highlight it and press (ENTER). When <New> menu opens below it, double-click on it, or press (ENTER); the Menu Insert menu appears.

Choose Action, and in the expanded Menu Definition dialog box that appears, enter the following for a keyword:

```
Add Inventory
```

For a description, enter **Enter new stock items**. Next, choose Select from the Action portion of the dialog box. When the Object Type list box appears, make sure Edit Session is highlighted, and choose OK. In the Select: Edit Session dialog box, choose New.

When prompted for a New Edit Session name, enter **ADD INVENTORY** and press (ENTER) or choose OK. When the Edit Session dialog box appears, choose Add to add a table to the workspace. In the Table field of the Edit Session – Table Information dialog box, enter **PRODUCTS** as the table name. In the Modes area of the dialog box, turn off the Delete and Edit check boxes, and then choose OK to close the dialog box. When the Edit Session dialog box reappears, turn on the DataEntry option in the Mode area of the dialog box. In the Prompt field, enter the following:

```
Add new records, press F2 when done.
```

Choose OK twice to close first the Edit Session and then the Menu Definition dialog box, and place the Add Inventory choice in the submenu.

Choose <New> in the submenu; then choose Action from the Menu Insert menu that appears. In the expanded Menu Definition dialog box, enter the following for a keyword:

```
Edit/Delete Inventory
```

For a description, enter **Edit or delete stock items**. Next, choose Select from the Action portion of the dialog box. When the Object Type list box appears, make sure Edit Session is highlighted, and choose OK. In the Select: Edit Session dialog box that appears, choose New.

When prompted for a New Edit Session name, enter **EDIT INVENTORY** and press (ENTER) or choose OK. When the Edit Session dialog box appears, choose Add to add a table to the workspace. In the Table field of the Edit Session – Table Information dialog box, enter **PRODUCTS** as the table name. In the Modes area of the dialog box, turn off the Insert check box. In the Initial View area, turn on the Table option. In the Allowable Views area, turn on the Table check box. Then choose OK to close the dialog box. When the Edit Session dialog box reappears, enter the following in the Prompt field:

```
Use Ctrl-Z to search a field, Alt-Z to search again.
```

16

Choose OK twice to close first the Edit Session and then the Menu Definition dialog box, and add Edit/Delete Inventory to the submenu.

Designing a Multiple-Action Object for the Sales Report

For the Sales Report, something different is needed. To enable the printing of reports for all sales based on a specific customer, you will combine a short PAL script that asks the user for a customer name, with a Query Form and a report. You may recall from Chapter 13 that the Multiple Actions choice in the Object Type list box lets you combine multiple actions and assign them to a single menu option.

First, you'll need to create the script. Open the ParadoxEdit menu of the Application Workshop, and choose Script. In a moment, a Select Script dialog box appears. In the Script field, enter TELLME as a script name, and choose New from the dialog box to create a new script by this name.

In a moment, you'll see a blank Editor window titled TELLME.sc. Enter the following PAL code in the window now:

```
@ 15,5
?? "Enter the customer code:"
ACCEPT "A4" TO tellme
@ 15,5
?? "Enter the starting date:"
ACCEPT "D" TO startday
@ 15,5
?? "  Enter the ending date:"
ACCEPT "D" TO endday
@ 15,5
?? "...working; one moment, please..."
```

Check your work for errors, and then choose DO-IT! to save the script. In a moment, the Select Script dialog box reappears; choose Cancel, since you do not need to create any more scripts.

When run, this short PAL program will ask the user of the application for a customer code, and starting and ending dates for sales; that information will later be stored in a field of a query (which you are about to design).

Open the ActionEdit menu of the Application Workshop, and choose Query. In a moment, an Edit: Query dialog box appears. Choose New from

Figure 16-3. *Query By Example dialog box for the QUERY SALES object*

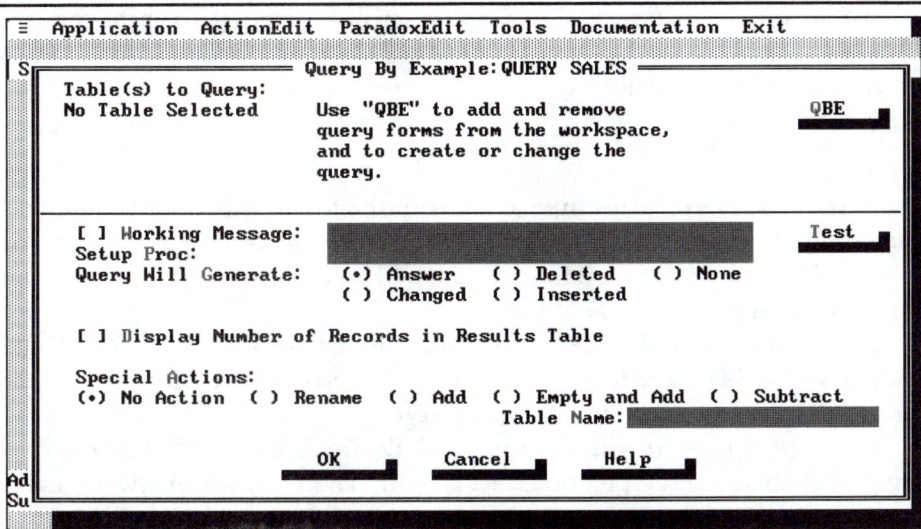

this dialog box, and when prompted for a new query name, enter QUERY SALES. Choose OK or press (ENTER), and in a moment the Query By Example dialog box appears, as shown in Figure 16-3.

Choose QBE from the dialog box, to create a new query. In a moment, the Application menu is replaced by the Query By Example menu, with choices of Add, Remove, Help, Done, and Cancel. Choose Add; when the Select Table dialog box appears, enter TRANSACT in the Table field, and choose OK. In a moment, a Query Form appears for the TRANSACT table.

Move the cursor to the Customer Code field of the Query Form, and press (F5) to begin an example element. Type the letters ABCD and a comma, and then type

```
~tellme
```

The comma, the tilde, and the "tellme" characters together serve as a query variable. Paradox will use this designation to represent the customer code typed by the user in response to the PAL script that you created earlier.

16

Next, move the cursor to the Product Code field. Press (F5) to begin an example element, and type **EFGH**. Use the arrow keys and (F6) (or the mouse) to place check marks in the Quantity Sold and Date of Sale fields. In the Date of Sale field, type the following:

```
>=~startday,<=~endday
```

Again, the tilde is used, this time along with the greater than, less than, and equal symbols, to form a query variable. Paradox will use this designation to represent the starting and ending dates typed by the user in response to the PAL script that you created earlier.

Choose Add from the menu, to add another Query Form. In the Table field, enter **CUSTOM** as the table name, and choose OK to place the Query Form for the customer table on the desktop.

Move the cursor to the Customer Code field, press (F5) to begin an example element, and type the letters **ABCD**. Then use the arrow keys and (F6) (or the mouse) to place a check mark in the Customer Name field.

Choose Add from the menu to add another Query Form. In the Table field, enter **PRODUCTS** as the table name, and choose OK to place the Query Form for the customer table on the desktop.

Move the cursor to the Product Code field, press (F5) to begin an example element, and type the letters **EFGH**. Then use the arrow keys and (F6) (or the mouse) to place check marks in the Description and Cost fields. At this point, your screen should resemble the example shown in Figure 16-4.

Finally, choose Done/Save from the menu to save the query. When the Query By Example dialog box reappears, click on Working Message to display a message that says "working" while the query is operating. Then choose OK from the dialog box.

Now you need to add a new action object for printing a report, based on the ANSWER table provided by the query. Open the ActionEdit menu again, and choose Report Print. In the Edit: Report Print dialog box that appears, choose New. When prompted for a new report print name, enter **ASK AND PRINT SALES**, and press (ENTER) to choose OK. In a moment, a Report Print dialog box appears.

In the Table field, enter **ANSWER** as a table name. Move the cursor to the Report Number field, and enter the letter **R** (for Standard Report). In the Send Report To portion of the dialog box, turn on the Screen option, and

Figure 16-4. *The completed Query Forms for your application*

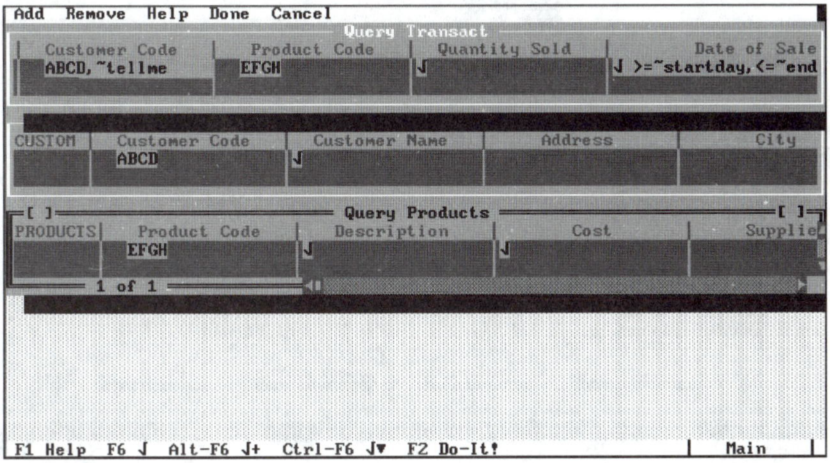

make sure that the Printer option, too, remains turned on. This will allow the user a choice of displaying the report on screen or printing it. Finally, choose OK from the dialog box, to save and put away the action object for printing the report.

Before completing your menu design, take a moment to design a report for the customer table. Names and addresses do not lend themselves well to the standard tabular report that Paradox produces as a default, so you will use the Reports option of the ParadoxEdit menu to design a new report.

Open the ParadoxEdit menu now, and choose Reports. In the Table field of the Report Selection dialog box that appears, enter **CUSTOM** as a table name. Press (TAB), and a report list for the CUSTOM table is displayed, showing that all the custom report designator numbers are currently unused, as shown in Figure 16-5.

Highlight 1, the first unused report in the list, and choose the Design button to begin designing the report. In a moment, you will be prompted for a report title; enter **Customer List**. Then choose FreeForm from the dialog box. In a moment, a default free-form report appears in the Report Designer window.

Figure 16-5. *The Report Selection dialog box for creating a customer table*

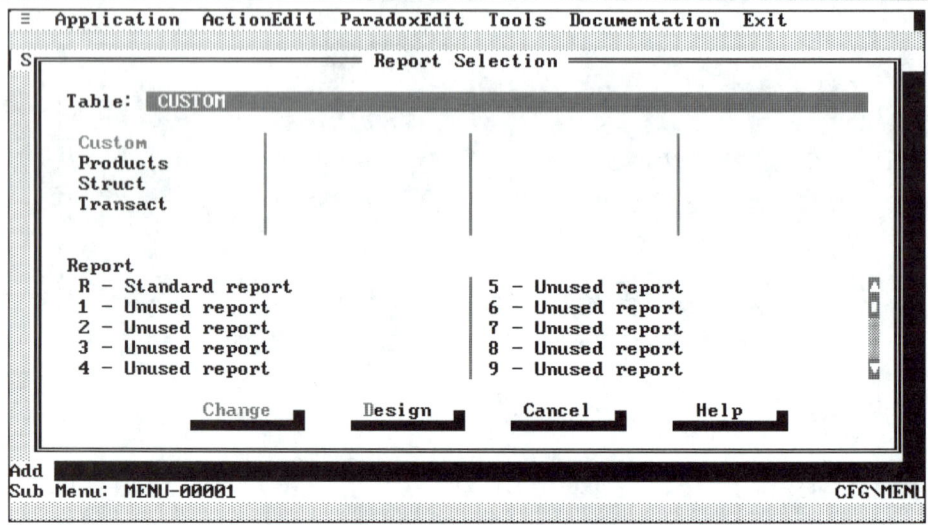

The free-form report style is fine to use as is for the report that's needed by this application. If you wish, however, you can make any "cosmetic" changes desired, using the techniques outlined in Chapters 7 and 12. When done, choose DO-IT! to save the report. In a moment, the application's menu bar will reappear on the desktop.

The next step is to define the actions for the options of the Print Reports submenu. Use ⊝ to highlight the Print Reports option and press (ENTER), or click on the Print Reports option. When you do so, another submenu with a single option, <New>, appears beneath the Print Reports menu option.

With the <New> submenu open, press (ENTER), or double-click on the <New> submenu. In the Menu Insert menu appears, choose Action. You'll see an expanded Menu Definition dialog box.

In the Keyword field, enter

```
Sales
```

and in the Description field, enter **Print sales transactions**. Choose the Select button. When the Object Type list box appears, choose Multiple Actions, and choose OK. In a moment, the Select: Multiple Actions dialog box appears.

Choose New from the dialog box, to define a new multiple-action object. When prompted, enter **SALES REPORT** for the object name, and press (ENTER) or click on OK. In a moment, a Multi-Action dialog box for SALES REPORT appears, as shown in Figure 16-6.

Choose the Add button from the dialog box, to add a new action. In the Object Type list box that appears, choose Play A Script, and then OK. When prompted for a script name, enter **TELLME** and choose OK. The Script dialog box vanishes, revealing the Multi-Action dialog box still underneath.

Choose Add again, to add a new action. In the Object Type list box, choose Query, and then OK. This causes a Select: Query dialog box to appear, displaying the name of the query you created and saved earlier, QUERY SALES. Make sure QUERY SALES is highlighted, and choose OK.

Choose Add once more from the Multi-Action dialog box. In the Object Type list box, choose Report Print, and then OK. In a moment, the Select: Report Print dialog box appears, displaying the name of the action object for printing a report that you created earlier, ASK AND PRINT SALES. Make sure ASK AND PRINT SALES is highlighted, and choose OK. At this point,

16

Figure 16-6. *Multi-Action dialog box for the sales report*

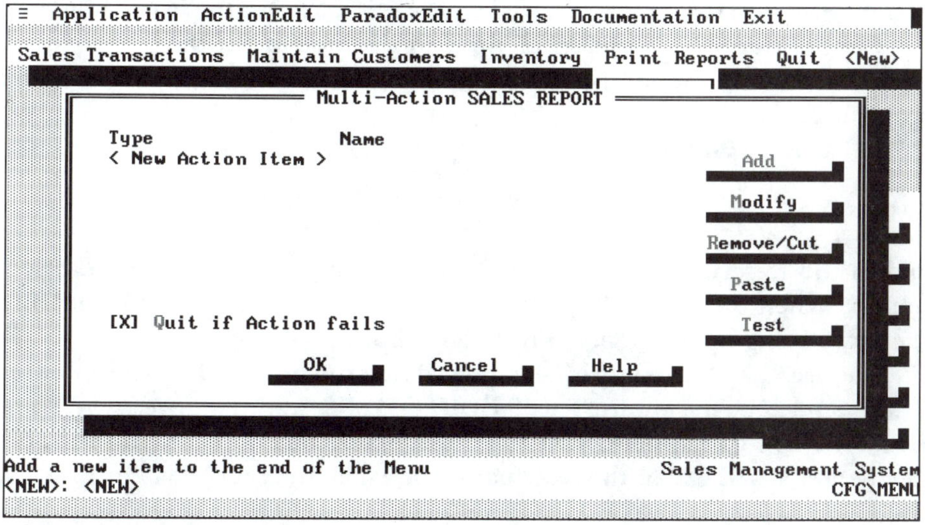

Figure 16-7.   *Completed Multi-Action dialog box for the sales report*

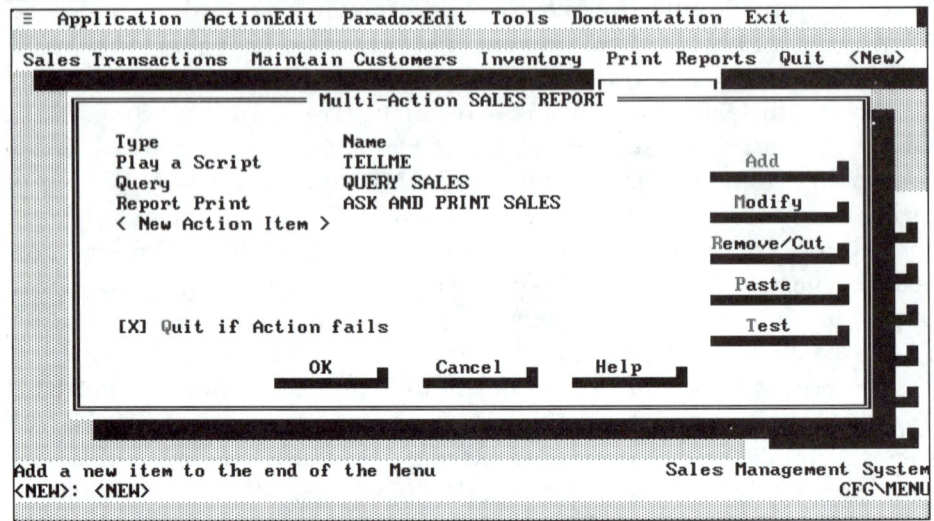

the Multi-Action dialog box will have all three items (for playing a script, performing a query, and printing a report), as shown in Figure 16-7.

Choose OK twice to close first the Multi-Action dialog box and then the Menu Definition dialog box. The Sales choice is added to the Print submenu.

Choose the <New> option of the Print submenu. In the Menu Insert menu, choose Action, and you'll again see the expanded Menu Definition dialog box.

In the Keyword field, enter

```
Customers
```

and in the Description field, enter **Print customer list**. Choose the Select button. When the Object Type list box appears, choose Report Print from the list to bring up the Report Print dialog box.

Choose <New> from the dialog box. When the prompt for a new Report Print name appears, enter **PRINT CUSTOMERS**, and then press (ENTER) or click on OK. In a moment, a Report Print dialog box appears. In the Table field, enter **CUSTOM** as the table name for which the report will be printed.

Then (TAB) to the Report Number field, and enter the number **1** (this indicates the custom report you created earlier in this chapter). In the Send Report To area, turn on the Screen option, and make sure the Printer option remains turned on. (This lets the user direct a report either to the screen or to a printer.) Finally, choose OK, and the Menu Definition dialog box reappears. Choose OK again to close the dialog box and add the Customers choice to the Print submenu.

Select the <New> option of the Print submenu again. When the Menu Insert menu again appears, choose Action, and the expanded Menu Definition dialog box is displayed once again.

In the Keyword field, enter

`Inventory`

and in the Description field, enter **Print inventory list**. Choose the Select button. When the Object Type list box appears, choose Report Print from the list to bring up the Report Print dialog box.

Choose the <New> option in the dialog box. When the prompt for a new Report Print name appears, enter **PRINT INVENTORY**, and then press (ENTER) or click on OK. In a moment, a Report Print dialog box appears. In the Table field, enter **PRODUCTS** as the table name for which the report is printed. Then (TAB) to the Report Number field, and enter the letter **R** (for Standard Report). In the Send Report To portion of the dialog box, turn on the Screen option, and make sure the Printer option remains turned on. Finally, choose OK twice to close the Report Print dialog box and then the Menu Definition dialog box. The Inventory choice is added to the Print submenu.

At this point, all the desired menu choices have been placed in the application, and all menu actions have been defined. All that remains is to generate the application. Open the Application menu (press (F10) and highlight Application, and then press (ENTER); or just click on the Application menu). Choose Finish from the Application menu.

Paradox will flash various messages on the screen as it builds the application. When it is done, choose Exit/To Paradox from the main menu to exit the Paradox Application Workshop. From the Paradox main menu, use Scripts/Play to run the application. (Remember, you assigned it a name of SALES.) Figure 16-8 shows the Sales Management System's main menu. Try

16

Figure 16-8.   *Main menu for the Sales Management System application*

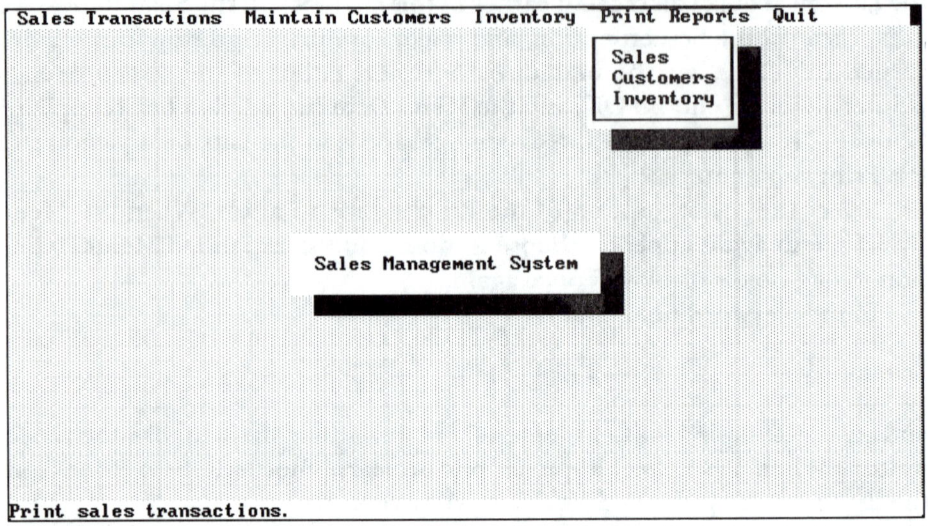

```
 Sales Transactions  Maintain Customers  Inventory  Print Reports  Quit
                                                    ┌──────────────┐
                                                    │ Sales        │
                                                    │ Customers    │
                                                    │ Inventory    │
                                                    └──────────────┘


                        ┌─────────────────────────┐
                        │ Sales Management System  │
                        └─────────────────────────┘




 Print sales transactions.
```

the various menu options; remember that you will need to add customers, inventory items, and sales records before a meaningful sales report can be printed.

You may want to try adding some features of your own to the application, using the various options of the Paradox Application Workshop.

A

Paradox Menu Options

This appendix provides a summary of the Paradox menu options. Use it to jog your memory—it will quickly show you which options are available for Paradox operations. Included with each menu option is a listing of the steps needed to perform the operation. Note that all options are selected from the main menu unless otherwise indicated.

Add

Sequence:
Tools/More/Add

The Add option lets you add records from one table to another table. Use Add to merge a single table into another table. Choose Tools/More/Add, and Paradox prompts you for the name of the source table (which will supply the records to be added) and the target table (which will receive the records). The fields in the two tables must be of compatible types and must be arranged in the same order.

All

Sequence (From the Edit Menu):
ValCheck/Clear/All

The All option lets you clear, from the table in use, all validity checks previously established with ValCheck. While in Edit mode, choose ValCheck/ Clear/All from the menu to clear the validity checks.

AppendDelimited

Sequence:
Tools/ExportImport/Import/ASCII/AppendDelimited

Use the AppendDelimited option to append data from a foreign file that uses delimited ASCII format into an existing Paradox table. Fields in such a foreign file are usually separated by commas, and may optionally be enclosed in single or double quotes; the ASCII text file should have an extension of .TXT. Choose Tools/ExportImport/Import/ASCII/AppendDelimited, and supply the name of the foreign file. Then supply the name of the table to which the data should be appended.

Area

Sequence (From the Form Design Menu):
Area/Erase
Area/Move

Use the Area option to move or erase portions of a form. To move an area, choose Area/Move from the Form Design menu. Place the cursor at one corner of the area to be moved and press (ENTER); move the cursor to the diagonal corner of the area and press (ENTER) again; finally, use the cursor keys to drag the area to its new location and press (ENTER).

To erase an area, from the Form Design menu choose Area/Erase. Place the cursor at one corner of the area to be erased and press (ENTER); then move the cursor to the diagonal corner of the area, and press (ENTER) again to erase the area.

Ask

Sequence:
Ask

Use the Ask option to compose a query that will let you select a subset of records based on various criteria and establish relationships between multiple tables. Choose Ask and enter the name of a table to display a Query Form containing the fields for that table. Place the cursor in any desired field, and press (F6) to include the fields in the answer. (To include every field in the answer, place the cursor at the extreme left and press (F6) for all fields or (ALT)-(F6) for all fields with duplicate records included.) To select certain records, enter the matching criteria in the fields. When the Query Form is completed, choose DO-IT! ((F2)) to produce the results, which are stored in a temporary ANSWER table.

AutoRefresh

Sequence:
Modify/CoEdit/*tablename*/AutoRefresh
Tools/Net/AutoRefresh

Use the AutoRefresh option to change the time interval (in seconds) that Paradox waits before refreshing the screen when you are in CoEdit mode. From the CoEdit menu, choose AutoRefresh. Enter a number for the desired value, from 1 to 3600 seconds (1 hour). The default value is 3 seconds.

Average

Sequence (From the Report Design Menu):
Field/Place/Summary/Calculated/*<expression>*/Average
Field/Place/Calculated/*<expression>*/Average

Use the Average option to average the values in a numeric field on a custom free-form or tabular report. From the Report Design menu, choose Field/Place/Summary/Calculated/Average if the field to be averaged in the report is a summary field. Then select PerGroup (if you want a summary each time the group changes) or Overall (if you only desire an overall summary).

A

Use the cursor to place the field in its desired band, and press (ENTER). Next, adjust the number of digits displayed (use (←) and (→)), and press (ENTER). Finally, adjust the number of decimal points displayed (with (←) and (→)), and press (ENTER) to complete the placement of the field.

BeginRecord

Sequence:
Scripts/BeginRecord

Use the BeginRecord option to begin recording a new script. Choose Scripts/BeginRecord, and enter a name for the new script. Paradox will record all further actions until you end the recording with Scripts/ EndRecord. Use Scripts/Play or Scripts/ShowPlay to play back a recorded script.

Border (To Add or Change Colors of an Existing Border)

Sequence (From the Form Design Menu):
Style/Color/Border

Use this Border option to add or change colors of an existing border. Place the cursor at one corner of the border and press (ENTER) to select it. Then move the cursor to the diagonal corner of the border and press (ENTER). Finally, use the arrow keys followed by (ENTER) to select the desired colors from the color palette that appears.

Border (To Add or Erase Borders in a Form)

Sequence (From the Form Design Menu):
Border

Use this Border option to add or erase borders in a form. To add a border, choose Border/Place from the Form Design menu. From the next menu, choose SingleLine, DoubleLine, or Other for the type of border. Place the cursor at one corner of the border and press (ENTER); move the cursor to the diagonal corner and press (ENTER) again to draw the border.

To remove a border, choose Border/Erase from the Form Design menu. Place the cursor at one corner of the border and press (ENTER) to select it.

Then move the cursor to the diagonal corner and press (ENTER) again to erase the border.

Borrow

Sequence:
Create/Borrow
Modify/Restructure/Borrow

Use the Borrow option to "borrow" the structure of an existing table while you are designing or restructuring another table. To borrow a table's structure, choose Create and enter the name of the table; then choose Borrow from the Create menu, and enter the name of the table to borrow the structure from. While restructuring, choose Borrow from the Create menu, and enter the name of the table from which to borrow the structure.

CalcEdit

Sequence (From the Form Design or Report Design Menu):
Field/CalcEdit

Use the CalcEdit option to edit an expression used in the calculated field of a form or report. From either the Form Design menu or the Report Design menu, choose Field/CalcEdit. Place the cursor at the desired field, and press (ENTER) to select the field. The existing expression will appear at the top of the screen, and you can edit the expression as desired.

Cancel

Sequence:
Cancel

Use the Cancel option to cancel the current Paradox operation. In most cases, Paradox will request confirmation by displaying an additional menu with Yes and No options. You must choose Yes to confirm the cancellation of the option.

A

Change

Sequence:
Forms/Change
Report/Change

Use the Change option to change existing forms or reports. To change a form, choose Forms/Change and enter a name for the table. Select an identifier for the form, and change the description or press (ENTER) to accept the existing description. Then make the desired changes to the form itself and choose DO-IT! ((F2)).

To change a Report Specification, choose Report/Change and enter a name for the table. Select a designator for the report, and the report description will appear. Make any desired changes to the report description and press (ENTER) to display the Report Specification. Make the desired changes, and choose DO-IT!.

Changes

Sequence:
Tools/Net/Changes

Use the Changes option to tell Paradox to restart a query or a report if the data used in the query or report changes during execution. Choose Tools/Net/Changes; then choose Restart (to restart the process if data changes), or Continue (to continue the process if data changes).

Clear

Sequence (From the Edit Menu):
ValCheck/Clear

Use the Clear option to clear validity check settings from a single field or from an entire table. To clear the validity check settings, begin editing, and then select ValCheck/Clear from the Edit menu. To clear the validity settings from all fields, choose All from the next menu. To clear the validity settings from a single field, choose Field, move the cursor to the desired field, and press (ENTER) to select the field.

ClearPasswords

Sequence:
Tools/More/Protect/ClearPasswords

Use the ClearPasswords option to clear all passwords used during a session. Choose Tools/More/Protect/ClearPasswords. The passwords you entered to access protected objects will be cleared from memory, and any further use of those objects will again require the entry of the passwords.

CoEdit

Sequence:
Modify/CoEdit

Use the CoEdit option to edit a table while other users may also be editing that table on a network. Choose Modify/CoEdit, and enter the name of the table to be coedited. When done editing, choose DO-IT!. Note that you cannot cancel a CoEdit session. The records must be deleted while in CoEdit mode, or emptied when in main mode. (Selecting Modify/CoEdit is functionally equivalent to pressing (ALT)-(F9), the CoEdit key combination.)

Color

Sequence (From the Form Design Menu):
Style/Color

Use this option to choose foreground or background colors for an area or border in a form. From the Form Design menu, choose Style/Color. From the next menu to appear, choose Area (to color an area of the form), or choose Border (to color a border). Place the cursor in one corner of the area or border and press (ENTER); then move the cursor to the diagonal corner of the area or border and press (ENTER) again. Finally, use the arrow keys followed by (ENTER) to select the desired colors from the color palette that appears.

ColumnSize

Sequence:
Image/ColumnSize

A

Use the ColumnSize option to change the width of a column in a table. To change the column size, choose Image/ColumnSize and then move the cursor to the column that is to be resized. Press (ENTER), and use (←) and (→) to adjust the column size. Then press (ENTER) to set the new column width.

Copy

Sequence:
Tools/Copy

Use this Copy option to copy Paradox objects, including tables, along with associated forms and reports or scripts. From the menu, choose Tools/Copy, and Paradox offers an additional menu with options of Table, Form, Report, Script, Graph, and JustFamily. Choose Form, Report, Script, or Graph to copy any of these specific objects; choose Just-Family to copy all associated objects except the table; and choose Table to copy the table and its family. Finally, enter the names of the source table and target table if prompted.

Note that if you choose Tools/Copy/JustFamily, the target table that will receive the copied objects must exist and have the same structure.

Copy (for Reports)

Sequence (From the Report Design Menu):
TableBand/Copy

Use this Copy option to copy columns from one location in a tabular report to another. From the Report Design menu, choose TableBand/Copy. Place the cursor in the desired column of the table band, and press (ENTER) to select the column. Then place the cursor in the desired location for the copy, and press (ENTER) again.

Count

Sequence (From the Report Design Menu):
Field/Place/Summary/Calculated/<*expression*>/Count

Use the Count option to count the number of values in a field on a custom free-form or tabular report. From the Report Design menu, choose Field/Place/Summary/Calculated/Count if the field to be counted is a summary field. Then select PerGroup (for a count of the number of values in a field for each group) or Overall (for an overall count). Use the cursor to place the field in the desired location and press (ENTER). Next, adjust the number of digits displayed (use (←) and (→)), and then press (ENTER). Finally, adjust the number of decimal points displayed (use (←) and (→)), and press (ENTER) to complete the placement of the field.

Create

Sequence:
Create

Use the Create option to create a new Paradox table. Choose Create from the menu, and enter a name for the new table. Paradox displays a table structure image, with entries for field names and corresponding field types. Fill in the desired fields and field types. Add an asterisk beside the field type to indicate a key field. (Key fields must be the first fields in a table.) After defining the fields, choose DO-IT! to store the completed table definition.

CrossTab

Sequence:
Image/Graph/CrossTab

Use the CrossTab option to build a crosstab table based on the current table. A crosstab is a cross-tabulation, or spreadsheet-like numeric analysis of data within a table. With the desired table to be cross-tabulated on the screen, choose Image/Graph/CrossTab. From the next menu, choose Sum, Min, Max, or Count. Move to the columns with the crosstab row labels, and press (ENTER). Finally, move to the column containing the crosstab values, and press (ENTER). A new table named CROSSTAB will appear, containing the summary values in crosstab form.

A

DataEntry

Sequence:
Modify/DataEntry

Use the DataEntry option to add records to a table without displaying existing records on the screen. Choose Modify/DataEntry, and enter the table name.

A new temporary table called ENTRY will appear, and you can proceed to add the necessary records. When done with the data entry, choose DO-IT! to store the records in the original table.

Date

Sequence (From the Report Design Menu):
Field/Place/Date

Use the Date option to place a field containing the current date in a custom free-form or tabular report. From the Report Design menu, choose Field/Place/Date. Select one of 12 possible date formats that appear as a menu. Move the cursor to the location on the report at which the date is to appear, and press (ENTER) to place the date field.

Default

Sequence (From the Edit Menu):
ValCheck/Define/Default

Use the Default option to set the default value for a field in the table. While in DataEntry or Edit mode, choose ValCheck/Define from the menu. Place the cursor in the field for which you want to set the default value, and press (ENTER). From the next menu, choose Default, and enter the value that Paradox is to insert if the field is left blank.

Delete (For Paradox Objects)

Sequence:
Tools/Delete

Use the Delete option to delete Paradox objects, including tables, forms, reports, scripts, index files, image settings, or validity checks. From the menu, choose Tools/Delete, and Paradox offers an additional menu with options of Table, Form, Report, Script, Index, KeepSet, ValCheck, and Graph. Select the object that is to be deleted. If you select Table, the table and all its associated objects will be deleted.

Delete (For Bands in a Custom Report)

Sequence (From the Report Design Menu):
Group/Delete
Setting/PageLayout/Delete

When designing reports, you can use the Delete option to delete group bands or to delete the last page-width setting. To delete a group, from the Report Design menu choose Group/Delete. Place the cursor at the group to be deleted, and press (ENTER).

To delete the last page width, choose Setting/PageLayout/Delete from the Report Design menu. Then choose OK from the next menu to confirm the operation.

Delete (For Pages in a Form)

Sequence:
Page/Delete

Use this Delete option to delete any page of a form. While designing or changing the form, place the cursor at the desired page. Choose Page/Delete from the menu, then choose OK to delete the unwanted page.

Design

Sequence:
Forms/Design
Report/Design

Use the Design option to design new forms or custom reports. To design a form, choose Forms/Design and enter a name for the table. Select an identifier for the form, and enter a description; then design the form as desired. When done with the design, choose DO-IT!.

To design a report, choose Report/Design and enter a name for the table. Select a designator for the report, and then enter a description. Choose Tabular or Free-Form for the desired type of report, and then design the report as desired. When done with the Report Specification, choose DO-IT!.

A

Directory

Sequence:
Tools/More/Directory

Use the Directory option to change the default directory being used by Paradox. Choose Tools/More/Directory, and enter the directory name that you desire. The name may be preceded by a disk drive identifier such as B:\FILES. Note that when you change directories, the workspace is cleared and any temporary tables are discarded.

DisplayOnly

Sequence (From the Form Design Menu):
Field/Place/DisplayOnly

Use the DisplayOnly option to place a display-only field at the desired location on a form. From the Form Design menu, choose Field/Place/DisplayOnly. Select the desired field from the list of fields that appears, and then place the cursor at the desired location for the display-only field. Press (ENTER) to anchor the starting location for the field. Adjust the field's width with (←) and (→), and then press (ENTER) again to complete the placement of the field.

DO-IT!

Sequence:
DO-IT!

Use the DO-IT! option to complete the current Paradox operation. Selecting DO-IT! from a menu or clicking it with the mouse is functionally equivalent to pressing (F2), the DO-IT! key.

Double-Line

Sequence (From the Form Design Menu):
Border/Place/Double-Line

Use the Double-Line option to add a double-line border in a form. To add the border, choose Border/Place/Double-Line from the Form Design menu.

Place the cursor at one corner of the border and press (ENTER); move the cursor to the diagonal corner and press (ENTER) again to draw the border.

Edit (For Modifying a Table)

Sequence:
Modify/Edit

Use this Edit option to edit an existing table. Choose Modify/Edit, and enter the name of the table you wish to edit. The cursor will appear in the first record of that table, and you can use the editing keys in Paradox to help you edit the desired records. To edit in a form layout, press the Form Toggle ((F7)) key. When done editing records, choose DO-IT!.

Editor

Sequence:
Scripts/Editor

See Scripts/Editor/New or Scripts/Editor/Open.

Empty

Sequence:
Tools/More/Empty

Use the Empty option to empty an entire table of all records. Choose Tools/More/Empty, and enter the name for the desired table. As a safeguard, Paradox will require confirmation by displaying a menu with Cancel and OK options. You must select OK to empty the table.

End-Record

Sequence:
Scripts/End-Record

Use this option to end the recording of a script. When you are done recording a script, choose Scripts/End-Record from the main menu. Use Scripts/Play or Scripts/ShowPlay to play back a recorded script.

A

Entry

Sequence:
Modify/MultiEntry/Entry

Use the Entry option to enter records into a single source table for storage in several target tables. Choose Modify/MultiEntry/Entry. Enter the name of the source table and then supply the name of the map table. You can then enter data into the source table. When you complete the data entry with DO-IT!, the data will be added to the appropriate fields in the target tables, as defined by the map table.

Erase (For Forms)

Sequence (From the Form Design Menu):
Field/Erase
Area/Erase

Use this Erase option to erase portions of a form. To erase a field, choose Field/Erase from the Form Design menu. Place the cursor anywhere in the desired field, and press (ENTER) to erase the field.

To erase an area, choose Area/Erase from the Form Design menu. Place the cursor at one corner of the area to be erased and press (ENTER); then move the cursor to the diagonal corner and press (ENTER) again to erase the area.

Erase (For Reports)

Sequence (From the Report Design Menu):
Field/Erase
TableBand/Erase

Use this Erase option to erase fields or columns from a tabular report. To erase a field within the report, choose Field/Erase from the Report Design menu. Place the cursor on the desired field, and press (ENTER) to erase the field. To erase a table band, choose TableBand/Erase from the Report Design menu. Place the cursor on the desired column, and press (ENTER) to erase the table band.

Exit

Sequence:
Exit

Use the Exit option to exit Paradox and return to the operating system. When you exit from Paradox, any data in temporary tables (such as ANSWER, ENTRY, and KEYVIOL) is discarded. When you select Exit, Paradox will confirm that you want to leave the program. Select Yes to proceed or No to cancel the command.

Export

Sequence:
Tools/ExportImport/Export

Use the Export option to export files from a Paradox table to other software. To export a file from Paradox, choose Tools/ExportImport/Export from the menu. Next, select the target software from the list of choices that appears. (Paradox lets you export files to Quattro/Quattro Pro, Lotus 1-2-3, Symphony, dBASE, PFS, Reflex, VisiCalc [DIF], and ASCII.) If another menu is displayed at this point, select the appropriate version of the target software; if you are exporting to ASCII, select Delimited or Text as the format of the file to be created. Enter the name of the Paradox table that is to be exported, and then enter a filename for the target file that will receive your Paradox data. Paradox will convert the table into a new file compatible with your other software.

Family

Sequence:
Tools/Info/Family

Use the Family option to list all forms and reports associated with a table. Choose Tools/Info/Family and enter a name for the desired table. Paradox will display a table named FAMILY, which contains the name and creation date of all reports and forms, along with the table name.

A

Fast

Sequence:
Scripts/ShowPlay/Fast

Use the Fast option to play back each step in a recorded script so that you can watch it at fast speed. Choose Scripts/ShowPlay, and enter the name of the desired script. Then select Fast to play the script rapidly.
See also Slow.

Field (To Clear Validity Checks)

Sequence (From the Edit Menu):
ValCheck/Clear/Field

Use this Field option to clear validity check settings from a single field. While in DataEntry or Edit mode, select ValCheck/Clear/Field from the Edit menu. Move the cursor to the desired field, and press (ENTER) to select the field.

Field (To Change Field Attributes in Forms or Reports)

Sequence (From the Form Design or Report Design Menu):
Field

Use this Field option to place, erase, reformat, justify, recalculate, or wordwrap fields while designing forms or reports. From the Form Design or Report Design menu, choose Field. From the next menu that appears, select the appropriate option from the menu, and then place the cursor on the field and press (ENTER) to carry out the desired operation. For more specifics on an option, see the option by name in this appendix.

Field (To Group Records in a Report Field)

Sequence (From the Report Design Menu):
Group/Insert/Field

Use this Field option to group together records that have the same field value within a report. From the Report Design menu, choose Group/Insert/Field.

From the list of fields that next appears, choose a field to group on. Place the cursor at the desired location for the group, and press (ENTER).

Field (In DataEntry or Edit Mode)

Sequence (From the Edit Menu):
Image/Zoom/Field

Use this Field option to locate the cursor at a specific field while adding or editing records. From the Edit menu, choose Image/Zoom/Field. Select the desired field from the list that appears. The cursor will move to that field.

Fieldnames

Sequence (From the Form Design Menu):
Style/Fieldnames

Use the Fieldnames option to display or hide the names of fields while you are placing the fields during the form design process. From the Form Design menu, choose Style/FieldNames. From the next menu that appears, choose Show to show the names of fields during form design or Hide to hide them.

FieldSqueeze

Sequence (From the Report Design Menu):
Setting/RemoveBlanks/FieldSqueeze

Use the FieldSqueeze option in a free-form custom report to suppress printing of leading and trailing blank spaces contained in a field. From the Report Design menu, choose Setting/RemoveBlanks /FieldSqueeze. From the next menu, choose Yes to confirm the suppression of blank spaces.

File (To Redirect a Finished Report to a Disk File)

Sequence:
Report/Output/File

Use this File option to redirect the output of a report to a disk file. Choose Report/Output and enter the name of the desired table. Next, choose from

A

among the available reports. Then choose File to direct the output to a disk file, and enter a filename. If you omit an extension, Paradox will supply a default extension of .RPT to the filename.

File (To Redirect a Report in Progress to a Disk File)

Sequence:
Report/Output/File

Use this File option to redirect the output of a report to a disk file while you are in the process of creating or modifying the report. From the Report Design menu, choose Output and then choose File to direct the output to a disk file. Paradox will prompt you for a filename. If you omit an extension, Paradox will supply a default extension of .RPT to the filename.

File (To Redirect a Select Range of a Report to a Disk File)

Sequence:
Report/RangeOutput/File

Use this File option to redirect a portion of a report to a disk file. Choose Report/RangeOutput, and enter the name of the desired table. Next, choose from among the available reports, choose File to direct the output to a disk file, and enter a filename. If you omit a file extension, Paradox will supply a default extension of .RPT. Finally, indicate the desired starting and ending page numbers of the report, which are to be included in the resulting file.

Files

Sequence:
Tools/Info/Inventory/Files

Use the Files option to display the names of all files located in a directory or on a disk. Choose Tools/Info/Inventory/Files. As an option, you can enter a pattern that can include drive identifiers or DOS wildcards. Press (ENTER) to see a table displaying the names of the files.

Fixed

Sequence (From the Main or Edit Menu):
Image/Format/Fixed

Use the Fixed option to specify a fixed format for a number field. Choose Image/Format, and place the cursor in the field you wish to reformat. Choose Fixed, and then enter the desired number of decimal places for the field.

Form (To Copy an Existing Form)

Sequence:
Tools/Copy/Form

Use this Form option to copy a form. From the menu, choose the option called Tools/Copy/Form. Choose SameTable to copy the form to the same table, or choose DifferentTable to copy the form to a different table. Then enter the names for the associated table. From the list of form designators that appears, select a form to copy; then, from the next list that appears, select another form designator to which you can copy the form.

Form (To Delete an Existing Form)

Sequence:
Tools/Delete/Form

Use this Form option to delete a form. From the menu, choose Tools/Delete/Form. Enter the name of the table associated with the desired form, and then, from the list of form designators that appears, choose the form that is to be deleted.

Form (To Rename an Existing Form)

Sequence:
Tools/Rename/Form

Use this Form option to rename a form. From the menu, choose Tools/Rename/Form. Enter the name of the table associated with the desired form. From the list of form designators that appears, select the form to be renamed;

A

then, from the next list that appears, select another form designator, which will serve as the new form name.

FormAdd

Sequence:
Tools/More/FormAdd

Use the FormAdd option to simultaneously add records to multiple tables using a form. Choose Tools/More/FormAdd, and enter the name of the target table. Choose the desired form from the list that appears next; then choose EntryTables (to add from one or more entry tables to the target table), or choose AnyTables (to add data from any tables to the target table).

Format (To Change the Display Format of a Field)

Sequence (From the Main or Edit Menu):
Image/Format

Use this Format option to specify a format for a number, currency, or date field. From the main menu, choose Image/Format, and place the cursor in the field you wish to reformat. Choose the desired format from the list of available formats. Depending on the type of field and the format chosen, Paradox may ask you for additional information, such as the number of decimal places to use.

Format (To Change the Overall Format of a Tabular Report)

Sequence (From the Report Design Menu):
Setting/Format

Use this Format option to specify whether tabular reports should be arranged in tables of groups or in groups of tables. From the Report Design menu, choose Setting/Format. Select GroupsOfTables or TablesOfGroups as desired. When arranged as tables of groups, the table header appears once at the top of each page, and group headers always appear under the table headers. By contrast, when arranged in groups of tables, the table header is repeated after every group header.

Forms

Sequence:
Forms

Use the Forms option of the main menu to design or change custom forms. Choose Forms, and then select Design to design a new form or Change to edit an existing form. Enter the name of the table with which the form will be used, select a designator to identify the form and then enter a description for the form. Design or change the form as desired, and then choose DO-IT! to store the design. To use the form, select Image/PickForm from the main menu and identify the form by name. Note that a table must contain records before the form can be used.

Free-Form

Sequence:
Report/Design/Free-Form

Use the Free-Form option to design a free-form custom report. Choose Report/Design, and enter the name of the table. Select a designator for the report, and then enter a description. Choose Free-Form for the type of report, and the Report Design menu will appear. Design the report as desired, and then choose DO-IT! to store it.

General

Sequence (From the Main or Edit Menu):
Image/Format/General

Use the General option to specify a general format for a selected number field. The general format shows only as many decimal places as necessary (trailing zeros are omitted), but aligns all decimals so that the column of numbers remains easy to read. From the menu, choose Image /Format, and place the cursor in the number field you wish to reformat. Choose General, and then enter the desired number of decimal places for the field.

A

Go

Sequence:
Scripts/Editor/New/Go
Scripts/Editor/Open/Go

Use the Go option to tell Paradox to exit from the Script Editor and play the script. While in the Script Editor, choose Go from the menu. Any changes made from the Script Editor will be saved, and the script will be played.

Graph

Sequence:
Image/Graph

Use the Graph option to view graphs or to send graphs to the printer or to a file. Also use this option to change, load, or save graph settings, or to create crosstabs. Choose Image/Graph. The next menu that appears provides the following options: Modify, to modify the current graph specification; Load, to load a stored graph specification; Save, to save the current graph specification; Reset, to reset the graph specifications to the default settings; Cross-Tab, to create a crosstab of the current image; and ViewGraph, to view a graph of the current image.

Select the desired option. For more specifics on an option, see the option by name in this appendix.

Group

Sequence (From the Report Design Menu):
Group

Use the Group option to insert a group, delete a group, or change the formats for a group within a custom report. From the Report Design menu, choose Group. The next menu that appears provides the following options: Insert, to insert a new group into a report; Delete, to delete an existing report group; Headings, to specify when group headings should be repeated; SortDirection, to change the sort direction for a group; and Regroup, to change the desired type of grouping used in the report.

Select the desired option. For more specifics on an option, see the option by name in this appendix.

GroupRepeats

Sequence (From the Report Design Menu):
Setting/GroupRepeats

Use the GroupRepeats option to allow or to suppress the printing of all occurrences of repeated field values within a group. From the Report Design menu, choose Setting/GroupRepeats. The next menu that appears will provide the choices of Retain and Suppress. Choose Retain to allow repeated field values to print within groups on the report, or choose Suppress to prevent such printings in the report.

GroupsOfTables

Sequence (From the Report Design Menu):
Setting/Format/GroupsOfTables

Use the GroupsOfTables option to arrange reports in groups of tables. When arranged in groups of tables, the table header gets repeated after every group header. To specify this formatting, from the Report Design menu, choose Setting/Format/GroupsOfTables.

Headings

Sequence (From the Report Design Menu):
Group/Headings

Use the Headings option to specify when group headings should be repeated within a custom report. From the Report Design menu, choose Group/ Headings. Move the cursor to the headings within the report that are to be changed, and press (ENTER) to select the group. The next menu that appears will offer two choices: Page and Group. Choose Page to print the group headings once per group and at the top of all spillover pages; choose Group to print the group headings only once per group.

A

Hide

Sequence (From the Form Design Menu):
Style/FieldNames/Hide

Use the Hide option to conceal the names of fields while you are placing them during the form-design process. From the Form Design menu, choose Style/Fieldnames/Hide to hide the names of the fields during form design.
See also Show.

HighValue

Sequence (From the Edit Menu):
ValCheck/Define/HighValue

Use the HighValue option to supply a maximum acceptable value when setting validity checks for a field. From the Edit menu, choose ValCheck/ Define, and place the cursor in the field to which the validity check must apply. Choose HighValue and enter the highest acceptable value for the field.

Image

Sequence:
Image

Use the Image option to change the way Paradox displays the information on the screen. Choose Image. The next menu that appears provides the following options: TableSize, to change the size of the table (by limiting the number of records visible at one time); ColumnSize, to change the width of a column; Format, to change the display format for a column; Zoom to go to a field, record, or value; Move, to move a column to a new position; PickForm, to select a form for the current image; KeepSet, to make the current image settings permanent; OrderTable, to change the index order of a table; and Graph, to display or print graphs.

   Select the desired option. For more specifics on an option, see the option by name in this appendix.

Import

Sequence:
Tools/ExportImport/Import

Use the Import option to import files from other software into a Paradox table. To import a file into Paradox, choose Tools/ExportImport/Import from the menu. Next, select the external software from the list of choices that appears. (Paradox lets you import files from Quattro/Quattro Pro, Lotus 1-2-3, Symphony, dBASE, PFS, Reflex, VisiCalc [DIF], and ASCII.) If another menu is displayed at this point, select the appropriate version of the software you have chosen; if you are importing from ASCII, select Delimited, AppendDelimited, or Text as the file format. Enter the name of the file to be imported, and then enter a filename for the new Paradox table that will receive the external data. Paradox will convert the file from your other software into a Paradox table and display the table in the workspace.

Index

Sequence:
Modify/Index

Use the Index option to add a secondary index to a table. Choose Modify/Index, and enter the desired table name. Choose the desired fields to index from the form that appears, then choose DO-IT! to build the index.

Info

Sequence:
Tools/Info

Use the Info option to display information about Paradox objects, DOS files, and network users. Choose Tools/Info. The next menu that appears provides the following options: Structure, to list the structure of a table; Inventory, to list tables, scripts, or DOS files; Family, to list forms and reports associated with a table; Who, to list users who are running Paradox on a network; and Lock, to list locks for a table.

A

Select the desired option. For more specifics on an option, see the option by name in this appendix.

Insert (To Insert Pages in a Form)

Sequence:
Page/Insert

Use this Insert option to insert a new page in a form. While designing or changing the form, with the cursor at the desired location, choose Page/Insert from the Form Design menu to insert a new page.

Insert (To Insert Pages or Bands in Reports)

Sequence (From the Report Design Menu):
Group/Insert
Setting/PageLayout/Insert
TableBand/Insert

Use the Insert option to insert group bands, a new page in a report, or new table bands in a tabular report. To insert a group, from the Report Design menu choose Group/Insert. Choose the type of group desired (by group of field values, range of field values, or specified number of records) from the next menu that appears. If you choose to group by either of the first two options, you must also supply a field name to group on. If you choose the third option, you must specify the number of records to include in each group. Finally, place the cursor at the desired location for the group and press (ENTER).

To insert a new page at the end of the report, the Report Design menu choose Setting/PageLayout/Insert. To insert a table band into a report, the Report Design menu choose TableBand/Insert. Place the cursor at the location where the new table band is to appear and press (ENTER).

InsertFile

Sequence:
Scripts/Editor/New/InsertFile
Scripts/Editor/Open/InsertFile

Use the InsertFile option to insert an existing script into a script that you are creating or editing with the Script Editor. While in the Script Editor, place the cursor where the new script is to appear, and choose File/InsertFile from the menu. Enter the name of the script you wish to insert into the Editor.

Inventory

Sequence:
Tools/Info/Inventory

Use the Inventory option to obtain information about tables, scripts, or DOS files. Choose Tools/Info/Inventory. From the next menu that appears, select Tables to list all tables, Scripts to list all scripts, or Files to list all DOS files.

JustFamily

Sequence:
Tools/Copy/JustFamily

Use the JustFamily option to copy a family of Paradox objects associated with a table to another table. From the menu, choose Tools/Copy/JustFamily. Enter the names for a source table and a target table when prompted. Note that the target table, which will receive the copied objects, must exist. Also, any objects in the target table that have the same names as objects in the source table will be overwritten.

KeepEntry

Sequence:
Modify/DataEntry/KeepEntry

Use the KeepEntry option when in DataEntry mode to keep the ENTRY table after completing the data entry. If you use KeepEntry, the added records are kept in the ENTRY table, rather than being added to the primary table. (Rename the ENTRY table or add the records to another table before exiting Paradox to avoid loss of data.) Choose Modify/DataEntry to enter DataEntry mode, and begin adding records. Once the records have been added, to keep the ENTRY table, choose KeepEntry from the Edit menu.

A

KeepSet

Sequence:
Image/KeepSet

Use the KeepSet option to make the current settings for the table image permanent. From the main menu or the Edit menu, choose Image/KeepSet. If you make the image settings permanent and later want to delete those settings, you can do so by choosing Tools/Delete/KeepSet and supplying the name of the appropriate table.

Labels

Sequence (From the Report Design Menu):
Setting/Labels

Use the Labels option to specify mailing-label format while you are designing a free-form report. From the Report Design menu, choose Setting/Labels. Then confirm with Yes at the next menu that appears.

Length

Sequence (From the Report Design Menu):
Setting/PageLayout/Length

Use the Length option to control the page length in a custom report. From the Report Design menu, choose Setting/PageLayout/Length. Enter a length, in number of lines per page, for the page length, or enter C for continuous length (useful with mailing labels or other continuous forms). Note that while the standard for 8.5-inch by 11-inch paper is 66 lines, some laser printers may eject the paper prematurely unless you set the page length of a report at no more than 62 lines.

LineSqueeze

Sequence (From the Report Design Menu):
Setting/RemoveBlanks/LineSqueeze

Use the LineSqueeze option in a free-form custom report to suppress the printing of blank lines when a field contains no data. From the Report Design menu, choose Setting/RemoveBlanks/LineSqueeze. From the next menu, choose Yes to confirm the suppression of blank lines. Then choose Fixed to place blank lines at the bottom of the record or Variable to delete blank lines, thereby varying the number of lines occupied by each record.

Load

Sequence:
Image/Graph/Load

Use the Load option to load graph settings from an existing graph file. Choose Image/Graph/Load. Paradox will prompt you for the name of the graph; enter the name, or press (ENTER) for a list of available graph names and select the desired name from the list.

Lock (To List Network Locks)

Sequence:
Tools/Info/Lock

Use this Lock option to list all locks for a table when you are operating on a network. Choose Tools/Info/Lock, and enter the desired table.

Lock (To Place or Remove Network Locks)

Sequence:
Tools/Net/Lock

Use this Lock option to place an explicit lock on a table, or unlock a table, while operating on a network. Choose Tools/Net/Lock. The next menu will provide choices for the type of lock (FullLock, WriteLock, and Dir Lock). Select the type of lock desired, and enter the name of the table to lock. Finally, choose Set to place the lock, or choose Clear to release an existing lock.

A

Lookup

Sequence (From the Report Design Menu):
Field/Lookup

Use the Lookup option to establish, change, or remove a relational link between a report and a table. From the Report Design menu, choose Field/Lookup. From the next menu to appear, choose Link (to add a relational link), Unlink (to remove an existing link), or Relink (to change an existing link). Then select the desired table and the name of the field when prompted.

LowValue

Sequence (From the Edit Menu):
ValCheck/Define/LowValue

Use the LowValue option to supply a minimum acceptable value when setting validity checks for a field. From the Edit menu, choose ValCheck/Define and place the cursor in the field to which the validity check must apply. Choose LowValue, and enter the lowest acceptable value for the field.

Margin

Sequence (From the Report Design Menu):
Setting/Margin

Use the Margin option to set the left margin in a custom report. From the Report Design menu, choose Setting/Margin. Enter the desired value for the left margin.

Modify (To Modify Graphs)

Sequence:
Image/Graph/Modify

Use this Modify option to modify the settings used for the current graph. Choose Image/Graph/Modify. Then change the graph settings by typing the desired settings in the Graph Type form that appears, or press (F10) to activate the Customize Graph Type menu and change the various graph settings.

Modify (To Modify Tables)

Sequence:
Modify

Use this Modify option to perform common operations that result in the modification of tables, such as sorting, adding, and editing records and restructuring a table. Choose Modify. The next menu that appears provides the following options: Sort, to sort or arrange records in a specific order; Edit, to insert, delete, or change records; CoEdit, to edit a table with other users concurrently; DataEntry, to add new records to a table; MultiEntry, to add records to a table that posts to two or more tables simultaneously; Restructure, to change the structure of an existing table; and Index, to add an index to a table.

Select the desired option. For more specifics on an option, see the option by name in this appendix.

Monochrome

Sequence (From the Form Design Menu):
Style/Monochrome

Use the Monochrome option to choose intensity, reverse video, blinking, or normal screen attributes for an area or border of a form. From the Form Design menu, choose Style/Monochrome. From the next menu to appear, choose Area (to change the attributes for an area) or choose Border (to change the attributes for a border). Place the cursor at one corner of the area or border and press (ENTER); then move the cursor to the diagonal corner of the area or border and press (ENTER). Finally, use (←) or (→) to switch between available styles. Press (ENTER) when the desired style appears.

More

Sequence:
Tools/More

Use the More option to display the second line of menu choices applicable to the Tools menu. Choose Tools/More. The menu that appears provides the following options: Add, to add records contained in one table to the records

in another table; MultiAdd, to add records to two or more tables simultaneously; FormAdd, to use a form to add records to one or more tables;
Subtract, to subtract the records of one table from those of another; Empty,
to remove all records from a table; Protect, to password-protect or write-
protect a table or script, or to clear passwords; Directory, to change the
working directory (also clears temporary tables and the workspace); and
ToDOS, to suspend Paradox and access DOS through a DOS "shell."

Select the desired option. For more specifics on an option, see the option
by name in this appendix.

Move (To Move Areas Within Custom Forms)

Sequence (From the Form Design Menu):
Area/Move

Use this Move option to move one area of a form to a different part of the
form. From the Form Design menu, choose Area/Move. Place the cursor at
one corner of the area to be moved, and press (ENTER); move the cursor to the
diagonal corner of the area and press (ENTER) again. Finally, use the cursor
keys to drag the area to its new location, and press (ENTER).

Move (To Move a Column)

Sequence (From the Main or Edit Menu):
Image/Move

Use this Move option to move a column to another location. From the main
or Edit menu, choose Image/Move. Paradox will display a list of columns by
name; choose the column to be moved from the list, and press (ENTER). Place
the cursor at the new location, and press (ENTER) again to move the column.

Move (To Move Table Bands Within a Tabular Report)

Sequence (From the Report Design Menu):
TableBand/Move

Use this Move option to move a column from one portion of a tabular report
to another. From the Report Design menu, choose TableBand/Move. Place
the cursor within the table band, in the column to be selected, and press

(ENTER) to choose the column. Then move the cursor to the new location for the column, and press (ENTER) again to move the table band.

Multi

Sequence (From the Form Design Menu):
Multi

Use the Multi option to design multitable forms or multirecord forms. While designing the form, choose Multi from the Form Design menu. From the next menu to appear, choose Tables (to place, remove, or move a form from another table) or choose Records (to place, remove, or adjust a multirecord region on the form).

MultiAdd

Sequence:
Tools/More/MultiAdd

Use the MultiAdd option to add records from a single source table to several target tables. Choose Tools/More/MultiAdd. Enter the name of the source table, and then supply the name of the map table (previously created with Modify/MultiEntry/Setup). The data in the source table will then be added to the appropriate fields in the target tables, as defined by the map table.

MultiEntry

Sequence:
Modify/MultiEntry

Use the MultiEntry option to enter records into a single source table for storage in several target tables. Both the source and map tables must be created before you use this command. Choose Modify/MultiEntry/Entry. Enter the name of the source table, and then supply the name of the map table. You can then enter data into the source table. When you complete the data entry with DO-IT! ((F2)), the data will be added to the appropriate fields in the target tables, as defined by the map table.

A

Net

Sequence:
Tools/Net

Use the Net option to lock or unlock tables, to prevent others from locking a table, to change your private directory or user name, or to change the AutoRefresh interval. Choose Tools/Net. The menu that appears provides the following options: Lock, to lock or unlock a table; PreventLock, to prevent others from locking tables; SetPrivate, to change your private directory; UserName, to change your user name; AutoRefresh, to change the delay time for automatic screen refreshing; and Changes, to restart or continue a query or report if the data changes.

Select the desired option. For more specifics on an option, see the option by name in this appendix.

New

Sequence:
Scripts/Editor/New

Use the New option to write a new script with the Script Editor. Choose Scripts/Editor/New, and enter a name for the script. If the name that you supply is already in use by a script, Paradox will warn you of this by requesting confirmation before overwriting the old script. When you have finished editing the script, choose DO-IT! to save the script and exit the Script Editor.

NewEntries

Sequence:
Tools/More/Add/NewEntries

Use the NewEntries option to add records in a source table to a keyed target table without disturbing any existing records in the target table. Choose Tools/More/Add. Enter the name of the source table and the target table. If the target table maintains a key field, the next menu provides the choice of NewEntries for adding records to the target table and Update for updating the target table records based on the source table records. Choose NewEntries to add the records to the target table without changing its existing records.

No

Sequence:
No

Use the No option to tell Paradox not to perform a specific type of operation.

#Record

Sequence (From the Form Design Menu):
Field/Place/#Record

Use the #Record option to place a record number field while designing a form. From the Form Design menu, choose Field/Place/#Record. Place the cursor at the desired form location for the record number and press (ENTER); then use (←) and (→) to adjust the width of the field, and press (ENTER).

NumberRecords

Sequence (From the Report Design Menu):
Group/Insert/NumberRecords

Use the NumberRecords option to specify how many records will be contained in a report grouping. From the Report Design menu, choose Group/Insert/NumberRecords. Next, specify the number of records to be contained in each group. Finally, place the cursor at the desired location for the new group to be inserted, and press (ENTER).

OK

Sequence:
OK

Use the OK option to tell Paradox to proceed with a specific type of operation.

A

Open

Sequence:
Scripts/Editor/Open

Use the Open option to edit an existing script. Choose Scripts/Editor/Open, and enter the name of the script you wish to modify. The script Editor will appear, and you can make the desired changes to the existing script. When done editing the script, choose DO-IT!.

OrderTable

Sequence:
Image/OrderTable

Use the OrderTable option to reorder (index) a table, based on a field of the table. Choose Image/OrderTable, then place the cursor in the desired field and press (ENTER). Choose OK from the dialog box that appears, and the table will be reordered based on the contents of the field.

Other

Sequence (From the Form Design Menu):
Border/Place/Other

Use the Other option to add borders to a form. From the Form Design menu, choose the Border /Place/Other option. Next, specify a character to be used as the border character. (You can specify graphics characters by holding down the (ALT) key and typing three-digit numbers on the numeric keypad that represent the ASCII code for the graphics character.) Place the cursor at one corner of the border and press (ENTER); move the cursor to the diagonal corner of the border and press (ENTER) again to draw the border.

Output (To Generate a Report)

Sequence:
Report/Output

Use this Output option to generate a report. Choose Report/Output, and then enter a name for the appropriate table. Next, select a report from the list of report designators that appears. Choose Printer, File, or Screen from the next menu for the report's output.

Output (To Generate a Report Being Designed or Changed)

Sequence (from the Report Design Menu):
Output

Use this Output option to generate a report while you are in the process of designing or changing the report. This is useful for proofing the report's design before you leave the design process. From the Report Design menu, choose Output. Then select Printer, Screen, or File as desired. The report will be produced and sent to the device you have selected.

Overall

Sequence (From the Customize Graph Type menu):
Overall

Use the Overall option of the Customize Graph Type menu to customize various settings that affect graphs. From the Customize Graph Type menu, select Overall. From the next menu, select one of the settings that can be changed: Titles, Colors, Axes, Grids, PrinterLayout (to define a page layout for printers or plotters), Device (to define the desired printer or plotter), and Wait (to specify a length of time that each graph will be displayed).

Page (For a Custom Report)

Sequence (From the Report Design Menu):
Field/Place/Page

Use this Page option to place a page number field on a custom report. From the Report Design menu, choose Field/Place/Page. Move the cursor to the location you want for the page number, and press (ENTER) to place the field. Note that the page number fields should be placed within the page bands. Placing page number fields elsewhere may produce bizarre results.

A

Page (For a Multipage Form)

Sequence (From the Form Design Menu):
Page

Use this Page option to add or remove a page from a multiple-page form. From the Form Design menu, choose Page. From the next menu to appear, choose Insert to add a page, or choose Delete to remove the current page of the form. If you choose Delete, you must confirm the deletion by choosing OK from the next menu. If you choose Insert, you will see another menu with Before and After options. Choose Before to place a new page before the current page of the form. Choose After to place the new page after the current page of the form.

PageLayout

Sequence (From the Report Design Menu):
Setting/PageLayout

Use the PageLayout option to set the page length and page width within a custom report. From the Report Design menu, choose Setting/PageLayout. From the next menu, choose Length, Width, Insert (to add a new page width at the end of the report), or Delete (to remove the last page width). If you choose Length or Width, Paradox will prompt you for a length value in number of lines per page, or a width value in characters. If you select Insert, Paradox will place a blank page width at the right side of the report specification. If you select Delete, Paradox will delete the last page width, along with any fields and literals contained within it.

Password

Sequence:
Tools/More/Protect/Password

Use the Password option to assign or remove a password. Choose Tools/More/Protect/Password, and then choose Table or Script. Next, enter the name of the table or script to be protected, followed by the desired password. If you are password-protecting a table, you will see an auxiliary

password form after you supply the initial password. The assignment of
auxiliary passwords is optional; it is generally not needed unless you are using
Paradox in a multiuser environment. Choose DO-IT! to store the changes and
assign the password.

PickForm

Sequence:
Image/PickForm

Use the PickForm option to select a form for viewing or editing records from
the current table. Choose Image/PickForm, and then select a form designator
from the list of forms that appears. Each time you switch to a form view with
Form Toggle ((F7)), the form you selected will appear. After you clear the
workspace or exit Paradox, the selected form is no longer in effect until you
choose it again. To make the form selection permanent, save the Image
settings with Image/KeepSet.

Picture

Sequence (From the Edit Menu):
ValCheck/Define/Picture

Use the Picture option to define a "picture" format, a format that data
entry must follow for a specific field. From the Edit menu, choose
ValCheck/Define and place the cursor in the desired field. Then choose
Picture, and enter the desired format, using a valid PAL picture format. Valid
format characters include the following:

#	Accept any numeric digit
?	Accept any letter
&	Accept any letter, convert to uppercase
!	Accept any character; if letter, convert to uppercase
;	Take literally
*	Repetition counts
[]	Optional items
{}	Grouping operator
,	Alternative values

A

Pies

Sequence (From the Customize Graph Type menu):
Pies

Use the Pies option of the Customize Graph Type menu to choose labels, exploding slicing, fill patterns, and colors for pie charts. From the Customize Graph Type menu, select Pie. Then fill in the desired options within the form that appears. When you finish filling in options in the form, choose a main menu option to continue defining other graph selections or choose DO-IT! to store the settings.

Place (When Designing Custom Forms)

Sequence (From the Form Design Menu):
Field/Place

Use this Place option to place fields while you are designing custom forms. From the Form Design menu, choose Field/Place. From the next menu that appears, select the desired field type (Regular, DisplayOnly, Calculated, or #Record). Identify the field or field format from the successive menus that may appear, depending upon your selection. Move the cursor to the desired location for the field, and press (ENTER) to place the field.

Place (When Designing Multitable Forms)

Sequence (From the Form Design Menu):
Multi/Tables/Place

Use this Place option to place another table's form within the current form when designing multitable forms. From the Form Design menu, choose Multi /Tables/Place. From the next menu to appear, choose Linked (if the forms are to be linked relationally) or choose Unlinked. Enter the name of the desired table at the next prompt, and place the form in the desired location with the arrow keys.

Place (When Designing Reports)

Sequence (From the Report Design Menu):
Field/Place

Use this Place option to place fields while you are designing custom reports. From the Report Design menu, choose Field/Place. From the next menu, select the desired field type (Regular, Summary, Calculated, Date, Time, Page, or #Record). Identify the field or field format from the successive menus that may appear, depending on your selection. Move the cursor to the desired location for the field, and press (ENTER) to place the field.

Play

Sequence:
Scripts/Play

Use the Play option to play back a script. Choose Scripts/Play, and enter the name of the script.

PreventLock

Sequence:
Tools/Net/PreventLock

Use the PreventLock option to prevent others from locking a table while you are on a network. Also use PreventLock to clear a prevent write lock or a prevent full lock. Choose Tools/Net/PreventLock. Select FullLock or WriteLock as the type of prevent lock desired, and enter the name of the table to which the prevent lock should be applied. Finally, choose Set to place the prevent lock or Clear to release an existing prevent lock. If your attempt to place or clear the prevent lock is successful, Paradox will display a message informing you of this fact.

Print

Sequence:
Scripts/Editor/New/Print
Scripts/Editor/Open/Print

Use the Print option to tell Paradox to print a script while you are using the Script Editor. While in the Script Editor, choose New/Print or Open/Print from the menu to print the script.

A

Printer (To Direct the Report Output to the Printer)

Sequence:
Report/Output/Printer

Use this Printer option to direct the output of a report to the printer. Choose Report/Output and enter the name of the desired table. Next, choose from among the available reports, and then choose Printer to direct the output to the printer. The output is directed to your PC's default printer. In most cases this is the printer connected to LPT1, unless you have used the DOS MODE command or your network operating system software to change this setting.

Printer (To Direct a Selected Report Range to the Printer)

Sequence:
Report/RangeOutput/Printer

Use this Printer option to direct a portion of a report to the printer. Choose Report/RangeOutput, and enter the name of the desired table. Next, choose from among the available reports, and then choose Printer. Enter the desired starting and ending page numbers of the report. The output is directed to your PC's default printer. In most cases this is the printer connected to LPT1, unless you have used the DOS MODE command or your network operating system software to change this setting.

Printer (To Print the Report While Designing or Modifying It)

Sequence (From the Report Design Menu):
Output/Printer

Use this Printer option to print a report while you are in the process of creating or modifying that report. This can be useful for ensuring, before you exit from the Report Specification, that the report you are designing will meet your needs. From the Report Design menu, choose Output and then Printer to direct the output to the printer. The output is directed to your PC's default printer. In most cases this is the printer connected to LPT1, unless you have used the DOS MODE command or your network operating system software to change this setting.

Protect

Sequence:
Tools/More/Protect

Use the Protect option to set and remove passwords for scripts or tables, temporarily clear passwords from memory, or write-protect tables. Choose Tools/More/Protect. The next menu provides you with three choices: Password, to set or remove passwords from a table or script; ClearPasswords, to clear passwords from memory; and Write-Protect, to write-protect a table. For additional details on these options, see each option by name in this appendix.

QuerySave

Sequence:
Scripts/QuerySave

Use the QuerySave option to save a Query Form that is currently in the workspace as a script. With a Query Form visible in the workspace, choose Scripts/QuerySave from the menu. Then enter a name for the script.

QuerySpeed

Sequence:
Tools/QuerySpeed

Use the QuerySpeed option to speed the performance of regularly used queries by building internal index files on non-key fields containing selection criteria in the query. Choose Tools/QuerySpeed.

Note that if the fields used in your query are key fields, no performance benefits can be gained with QuerySpeed. In such cases, Paradox will respond with a "No speedup possible" message if you try to use the QuerySpeed option.

Range

Sequence (From the Report Design Menu):
Group/Insert/Range

A

Use the Range option within a report to group together records that have values within a specified range. From the Report Design menu, choose Group/Insert/Range. From the list of fields that appears next, choose a field to group on, and then specify the size or scope of the range. Place the cursor at the desired location for the group, and press (ENTER).

RangeOutput

Sequence:
Report/RangeOutput

Use the RangeOutput option to send specified pages of a report to the printer, the screen, or a disk file. Choose Report/RangeOutput, and then enter a name for the appropriate table. Next, select a report from the list of report designators that appears, and then choose Printer, File, or Screen as desired. If prompted, enter the starting and ending page numbers for the report.

Record

Sequence (From the Main or Edit Menu):
Image/Zoom/Record

Use the Record option to locate the cursor at a specific record number. From the main menu or the Edit menu, choose Image/Zoom/Record. Enter a record number, and the cursor will move to that record.

Records

Sequence (From the Form Design Menu):
Multi/Records

Use the Records option to place, remove, or adjust a multirecord region on a form. From the Form Design menu, choose Multi/Records. From the next menu to appear, choose Define (to define a multirecord region on the form), Remove (to remove an existing multirecord region), or Adjust (to adjust the size of an existing multirecord region).

Reformat

Sequence (From the Form Design or Report Design Menu):
Field/Reformat

Use the Reformat option to reformat fields while you are designing forms or reports. From the Form Design or Report Design menu, choose Field/Reformat. Place the cursor on the field you wish to reformat, and press (ENTER) to select the field. Choose the desired options from the choices that appear for reformatting the field. Note that you can change field widths only in forms.

Regroup

Sequence (From the Report Design Menu):
Group/Regroup

Use the Regroup option to change the type of grouping used in a custom report. From the Report Design menu, choose Group/Regroup. Place the cursor at the desired group, and press (ENTER) to select it. Then choose the appropriate grouping method (Field, Range, or NumberRecords) and provide the required information when prompted.

RemoveBlanks

Sequence (From the Report Design Menu):
Setting/RemoveBlanks

Use the RemoveBlanks option to suppress the printing of blank lines or blank fields within the form band in a custom free-form report. From the Report Design menu, choose Setting/RemoveBlanks. From the next menu that appears, choose LineSqueeze to suppress blank lines when fields are empty, or choose FieldSqueeze to suppress blank characters when field data contains leading or trailing blank spaces.

Rename

Sequence:
Tools/Rename

A

Use the Rename option to rename tables, forms, reports, scripts, or graphs. Choose Tools/Rename. From the next menu that appears, choose Table, Form, Report, Script or Graph, and enter the old and then the new name for the object.

RepeatPlay

Sequence:
Scripts/RepeatPlay

Use this option to play a script a set number of times, or to play the script continuously. Choose Scripts/RepeatPlay. Next, enter the name of the desired script. At the next prompt, enter the number of times to play the script, or enter **C** for continuous play.

Report

Sequence:
Report

Use the Report option of the main menu to create and modify reports. Choose Report, and the menu that appears provides the following options: Output, to send a report to the printer, screen, or disk file; Design, to design a new Report Specification; Change, to change an existing Report Specification; RangeOutput, to send specified report pages to the printer, screen, or disk file; and SetPrinter, to select a printer port or enter a setup string.

Select the desired option. For more specifics on an option, see the option by name in this appendix.

Required

Sequence (From the Edit Menu):
ValCheck/Define/Required

Use the Required option to tell Paradox that all new or edited records must contain an entry in a specific field. Paradox will display an error message if you press (ENTER) after leaving the field blank during data entry. While in DataEntry or Edit mode, choose ValCheck/Define. Place the cursor in the desired field and press (ENTER). From the next menu, choose Required, and then Yes. (The No option from this menu may be used later, if you want to remove the Required status from the field.) Choose DO-IT! to save the validity check to the table, or else it will be discarded.

Reset

Sequence:
Image/Graph/Reset

Use the Reset option to restore graph settings to their default values, as defined by the Custom Configuration Program (CCP). Choose Image/Graph/ Reset, and then choose OK to restore the graph settings to the default values.

Resize

Sequence (From the Report Design Menu):
TableBand/Resize

Use the Resize option to change the size of a table band in a custom tabular report. From the Report Design menu, choose TableBand/Resize. Move the cursor to the column to be resized, and press (ENTER). Use (←) and (→) to resize the column, and then press (ENTER) to set the new size.

Restructure

Sequence:
Modify/Restructure

Use the Restructure option to change a table's structure. Choose the option called Modify/Restructure, and enter the name of the desired table. Make the desired changes to the field names and field types, and choose DO-IT! to store the changes.

Retain

Sequence (From the Report Design Menu):
Setting/GroupRepeats/Retain

A

Use the Retain option to allow the printing of repeated field values within a group. From the Report Design menu, choose Setting/GroupRepeats/Retain to allow repeated field values to print within groups on the report.

Save

Sequence:
Image/Graph/Save

Use the Save option to save graph settings to a file. Choose Image/Graph/Save. Paradox will prompt you for the name of the file; enter the name, and the current graph settings will be saved to a settings file. Note that to save an image of the graph itself, you should use Image/ViewGraph/File.

Scientific

Sequence (From the Main or Edit Menu):
Image/Format/Scientific

Use the Scientific option to select scientific (exponential) format for the display of number fields. From the main menu or the Edit menu, choose Image/Format. Place the cursor in the number field you wish to reformat, and press (ENTER) to select the field. Choose Scientific from the next menu, and specify the number of decimal places you desire.

Screen (To Direct a Finished Report to the Screen)

Sequence:
Report/Output/Screen

Use this Screen option to direct the output of a report to the screen. Choose Report/Output, and enter the name of the desired table. Next, choose from among the available reports, and then choose Screen to display the report.

Screen (To Direct a Report in Progress to the Screen)

Sequence (From the Report Design Menu):
Output/Screen

Use this Screen option to display the output of a report while you are in the process of creating or modifying the report. This can be useful for ensuring, before you exit from the Report Design menu that the report you are designing will meet your needs. From the Report Design menu, choose Output. Then choose Screen to direct the output to the screen.

Screen (To Direct a Selected Report Range to the Screen)

Sequence:
Report/RangeOutput/Screen

Use this Screen option to direct a portion of a report to the screen. Choose Report/RangeOutput, and enter the name of the desired table. Choose from among the available reports, and then choose Screen. Then indicate the desired starting and ending page numbers of the report.

Script

Sequence:
Tools/Copy/Script
Tools/Delete/Script
Tools/Rename/Script
Tools/More/Protect/Password/Script

Use these Tools options to copy, rename, delete, or password-protect scripts. To copy a script, choose Tools/Copy/Script. Enter the name of the script to copy, followed by the new name for the copy. To delete a script, choose Tools/Delete/Script, enter the name of the script, and confirm the deletion by choosing OK from the next menu. To rename a script, choose Tools/ Rename/Script and enter the name of the script, followed by the new name.

To password-protect a script, or to clear password protection from a script, choose Tools/More/Protect/Password/Script, and enter the name of the desired script. Enter the password when prompted to do so, and enter it a second time to confirm the correct spelling (or press (ENTER) without entering any passwords to clear the password from a protected script).

A

Scripts (To List Scripts)

Sequence:
Tools/Info/Inventory/Scripts

Use this Scripts option to list all available scripts in the current directory. Choose Tools/Info/Inventory/Scripts. Enter a directory name, or press (ENTER) without a name to list scripts in the current directory.

Scripts (To Play, Record, Save, or Change)

Sequence:
Scripts

Use this Scripts option to play and record scripts, to save a query as a script, to play scripts repeatedly or at slow speeds, or to change scripts with the Editor. From the menu, choose Scripts. The following menu options then become available: Play, to play a script; BeginRecord, to begin recording a script; QuerySave, to save a query as a script; ShowPlay, to play a script slowly; RepeatPlay, to play a script a designated number of times; and Editor, to write or edit a script.

Select the desired option. For more specifics on an option, see the option by name in this appendix.

Series

Sequence (From the Customize Graph Type menu):
Series

Use the Series option of the Customize Graph Type menu to define legends, labels, markers, fill patterns, and colors for each data series within the graph. From the Customize Graph Type menu, select Series. From the next menu to appear, choose LegendsAndLabels, MarkersAndFills, or Colors. Use LegendsAndLabels to define whether a legend will appear and to choose the placement of labels. Use MarkersAndFills to choose the markers and fill patterns for bars or points within a graph. Use Colors to define the colors that will be displayed or printed.

SetPrinter

Sequence:
Report/SetPrinter

Use the SetPrinter option to select a setup string or a printer port for printed output. Choose Report/SetPrinter. The next menu that appears offers the choice of Regular, to use the printer port and setup string stored with the report, or Override, to override the printer port and setup string stored with the report. If you choose Override, you must either enter a setup string, choose a printer port, specify a printer reset string, or specify formfeeds or linefeeds for the end of a page.

SetPrivate

Sequence:
Tools/Net/SetPrivate

Use the SetPrivate option to change your private directory while you are using Paradox on a network. Choose Tools/Net/SetPrivate, and enter the directory name (including the drive identifier and path). Paradox will display a menu requiring confirmation; you must choose OK to change your private directory.

Setting (With Free-Form Custom Reports)

Sequence (From the Report Design Menu):
Setting

Use this Setting option to change the settings of a free-form custom report. From the Report Design menu, choose Setting. The following menu options then become available: RemoveBlanks, to suppress blank lines or fields; PageLayout, to set page lengths and widths, and to insert or delete page widths; Margin, to change the left margin of the report; Setup, to specify a setup string, a reset string, or set the printer port; Wait, to pause report printing after each page; and Labels, to specify the printing of mailing labels.

Select the desired option. For more specifics on an option, see the option by name in this appendix.

A

Setting (With Tabular Custom Reports)

Sequence (From the Report Design Menu):
Setting

Use this Setting option to change the settings of a tabular custom report. From the Report Design menu, choose Setting. The following menu options then become available: Format, used to specify the overall report format; GroupRepeats, to suppress or retain printing of repeated values in a group; PageLayout, to set page lengths and widths, and to insert or delete page widths; Margin, to change the left margin of the report; Setup, to specify a setup string or set the printer port; Wait, to pause report printing after each page.

Select the desired option. For more specifics on an option, see the option by name in this appendix.

Setup (When Adding Data to Multiple Tables)

Sequence:
Modify/MultiEntry/Setup

Use this Setup option to set up the source and map tables used with the MultiEntry option. Remember that the Query Form used for each of the target tables should be in the workspace before you use the Setup option. Choose Modify/MultiEntry/Setup. Enter the name of the new source table, and then enter the name of the new map table. Paradox will create the source and map tables, and you can then use Modify/MultiEntry/Entry or Tools/More/MultiAdd to add records to multiple tables simultaneously.

Setup (When Designing Reports)

Sequence (From the Report Design Menu):
Setting/Setup

Use this Setup option to specify the printer port and/or setup string to be sent to the printer. From the Report Design menu, choose Setting/Setup. Select Predefined to choose a setup string from a predefined list, or choose Custom to enter a custom printer port and setup string.

Show

Sequence (From the Form Design Menu):
Style/Fieldnames/Show

Use the Show option to show the names of fields while you are placing them during the form design process. From the Form Design menu, choose the Style/Fieldnames/Show option.

ShowHighlight

Sequence (From the Form Design Menu):
Style/ShowHighlight

Use the ShowHighlight option with multirecord forms to show or hide the highlight of a multirecord region. From the Form Design menu, choose Style/ShowHighlight. From the next menu that appears, choose Show (to show the multirecord region in a highlighted intensity) or Hide (to display the mutirecord region in the same intensity as the initial record in the form).

ShowPlay

Sequence:
Scripts/ShowPlay

Use the ShowPlay option to play a script at a speed that is sufficiently slow for you to observe the effects. Choose Scripts/ShowPlay, and enter the name of the script. The next menu that appears provides the choice of Fast (to play the script rapidly) or Slow (to play the script slowly). Choose the desired speed at which to play the script.

Single-Line

Sequence (From the Form Design Menu):
Border/Place/Single-Line

Use the Single-Line option to add a single-line border in a form. To add the border, choose Border/Place/Single-Line from the Form Design menu. Place the cursor at one desired corner of the border, and press (ENTER); move the

A

cursor to the diagonal corner of the desired border, and press (ENTER) again to draw the border.

Slow

Sequence:
Scripts/ShowPlay/Slow

Use the Slow option to play a script at the slowest possible speed. Choose Scripts/ShowPlay, and enter the name of the script. Then choose Slow to play the script slowly.

Sort

Sequence:
Modify/Sort

Use the Sort option to sort the records in a table. Choose Modify/Sort, and enter the name of the table to sort. If the table is keyed, you must also enter a name for the new table that will result from the sort. Fill in the sort screen by placing numbers to indicate the priority for the sort order next to the desired fields and, if desired, placing the letter D (for "descending") to the right of the number. Then choose DO-IT! to perform the sort.

SortDirection

Sequence (From the Report Design Menu):
Group/SortDirection

Use the SortDirection option to specify the sort direction you prefer when groups are included in a custom report. From the Report Design menu, choose Group/SortDirection. Move the cursor to the group whose sort order is to be changed, and press (ENTER) to select that group. Then choose Ascending or Descending for the sort order.

Structure

Sequence:
Tools/Info/Structure

Use the Structure option to display the structure of a table. Choose Tools/ Info/Structure, and enter the name of the desired table.

Style

Sequence (From the Form Design Menu):
Style

Use the Style option to choose the style of text when you are designing a custom form. From the Form Design menu, choose Style. The menu that appears next displays the following options: Color, to select desired colors; Monochrome, to various select monochrome display attributes; ShowHighlight, to show or hide the highlight in a multirecord form; and Fieldnames, to show or hide field names during form design.

Select the desired option. For more specifics on an option, see the option by name in this appendix.

Subtract

Sequence:
Tools/More/Subtract

Use the Subtract option to remove all records in one table that match records in another table. Choose Tools/More/Subtract, and then enter the name of the source table (the table containing the records to be subtracted from the other table). Next, enter the name of the target table (the table from which to subtract the records). If the target table is not keyed, Paradox will remove all records that exactly match records in the source table. If the target table is keyed, Paradox will remove all records in which the key fields match the key fields of any record in the source table.

Sum

Sequence (From the Report Design Menu):
Field/Place/Summary/Calculated/Sum
Field/Place/Summary/Regular/Sum

Use the Sum option to sum the values in the summary field of a custom free-form or tabular report. From the Report Design menu, choose Field/

Place/Summary/Calculated/Sum or Field/Place/Regular/Sum. Select Per-Group for a summary each time the group changes or Overall for an overall summary. Use the cursor to place the field in its desired location, and press (ENTER). Adjust the number of digits displayed (use (←) and (→)). Then press (ENTER). Adjust the number of decimal points displayed (use (←) and (→)), and then press (ENTER) to complete the placement of the field.

Summary

Sequence (From the Report Design Menu):
Field/Place/Summary

Use the Summary option to place a summary field within a custom report. From the Report Design menu, choose Field/Place/Summary. From the next menu that appears, select Regular to place a regular field or Calculated to place a calculated field, based on an expression. If you choose Regular, you must next choose the field to be placed from a list of fields; if you choose Calculated, you must enter an expression as the basis for the calculation.

From the next menu that appears, choose Sum, Average, Count, High, or Low, depending upon the type of summary you desire. Then select PerGroup for a summary each time the group changes or Overall for an overall summary. Use the cursor to place the field in its desired location, and press (ENTER). Next, adjust the number of digits displayed (use (←) and (→)), and then press (ENTER). Finally, adjust the number of decimal points displayed (with (←) and (→)), and press (ENTER) to complete the placement of the field.

Suppress

Sequence (From the Report Design Menu):
Setting/GroupRepeats/Suppress

Use the Suppress option to prevent the printing of all occurrences of repeated field values within a group. From the Report Design menu, choose Setting/GroupRepeats/Suppress.

Table

Sequence:
Tools/Copy/Table
Tools/Delete/Table
Tools/Rename/Table
Tools/More/Protect/Password/Table

Use these versions of the Table option to copy, rename, delete, or password-protect tables. To copy a table, choose Tools/Copy/Table, and enter the name of the table to copy, followed by the new name for the copy. To delete a table, choose Tools/Delete/Table, enter the name for the table, and confirm the deletion by choosing OK from the next menu. To rename a table, choose the Tools/Rename/Table option and enter the name of the table, followed by the new name for the table.

To password-protect a table, choose Tools/More/Protect/Password/Table, and enter the name of the table. Enter the password when prompted to do so, and enter it a second time to confirm the correct spelling. If you wish, fill in the auxiliary password from the next screen that appears and then choose DO-IT!; if no auxiliary passwords are necessary, simply choose DO-IT!.

TableBand

Sequence (From the Report Design Menu):
TableBand

Use the TableBand option, while you are designing or changing tabular reports, to insert, erase, resize, move, or copy columns. From the Report Design menu, choose TableBand. The following menu options will appear: Insert, to insert a new column; Erase, to erase a column; Resize, to change the width of a column; Move, to move a column to another location; and Copy, to copy a column to a new location.

Select the desired option. For more specifics on an option, see the option by name in this appendix.

A

TableLookup

Sequence (From the Edit Menu):
ValCheck/Define/TableLookup

Use the TableLookup option to compare field entries to a lookup table to determine their validity. From the Edit menu, choose ValCheck/Define. Place the cursor in the field that is to be compared to the lookup table, and press (ENTER). Choose TableLookup, and enter the name of the table that contains the lookup values. The field in the lookup table must be the first field in the table and must have the same name and characteristics as the field to which it is being compared.

From the next menu that appears, select JustCurrentField to check entered values in the current field against the lookup table, or select All-CorrespondingFields to check and fill in values from all corresponding fields in the lookup table.

Finally, choose PrivateLookup (or FillNoHelp, if you last chose All-CorrespondingFields) to check the validity while denying access to the lookup table, or choose HelpAndFill to check the validity while allowing browsing of the lookup table.

Tables (for Forms)

Sequence (From the Form Design Menu):
Multi/Tables

Use this Tables option to place, remove, or move a form from another table to the form you are designing. From the Form Design menu, choose Multi/Tables. From the next menu to appear, choose Place (to add another table's form to the current form), Remove (to remove another table's form from the current form), Move (to move a form already placed), or DisplayOnly (to specify that a form is to be used for editing or just for display).

Tables (To List Available Tables)

Sequence:
Tools/Info/Inventory/Tables

Use this Tables option to list all available tables in a directory. Choose Tools/ Info/Inventory/Tables. Enter a directory name, or press (ENTER) without a name for the current directory. All available tables will appear by name within a temporary table, along with the creation dates for each table.

TableSize

Sequence:
Image/TableSize

Use the TableSize option to change the current table's size (in rows) in the workspace. Choose Image/TableSize. Use the (↑) and (↓) to increase or decrease the number of visible rows, and then press (ENTER) to set the desired table size. Tables must occupy a minimum of two rows.

TablesOfGroups

Sequence (From the Report Design Menu):
Setting/Format/TablesOfGroups

Use the TablesOfGroups option to arrange reports in tables of groups. When arranged in tables of groups, the table header appears just once, at the top of the page. To specify this formatting, choose Setting/Format/ TablesOfGroups from the Report Design menu.

Tabular

Sequence:
Report/Design/Tabular

Use the Tabular option to design a tabular custom report. Choose Report/ Design, and enter the name of the table. Select a designator for the report, and then enter a description. Choose Tabular for the type of report, and the Report Design menu will appear. Design the report as desired, and then choose DO-IT! ((F2)) to store the report.

A

Time

Sequence (From the Report Design Menu):
Field/Place/Time

Use the Time option to place a field containing the current time in a custom free-form or tabular report. From the Report Design menu, choose Field/Place/Time, and select one of two possible time formats that appear. Move the cursor to the desired location, and press (ENTER) to place the time field.

ToDOS

Sequence:
Tools/More/ToDOS

Use the ToDOS option to temporarily suspend Paradox and access DOS through a DOS "shell." Choose Tools/More/ToDOS, and in a moment the DOS prompt will appear. From the DOS prompt, enter **EXIT** to return to Paradox. (Note that the (CTRL)-(O) or (ALT)-(O) key combinations can also be used to access DOS.)

Tools

Sequence:
Tools

Choose the Tools option of the main menu to choose from among various Paradox tools. The menu that appears provides the following options: Rename, to rename Paradox objects; QuerySpeed, to speed the performance of queries; ExportImport, to exchange data between Paradox and other software; Copy, to copy Paradox objects; Delete, to delete Paradox objects; Info, to show information such as filenames, table fields, and network users; Net, to perform common network functions; and More, to provide access to additional tools through another menu.

Select the desired option. For more specifics on an option, see the option by name in this appendix.

Type

Sequence (From the Customize Graph Type menu):
Type

Use the Type option of the Customize Graph Type menu to choose the type of graph to display, or to mix types within a single graph. From the Customize Graph Type menu, select Type. Then select the desired type of graph from the next menu to appear. The available types are Stacked Bar, Bar, 3-D Bar, Rotated Bar, Line, Markers, Combined Lines and Markers, X-Y Graph, Pie Graph, and Area Graph.

Undo

Sequence (From the Edit Menu):
Undo

[CTRL]-[U]

Use the Undo option, while you are editing, to undo changes made to a record. From the Edit menu, choose Undo. From the next menu that appears, choose Yes to undo your most recent edit. You can repeat the Undo option to undo successive changes, all the way back to the start of a session. (Note that while in CoEdit mode, you can only undo the most recent action.)

Update

Sequence:
Tools/More/Add/Update
Tools/More/MultiAdd/Update

Use the Update option to update a keyed table, using the records in another table as the source of the update. Choose Tools/More/Add; or to update more than one table simultaneously, choose Tools/More/MultiAdd. Enter a name for the source table (the table with records to be added); and in the case of MultiAdd, enter the name of the map table. Then enter a name for the target table (the table to add the records to).

    If the target table has a key field, another menu will provide the choice of NewEntries, for adding records to the target table, and Update, for

A

updating the target table records based on the source table records. Choose Update, and the target table(s) will be updated.

UserName

Sequence:
Tools/Net/UserName

Use the UserName option to change your user name while you are using Paradox on a network. Choose Tools/Net/UserName, and enter the new user name (of up to 15 characters). Then confirm the new name by choosing OK from the next menu that appears.

ValCheck (To Clear All Validity Checks for a Table)

Sequence:
Tools/Delete/ValCheck

Use this ValCheck option to clear all validity checks from a table by deleting the validity check file. Choose Tools/Delete/ValCheck, and enter the name of the table. Paradox will proceed to delete the file that contains all of the validity checks for that table.

ValCheck (To Set or Clear Validity Checks)

Sequence (From the Edit Menu):
ValCheck

Use this ValCheck option to set validity checks on fields or to clear one or more validity checks from a field. From the Edit menu, choose ValCheck. Then choose Define to define or Clear to clear a validity check.

View

Sequence:
View

Use the View option to view an existing table. Choose View, and enter the name of the desired table. If a table is already visible on the desktop, the table that you select with View will appear atop the existing table.

ViewGraph

Sequence (From the Customize Graph Type menu):
ViewGraph

Use the ViewGraph option of the Customize Graph Type menu to show the current graph on the screen, to print the current graph, or to store an image of the graph in a disk file. From the Customize Graph Type menu, select ViewGraph. From the next menu that appears, select Screen (to display the graph), Printer (to print the graph at the default print device), or File (to store the graph in a disk file).

Wait

Sequence (From the Report Design Menu):
Setting/Wait

Use the Wait option to force the printer to pause after each page of a custom report. With this option chosen, the user will be prompted to press a key before each successive page is printed. From the Report Design menu, choose Setting/Wait. Then confirm the selection by choosing Yes from the next menu that appears.

Who

Sequence:
Tools/Info/Who

Use the Who option to list all users currently running Paradox on a network. Choose Tools/Info/Who, and a list of network users will appear in the form of a temporary table.

A

Width

Sequence (From the Report Design Menu):
Setting/PageLayout/Width

Use the Width option to control the page width in a custom report. From the Report Design menu, choose **Setting/PageLayout/Width**. Enter the desired width, measured in number of characters (from 2 to 2000).

Write-Protect

Sequence:
Tools/More/Protect/Write-Protect

Use the Write-Protect option to protect a table against changes or to remove write protection. Choose **Tools/More/Protect/Write-Protect**, and enter the name of the desired table. From the next menu that appears, choose Set to write-protect the table, or choose Clear to remove the write protection.

Yes

Sequence:
Yes

Use the Yes option to tell Paradox to perform a specific type of operation.

Zoom

Sequence:
Image/Zoom

Use the Zoom option to locate the cursor at a specific field, record number, or matching value. Choose **Image/Zoom**. From the next menu that appears, choose Field, Record, or Value to go to a specific field, record number, or value.

B

Running Paradox 4 Under Microsoft Windows

Paradox 4 is fully compatible with Microsoft Windows (versions 3.0 and above), and can be run either in full-screen mode or within a window under Windows. Note that you must have a minimum of 4MB of RAM installed on your computer to run Paradox 4 under Windows.

To optimize the performance of Paradox 4 in the Windows environment, a PIF (Program Information File) file is included in the Paradox directory that contains your system files. (PIF files are commonly used to run DOS applications under Windows. For a detailed explanation of PIF files, see your Windows documentation.) The instructions that follow will step you through the process of placing the PIF file provided by Borland into the appropriate Windows program group.

Installing Paradox 4 Under Windows

First, if you plan to install Paradox 4 in a directory other than C:\PDOX40, you must edit the PIF file to indicate this change. Start Windows in the usual manner. Next, choose PIF EDITOR from the Program Manager. Choose File/Open, and use the dialog box to locate the directory where Paradox 4 is installed. Choose PDOXDOS.PIF from the list of available PIF files, and then choose OK.

Once the PIF settings are visible in the Windows PIF Editor, replace the existing directory (C:\PDOX40) with the name of the directory where Paradox 4 is to be installed (or is already installed). Also, change the startup directory to this same directory name. If you prefer to start Paradox 4 inside a window rather than full screen, change the Display Usage setting from Full Screen to Windowed. When done, choose File/Save to save your changes. Exit the PIF Editor, by pressing (ALT)-(F4).

To install Paradox 4 under Windows, perform the following steps:

1. Exit Windows, and install Paradox 4 in the usual manner (if you have not already done so), following the instructions in the Installation booklet provided with your Paradox documentation.

2. If you have just installed Paradox, reboot your computer, and make sure that Paradox operates properly under DOS. Exit Paradox.

3. Start Windows in the usual manner.

4. Open the File Manager, and resize the File Manager window so that it occupies the top half of the screen. Open the program group in which you want to place Paradox 4, and resize its window so that it occupies the bottom half of the screen.

5. In the File Manager, find the directory where Paradox 4 is currently installed. Locate the file called PDOXDOS.PIF. Using the mouse, drag the PDOXDOS.PIF file into the program group where you want to install Paradox 4. When you release the mouse button, a DOS icon will appear.

6. (Optional) If desired, you can change the DOS icon to the Paradox 4 icon (supplied by Borland). Click once on the DOS icon that just appeared to select it. From the Program Manager menu, choose File/Properties, and select choose Change/Icon from the dialog

box that appears. (If you see a message box stating, "No icons are available," click on OK to proceed. In the dialog box that next appears, enter the drive and directory name where Paradox 4 is installed, followed by **PDOXDOS.ICO**. Choose the OK button twice to close the dialog boxes, and the Paradox 4 icon will appear.

Starting Paradox 4 Under Windows

To start Paradox 4 under Windows, first open the program group containing the Paradox 4 icon, and then double-click on the icon. Paradox will load and start in a window or full screen, depending on the setting in your PIF file (see the earlier section, "Installing Paradox 4 Under Windows," for details on PIF files).

If you are using Windows 3.0, you will not be able to use the mouse within Paradox 4 unless you are running Paradox 4 in full-screen mode. With Windows 3.1, you can use the mouse in Paradox 4 running either in a window or full screen.

While running Paradox under Windows, keep in mind that you can use (ALT)-(ENTER) to switch between windowed mode and full-screen mode. And you can use (ALT)-(TAB) to switch between Paradox 4 and other applications that are running under Windows. For a full description of keys available for navigating in Windows, refer to your Windows documentation.

A Warning About Loading Paradox 4 from DOS

Do not ever attempt to load Paradox 4 from a DOS prompt within Windows; that is, do not click on the DOS Prompt icon within Windows to jump to DOS, and then attempt to load Paradox 4 from there. When you use the DOS Prompt icon in Windows, you are jumping into a DOS "shell," but major portions of Windows remain in memory. An attempt to load Paradox 4 from the Windows/DOS prompt may overwrite part of the Windows program in memory, causing your system to hang. If you want to run Paradox from DOS, exit Windows *completely*, and then start Paradox.

B

Index

G

Q

LAN Times Buyers Directory

How many network products are there to choose from?

THOUSANDS!

How do you find and compare them?

There is only ONE SOURCE—The LAN Times Buyers Directory. IT'S NEW!

The LAN Times Buyers Directory contains descriptions of thousands network hardware and software products and network services. Each listing contains product specifications, pricing, and company contact information. If you only want to have one resource for network products and services, the LAN Times Buyers Directory is it!

And now its available in two formats: PRINTED and ELECTRONIC.

The printed version includes all descriptions of products and services plus indexes by product type, company, and region. It is printed annually.

The electronic version comes as a runtime hypertext diskette (DOS / Folio). You can instantly search on product names, specifications, or compatibility standards as well as company names or locations. It's simple and intuitive to use. The electronic version is available on a subscription basis with monthly updates.

ORDER TODAY! Call (801) 565-5812 or mail the attatched form.

LAN TIMES BUYERS DIRECTORY
7050 Union Park Center
Suite 240
Midvale, UT 84047